COMPENSATION COMMITTEE HANDBOOK

Second Edition

JAMES F. REDA
STEWART REIFLER
LAURA G. THATCHER

WILEY

JOHN WILEY & SONS, INC.

The authors dedicate this book to their spouses
for all of their patience and support of this project:

Deborah Reda
Sheryl Reifler
Brad Thatcher

Contents

Foreword

The compensation committee and executive leadership are central to the critical task of aligning compensation with the mission of a business in the way that provides maximum benefit to shareholders. A typical Fortune 500 CEO makes more than $10 million in total annual compensation, of which as much as 90% comes from incentive systems put in place by the compensation committee and the board, often with shareholder consent and within strict regulatory guidelines mandated by the U.S. Securities and Exchange Commission, the Internal Revenue Service, stock exchange listing rules, the Department of Labor, and the Sarbanes-Oxley legislation. At the same time, the level of pay of the CEO and senior executives must be consistent with corporate performance and meet the test of reasonableness; this requires a constant check of industry practices and emerging trends.

Compensation systems must be transparent in that they should be disclosed and easily understood by shareholders. Most importantly, they must be effective in motivating management for both the short- and long-term. In addition to these important roles, today's compensation committees must have profound expertise in finance, governance and legal matters that are inherent in compensation systems. They have to walk the line between maintaining the flexibility to adapt to a changing business environment while at the same time maintaining a level of consistency that satisfies the regulators and serves the goals of shareholders.

Increasingly, the overlapping or boundary issues between the compensation, governance, and audit committees require coordination and a thoughtful response. One example of this teamwork is the CEO evaluation process. Typically, the CEO is also the board chair; thus it is imperative that the chairs of the compensation and governance committees work together to provide for a meaningful CEO evaluation process.

This handbook was written to provide compensation committee members with the tools needed to meet their responsibilities to the shareholders while complying with innumerable regulations. It provides valuable advice and insights into today's evolving issues and is straightforward in its approach, offering practical examples to clarify more complicated issues. Overall, it is an excellent resource for compensation committee members as well as other corporate directors and executive management.

Charles R. Shoemate

Charles R. Shoemate

Charles R. ("Dick") Shoemate is retired chairman of the board, president and chief executive officer of Bestfoods. He has over 40 years of substantial business experience and serves on the boards of CIGNA Corporation, ChevronTexaco Corporation and International Paper Company. He has over 15 years of Fortune-500 board experience. Currently, he serves as the chair of International Paper's Management Development and Compensation Committee.

Preface

Concern about executive pay is hardly a new phenomenon. Rather, it has tended to ebb and flow with overall economic fortunes. Attention tends to decline in periods of economic plenty—as long as most Americans perceive themselves as doing well, they worry less that chief executive officers (CEOs) might be doing better still. As general economic fortunes subside, however, the relatively large earnings of corporate leaders invoke public ire.

Today, almost five years after the end of the bull market of the 1990s, the pendulum has swung, and attention is again focusing on executive pay. There is a growing perception that the gap between CEO pay and the earnings of the average worker is too large. Many believe that executives are shielded from financial loss even as the average worker faces layoff, loss of income, and cuts in benefits.

"One big [corporate] governance problem yet to be tackled is executive compensation," *The Wall Street Journal* observed in a July 2003 article on changes in the boardroom. "CEO candidates and incumbents still command enormous packages that reward them regardless of performance."[1]

This mood is a remarkable contrast from a few years before, when some CEOs had achieved iconic status as admired symbols of America's economic leadership. In hindsight, we can see that the economic euphoria of the 1990s resulted in some worrisome trends. Many believe linkage between performance and compensation eroded during the decade. When executives failed to qualify for performance-based bonuses or when stock price declines rendered options worthless, some compensation committees and boards restructured the terms to make sure executives' benefits were protected.

Moreover, the use of stock options to align the interests of executives and shareholders did not work as anticipated. As the stock market sped higher, the value of options increased almost irrespective of executive performance. Shareholder activists who pressed for the use of options ten years ago now acknowledge that the concept was flawed. According to Ken West, Chairman of the National Associa-

---

[1]"Boardrooms Under Renovation," *The Wall Street Journal,* July 22, 2003.

tion of Corporate Directors (NACD), the problem is that "option holders think like option holders, not necessarily like shareholders."[2]

Adding to the sense of public distrust has been the round of high-profile corporate failures and fraud that took place in the last few years. The Sarbanes-Oxley of 2002, the new Public Company Accounting Oversight Board, and new rules from the stock exchanges have responded to these failures by focusing on measures that make it more difficult for corporate officers to commit fraud, and that strengthen the ability of corporate boards to detect misconduct. Now, public policymakers, public and private oversight bodies, and shareholder groups are shifting their focus to enhancing the ability of corporate boards of directors to ensure that businesses operate ethically and effectively.

The role of the compensation committee has taken on added importance over the past few years. The new NYSE listing rules require the compensation committee to be the main arbiter of CEO pay and the main clearinghouse for pay decisions. A recent survey shows that compensation committee oversight is expanded in two ways, horizontal and vertical. First, compensation committees are expanding their oversight to include more plans and programs such as medical benefits, qualified pension, and other plans. Second, the compensation committees are expanding their oversight further down the organization, covering more employees with regard to compensation.

The Conference Board, the NACD, the American Society of Corporate Secretaries, and the Business Roundtable have all provided very thoughtful comments and leadership on issues of executive compensation and the role of the compensation committee. Furthermore, major corporations such as General Electric, MCI, General Motors, and Pfizer all have provided leadership in this area. We rely substantially on this leadership to provide the best practice guidance throughout this book.

While recognizing that there is no single "correct" model for executive pay that will fit every business organization, there is an identifiable set of evolving "best practices" that compensation committees and boards of directors can apply. The practices discussed in this new edition reflect current and pending regulations, including new rules by the Securities and Exchange Commission, the New York Stock Exchange, and Nasdaq. They also reflect the experience of compensation committee members and the knowledge gained in careers as business executives, government officials, corporate board members, governance experts, compensation consultants, and academics engaged in the study of business history and practices.

It is hoped that this handbook will stimulate useful and vigorous dialogue within compensation committees and boards of directors on valid measurements of executive performance, the appropriate level of compensation, and the proper mix of compensation elements and incentives, including base pay, performance

[2]"Are Compensation Committees Doing Their Jobs," by Ken West, *Director's Monthly,* October 2001.

bonuses, equity grants, retirement benefits, welfare benefits, perquisites, and other benefits.

We also hope that the best practices identified in this book will encourage compensation committees to establish a set of values that guides compensation discussions. This process should include identifying the goals that the pay package is designed to achieve, carefully examining each element of compensation, and considering the potential costs of the package in a variety of scenarios. Our fundamental point is that every company should have a compensation system based on a core set of clearly established principles, not one based on ad hoc decision-making.

However, more important than any best practice is the attitude and rigor that the compensation committee brings to its task. What is needed most is courage, leadership, and a spirit of independence—the willingness to ask uncomfortable questions, test the assumptions that underlie traditional past practices, strengthen accepted practices that work, say "no" when the situation warrants, and chart new courses when the rationale for old habits falls short. These characteristics, combined with the best practices discussed in the book, will ensure best-in-class performance for compensation committees.

Acknowledgments

The authors have worked together from three distinct perspectives to create this second edition of the *Compensation Committee Handbook*. Each of the authors would like to thank certain individuals who contributed to this edition.

Laura Thatcher sends special thanks to Brad and Ryan who ran the farm in her absence—all the while worrying ceaselessly about her ability to write a book of any kind, much less a serious one. She also acknowledges with admiration and appreciation the assistance of her law partners Nils Okeson, whose unparalleled expertise on fiduciary duties of directors is reflected liberally in Chapter 5, and Mitchel Pahl for his invaluable counsel on employment and severance arrangements. She thanks colleagues Mike Stevens, John Shannon, and Kerry Tynan for reading and re-reading voluminous text on pretty weekends and generally keeping things on the straight and narrow. Lastly, she thanks her law firm of 25 years, Alston & Bird, for encouraging her to embark on this engaging and professionally rewarding adventure.

Stewart Reifler expresses his appreciation to all the boards of directors, compensation committees, CEOs, COOs, CFOs, GCs, senior HR, and other executives whom he has advised over the years and who have indirectly but immeasurably contributed to this book. In addition, he wishes to thank the executive compensation attorneys at Vedder Price who—in one way or another—participated with him in discussing and developing compensation committee strategies for the 21st century. Finally, he particularly wants to thank Kevin Hassan and Michael Joyce for their time and attention spent in meticulously reviewing this book.

Jim Reda thanks Laura Thatcher and Stewart Reifler who agreed to revise the first edition of this book, as the second edition covers more and different topics, particularly in light of the swirl of regulatory action over the past few years. He also would like to thank his colleague, Matthew Miesionczek, who assisted in the review of the book. He would also like to thank outstanding directors and compensation committee chairs such as Jane Pfeiffer, Robert Womack, Charles Shoemate, Earnest Deavenport, Barbara Diamond, and Roger Drury who have made corporate America a better place with their time and energy in designing and implementing shareholder-friendly performance plans that encourage outstanding corporate performance. The knowledge gained in working with these outstanding directors is the basis of this book and his consulting practice.

Finally, the authors all want to thank Timothy Burgard at John Wiley & Sons, who kept the book on track and added infinitely to the final product.

About the Authors

JAMES F. REDA
Managing Director, James F. Reda & Associates, LLC

Mr. Reda has served for more than 17 years as advisor to the top managements and boards of major corporations in the United States and abroad in matters of executive compensation, performance, organization, and corporate governance. Mr. Reda has played an integral role in the field of executive compensation and the formation of the role of the compensation committee. As a recognized authority on corporate governance, he also serves as expert witness in executive compensation litigation and is typically retained by compensation committees as an outside independent advisor. Mr. Reda has a B.S. in Industrial Engineering from Columbia University, and a S.M. in Management from Massachusetts Institute of Technology, Sloan School of Management. He is a member of the American Society of Corporate Secretaries; WorldatWork; The National Association of Stock Plan Professionals; National Association of Corporate Directors (NACD); and the New York Society of Security Analysts, for which he serves on the corporate governance committee. He is chair of the Atlanta Chapter of NACD and was a commissioner member of the NACD Blue Ribbon Commission entitled "Executive Compensation and the Role of the Compensation Committee."

STEWART REIFLER
Shareholder, Vedder, Price, Kaufman & Kammholz, P.C.

Stewart Reifler is a shareholder of Vedder, Price, Kaufman & Kammholz, P.C. and heads its executive compensation practice in New York. He has extensive experience in representing companies, their boards, and their executives, both as an attorney with Weil, Gotshal & Manges and the Law Offices of Joseph E. Bachelder and as a compensation consultant with PricewaterhouseCoopers. He is a member of the executive compensation steering committee of the American Institute of Certified Public Accountants. He is a frequent speaker on executive compensation topics, and his articles have appeared in the *National Law Journal, The Metropolitan Corporate Counsel, The Tax Executive, The Journal of Compensation and Benefits, Mergers and Acquisitions, Director's Monthly, Securities Regulatory Update, Corporate Business Taxation Monthly, Estate Tax Planning Advisor,* and *The Journal of Taxation of Employee Benefits.*

LAURA G. THATCHER
Partner, Alston & Bird LLP

Laura Thatcher heads Alston & Bird LLP's executive compensation practice and works in its Atlanta office. Having over 20 years' experience in securities and business law, Ms. Thatcher developed executive compensation as a separate specialty area of the firm's tax practice in 1995 and now works exclusively in that area. She serves on the Editorial Board of the *Journal of Deferred Compensation,* and the Advisory Board of the Certified Equity Professional Institute of Santa Clara University. A frequent speaker and author on topics relating to executive compensation, her articles and interviews appear in various publications of the Bureau of National Affairs (BNA), including the *BNA Corporate Accountability Report, BNA Daily Tax Report,* and *BNA Executive Compensation Library.* She has addressed national and local conferences of the National Association of Stock Plan Professionals (NASPP), Institute for International Research (IIR) National Forum on Financing and Managing Executive Compensation Plans, and the ICLE Business Law Institute, and she participated as a speaker in the first nationwide PLI teleseminar on Sarbanes-Oxley issues affecting executive compensation.

All three of the authors are members of the *Executive Compensation Task Force* created in 2004 under the auspices of The Corporate Counsel, The Corporate Executive, and the NASPP.

The 21st Century Compensation Committee

Chapter 1

The Compensation Committee

One of the most important determinants of a successful corporate strategy is the quality of the compensation committee. The committee is charged with designing and implementing a compensation system that effectively rewards key players and encourages direct participation in the achievement of the organization's core business objectives.

Outstanding, well-integrated compensation strategy does not just happen. Rather, it is the product of the hard work of independent, experienced compensation committee members. The most effective pay strategies are simple in design, straightforward in application, and easy to communicate to management and investors. The pay program for the chief executive officer (CEO) should be in line with pay programs for the company's other executives and with its broad-based incentive programs. In other words, there should be no conflict in the achievement of objectives, and the potential rewards should be as meaningful to all participants as to the CEO.

The United States is unique in its vast number of high-earning entrepreneurs, entertainers, athletes, lawyers, consultants, Wall Street traders, bankers, analysts, investment managers, and other professionals. Yet, it is the pay levels of corporate executives, in particular CEOs, that stir the most heated debate and controversy. It is estimated that the bull market of the 1990s created over 10 million new millionaires whose wealth was derived almost solely from stock options. During this period, many CEOs made hundreds of millions in option gains and other compensation—often making as much as 400 times the earnings of the average workers in their companies. Beginning in late 2001, the business world changed dramatically. Now, with the public's and investors' direct focus on corporate governance and compensation philosophy, and anticipated changes in accounting rules affecting equity-based compensation, CEOs and other executives should not expect to sustain historic rates of wealth accumulation, absent substantial performance that is no longer linked solely to the price of the company's stock.

While the proxy statement compensation tables provide historical information and raw data about the company's remuneration of its top executive officers, the compensation committee's report in the proxy statement provides a window into the company's compensation philosophy and a means for investors to assess whether and how closely pay is related to performance. A thoughtfully prepared compensation committee report is good evidence of a well-functioning compensation committee that takes its work seriously.

Among the topics covered in this chapter are:

- Board and board committee structure
- Independence measures
- Compensation committee size
- Compensation committee charter
- Role of the compensation committee and its chair
- Duties and responsibilities
- Precepts for responsible performance
- Compensation benchmarking
- The importance of meeting minutes

BOARD STRUCTURE; THE FOCUS ON INDEPENDENCE

Much of the recent public scrutiny of corporate governance issues has focused on structural issues as they relate to corporate boards—questions related to independence from management; separation of the chair and CEO positions; issues related to the composition and function of board committees; and renewed efforts to create a framework in which outside directors can obtain impartial advice and analysis, free of undue influence from corporate management.

While it has always been desirable to have a healthy complement of outside directors on the board, new corporate governance rules adopted by the New York Stock Exchange (NYSE) and Nasdaq in 2003 require that a majority of a listed company's board consist of independent directors and, with limited exceptions, that such board appoint fully independent compensation, audit, and nominating/corporate governance committees. The new NYSE and Nasdaq rules also prescribe standards for determining the independence of individual directors, which, when layered over the director independence standards under Section 162(m) of the Internal Revenue Code (Code) and Rule 16b-3 of the Securities Exchange Act of 1934 (Exchange Act), make the nomination and selection of compensation committee members a challenging exercise.

COMPENSATION COMMITTEE COMPOSITION AND MULTIPLE INDEPENDENCE REQUIREMENTS

When selecting directors to serve on the compensation committee of a public company, the nominating committee should choose only those persons who meet all the relevant independence requirements that will permit the committee to fulfill its intended function. For example, a compensation committee member must be an "independent director," as defined under NYSE or Nasdaq rules, where applicable. In addition, a public company is well served to have a compensation committee consisting solely of two or more directors who meet (i) the definitional requirements of "outside director" under Code Section 162(m), and (ii) the definitional requirements of "non-employee director" under Rule 16b-3 of the Exchange Act. This often leads to a lowest common denominator approach of identifying director candidates who satisfy the requirements of all three definitions. Unfortunately, the three tests are not identical, and it is indeed possible to have a director who meets one or more independence tests but not another.

NYSE/Nasdaq Independence Tests

Under the 2003 NYSE listing rules, an independent director is defined as a director who has no material relationship with the company. Nasdaq defines independence as the absence of any relationship that would interfere with the exercise of independent judgment in carrying out the director's responsibilities. In both cases, the board has a responsibility to make an affirmative determination that no such relationships exist. The rules list specific conditions or relationships that will render a director nonindependent. These are summarized in Exhibit 5.1 in Chapter 5.

Rule 16b-3 Independence Test

Awards of stock options and other equity awards to directors and officers of a public company, generally referred to as "Section 16 insiders," are exempt from the short-swing profit provisions of Section 16 of the Exchange Act if such awards are made by a compensation committee consisting solely of two or more "non-employee directors" (as defined in Rule 16b-3 under the Exchange Act). In addition to such compensation committee approval, there are three alternative exemptions under Rule 16b-3: (i) such awards to Section 16 insiders can be preapproved by the full board of directors, (ii) the awards can be made subject to a six-month holding period (measured from the date of grant), or (iii) specific awards can be ratified by the shareholders (which alternative is, for obvious reasons, rarely taken).

Disadvantages of relying on full board approval for the Rule 16b-3 exemption are that (i) it is administratively awkward to single out awards to Section 16 insiders for special full board approval, and (ii) if the full board takes on that role, the proxy statement report on executive compensation must be made over the names of all the directors. Therefore, prevalent practice is for the compensation committee to be staffed exclusively with directors who meet the Rule 16b-3 definition of "non-employee director," and to have the compensation committee approve all equity awards to Section 16 insiders.

To qualify as a "non-employee director" under Rule 16b-3, a director cannot (i) be a current officer or employee of the company or a parent or subsidiary of the company; (ii) receive more than $60,000 in compensation, directly or indirectly, from the company or a parent or subsidiary of the company for services rendered as a consultant or in any capacity other than as a director; or (iii) have a reportable transaction under Regulation S-K 404(a) or a reportable business relationship under Regulation S-K 404(b) of the Securities and Exchange Commission (SEC), as outlined in Exhibit 1.1.

IRC Section 162(m) Independence Test

For any performance-based compensation granted to a public company's CEO or its next four most highly compensated executive officers ("covered employees") to be excluded from the $1 million deduction limit of Code Section 162(m), such compensation must have been approved in advance by a compensation committee consisting solely of two or more "outside directors" (as defined under the Code Section 162(m) regulations). Full board approval of such compensation will not suffice for this purpose, unless all directors who do not qualify as outside directors abstain from voting. Therefore, prevalent practice is for the compensation committee to be staffed exclusively with directors who meet the Code Section 162(m) definition of "outside director," and to have such compensation committee approve all performance-based awards to executive officers and others who might reasonably be expected to become covered employees during the life of the award.

To qualify as an "outside director" under Code Section 162(m), a director (i) cannot be a current employee of the company, (ii) cannot be a former employee of the company who receives compensation for services in the current fiscal year (other than tax-qualified retirement plan benefits), (iii) cannot be a current or former officer of the company, and (iv) cannot receive remuneration from the company, directly or indirectly, in any capacity other than as a director. Exhibit 1.2 outlines the Code Section 162(m) independence test, including a summary of what constitutes "indirect" remuneration.

State Law Interested Director Test

To further complicate the analysis, the concept of independence is also applied in determining whether a director is "interested" in a particular transaction under consideration by the board or the committee. A director who meets all of the regulatory definitions of independence under the NYSE/Nasdaq rules, Code Section 162(m),

Exhibit 1.1   Regulation S-K 404(a) Transactions with Management and Others

When	Transaction occurred in last fiscal year or is currently proposed
Between Whom	(1) The company or its subsidiaries, and (2) the director or nominee or his or her immediate family member
Threshold Amount	$60,000
Nature of Interest	Direct or indirect material interest in the transaction or other entity
Exceptions	Instructions provide guidance as to whether an indirect interest is material

Regulation S-K 404(b) Certain Business Relationships

When	Now existing, during last fiscal year, or proposed in current fiscal year
Who	(1) The director or nominee for director, and (2) an entity that has a relationship with the company
Category 1 Relationship	*Other entity pays the company for property or services:* (a) The director or nominee is or has been in the last fiscal year either an executive officer, or 10% owner, of the other entity, and (b) Payment exceeds 5% of either (i) company's consolidated gross revenues for last fiscal year, or (ii) other entity's consolidated gross revenues for its last fiscal year.
Category 2 Relationship	*The company pays the other entity for property or services:* (a) The director or nominee is or has been in the last fiscal year either an executive officer, or 10% owner, of the other entity, and (b) Payment exceeds 5% of either (i) company's consolidated gross revenues for last fiscal year, or (ii) other entity's consolidated gross revenues for its last fiscal year.
Category 3 Relationship	*The company was indebted to the other entity at end of company's last fiscal year:* (a) The director or nominee is or has been in the last fiscal year either an executive officer, or 10% owner, of the other entity, and (b) Indebtedness exceeds 5% of company's total consolidated assets at the end of last fiscal year.
Category 4 Relationship	*The director is a member of the company's law firm:* The director or nominee is a member of or counsel to a law firm that the company has retained in the last fiscal year or proposes to retain in the current fiscal year.
Category 5 Relationship	*The director is a member of the company's investment banking firm:* The director or nominee is a partner or executive officer of an investment banking firm that has performed services for the company (other than as a syndicate member) in the last fiscal year or proposed for the current fiscal year.
Category 6 Relationship	Any other relationships substantially similar in nature and scope to those specifically identified.

Exhibit 1.2   Outside Director Requirements under Code §162(m) Regulations

Current Employee	The director cannot be a current employee of the publicly held company.
Former Employee	The director cannot be a former employee of the publicly held company who receives compensation for services in the current fiscal year (other than tax-qualified retirement plan benefits).
Officer	The director cannot be a current or former officer of the publicly held company.
Remuneration	The director cannot receive remuneration from the company, directly or indirectly, in any capacity other than as a director. See categories 1–4 for what constitutes "indirect" remuneration.
Category 1	If remuneration is paid directly to the director, he or she is disqualified. No *de minimis* exception.
Category 2	If remuneration is paid to an entity of which the director is a 50% or greater beneficial owner, he or she is disqualified. No *de minimis* exception.
Category 3	If remuneration (other than a *de minimis* amount) was paid in the last fiscal year to an entity in which the director beneficially owns between 5% and 50%, he or she is disqualified. See below for definition of a *de minimis* amount.
Category 4	If remuneration (other than *de minimis* amount) was paid in the last fiscal year to an entity by which the director is employed (or self-employed) other than as a director, he or she is disqualified. See below for definition of *de minimis* amount.
De minimis **amount other than for personal services**	Payments not for personal services are *de minimis* if they did not exceed 5% of the gross revenue of the other entity for its last fiscal year ending with or within the company's last fiscal year.
De minimis **amount for personal services**	Payments for personal services are *de minimis* if they do not exceed $60,000.
Personal Services	Remuneration is for personal services if it (i) is paid to an entity for personal services consisting of legal, accounting, investment banking, or management consulting services (or similar services) and is not for services that are incidental to the purchase of goods or nonpersonal services; and (ii) the director performs significant services (whether or not as an employee) for the corporation, division, or similar organization (within the third-party entity) that actually provides the legal, accounting, investment banking, or management consulting services (or similar services) to the company, or more than 50% of the third-party entity's gross revenues are derived from that corporation, division, subsidiary, or similar organization.

Exhibit 1.2 Continued

Former Officer Defined	A director is not precluded from being an outside director solely because he or she is a former officer of a corporation that previously was an affiliated corporation of the publicly held corporation. For example, a director of a parent corporation of an affiliated group is not precluded from being an outside director solely because that director is a former officer of an affiliated subsidiary that was spun off or liquidated. However, an outside director would cease to be an outside director if a corporation in which the director was previously an officer became an affiliated corporation of the publicly held corporation.

and Rule 16b-3 can still have a personal interest in a particular transaction that can interfere with his or her ability to render impartial judgment with respect to that transaction. This type of nonindependence will not render the director unsuitable to serve on the compensation committee, but he or she may need to be excused from voting on the particular matter. An example of this might be a situation in which the compensation committee is determining whether to hire a particular consulting firm to advise the committee with respect to a particular matter and one of the committee members has a relative at such consulting firm. This relationship would not necessarily bar the committee member from satisfying any of the regulatory definitions of independence (particularly if the amount of the consultant's fee is less than $60,000), but the director might have a personal interest in having the committee hire that consulting firm over another. In that case, the interested director should disclose the nature of his or her interest in the matter and abstain from voting on the hiring question. Once that consulting firm has been hired to represent the committee, the matter is over, and the originally interested director may resume active participation in the business of the committee.

Full Disclosure of Pertinent Information

The SEC's proxy rules require disclosure of relevant background information about each director that is intended to give shareholders an indication of the director's unique qualifications and any relationships or affiliations that might affect his or her judgment or independence. For example, disclosure is required regarding:

- All positions and offices the director holds with the company.
- Any arrangement or understanding between the director and any other person pursuant to which he or she is to be selected as a director or nominee.
- The nature of any family relationship (by blood, marriage, or adoption, not more remote than first cousin) between the director and any executive officer or other director.

- The director's business experience during the past five years.
- Any other public company directorships held by the director.
- The director's involvement in certain legal proceedings.
- Any standard arrangements pursuant to which directors are compensated, and any other arrangements pursuant to which a director was compensated during the company's last fiscal year for any service provided as a director.
- Any transaction, or series of similar transactions, occurring in the last year or currently proposed, to which the company or any of its affiliates is a party, in which the amount involved exceeds $60,000 and in which the director had, or will have, a direct or indirect material interest.
- Certain business relationships that currently exist, or existed during the last fiscal year, between the company and an entity affiliated with the director or nominee, and the nature of such director's or nominee's affiliation, the relationship between such entity and the company and the amount of the business done between the company and the entity during the company's last full fiscal year or proposed to be done during the company's current fiscal year.
- Any indebtedness of the director in excess of $60,000 to the company or its subsidiaries at any time in the last fiscal year.
- Any failure by the director to make a timely filing of any Section 16 report during the last fiscal year.
- Any director interlocking relationships.

Director Interlocks

As a reflection of the current insistence on unbiased, independent analysis in setting executive pay, there is a special sensitivity to so-called "director interlocks." A director interlock exists where any of the following relationships is in evidence:

- An executive officer of the company serves as a member of the compensation committee of another entity, one of whose executive officers serves on the compensation committee of the company.
- An executive officer of the company serves as a director of another entity, one of whose executive officers serves on the compensation committee of the company.
- An executive officer of the company serves as a member of the compensation committee of another entity, one of whose executive officers serves as a director of the company.
- NYSE/Nasdaq description—A director of the listed company is, or has a family member who is, employed as an executive officer of another entity where at any time during the last three years any executive officers of the listed company served on the compensation committee of such other entity.

While not prohibited as a legal matter, director interlocks are suspect due to the possibility that they could engender a "you-scratch-my-back, I'll-scratch-yours" influence or other *quid pro quo* situation affecting executive compensation decisions. For that reason, a director who has an interlock of the nature described under applicable NYSE or Nasdaq rules will not be deemed an independent director until three years after such interlocking employment relationship has terminated. During that time, he or she would not be eligible to serve on the compensation committee.

An interlocking relationship will be evident to the public. The SEC's rules for public companies require disclosure in the proxy statement, under the specific caption "Compensation Committee Interlocks and Insider Participation," of each person who served as a member of the compensation committee (or board committee performing equivalent functions) during the last fiscal year, indicating each committee member who is or was an employee or officer of the company, had a disclosable transaction with the company, or had an interlocking relationship.

COMPENSATION COMMITTEE SIZE

State law has little to say about the size of a board of directors, and even less about the size of its oversight committees such as the compensation committee. The Revised Model Business Corporation Act (Model Act), on which a majority of states base their corporation laws, provides that a board must consist of one or more individuals, with the number to be specified or fixed in accordance with the corporation's charter or bylaws. Under the Model Act, a company's charter or bylaws may fix a minimum and maximum number of directors and allow the actual number of directors within the range to be fixed or changed from time to time by the shareholders or the board. Delaware, which does not follow the Model Act but is the state of incorporation for many U.S. companies, has similar requirements for determining the size of the board.

Corporations should attempt to assemble a board that reflects a diversity of viewpoints and talents, but is not so large as to frustrate the accomplishment of business at meetings. Smaller boards (those with 12 or fewer members) may allow more free interchange among directors who might otherwise be reticent to express their views in a larger group. However, when considering the appropriate size for a public company board, it is important to include a sufficient number of independent directors to staff the audit, compensation, and nominating/corporate governance committees, each of which is now required by applicable rules to consist solely of independent directors.

Given the interplay of three separate independence requirements for compensation committee members, as discussed previously, it is unusual for a public company's compensation committee to have more than five members. A compensation committee of three to five members should provide an adequate forum for a useful exchange of ideas and healthy debate.

COMPENSATION COMMITTEE CHARTER

The compensation committee (whether it is called such or by some other name—e.g., the human resources committee) generally is established through a formal board resolution, in accordance with applicable state corporate law, the company's articles/certificate of incorporation, and/or the company's bylaws. In the past, some compensation committees had a written charter, while others did not. However, today most compensation committees have a written charter, largely due to recent changes in stock exchange listing rules. As discussed in more detail later, new rules at the NYSE require that both the audit committee and the compensation committee have a written charter, while the new Nasdaq rules only require that audit committees have a written charter. Nevertheless, compensation committees at most Nasdaq companies have or are in the process of adopting a written charter, in the spirit of good corporate governance. In addition, there may be other federal or state statutory or regulatory requirements for such a charter with respect to specific regulated industries.

Some companies use a short-form charter (often less than a page) that grants the compensation committee authority in very broad strokes. Others adopt a long-form charter that spells out the duties and responsibilities of the committee, the procedures to be followed, and a variety of other specifications and requirements (such as number of members, number of scheduled meetings per year, and so forth). While the long-form charter is often favored as providing an aura of good corporate governance practice, one drawback is that the details in the charter must in fact be followed. For example, if the charter provides that the committee shall meet at least once every quarter, then the committee must do so or be in violation. Another consequence of the long-form charter is the need for more frequent review and adjustment. Any adjustments must follow an appropriate amendment procedure and will require subsequent disclosure.

See Appendix D for a sample compensation committee charter and selected examples of a variety of compensation committee charters at NYSE and Nasdaq companies.

NYSE Compensation Committee Requirements

Under NYSE rules, the compensation committee must have a written charter that addresses the committee's purpose and responsibilities and requires an annual performance evaluation of the committee. The compensation committee of an NYSE listed company must, at a minimum, have direct responsibility to:

- Review and approve corporate goals and objectives relevant to CEO compensation, evaluate the CEO's performance in light of those goals and objectives, and, either as a committee or, if the board so directs, together with the other independent directors, determine and approve the CEO's compensation level based on that evaluation. The committee is free to discuss CEO compensation with the board generally, as long as the committee shoulders these absolute responsibilities.

- Make recommendations to the board with respect to (i) compensation of the company's executive officers other than the CEO, (ii) incentive compensation plans, and (iii) equity-based plans.
- Produce a compensation committee report on executive compensation as required by the SEC to be included in the company's annual proxy statement or annual report on Form 10-K filed with the SEC.

The compensation committee charter should also address: (i) committee member qualifications, (ii) committee member appointment and removal, (iii) committee structure and operations (including authority to delegate to subcommittees), and (iv) committee reporting to the board.

If a compensation consultant is to assist in the evaluation of director, CEO, or senior executive compensation, the compensation committee charter should give that committee sole authority to retain and terminate the consulting firm, including sole authority to approve the firm's fees and other engagement terms.

Nasdaq Compensation Committee Requirements

Under Nasdaq rules, compensation of the CEO and all other executive officers of the company must be determined, or recommended to the board for determination, either by a majority of the independent directors, or a compensation committee comprised solely of independent directors. The CEO may not be present during voting or deliberations with respect to his or her own compensation.

Unlike the NYSE, Nasdaq rules do not specifically require the compensation committee to have and publish a charter. However, it is generally a matter of good corporate governance that a charter be established and followed. The first model compensation committee charter appearing in Appendix D is annotated to conform to both the NYSE and Nasdaq rules as currently in effect.

ROLE OF THE COMPENSATION COMMITTEE

Over time, the role of the compensation committee as a core oversight committee of the board has crystallized. As indicated previously, the new NYSE and Nasdaq corporate governance rules require all listed companies to have a compensation committee (or a committee having that function, regardless of the name) composed entirely of independent directors.

The tenets of sound corporate governance embodied in the NYSE and Nasdaq rules should be heeded by any company, whether public or private. In the shareholder-savvy climate of the 21st century, it would be hard to justify a nonindependent compensation committee in which the CEO is allowed to vote on or otherwise participate in decisions regarding his or her own compensation. The NYSE and Nasdaq rules set out minimum standards governing the deliberative process of the compensation committee. A good committee will not stop there. As discussed more fully in Chapter 5, a host of influential business and investor groups have published their own concepts of best practices for the compensation committee. While none is binding or has the force of law, and while one might not agree with all the views in each report, these best practice guidelines are a "must read" for every compensation committee member who undertakes seriously to consider the proper role of the committee.

The basic role of the compensation committee is twofold. First is to be the "owner" of the company's executive and director compensation philosophy and programs. Second is to provide the primary forum in which core compensation issues are fully and vigorously reviewed, analyzed, and acted upon (either by the committee itself or by way of recommendation to the full board or the independent directors as a group). The decisions and actions of the compensation committee may make the difference between mediocre and outstanding corporate performance.

The more defined role of the compensation committee varies from company to company, and is contingent on various factors such as ownership structure, concerns of shareholders (and perhaps stakeholders—as broadly defined), director capabilities, board values, market dynamics, the company's maturity and financial condition, and other intrinsic and extrinsic factors. The compensation committee, more than any other oversight committee, is charged with the all-important task of balancing the interests of shareholders with those of management. The essential conflict between these two interests is generally not over pay levels, but rather the relationship of pay to performance. Shareholders favor a compensation plan strongly tied to corporate performance, while managers have a natural tendency to prefer a compensation plan with maximum security.

Exhibit 1.3 is a matrix illustrating a typical division of responsibilities among the full board, the nominating committee, and the compensation committee relative to certain matters. Where the responsibilities overlap, it generally implies committee recommendation followed by board ratification.

ROLE OF THE COMPENSATION COMMITTEE CHAIR

The chair's role is to lead the committee and initiate its agenda. The chair of the compensation committee may be selected by the members of the compensation

Exhibit 1.3   Board/Compensation Committee Responsibility Matrix

	Approval/Review Required	
	Full Board	Committee
Corporate Organization		
• Certificate of Incorporation (adoption or amendment)	X	
• Corporate bylaws (adoption or amendment)	X	
• Stock: all authorization to issue or buy back shares	X	
Board Organization		
• Board membership qualification		Nominating
• Board committee memberships		Nominating
• New member selection		Nominating
Compensation Matters: ***Base Salary***		
• Salaries of CEO and executive officers		Compensation
Officer Employment Agreements		
• Severance agreements	X	Compensation
• Retention agreements	X	Compensation
• Change in control agreements	X	Compensation
Fringe Benefits		
• Establishment of new plans or amendments to existing plans	X	Compensation
Incentive Compensation		
• All arrangements for corporate officers		Compensation
• Approval of specific financial targets		Compensation
• Determination of payouts		Compensation
Long-term (Cash) Incentive Plans		
• Establishment of performance targets		Compensation
• Award sizing		Compensation
Stock Plans		
• Establishment of, or amendment to, equity compensation plans	X	Compensation
• Administration of stock plans		Compensation
• Grants of all stock plans		Compensation

committee, by the nominating committee, or as otherwise provided in the committee's charter. The responsibilities of the chair might appropriately include:

- To suggest the calendar and overall outline of the annual agenda for the committee
- To convene and prepare the agenda for regular and special meetings
- To preside over meetings of the committee, keeping the discussion orderly and focused, while encouraging questions, debate, and input from all members on each topic under discussion
- To provide leadership in developing the committee's compensation philosophy and policy
- To counsel collectively and individually with members of the committee and the other independent directors
- To interview, retain, and provide interface between the committee and outside experts, consultants, and advisors

DUTIES AND RESPONSIBILITIES OF THE COMPENSATION COMMITTEE

The fundamental task of the compensation committee is to establish the compensation philosophy of the company. Having done so, it should design programs to advance that philosophy. In almost all cases, this will require the advice of outside experts, to assure that specific performance metrics and performance goals are established that promote desired performance and that pay is in line with such performance.

The compensation committee should assume primary responsibility for the following general areas:

- Compensation philosophy and strategy
- Compensation of the CEO and other executive officers
- Compensation of nonexecutive officers (or the oversight of such compensation if delegated to others)
- Compensation of directors (this function is sometimes housed at the board level or with the governance committee)
- Management development and succession (this function is sometimes placed with the full board or the governance committee)
- Equity compensation plans
- Retirement plans, benefits, and perquisites (this function is sometimes shared with, or performed by, a separate benefits plan committee):
  - Qualified retirement plans, profit sharing, and savings plans

- Nonqualified plans such as supplemental executive retirement plans (SERPs), nonqualified deferred compensation, and pension restoration plans
- Welfare benefits, including medical, life insurance, accidental death and disability insurance
- Executive benefits such as supplemental medical coverage and supplemental life insurance
- Perquisites
- Contractual arrangements with management, including employment and severance agreements
- For public companies, preparation of the report to shareholders on executive compensation that is required by the SEC to be included in the company's annual proxy statement or annual report

The decision as to how far compensation committee oversight should be extended depends on various factors, including the corporate culture, strength of management, the size of the committee, members' time availability, the regulatory environment in which the company operates, and prior corporate performance in these areas.

Exhibit 1.4 contains a checklist covering typical duties of the compensation committee.

SIX PRECEPTS FOR RESPONSIBLE COMMITTEE PERFORMANCE

To execute its duties responsibly, the compensation committee must be able to efficiently synthesize highly technical information and apply sound business judgment. As the field of executive compensation becomes increasingly complex and more in the focus of public attention, the committee's job grows more and more challenging. Adherence to the following six precepts will pave the way to optimal performance by the committee:

1. Get organized
2. Get and stay informed
3. Keep an eye on the big picture
4. Return to reason
5. Consider the shareholders' perspective
6. Communicate effectively

1. Getting Organized

Set the agenda. As noted previously, many topics generally fall within the purview of the compensation committee. To make sure that all are considered in a timely and effective manner, the compensation committee chair should at the beginning

Exhibit 1.4   Checklist for the Compensation Committee

• Ensure disinterest and independence from management	• Understand and coordinate all elements of executive pay
• Retain and maintain direct access to outside experts/consultants	• Assess the real dollar value/cost of executives' total pay packages
• Establish and periodically review/update compensation philosophy	• Carefully select recognized industry index and/or an appropriate peer group for the performance group
• Establish a compensation strategy (including pay plans) consistent with overall compensation philosophy and corporate objectives	• Compare pay programs with relevant peer group
	• Link payments with performance goals
• Ensure that shareholder and corporate economic values are prime drivers of the executive pay program	• Set goals for CEO, evaluation performance against such goals, and set CEO pay levels
• Be sensitive to external pressures	• Draft compensation committee report for proxy statement. Use detailed, individualized disclosures—avoid boilerplate
• Be mindful of controversial pay practices	
• Balance fixed versus variable rewards	• Prepare other disclosures, both required and more if necessary or appropriate
• Define equity participation strategy	

of the year prepare a schedule of meetings for the whole year, along with a tentative agenda for each meeting. To accommodate new topics arising over the ensuing months, specific agenda should be prepared and circulated before each meeting. An example of such an annual schedule, along with possible recurring agenda items, is shown in Exhibit 1.5.

Exhibit 1.5   Illustrative Compensation Committee Agenda

Event	Meeting Date	Recurring Agenda Items
End of calendar/ fiscal year in December	Late February	• Approve minutes of prior meeting • Review prior year operating results presented as required by bonus plan criteria • Evaluate performance of CEO for prior year, and review and approve recommended bonus plan payments • Review and approve recommendations related to current year participation in bonus plan

Exhibit 1.5 Continued

Event	Meeting Date	Recurring Agenda Items
		• Review and approve current year bonus plan targets for organization units and plan participants
		• Review and approve personal goals of CEO for current year
		• Review and discuss draft of compensation committee report for inclusion in proxy
		• Review executive compensation disclosures for inclusion in proxy
		• Review new plan proposals for inclusion in proxy
After annual shareholders' meeting and approval of stock-related plans	June/July or September/ October	• Approve minutes of prior meeting
		• Review and approve recommendations for annual equity grants
		• Review and approve mid-year promotions, new hires
		• Receive consultant's report on fringe benefits and benefit costs; competitive practices and recommended changes and costs
		• Receive annual management development and succession planning overview from CEO
		• Engage outside studies for various matters
		• Review performance of outside advisors
Late in year	November/early December	• Approve minutes of prior meeting
		• Review consultant's report on compensation levels and competitive pay practices
		• Review and approve recommended changes in salary structure and bonus plan provisions
		• Approve additions and removals from bonus plan participation
		• Review executive compensation budget, and approve annual salary increases for next year
		• New ideas session (planning session for new ideas, plans, and programs)
		• Discuss incentive measures for upcoming year
		• Annual review of executive severance plans
		• Review corporate compensation philosophy and pay strategy

Provide timely information. It is best to provide written materials to each committee member at least a week before each meeting so that he or she will have ample opportunity to review them in advance and will be able to come to the meeting fully prepared to ask pertinent questions and move the discussion forward. Such materials should include minutes of the prior meeting, and materials and information pertinent to the agenda for the current meeting—such as copies of any plans or agreements to be considered by the committee, reports and analysis from outside experts, internally prepared information relevant to the matter, and proposed resolutions.

Engage outside experts. Issues faced by compensation committees today involve sophisticated techniques and require a facile understanding of financial measures tax and accounting applications. The "level playing field" that will result from stock option expensing is causing widespread use of alternative types of equity compensation vehicles, many of which may be unfamiliar to compensation committee members. The array of choices alone can be bewildering. Moreover, the role of the committee itself is becoming imbued with an overlay of regulatory requirements and legal nuances, while trends in shareholder litigation underscore the importance of relying on the advice of outside experts. Delaware courts in the recent *Disney* and *Cendant* cases focused on the alleged failure of those compensation committees to seek expert advice in advance of important compensation decisions.

For these and other reasons, it is all but essential that the compensation committee look to competent outside compensation consultants and legal advisors. While it may be appropriate for the committee to engage its own legal counsel for special assignments, the relationship with the compensation consultant should be of an ongoing nature. It is axiomatic that it should be the committee, and not management, that interviews and hires outside experts. The allegiance of such experts should be to the committee, and ultimately to the company, rather than to management.

Establish a meaningful CEO evaluation program. The compensation committee should create and adhere to an effective CEO evaluation program. NYSE and Nasdaq corporate governance rules require the compensation committee to review the CEO's performance on an annual basis, but this should be done regardless of any regulatory requirement. Such an evaluation is essential for the proxy statement compensation committee report, and provides a basis for determining whether the company's executive incentive compensation programs are achieving intended results. Chapter 3 addresses the CEO evaluation process.

Establish annual compensation committee (and perhaps board) evaluation programs. Recent NYSE corporate governance rules require an annual self-performance evaluation by the compensation committee. If board compensation is within the purview of the compensation committee rather than the nominating/governance committee, it may also make sense for the compensation committee to implement the board evaluation program. The program should include feedback solicited from other directors, the CEO, other senior executives, and other interested parties. See Exhibit 1.6 for a sample board evaluation form.

2. Getting and Staying Informed

Understand the context. The committee cannot make valid compensation decisions in a vacuum. Even where the committee does not have direct oversight or responsibility for all aspects of compensation and benefits, it is imperative that the

Exhibit 1.6 Sample Form for Board Evaluation

Rate the following statements in relation to our board of directors

Topic	Description	Rating*
1.	The board knows and understands the company's beliefs, values, philosophy, mission, strategic plan, and business plan, and reflects this understanding on key issues throughout the year.	
2.	The board has and follows procedures for effective meetings.	
3.	Board meetings are conducted in a manner that ensures open communication, meaningful participation, and timely resolution of issues.	
4.	Board members receive timely materials for consideration prior to meetings.	
5.	Board members receive accurate minutes.	
6.	The board reviews and adopts annual capital and operating budgets.	
7.	The board monitors cash flow, profitability, net revenue and expenses, productivity, and other financially driven indicators to ensure the company performs as expected.	
8.	The board monitors company performance with industry comparative data.	
9.	Board members stay abreast of issues and trends affecting the company, and use this information to assess and guide the company's performance not just year to year, but in the long term.	
10.	Board members comprehend and respect the difference between the board's policy-making role and the CEO's management role.	
11.	The board acts to help the CEO by setting clear policy.	
12.	Board goals, expectations, and concerns are honestly communicated with the CEO.	

*Rating 1 to 5, with 1 for "not performing" to 5 for "outstanding"

committee have an understanding of how all pieces of the puzzle fit together. The committee should have access to information necessary to calculate the value of an executive's total compensation arrangement at any given time. For example, if the committee is considering one element of pay for the CEO, such as a long-term equity award, it must be able to do so in the context of the CEO's total pay, including all forms of compensation and benefits (such as base salary, short-term incentive opportunity, qualified and nonqualified deferred compensation, SERPs, perquisites, severance arrangements, and other previously granted long-term incentives), to ensure that the total compensation is reasonable and not excessive.

Naturally, not all elements of pay will be considered at a single committee meeting, and not all information before the committee at a given time will be presented with equal detail or emphasis. However, as baseline contextual information, the committee should insist on regularly being provided with the senior executives' total compensation tallies—perhaps in the form of a simple spreadsheet showing each element of pay and benefits, a brief summary of how each pay program operates, and an estimate of current rates, benefit levels, or balances.

Understand each element of the compensation program. The compensation committee, not management or the human resources department, is the "owner" of the company's executive compensation and employment plans, programs, and arrangements. As such, it is the compensation committee's duty to thoroughly understand all compensation programs, both simple and complex.

There is no one "correct" way to conduct this review, as long as it results in a full and thorough examination of each program. Generally, this review will involve management (including the human resources department), the company's auditors, and the committee's independent advisors. Only when the committee has its arms around all aspects of each program can it make informed and appropriate decisions in implementing (and perhaps restructuring) the overall compensation strategy.

Regularly review and quantify the impact of change-in-control provisions in all compensation plans and programs. Change-in-control (CIC) arrangements have become almost universal for senior executives in the largest public companies. At some companies, CIC agreements or policies extend protections deeper into employee ranks, and in some cases, cover all employees. The committee must keep sight of the estimated aggregate cost of all such CIC protections, including tax gross-ups and lost deductions, under various circumstances. Because circumstances change and compensation programs can dramatically affect the cost of CIC arrangements in not-so-obvious ways, this exercise should be undertaken on a regular basis to guard against surprises if and when an actual CIC situation arises. In assessing the potential cost, the committee should consider that aggregate CIC payments of 1% to 3% of the transaction amount are generally within standard practice.

3. Keeping an Eye on the Big Picture

Compensation plans and programs should be consistent with the achievement of corporate strategy. This is especially true with incentive-based compensation. It makes little sense for the compensation programs to be motivating executives to achieve goals that do not enhance overall corporate objectives.

The committee must take an active hand in the process. For example, with the aid of management and outside advisors, each member of the committee should learn and understand the financial measures that are most relevant to the company's success and design incentive programs on the basis of those measures. The committee should understand how any year-end financial reporting adjustments (or other events) might affect such measures and thereby affect compensation based on those measures. Where feasible, performance compensation programs should be designed to minimize the possibility of manipulation to achieve certain results—not on the assumption that management would do so, but more as evidence of a sound and reliable program.

The compensation committee should be prepared to explain to investors in its annual report on executive compensation how the short-term and long-term incentive programs for executive officers relate specifically to and complement the company's overall strategy. Moreover, the committee should be thoughtful in setting and explaining goals for incentive compensation. For example, setting "stretch" or very demanding goals and being prepared to pay commensurate with achieving this level of performance, can be an effective driver of performance.

4. Returning to Reason

There is no denying that executive compensation in the 1990s soared to unsustainable levels. Fueled by the seemingly endless bull market, the investing public's "irrational exuberance" (as dubbed by Alan Greenspan as early as 1996) and perhaps even unintentionally by the then-prevailing benchmarking practices of compensation consultants in which all executives were slated for above-average pay levels, executive compensation simply got out of hand. In the sobering post-scandal environment of the new century, boards and management alike recognize that something dramatic must be done to restore investor confidence and return compensation to sensible, sustainable levels. If the private sector cannot be disciplined and effective in achieving this, it is likely that the nose of Congress will once again creep under the tent.

Outside experts and advisors cannot be expected to right the ship—that requires the attention, support, and serious direction of the compensation committee. Consultants and advisors should be given free reign and encouragement to give an honest review and assessment of the company's pay practices and to speak up when changes are in order. The compensation committee must then be prepared to make hard decisions or negotiate with management if cutbacks on existing compensation are recommended in one area or another. Evidence of real negotiations with management can be of evidentiary importance in future shareholder litigation.

All this is not to say that executive pay is evil or unnecessary. It is, of course, still true that competitive compensation is needed to attract and retain the best executive talent. The compensation committee will continue to need to understand the "market" for executive compensation, both in form and levels of pay. Independent compensation specialists are best equipped to provide this information. However, the common practice of setting pay based on benchmarking for comparable positions gleaned from survey data is one of the main culprits for runaway compensation in the 1990s. This is because so many companies targeted executive pay at the 75th percentile of the selected peer group. It is easy to see, in hindsight, that this annual ratcheting effect—where this year's 75th percentile becomes the next year's 50th percentile—led to unrealistically high competitive data. Moreover, there is considerable room for manipulation of such studies, by cherry picking the peer companies, for example, to include those that recently experienced aberrational strong performance, those that emphasize one element of pay over others, or those that are not appropriate peers of the company based on revenue, market cap, or other factors. While the committee need not turn away from considering objective outside data as a legitimate measure of competitive practice, it can safeguard the process by making sure its consultants understand the committee's expectation of candor and objectivity, and by asking the right questions about how and why the data were selected. The mechanical process of compensation benchmarking is discussed later in this chapter.

5. Considering the Shareholders' Perspective

The compensation committee must consistently ask the question, "is this in the shareholders' best interests and how will shareholders view it?" In today's business environment, shareholders are taking a greater interest than ever before in matters of executive compensation. While this does not change the duty or allegiance of the committee, it does provide a useful focus to its deliberations.

Shareholder value is paramount. In general, executive compensation should be accretive to shareholder value. Existing and new programs should be considered by the compensation committee in this context. The committee should analyze each compensation program with a view to its potential effects on financial results and shareholder dilution, and whether such effects can be managed or mitigated. For example, in the case of an equity-based compensation plan, the source of shares to pay participants (i.e., newly issued shares or repurchases in the market) can affect the dilution analysis.

Understand and consider institutional investor concerns. Institutional investors are making their voices heard loud and clear, aided by a number of factors, including new NYSE and Nasdaq rules that require shareholder approval for all new or materially modified equity compensation plans, new rules that prohibit brokers from voting street-name shares on compensation plan proposals without the express direction of the beneficial owners, and the increasingly high approval rate of shareholder proposals in recent proxy seasons. Shareholder activism has matured considerably from its roots in the 1970s. Independent research firms such as Investor Responsibility Research Center glean, organize, and make available information on corporate governance and social responsibility issues affecting investors. IRRC does not advocate on any side of the issues it covers. A host of institutional investor advisory groups, such as Institutional Shareholder Services, Glass-Lewis & Co., and The Council of Institutional Investors, as well as large investor pension funds such as TIAA-CREF, CalPERs, SWIB, and NYCERS, take a more confrontational stance on issues. Most have formulated complex models for assessing the potential dilution and "value transfer" of proposed compensation plans. Together or individually, these groups make possible powerful voting and economic blocks that cannot be ignored.

The compensation committee should be proactive in anticipating institutional investor concerns. Corporate governance issues, such as the independence of directors, organization of the board, incentive plans and programs, CEO selection and succession, employment agreements, executive stock ownership, insider trading actions, compensation levels, and other related issues are fair game for shareholder comment. It is usually productive to seek the input of the company's largest institutional investors on compensation proposals well in advance of putting them up for shareholder vote. Often, it is possible to adjust proposed plan provisions in a way that will make the difference in the plan being approved or voted down.

6. Communicating Effectively

Take control of the compensation committee report. The committee's report on executive compensation that appears in the annual proxy statement provides the best window into the work of the committee. The amount of candor, care, and detail that goes into that report speaks volumes about how seriously the committee takes its role and responsibility. The preparation of this report should not be relegated to management, the compensation consultant, or legal counsel. Rather, it should reflect the independent and thoughtful analysis of the committee, even if others participate in the drafting. Boilerplate language is not a substitute for the actual voice of the committee, nor should the report say the same thing every year—assuming that new thought and analysis takes place each year, as it should. A straightforward and thorough explanation of the committee's actions and philosophy is critical to a meaningful report. Remember that the report goes over the names of the individual committee members, which is meant to assure that they personally stand behind its content.

See Appendix E for sample compensation committee reports taken from several 2004 proxy statements.

Prepare for increased disclosure and accountability. It has been well over a decade since the SEC's 1992 overhaul of the executive compensation disclosure rules. When the SEC revisits these rules, as it surely will before long, we can expect to see more tabular disclosure of common compensation programs, such as deferred compensation, SERPs, and life insurance programs, as well as disclosure rules that more closely fit the array of equity-based incentive vehicles that are finding their way into compensation plans as replacements for traditional stock options and restricted stock awards. The compensation committee can and should get out in front of that wave by collecting information now about its current programs and policies, considering whether and how all elements work together for a cohesive whole, and thinking about how to effectively communicate this to shareholders. In fact, there is no need to wait until SEC rules require specific disclosures. Effective communication is always timely and can go a long way to building investor confidence that the company's compensation strategy is in good hands.

COMPENSATION BENCHMARKING

Compensation committees are constantly examining whether the compensation levels of the top executives are reasonable and adequate. This is done for two reasons. First is to ensure that the pay levels are competitive, because if they are not (otherwise referred to as "below market"), another company may try to "raid" the executive talent pool. Second is to ensure that the compensation levels are neither too high nor too disproportionate (i.e., there is reasonable balance between salary, annual bonus, long-term incentives, pension, and so on).

This examination generally entails two processes. First is to collect and review recent and reputable surveys (usually published by compensation consulting or accounting firms). These surveys must be carefully reviewed to determine the methodology used and the quality of the data. For example, a survey might say that the median salary of CEOs in the biotechnology industry is $400,000; however, upon closer review, it may be discovered that only three companies were included, and that one of the companies has a founder CEO who receives a nominal salary. Accordingly, these surveys are helpful but cannot—in and of themselves—be used to set executive compensation levels without full and careful analysis.

The second process is to prepare a benchmarking or comparison study. This can be done in-house, but most companies prefer to use outside advisors. The most important aspect of these studies is to construct a peer group of companies that both the compensation committee and management agree represents "market." In addition, there should be a minimum of 10 peer companies. Generally, 15 to 30 companies would be preferred to ensure that any anomaly (known as an "outlier" or a "red circle") would not significantly impair the overall results.

Peer companies generally are selected based on similarities to the subject company in terms of revenues, market capitalization, and/or industry, oftentimes using Standard Industrial Classification (SIC) codes that are the same as or similar to the subject company. Sometimes, other aspects are considered, such as geography, company age, financial performance, and so forth. No matter what and how many characteristics are used to construct the peer group, the key is for all parties to agree that the peer group is representative of an appropriate "market."

After the peer group is finalized, the next step is to collect and collate executive compensation data, either from private databases or culled from publicly filed documents, such as proxy statements and Form 10-Ks. Of course, each data point must be reviewed to ensure that it is correct. For example, some benchmarking studies will mingle different fiscal years. Other benchmarking studies may mechanically cull data from a proxy statement without any analysis, and thus could, for example, use an "annual salary" amount that actually is for a partial year. Other benchmarking studies may apply inconsistent valuation methodologies (such as valuation of stock options or other long-term incentive awards). In addition, more and more benchmarking studies are including performance analysis of each peer company. This is then used to determine whether the compensation level should be set at, below, or above the peer group's median level. For example, if the subject company is performing well below the median of the peer group, then arguably the compensation levels should also be below the median of the peer group.

Finally, after all the data are collected, reviewed, and otherwise "scrubbed," it is placed into a model that typically shows quartiles and what percentile levels apply to the company's existing executives or candidates. An example of such a model is shown in Exhibit 1.7.

These models also typically show ratios, such as between target annual bonus and salary, long-term incentives (LTI) and salary, and LTI and total compensation. In addition, some companies use ratios to set executive compensation levels below the CEO (e.g., the COO's salary level is set at 75% of the CEO's salary level).

While many companies have used these benchmarking studies as a rigid guide to setting executive compensation, there is a trend to apply both an objective and subjective analysis of the data. In other words, the data are first quantitatively reviewed, and then qualitatively reviewed. The reason for this is that each company has its own particular set of facts and circumstances, and square pegs should not be forced into round holes. For example, assume a company wants to pay its CEO at "market median," that the median CEO salary of the peer group is determined to be $500,000, and the salary of the subject company's CEO is $650,000.

Exhibit 1.7 CEO Benchmarking Study Template

Company	CEO	Salary	Target Bonus	Total Actual Bonus	Cash Comp	Restricted Stock	Stock Options	Other LTI	Total LTI	Other Comp	Total Comp
# 1											
# 2											
# 3											
...											
# 20											
Subject Company											
Minimum											
25th Percentile											
50th Percentile											
75th Percentile											
Maximum											
Average											

The compensation committee, however, when it hired the CEO, agreed to the $650,000 salary level because that was the CEO's salary level at the previous employer. Accordingly, the salary level will be in the upper quartile, and the compensation committee will most likely need to adjust other components of this CEO's compensation (but not the salary) to bring it within "market median."

THE IMPORTANCE OF COMPENSATION COMMITTEE MEETING MINUTES

Today's heightened focus on corporate governance in general, and executive compensation in particular, justifies a close review of the processes of the compensation committee, and its documentation of the same. It has always been customary corporate practice to keep minutes of committee meetings. However, it is important to recognize that minutes, which are easily attainable by shareholders, are as important in what they don't say as what they do.

Historically, many companies have taken the view that perfunctory, bare-bones minutes were adequate and even preferred—a means of satisfying minimum corporate procedural requirements without airing dirty laundry in the form of dissenting opinions or serious debate that might suggest lack of unanimity or weakness of resolve. However, recent shareholder litigation and apparent trends in judicial review, as discussed more fully in Chapter 5, suggest that the better approach favors thoughtful minutes that reflect in detail the ultimate action taken, the discussion of each topic, the time devoted to the discussion, the alternatives reviewed, the consideration of relevant materials and outside advice, and the rationale for each decision reached. Two recent Delaware court cases illustrate how the quality of minutes can make a difference very early in the litigation process.

In 2003, the Delaware Chancery Court refused to dismiss a complaint by shareholders in *In re Walt Disney Co. Derivative Litigation,* 825 A.2d 275 (Del Ch. 2003), alleging that Disney's directors breached their fiduciary duties when they approved an employment agreement with its president, Michael Ovitz, which ultimately resulted in an award to him allegedly exceeding $140 million after barely one year of employment. The court focused heavily on what was reflected in the minutes of the compensation committee, from which it appeared that (i) no draft employment agreement was presented to the compensation committee for review before the meeting; (ii) the committee received only a summary of the employment agreement and no questions were asked about the agreement; (iii) no expert consultant was present to advise the compensation committee; (iv) the compensation committee met for less than an hour and spent most of its time on two other topics, including the compensation of one director for helping secure Ovitz's employment; (v) no time was taken to review the documents for approval; and (vi) the committee approved the hiring in principle but directed Mr. Eisner, Ovitz's close friend, to carry out the negotiations with regard to certain still unresolved and significant details. Referring to the board meeting that followed the compensation committee meeting, the court further noted that less than 2 of 15 pages of minutes were devoted to discussions of hiring the new president and that, so far as such minutes reflected, no presentations were made to the board regarding the terms of the draft agreement, no questions were raised, and no expert consultant was present to give advice.

The *Disney* court concluded that the alleged facts, if true, could support a determination that the defendant directors' action went beyond a mere breach of the duty of care to amount to a lack of good faith, such that their action would not be protected by the business judgment rule or by the company's director exculpation provision in its charter. If so, the directors could be held personally liable and unindemnifiable.

Also to the point is the April 2004 settlement of shareholder litigation against Cendant Corporation. The complaint alleged the directors breached their fiduciary duties in approving an amendment to the CEO's employment agreement that would have provided, among other things, an uncapped annual bonus stated as a percentage of the company's pretax earnings, $100 million of life insurance for life, and severance benefits that could have exceeded $140 million. According to the complaint, the minutes of the compensation committee reflected (i) no analysis of the potential cost to Cendant of the new agreement, (ii) no discussion of the committee's deliberation on various aspects of the proposed changes to the agreement, (iii) no advice from outside advisors, such as compensation experts or independent legal advisors, (iv) no questions raised about the financial consequences to the company under various severance scenarios, and (v) no involvement by any member of the compensation committee in the negotiation of the agreement. Even if the directors did in fact exercise more care and deliberation than alleged, the quick settlement of this lawsuit (the month after it was filed) might indicate the defendants' recognition of the damning potential of scant minutes on their ability to establish adequate proof to the contrary.

The lesson from these cases and others sure to come is this: Adherence to fiduciary duties is an absolute requirement and keeping minutes that reflect the proper amount of attention, deliberation, and consideration of compensation decisions can be of pivotal evidentiary value in shielding directors from personal liability.

Accordingly, compensation committee meeting minutes should reflect:

- Each discussion topic and the approximate time that the matter was considered
- Whether outside advisors were present or consulted, and the extent of their involvement
- The committee's consideration of any cost analyses for specific proposals, such as financial modeling of employment and severance contracts under various scenarios

- Whether questions were asked, about what, and by whom
- Due consideration by the committee of the reasonableness of the particular element of pay being voted on, when viewed in context with the executive's overall compensation package

CALL TO ACTION

The work of the modern compensation committee is not "business as usual." To take a lofty view (and to borrow the words of former SEC chairman and "MCI Corporate Monitor" Richard Breeden in his well-publicized report to the board of directors of MCI Corporation), theirs is the job of restoring trust in corporate America, by reversing the compensation excesses of the late 20th century that have so evoked the public's ire. On a more pedestrian level, to the extent that compensation committees across the country are in fact successful in reestablishing realistic and effective compensation practices through their own disciplined approaches, Congress may be persuaded to stay out of the mix. Ultimately, the compensation committee of the 21st century has the opportunity now to shape its own future.

Chapter 2

Selecting and Training Compensation Committee Members

For purposes of this chapter, it will be assumed that the company seeks new independent directors to round out the board and staff its core oversight committees, including the compensation committee. The chapter will first discuss the processes the nominating committee should follow to identify and attract qualified independent individuals who are best suited to serve as independent directors for their particular company. Later, the chapter will discuss the orientation and training of the individuals who are selected to fill that role.

As previously discussed in Chapter 1, independence is the core requirement for the compensation committee. However, independence is not the sole determinant of its success. Particularly now, as compensation programs are under intense public scrutiny and most likely will move well beyond the traditional reliance on "plain vanilla" stock options and cash bonuses, it is imperative that compensation committee members have a facile understanding of the evolving landscape of executive pay and the expanding array of compensation vehicles available to shape desired results. They must be able to use this knowledge to devise programs that are straightforward, transparent, and effective. To this end, the committee should receive continuing training and employ the advice of independent experts and advisors.

THE ROLE OF THE NOMINATING COMMITTEE

The New York Stock Exchange (NYSE) and Nasdaq recognize that a fully independent nominating committee is central to the effective functioning of the board, and that director and board committee nominations are among the board's most important functions. NYSE-listed companies must have a nominating/corporate governance committee, which is made up exclusively of independent directors. This committee is charged with identifying individuals qualified to become board members, consistent with criteria approved by the board, and to select, or to recommend that the board select, the director nominees for the next annual meeting of shareholders. Under Nasdaq rules, director nominees must be selected, or recommended for the full board's selection, either by a nominating committee comprised solely of independent directors or by a majority of the independent directors.

The rationale for this is that an independent nominating committee enhances the independence and quality of the nominees. This notion holds true for nonlisted companies as well. Given today's focus on sound corporate governance principles, it makes sense for private and other nonlisted companies to take advantage of the careful thought that has been applied to these issues by the NYSE, Nasdaq, the Securities and Exchange Commission (SEC), and influential business and investor groups.

While the nominating committee may be separate from a corporate governance committee, those functions are often combined in a single committee under a combined designation. Either such committee (or the combined committee) may be assigned to periodically review and make recommendations regarding the size of the board, committee structure and committee assignments, and frequency of regular board and committee meetings. In some cases, the nominating or corporate governance committee also specifies the roles and responsibilities of each board committee, in keeping with the corporate charter and bylaws and the specific requirements for the composition and function of committees as imposed by the NYSE, Nasdaq, and the SEC, where applicable. Management's input to these decisions may be considered, but predominant and best practice is to leave the ultimate decisions to the independent nominating or corporate governance committee.

NOMINATION AND SELECTION OF NEW COMPENSATION COMMITTEE MEMBERS

Finding and selecting qualified outside directors is one of the most challenging and rewarding dimensions of building an effective compensation committee. Before beginning the search for new directors, the company should develop a board prospectus. The board prospectus can be a helpful tool in recruiting director candidates, and can assist the company in networking with lenders, advisors, and others who might know of attractive director candidates. A sample board prospectus is shown in Exhibit 2.1.

The board prospectus should describe clearly the purpose and goals of the board. It should convey the qualities and capabilities the board is seeking in directors, and describe the board structure, director compensation, and anticipated time demands on members. The board prospectus should convey the business, culture,

Exhibit 2.1   Sample Board Prospectus

We seek one independent director to round out our board of directors and help us manage the future of our successful corporation. We believe our business and industry will face new issues more complex and challenging than we have confronted before. We believe a board consisting of a majority of qualified independent and experienced directors to be an invaluable resource to aid us in providing the very best return to our shareholders. The following describes our company and the roles and purpose we envision for our board.

OUR COMPANY

We are the largest company of its kind in the southeastern part of the United States. We have 25 locations and a significant investment in real estate through three real-estate holding companies. We have several separate but related lines of business. In all, we are a $450-million enterprise with 3,200 employees.

We provide the highest quality and broadest line of high-end products and services to our customers. We are proud to have recently received the very first "Blue Ribbon" award in our industry. We reach our customers through a valued 100-year-old reputation and well-managed public relations. Market reputation in this business, however, can be overturned by only one year of poor performance.

THE IMMEDIATE NEEDS OF THE BOARD

The company's local and traditional market has matured. The changing attitudes of consumers to our industry and products require major changes to our company. Recent federal legislation will greatly affect the structure of our industry and how firms in our industry compete. The company must invent new ways of designing, manufacturing, distributing, selling, and servicing our products. To do this, we need to refocus the company's business while at the same time raise significant capital.

THE PURPOSE OF THE BOARD

The primary purpose of the board is to help management to increase shareholder value. The company will benefit from successful independent directors who bring their diverse experience to bear on the best interests of the company.

The board will help management evaluate the key issues and decisions facing our business. The board will offer a forum to discuss important and strategic decisions, while bringing a fresher perspective that will encourage corporate management to consider additional alternatives.

THE NATURE OF THE BOARD

Our board will comprise eight members: the CEO and seven outside directors. You will be replacing a 62-year old director who is not standing for renomination. Of the six other outside directors, four are current or former CEOs of their own businesses, one is the president of a major local university, and one is the managing partner of a large, local law firm.

Exhibit 2.1   Continued

Our board will formally meet four times per year at a morning meeting. The day usually begins very early at 7:30 A.M., and ends in mid-afternoon. Each independent director will serve on one or more of the following committees: audit, compensation, and nominating/corporate governance. Committees meet an average of four times a year.

CONCLUSION

We believe an additional experienced independent director will assist corporate management in this challenging time in the company's evolution.

---

philosophy, and values of the company. This prospectus usually includes the information in Exhibit 2.2.

The search for new directors begins typically with the nominating committee, which may request recommendations from the chief executive officer (CEO) and other directors. Whatever the source of the recommendation, the nominating com-

Exhibit 2.2   Typical Elements of a Board Prospectus

I.   Overview of the Company
    A. Industry
    B. Most important products and types of consumers
    C. Size
    D. Major shareholders
II.   Board Profile
    A. Character of business
    • Stage of life cycle (startup, rapidly growing, mature)
    • Relative strengths or weaknesses (highest quality producer in the region, need to develop more cost-conscious culture)
    • Strategic thrust (developing an international presence, seeking to grow by acquisition, committed to increasing market share)
    B. Relationship of the board with management
    C. Personal criteria of candidates
    • Desired background, personal characteristics, and experience of board candidates
III.   Structure of the Board
    A. Number of independent directors and management/investor directors on the board
    B. Committee structure
    C. Number of meetings (board and committee)
    D. Time commitment
    E. Compensation
    F. Director indemnification and insurance
    G. Term of office
    H. Mandatory retirement age or term limitations

---

mittee should carefully evaluate each candidate. Politics, bolstering egos, repaying debts, conveying thanks, rewarding performance, and satisfying interest groups should not play a role in selecting directors. The nominating committee should select new board members—and renominate existing board members—with one purpose in mind: to meet the specific needs and best interests of the company as they evolve over time.

A typical search for independent directors begins with an overview of the needs of the board—representation that may be lacking or need more emphasis. For example, the company may seek greater diversity on its board, or may seek a new director with experience in a particular sector (e.g., academic, public service, business, nonprofit) or area of useful expertise. Perhaps the board would benefit from directors with more time availability or higher profile in the company's industry or community.

The following sections illustrate possible strengths and weaknesses of various categories of outside board candidates.

Competitors

Directors or officers of current or potential competitors generally do not make ideal candidates because of their inherent conflict of interest. This is another reason to seek directors from other industries so as to take advantage of their fresh perspectives and new insights, rather than an affirmation of what management already knows. Oftentimes, the best place to find such insight is from directors with backgrounds in different industries facing analogous challenges and problems.

Consultants

Paid advisors are not usually good candidates for board service. Such status would render them nonindependent under NYSE and Nasdaq rules and ineligible to serve on any core committees of the board. The services of outside consultants are readily available to the board in any event; as directors they bring to the boardroom an inherent conflict of interest. The board can always invite trusted advisors to attend board sessions—it is not necessary to make them directors to reap the benefits of their knowledge.

Where technical "independence" is not a requirement, some boards may make an exception for advisors who have broad exposure to top executives in a wide range of companies. These professionals often develop executive skills and can be a valuable resource, even if they lack first-hand executive experience.

Friends

Directors should never be selected on the basis of friendships with management or existing directors. Such personal ties can lead to allegations of cronyism (whether or not true) and jeopardize the independence and effectiveness of the board. More-over, the candid exchange of viewpoints needed from directors can put a strain on friendships. Even at the recruitment stage, it may be difficult to objectively inter-view and assess the references of such candidates.

Retirees

Retired executives from other industries often make promising director candidates. For example, many retirees enjoy high visibility, generous time availability, and use-ful experience. However, there can be drawbacks. A retiree may eventually lose touch with the mainstream of business or become overly enamored with board ser-vice as a source of retirement income, ego support, or stimulation. If a retiree be-comes beholden to management and the other directors to maintain his or her seat on the board, it may compromise the independent contribution he or she might other-wise make.

Academics

Academics can be good director candidates for the right board. They provide an excellent source of intellectual capital, tend to have reasonable time availability, and oftentimes are skillful in consensus building and tactful interaction among those having divergent viewpoints. However, they may lack the "real world" experience that can be useful in a profit-driven business environment.

People Who Hold Other Directorships

People who serve on other boards make tempting director candidates, due to their relevant experience. However, serving on too many boards at once can curtail the effectiveness of directors.

Other CEOs, Entrepreneurs, or Business Owners

Risk-taking peers often make excellent outside directors. Executives from other companies who have weathered crises at their own companies can provide invalu-able counsel to the board facing similar or even dissimilar business challenges. However, the nominating committee should avoid creating interlocking relation-ships where, for example, any of the company's executive officers serve on the candidate's board. As previously discussed in Chapter 1, overlapping (or interlock-ing) directorships can compromise a director's independence, causing him or her to temper decisions and comments to protect the other relationship. Another issue to guard against in selecting directors who are CEOs of another company is the so-called "kindred spirit" phenomenon, in which the director may be disinclined to be critical of management because he or she sympathizes with the discomfort of dealing with a "difficult" board.

TIME COMMITMENT

At a minimum, attendance at four board meetings per year, including preparation and travel time, would take about eight days per year. However, all outside directors will most likely serve on one or more oversight committees, which require a substantially greater time commitment in terms of preparation for and attendance at meetings, interaction with management and outside advisors, ongoing training, and taking a leadership role in special projects. In that case, the minimum time commitment can quickly balloon to 30 days per year.

A key issue to consider in the selection of board members is time availability. Directors who do not have time to attend and adequately prepare for board meetings and devote concentrated effort to committee work will contribute to an ineffective board. Spreading committee assignments effectively among board members can alleviate the time commitment required of well-qualified directors.

Ideally, all directors will have equal time and energy to devote to the business of the board and committees on which they serve. However, in the real world, some will have more time availability and others will provide more value for other characteristics. In selecting outside directors, the nominating committee would do well to acknowledge and plan for this. For example, outside directors who have full-time positions elsewhere or serve on a number of other boards may make invaluable contributions but may have minimal time to devote to the company's board, while directors who are retired or are in academia may have more time. If possible, the nominating committee should try to balance the board and its committee assignments accordingly to provide the most effective allocation of director resources.

In the nomination process, it is important that all candidates fully understand and buy into the notion that they must be prepared to devote the time, regardless of personal or professional inconvenience, to meet their responsibilities to the board, particularly in times of unexpected activity such as major litigation, responding to a takeover proposal, or considering strategic business alternatives for the company.

DIVERSITY

Diversity of the board and its compensation committee allows for a variety of experiences and knowledge to bring to bear on the issues under consideration by the committee. A diverse board or committee is in a position to make better decisions, because issues must be considered from a variety of perspectives. The move toward organizational diversity begins with commitment and open-mindedness.

As companies demand more of their board members, both in terms of time and technical expertise, and as shareholders become more active in governance, the pressures are intensifying to diversify and broaden board and committee membership. More and more major institutional investors are citing diversity as a criterion in making or maintaining investment positions.

ATTRACTING CANDIDATES

Quality boards and quality companies attract quality directors. Having excellent outside advisors available to the board (auditors, legal advisors, and compensation consultants) will serve to allay any concerns that a good director candidate may have about personal liability arising from legal or accounting irregularities. A healthy diversity of industries represented on the board may also help attract director candidates who are senior executives from outside of the company's industry. For example, a CEO from another industry serving on the company's board can profit personally from the exchange of ideas among fellow board members hailing from industries other than his or her own.

In general, the following factors attract good directors:

- Quality of management
- Ethics of the company
- Prospect of serving with respected peers
- Opportunity to learn
- Opportunity to make a difference; to make an impact on the future direction of an organization in a measurable way
- Opportunity to use his or her own knowledge and expertise
- Opportunity to network with top business leaders
- Opportunity to serve in a prestigious position
- Compensation—to a limited degree
- Entrepreneurial spirit, an opportunity to create something special
- Personal challenge

A proactive, enthusiastic approach to the director search goes a long way to attracting superlative directors.

CONDUCTING THE SEARCH

Conducting a successful search for directors is a time-consuming process, including researching and educating potential candidates and conducting initial and callback interviews. Using a professional search firm can be an effective and efficient way to guide the process, although not inexpensive. In general, the company should be prepared to pay up to the equivalent of one year's director's fees for the service.

In practice, large public companies tend to use professional search firms to find new directors, particularly now that there is high demand for independent directors who have an advanced level of expertise in one or more substantive areas. Small to mid-sized firms and private companies use such firms more sparingly. These companies most often select directors who are personally known to current board members. Other prevalent sources of referral are directors of other companies and professional trade organizations.

Professional trade organizations (such as the National Association of Corporate Directors [NACD] and Catalyst), local chambers of commerce, business roundtables, and other similar organizations can be a useful starting place for a search for appropriate director candidates. These organizations typically keep biographies of their members, which can be prescreened by the company for promising director candidates. The NACD, for example, makes available a confidential directory service for companies recruiting directors.

Whatever search method is employed, a typical search may result in consideration of 20 to 25 candidates to derive a list of three to five finalists who are acceptable for board service. The nominating committee should review the list to cull out any who may be unacceptable, for one reason or another. Then, the nominating committee, perhaps with the CEO and/or search firm representative, should meet with the finalists for more in-depth interviews.

A search for new board members can take several months. This process can be shortened if board recruiting is an ongoing process. The nominating committee should always have three to five promising candidates in mind should there be a need to replace directors or expand the board.

Using an outside search firm allows the nominating committee to select among prequalified, available candidates, best using the committee's time to focus on the culture, the fit, and the vision. The following are some of the other advantages of using a competent outside recruiter:

- Allows the company to proactively recruit to its strategic plan and critical issues
- Gives access to the broadest spectrum of targeted, qualified candidates
- Allows the search to extend beyond the board's own circle of influence
- Provides a more extensive choice among highly qualified candidates
- Validates the board to potential director candidates
- Validates the board to the company's constituents (shareholders, senior officers, alliance partners)
- Provides an objective point of reference and interview process

- Promotes integrity, confidentiality, and discretion in the director search
- Increases the efficiency of the search by eliminating less-qualified candidates early in the process
- Promotes the goodwill of the CEO, candidates, directors, and constituents

HOW TO APPROACH CANDIDATES

Once a list of qualified candidates has emerged, the focus shifts to seeking information from the candidates to narrow the field to those with the best fit. Some of the following questions can solicit useful information from the candidates:

- Why do you want to serve on the board of this company?
- What is your opinion of the company? (Does he or she have knowledge of how the company competes, how it markets, who its competition is, who its customers are, what its critical issues are?)
- How will you contribute to the board? (Ask for clear and simple examples of how the candidate can contribute.)
- What are your specific areas of expertise? How will your expertise add value to the board?
- What is your financial acumen? (Each director should have the ability to read and understand financial analysis, but need not have a professional financial or accounting background.)
- On how many other boards do you serve? (List for-profit and not-for-profit separately.) What role do you play on those boards?
- What is your view of the role of the board and corporate governance?
- What has been your most rewarding experience as a director?
- How specifically have you added value to the boards on which you serve?
- What has been your most difficult experience as a director?
- Are you willing and able to commit to the level of participation we require?
- What are your concerns?

CEO INVOLVEMENT IN THE SELECTION PROCESS

Current NYSE and Nasdaq rules require a nominating committee of independent directors to take the lead in nominating and renominating directors. That duty often includes assigning directors to oversight committees, such as the compensation committee, and selecting committee chairs. However, management, and in particular the CEO, should have an opportunity to provide input to these decisions. It is important that all key constituents (nominating committee, other board members, management, and the new director) be comfortable with the process. If managed well, the new board member should begin on a positive footing, knowing that he or she has the backing of several constituencies participating in the selection.

MAKING THE FINAL SELECTION

In screening director candidates, some of the most important qualities to consider are also the simplest. At a minimum, the candidate should exhibit integrity and the ability to make thoughtful and sometimes difficult decisions.

The candidate should show candor, an eagerness to learn, and a lively interest in the business and work of the board and the committees on which he or she is likely to serve. The candidate should demonstrate courage of conviction, readiness to express his or her viewpoint, and the kind of personality that can be effective in a boardroom setting—an ability to be a team player, for instance.

With respect to each serious candidate for director, the nominating committee should conduct a personal interview and a comprehensive review of his or her background and experience and compare the findings with the needs of the board. A successful board selection process can make the difference in the company's ability to recruit other qualified directors. Every director nominated to the board serves as an incentive or disincentive for other prospective directors to serve.

In identifying and selecting directors for an effective board, the following criteria should be considered and weighed as appropriate:

1. *Availability*. With the increased focus on corporate governance, serving as a director, particularly a director of a public company, requires a serious time commitment, as discussed previously. The days are gone for "social" directorships, in which the primary time commitment is for perfunctory quarterly meetings followed by an afternoon of golf and dinner. Even the best qualified directors will not be effective if they do not have the time to devote serious attention to the business of the board and the committees on which they serve.
2. *Intelligence*. Intelligence is a baseline requirement, but it comes in many different forms. One aspect is the director's ability to offer a fresh look at an old problem, even in an area in which he or she lacks practical experience. For directors who are not experienced in the company's business sector or with board service in general, the company can provide education and training opportunities to make them more effective directors. Director training sessions are offered by many educational institutions, including Harvard, Wharton, Uni-

versity of Chicago, Stanford, Yale, and Duke University, and by independent business groups such as the NACD.

3. *Reputation.* A director's high-profile reputation in the business community can be especially important for the board of an emerging company, a company in a turnaround situation, or a company moving toward a broadly held shareholder base. Oftentimes, however, there is a trade-off between a director's reputation and availability, which should be taken into consideration. Reputation is always hard to measure, and can be favorable or unfavorable. A review of the candidate's own publications and references to the candidate in the media can be enlightening in assessing his or her business or professional reputation. It is also useful to check the references of the candidate with peers in his or her respective field.

4. *Communication skills.* The ability to communicate effectively—especially extemporaneously in a group setting—is an important quality for a corporate director. Personal interviews with the candidate can be particularly instructive as to this ability. It is not always true that a polished public speaker is also an effective communicator in a give-and-take setting, such as the boardroom.

5. *Experience.* Relevant experience can be an important determinant of the effectiveness of a potential director, whether it be:

   – Direct experience in the company's industry

   – Prior experience as a director in other companies

   – Executive managerial experience in another company

6. *Leverage.* Leverage denotes the ability of the director to use his or her professional affiliations to expand the company's relationships (such as the ability of an investment banker director to introduce the company into the capital markets), and to provide additional management expertise in areas identified as lacking on the board (such as the ability of a director experienced in marketing to provide insight to an industrial company seeking to expand into consumer products). In some cases, especially for emerging companies or companies undergoing a transformation, a director's leverage can be an important factor.

The weight placed on each of these factors should be guided by the company's needs, the strengths and shortcomings of other board members, and the urgency of finding a new board member. To organize an evaluation of several director candidates, the company should rank the criteria and then rank the candidates.

An illustration of such an evaluation appears in the following paragraphs and in Exhibit 2.3.

A middle-market public company is searching for an outside director to fill the role of the retiring chairman of the compensation committee. The company's current board is comprised of a majority of high-profile, independent directors drawn

Exhibit 2.3   Illustration of a Candidate Evaluation Summary

		Outside Director Candidates			
	Weight	A	B	C	D
Availability	10	4	10	7	9
Communication Skills	10	8	6	8	7
Intelligence	8	6	10	10	6
Reputation	7	8	4	7	7
Experience	4	10	4	6	8
Leverage	2	8	3	7	4
Total Weighted Score		280	290	317	297

from locally based, large public companies. The retiring director noted as one reason for her retirement from the board her lack of adequate time to devote to the business of the compensation committee.

A primary focus of the nominating committee, therefore, is that the new director have available time to serve as chairman of the compensation committee. In addition, the nominating committee is seeking a candidate ranking high in intelligence, communication skills, and professional reputation, but experience and leverage are not strong criteria in the search.

The candidates making the final cut are:

- *Candidate A.* The new CEO of the retiring board member's company. This candidate comes from outside of the company's industry and outside of the local area. He is very well regarded professionally and gets high marks for relevant experience.
- *Candidate B.* A business school professor in her mid-40s. She has a reasonably successful academic career, and has a PhD in economics from Stanford University. She has little relevant experience other than her role as a department chairperson at her business school.
- *Candidate C.* A local lawyer who does no work for the company and specializes in intellectual property law (a particularly important matter with the company). This lawyer also serves on the board of another publicly held company. She is a Rhodes Scholar who graduated first in her class at Harvard University. She also has served as head of her law firm's executive committee.
- *Candidate D.* A prematurely retired senior executive from a large local company. After his retirement, this executive went on to run an emerging company

for two years, and has since left that firm. He is in his late-50s, currently serves on two boards, and wants to serve on one more to round out his work schedule.

According to Exhibit 2.3, candidate C is the best qualified closely followed by candidates B and D. While candidate C does not have as much availability as B and D, her high ranks in intelligence and communication skills and moderately high rank in professional reputation make her the first choice overall.

HOW TO SAY NO

For every candidate who is ultimately selected for the board, there are others who will need to be rejected. This task can be made easier if the process is managed responsibly. For example, a thorough prescreening process will reduce the number of candidates who reach the final stages of consideration. The board should not let the screening process go too far unless there is strong interest in the candidate. It would be a mistake, for example, to set up more than one meeting with a candidate or ask him or her to the company to "meet and greet" the board and senior executives unless the nominating committee considers the person a serious and well qualified contender for the position.

When the time comes to end the solicitation of a particular candidate, the best approach is to emphasize the goals communicated at the outset of the screening process—to select a complementary group of people with a mix of backgrounds and expertise to match the needs of the company.

WHAT IF THE NEW DIRECTOR DOES NOT WORK OUT?

Despite the favorable odds associated with a well-planned and thorough director search or committee assignment, boards sometimes make mistakes in selecting or assigning directors. Errors usually do not become clear immediately. It may take as much as a year or two for a board to conclude that a particular director is not making an adequate contribution. Annual director performance evaluations will hasten the determination and allow corrections to be made on a more timely basis.

Once mistakes are discovered, boards should act promptly to make corrections or reassignments, however uncomfortable that process may be. Most often, the best way to deal with the problem is for the chair of the nominating committee (or other appropriate board representative) to approach the nonperforming director directly and explain that he or she will not be nominated for reelection (or in some cases to ask for an early resignation), and the reason for that decision. Sometimes, the explanation may be that the needs of the business are changing and the board needs new directors having skills and backgrounds different from his or her own.

Other times, the explanation must be more direct, but can still be delivered in a nonthreatening and congenial manner.

In most cases, an under-performing but honest director will be asked to serve out the remainder of his or her current term and not stand for reelection. The company's public relations team can help to manage communications about the reason for the director's departure from the board.

The nominating committee may turn to professional advisors, such as director search firms, in reconfiguring the company's board, particularly if more than one director needs to be removed. In addition to assisting with the director assessment, such firms can also meet with the soon-to-be removed director to lessen the tension in a delicate situation.

BENEFITS OF AN EDUCATED BOARD

The most effective directors understand the specific business concerns of the company or the committees they serve, and the overall economic, political, and social environment in which the company exists and competes. All directors should be prepared to consider and discuss a multitude of complex issues in appropriate context. Membership on a board, particularly in today's environment, is more than just a position of honor—it is a position of public trust. Effective participation on a board can be enhanced through training and continuing education on topics ranging from new technologies and developments in the company's particular business, to new approaches in effective organizational leadership and corporate governance.

Through systematic and appropriately focused training, board members can enhance their own leadership skills and competencies and increase their knowledge. A skilled and knowledgeable board results in an organization better able to serve its shareholders, employees, and community.

ORIENTATION OF NEW MEMBERS

While the director recruitment process serves as an initial stage of orientation, the process should not stop there. A proper board orientation program should entail more than introductions to other board members and management and a summary of the logistics of board meetings. New board members should be instructed as to the organization's mission, goals, products, and services, and the company's expectations of its board of directors. Some organizations conduct orientation sessions for prospective members; others hold them for new members only once they come on the board. In either case, a primary purpose of board orientation is to give new members information about the organization's operations and their roles as board members.

Directors who serve on core committees, such as the compensation committee, should receive ongoing topical training of relevance to the mission of the committee. Compensation committees are encouraged to engage outside consultants and advisors (independent of management) to assist the committee in understanding and designing compensation programs that effectively drive performance, while reflecting current compensation philosophies and evolutions in relevant legal and accounting rules.

Some companies maintain a checklist for new board members whereby the director must spend time with various executives throughout the company, such as executives in the legal and human resources departments and the corporate secretary. Other companies provide paid educational opportunities for directors in programs offered by major universities and organizations such as the NACD.

A planned, systematic approach to orientation is most effective. Exhibit 2.4 suggests one orientation approach that can be modified to suit different circumstances.

Exhibit 2.4   Suggestions for Director Orientation Program

I. Plan the orientation program.
   A. During recruitment, prospects should have learned what is generally expected of them as members of the board of directors. The board's written job description should include a statement that participation in orientation is mandatory, so it will not come as a surprise when one or two days (not necessarily consecutive) are spent on orientation activities.
   B. Plan the distribution of materials in accordance with each orientation activity. Too much written material too soon is overwhelming.
   C. Use the background data gathered during recruitment to tailor presentations according to a new member's personal and professional interests.
   D. Consider assigning a sponsor—an experienced board member—to each new director, making sure the purpose of this relationship is clear to both.
II. Orient new members to the organization.
   A. Schedule a meeting with the CEO to give the new board member an opportunity to ask specific questions about the organization's operations, culture, and most important current issues. For the CEO, meeting with new board members provides a chance to establish a good working relationship early on.
   B. Board members will be called upon to make decisions regarding the company's physical plant and employees, so onsite visits are vital to the role of the director. With this in mind, plan a tour of a representative sample of the company's various facilities (e.g., factory, headquarters building, training facility, sales office, distribution warehouse, etc.). Even if the organization is not a facilities-based business, a visit to the main office where the organization conducts its business is highly recommended.

(*continues*)

Exhibit 2.4   Continued

    C. Prepare a brief two- or three-page synopsis of key organizational demographics: customers, employees, suppliers, company milestones, major changes over the past five years, executive officer roster (with photos and detailed biographies), trends, and other appropriate data to supplement oral presentations.

    D. Arrange for new members to attend an executive staff meeting or briefing session by the CEO's staff. The directors should have the opportunity to meet key personnel, learn about their respective areas of responsibility, and ask questions.

III. Orient members to the board.

    A. Have the board chair make a welcoming call or visit to all new members.

    B. Distribute a biographical sketch of the new members to the full board, including members' terms and committee assignments, places and positions of employment, contact information, and other relevant information.

    C. Hold an informal social function to help integrate new members with the rest of the board.

    D. Schedule a meeting for all new board members with the executive committee and other committee chairs. This gives newcomers an opportunity to become acquainted with the board's leadership and with the activities of the committees. A discussion of board procedures, directors' roles, responsibilities and liabilities, and major issues facing the organization provides new members with useful perspectives on the whole organization.

    E. Distribute the board manual (or briefing book), which should include some or all of the following information to the new directors, as relevant:

       1. Company organization chart with officer biographies

       2. Mission statements

       3. Strategic plans

       4. Most recent proxy statement and annual report to shareholders

       5. Core strategies

       6. Company history

       7. Board materials, including the board charter, structure, needs matrix, directors' biographies, meeting dates, locations, committee assignments, summaries and processes, and profiles for any open board seats

       8. Marketing materials

       9. Customer profiles

     10. Articles, information sources on the industry

     11. Competition data

     12. Financial statements

     13. Insider trading policy

     14. Analyst reports

     15. Corporate bylaws and committee charters

     16. Corporate calendar

     17. Board and committee meeting minutes

     18. Director compensation package

     19. Director evaluation program

Exhibit 2.4   Continued

20. Management succession plan
21. Short-term and long-term incentive plans

F. Provide time for a debriefing among the new members, board chair, and CEO so any questions and concerns can be clarified. Debriefing sessions also can be an opportunity to ask new board members which parts of the orientation were most helpful, which were the least helpful, and how future board orientations might be improved.

ONGOING TRAINING

Initial board orientation should be followed by systematic and focused training opportunities, including regularly scheduled retreats or renewal sessions, and occasional training programs or workshops on special topics.

Some companies charge the nominating/corporate governance committee with the oversight responsibility for board education. Others may select an ad hoc committee to plan board educational activities. Either type of planning group can more effectively fulfill its function by adhering to the following principles of board development:

- Carefully formulate a purpose for all board development activities.
- Set realistic training objectives.
- When planning an activity, consider the unique needs and interests of all members of the board.
- Consider different types of development activities, such as in-house training, guest speakers or consultants, and workshops or conferences.
- Evaluate each educational activity.

The full board should be involved in the selection of issues to be addressed in board development training. The committee should set specific training objectives, decide on appropriate content and formats, manage the logistics, and perform other related tasks. Approaching board development in this way increases the likelihood of full participation.

In addition to helping a board learn how to operate more effectively, a good program of board development sustains members' interest in the organization and in the board. When board members are well informed and trained to carry out the board's primary functions, they are more comfortable with, and are more likely to remain committed to, their roles.

An organized development program for a board sends a positive message to its members that the organization values the directors' contributions enough to invest time and resources to their continuing excellence. Development programs give board members an opportunity for self-renewal and for quality time away from business as usual. In short, the ongoing education of a board is an excellent strategy for keeping board members motivated, focused, and energetic.

A development program might include the introduction of an outside advisor/ expert at each board meeting. For example, in a typical meeting schedule over the course of a year, the board might schedule presentations from the following types of outside groups:

January	Executive Compensation Consultant
April	Outside Legal Counsel
June	Outside Auditor Engagement Partner
September	Leading Expert on Corporate Governance
November	Prominent Business School Professor

OUTSIDE EXPERTS AND ADVISORS

While boards have for decades sought the advice of outside consultants and advisors, the concerns of spiraling executive pay and allegations of executive malfeasance over the last few years have led to an insistence that boards exercise autonomy in the hiring and firing of such outside advisors.

New NYSE rules require that if the compensation committee uses a compensation consultant to assist in the evaluation of director, CEO, or other senior executive compensation, the compensation committee must have sole authority to retain and terminate the consulting firm and to approve its fees. These rules are designed to avoid even the appearance of undue influence by the payee over his or her own compensation. While outside advisors should have access to management and other corporate resources, such as the human resources department, for input and consultation, the advisors' allegiance and reporting relationship should be to the compensation committee.

Oftentimes, large companies engage more than one outside compensation consultant in an effort to enhance objectivity and compare advice, or to participate in independent projects for fresh opinions and outlook. In selecting an appropriate outside compensation consultant, the compensation committee should look for the following criteria:

- *Industry expertise*. This expertise should include a solid understanding of the overall industry in which the company is engaged, its competitive market forces, key dynamics that influence individual company and overall industry performance, and the competitive talent pools.

- *Direct and relevant experience.* Advisors should be highly experienced and have successful track records in assisting similar companies. Generally speaking, the prospective consultant should have several years of executive compensation consulting experience.
- *Executive compensation consulting resources.* The consulting firm should have an extensive survey library, data resources, and secondary consulting resources in the event that the lead consultant is not available.
- *Visibility and good reputation.* Particularly for large companies, the consulting firm and its lead consultants should be nationally recognized and well regarded.
- *Seamless integration of resources.* The lead consultant and consulting firm should be able to deliver, or arrange for, accounting, tax, actuarial, pension, and financial advice in a seamless manner.
- *Nationwide and worldwide coverage.* A company with international operations should also look for international consulting capabilities. It is appropriate to inquire about the consultant's offices in the United States and outside the United States and whether it has expertise in the countries in which the company operates.
- *Proficiency in all elements of total compensation.* The consulting firm and its consultants should have knowledge of salary, short-term incentive programs, long-term incentive programs, and pension-benefit, welfare-benefit, and perquisite programs. A consultant who is not personally proficient in all elements of total compensation should be able to recognize issues and access expertise in all such areas.
- *Business goals and executive compensation strategy alignment.* The philosophy of the consulting firm should be compatible with the company's philosophy. Some consultants have a specific philosophy and approach toward compensation and may be reluctant to or unable to acknowledge the merits of a different but legitimate approach favored by the compensation committee. This would be a poor fit.
- *Performance measurement expertise.* The consultant must be expert at interpreting financial statements and correctly applying financial ratios and measures in light of the company's industry and business plan and other pertinent facts and circumstances.
- *Creativity and capability to create custom designs.* The consulting firm should be able to provide creative solutions in the context of shifting economic trends and business models.

Different types of advisors serve different purposes, ranging from advice with respect to trends in corporate governance, accounting rules or securities compliance and disclosure issues, to specific advise on peer group competitive practices. The following is a summary of some of the broad types of outside advisors a compensation committee might choose to consult. In many cases, the fields of expertise overlap or complement one another.

Law Firm

A law firm with a broad business practice can generally provide a compensation committee advice with respect to historic practices and recent developments in the areas of corporate governance and board duties and responsibilities, securities compliance and disclosure, tax, special concerns and planning opportunities in the context of mergers and acquisitions, and executive employment and severance arrangements. Unlike executive compensation consultants, law firms generally do not have access to databases or survey data to be used in developing specific compensation programs. Because compensation consultants are not usually lawyers, the two disciplines frequently work together to assist a compensation committee in developing and implementing a sound compensation strategy and program in keeping with current legal parameters.

Specialized Executive Compensation Consulting Firm

Executive compensation consulting firms generally focus on cutting-edge issues in executive compensation practices. Using extensive databases and survey data, they can help the compensation committee identify appropriate trends and to design a compensation program that will drive desired performance, encourage retention, and manage shareholder dilution. While generally well versed in governmental and regulatory trends and issues, most consulting firms do not render legal or tax advice.

Human Resources/General Compensation and Benefits Firm

These types of firms provide actuarial, benefits, compensation, organizational dynamics, and pension plan advice, outsourcing of human resources functions, and employee communications. Such firms tend not to be highly specialized in technical/regulatory areas and generally do not provide tax or legal advice.

Insurance Specialist

Insurance specialists often offer innovative approaches to specific needs. Because their solutions are typically oriented to the sale of various types of insurance products, the focus is somewhat narrow. While they can play a valuable role, it is not likely that an insurance specialist would be equipped to provide the broad range of advice that a compensation committee needs to design and implement a total compensation program.

Accounting Firm

Accounting firms can be an outstanding source of technical know-how, as they typically have subject matter experts in all aspects of business and commerce, with a focus on accounting and tax rules. However, the Sarbanes-Oxley Act imposes significant limitations on a company's ability to use the nonaudit services of its outside auditor. More and more frequently, public companies are using one major accounting firm for auditing services and a competitor firm for nonaudit services, including compensation advice. Again, most accounting firms do not presume to give legal advice.

Chapter 3

CEO Succession and Evaluation

The most important responsibility of a board of directors is management succession. This primarily concerns the hiring and firing of the chief executive officer (CEO), as the CEO usually takes the lead in the hiring and firing of all other executives. In addition, woven into the fabric of this responsibility is the responsibility of evaluating the CEO. Simply put, CEO evaluations must be done to determine whether the CEO's employment should be continued or terminated. Accordingly, proper and timely CEO evaluations are critical to the company and its shareholders, since the evaluation often will trigger the initial implementation of the CEO succession plan.

While succession planning and CEO evaluation are the responsibilities of the entire board, these responsibilities typically fall on the shoulders of the compensation committee, the governance committee, or on a committee that usually includes all or most of the members of the compensation committee.

SUCCESSION PLANNING

In its "Corporate Governance Best Practices: A Blueprint for the Post-Enron Era" released in 2003, The Conference Board stated that a successful succession planning process should:

- Be a continuous process.
- Be driven and controlled by the board.
- Involve CEO input.
- Be easily executable in the event of a crisis.
- Consider succession requirements based on corporate strategy.

- Be geared toward finding the right leader at the right time.
- Develop talent pools at lower levels.
- Avoid a "horse race" mentality that may lead to the loss of key deputies when the new CEO is chosen.

These generalizations apply both to management and CEO succession. However, they do not—in and of themselves—constitute a succession plan, and there is no standard "one-size-fits-all" succession plan. Instead, each board must determine the processes and methods that will produce such a plan and shape it into the best plan for its purposes. Generally, this will involve developing the existing executive talent pool of the company and the use of executive recruiting firms, directors' personal contacts, and an overall "ear-to-the-ground" approach. No matter what, the most important point is that there be a CEO succession plan in place at all times.

CEO EVALUATION

CEO evaluations are now required as part of the new New York Stock Exchange (NYSE) listing requirements. However, these rules only require that a CEO evaluation be completed and that there be a process in place. They do not require that the results of the evaluation process be disclosed. In addition, the new NYSE rules do not require that an evaluation form be written or that the results be written; they only require that the CEO evaluation be completed according to a process and duly noted. However, it is recommended—in most cases—that the evaluation process not be completely oral, since there are inherent fundamental flaws in a completely oral process. The pros and cons of a written versus oral evaluation is discussed later in this chapter.

Unlike the new NYSE rules, the new Nasdaq listing requirements are silent with respect to CEO evaluations. However, many Nasdaq companies look to both the Nasdaq and the NYSE rules to discern good corporate governance practice and behavior. Accordingly, it is expected that most Nasdaq companies will perform CEO evaluations similar to those performed at NYSE companies (although self-imposed).

Currently, the executive compensation disclosure rules issued by the Securities and Exchange Commission (SEC) require only that the CEO pay decisions be explained in the compensation committee's report with specificity. However, there is no current requirement that a CEO evaluation be completed or that the results be publicly disclosed in the compensation committee report or in any other publicly filed document. Thus, at the moment, CEO evaluations generally remain private and confidential, unless disclosure is required by subpoena or other imposed discovery processes.

A meaningful CEO evaluation includes the following important points:

* Regular executive sessions culminating in a formal annual evaluation
* Good planning
* Objective analysis
* Effective tying of the evaluation to the CEO's pay package

CEO evaluations are closely linked with director evaluations and, when properly conducted, can help foster a sense of teamwork between the board and the CEO. Good chemistry between the board and the CEO is extremely important, and it starts with an attitude that fosters a sense of respect, worthiness, and direct and clear communication. Once the board and the CEO "bond," they can more easily share their visions of the future and get a buy-in from one another. This meeting of the minds goes a long way in keeping the company on track under adversity and conflict.

To open and maintain the channels of communication, the board or lead director of the board should meet with the CEO on a regular basis to go over the evaluation and the evaluation process. These evaluation sessions should be a part of the board process, and not hurried or shortened.

A major obstacle to the CEO evaluation process is that most directors have limited interaction with the CEO, usually occurring only during board or committee meetings. Observations of the CEO by the directors are important for that part of the evaluation that is based on qualitative and personal traits. In other words, it is difficult for directors to fairly evaluate a CEO when they have not observed the CEO performing his or her daily work. Accordingly, it is important for each director involved in the evaluation process to interact with the CEO outside of board and committee meetings.

Barriers to Effective CEO Evaluation

A number of factors can inhibit the effectiveness of a CEO evaluation:

* *Discomfort.* Some board members find evaluating the CEO neither enjoyable nor comfortable. The majority of CEOs feel the same way.
* *Misunderstood purpose.* Some directors misuse the evaluation to find fault rather than use the process for constructive purposes.
* *Ambiguity.* This is a major impediment to implementing an effective board evaluation process. Ambiguity can come from a "squishy" statement of the organization's strategic goals, the CEO's job description and goals, how the process is designed, or the way in which evaluation results are shared with the CEO.

- *Low priority.* The CEO evaluation should be given a high priority, and a sufficient amount of time and energy must be dedicated to the process.
- *Objective measurements.* There is often difficulty in rating the CEO on qualitative factors, such as the CEO's ability to develop the leadership pipeline or growth as a continuously learning organization.
- *Being critical of the CEO.* Some boards fear that being critical in an evaluation could result in the loss of an overall effective CEO.

These factors, of course, should not inhibit the CEO evaluation process, and directors must take appropriate action to ensure that they do not.

CEO Evaluation Process

An appropriate CEO evaluation has two important components: the process itself and the evaluation criteria. An excellent process with a poorly designed evaluation form is oftentimes superior to a weak process with a well-designed evaluation form.

The evaluation process includes laying out the evaluation approval authority, the administration of the evaluation (including the form of the summary report), the type of evaluation (oral versus written), the disposition of the evaluation worksheets, the timing of the evaluation, and most important, the feedback to the CEO. Furthermore, there is interplay between the board evaluation process and the CEO evaluation process and measurement criteria. These sets of criteria and processes should be integrated to ensure a smooth evaluation process and to avoid disconnects between the board and management.

To make the evaluation process more objective, the board should create a job description for the CEO, and a solid basis for performance measures and targets. The job description and performance targets should be finalized during the first fiscal quarter. That will provide an objective reference to evaluate the CEO once the year is complete. Progress against these objective reference points will be used to provide feedback to the CEO.

The CEO's job description should explicitly state what the board wants from the CEO. A basic CEO job description stipulates the executive's duties, responsibilities, and powers. The job description should also prescribe a set of priorities. Essentially, the job description will provide a solid footprint for a performance evaluation system. Exhibit 3.1 shows a sample job description.

Confidentiality Is Paramount

The CEO evaluation should be conducted with utmost confidentiality. Thus, great care must be taken to maintain this confidentiality. Completed evaluation forms should be returned only to the director in charge of the evaluation, who should then

Exhibit 3.1   Sample CEO Job Description

Major Task	Benchmark for Achievement
Corporate leader	Lead the innovative process that takes the company into new, more profitable markets. Lead the business planning process.
Chief communicator	Be the chief representative for the company. Keep visions, values, and missions in front of the public, shareholders, stock analysts, employees, suppliers, and alliance members. Promote quality communication within the company. Be able to express ideas, plans, strategies, and reasons for change in a clear, persuasive, concise, and effective manner.
Attitude leader	The CEO should have a positive attitude toward the board, with a particular emphasis on the need to engage the board. Behaviors that encourage good board relations are: • Providing enough information for board members to be effective and timely in their input. • Staying in touch with the board. • Fostering honesty, candor, frankness, and openness in communications with all board members. • Responding to the board's advice in a clear and convincing manner. If the CEO and the board agree on something to be done, the CEO should make sure it happens. • Being willing to be held accountable. • Share in the credit with the board, when the company is successful.
Cultural leader	Set the tone of the company's culture by example. Encourage behavior that will grow the business, such as entrepreneurial spirit, as well as accountability for results.
Executive team leader	Lead the executive team. Demand success and be willing to reorganize executive team based on results.
Corporate resource manager	Use corporate resources effectively and efficiently. Strike an optimum balance between long-term and short-term needs. Pay particular attention to human resources issues, especially with regard to executive succession planning. Ensure that proper measurement and control processes are in place, especially the performance appraisal system.

Exhibit 3.1 Continued

Major Task	Benchmark for Achievement
Continual learner	Seek ways to improve the company, as reflected in improved corporate results. Always seek feedback for the purpose of positive change and improvement.
Strategic planner	Form the company's structure and processes to fit the strategy and culture sought by the board. Encourage various corporate sectors to work together for a common, strategic goal. Be willing to restructure the company, when necessary, based on clear strategic needs.

arrange to compile a summary of the responses. It is recommended that an outside consultant (perhaps the same organization that is assisting with the director evaluation program) help manage this process. Management (especially the CEO) generally should not see the raw information, as it may be taken out of context and have an unintended effect on the CEO's performance.

To assure confidentiality and to encourage an objective evaluation and associated comments, worksheet forms should be destroyed after the evaluations are summarized. The retention of notes and comments relating to the CEO's performance—just like hand-written notes on board materials—may be taken out of context upon review.

While there is a concern that the destruction of written CEO evaluation forms completed by directors might somehow deprive shareholders of information or rights, most would agree that shareholders are not entitled to this information. There is no rule, law, or requirement that this information be retained or disclosed to shareholders. Moreover, requiring such retention or disclosure would make the evaluation process more cumbersome than necessary.

Oral versus Written Process

As stated earlier, there is no requirement that the CEO evaluation be written. It is possible for the outside directors to conduct an oral evaluation of the CEO. This process would be similar to the recommended process for written evaluations. For example, there would still be a CEO evaluation form outlining goals and objectives, and the CEO would discuss his or her performance before the full board. The full board would ask the CEO questions about his or her performance and then meet in executive session to discuss the CEO's performance. The results of these discussions would be summarized and shared with the CEO shortly after the executive session.

This discussion would not be conducted by the full board, but by one or two directors.

The primary advantage of an oral-based CEO evaluation process is that the interplay between directors is conducted in executive session without written comments that may be misunderstood. Moreover, group discussion among the directors may help some directors articulate their own evaluations of the CEO. Finally, oral evaluation generally take less time than written evaluations.

The disadvantage of an oral-based CEO evaluation process is that a few very vocal directors may unduly influence other directors, which can undermine a fair and objective evaluation of the CEO. Directors are more likely to be objective and fair if they do not have to debate the performance in full session prior to completing their own evaluations of the CEO. Another problem with an oral process is that it may not allow for in-depth review of the performance, since the evaluation usually occurs all at one meeting.

Some pointers for a well-organized oral CEO evaluation are:

- Before the process begins, the board should agree to a list of objectives and goals to guide the discussion. This typically is the same guide that the CEO used for discussion of his or her performance before the board. Generally, it is difficult to have a meaningful evaluation if the discussion jumps to and from various sections of the evaluation.
- The board discussion should be organized, managed, and controlled. Typically, one board member leads the discussion, and the chairs of the compensation and corporate governance committees are consulted at the end of each section of the CEO's performance that is discussed.
- All members of the board should be given an opportunity to contribute to the discussion. To promote this objective, different outside directors could lead the discussion for different sections of the evaluation. Providing the opportunity for active participation by all directors is important to the integrity of the evaluation process.

To counteract some of the disadvantages of an oral process, many companies use written CEO evaluations that—even though destroyed when the evaluation process is completed—nevertheless were in writing, and thus the board will not have to defend the oral evaluation process before shareholders.

Overall, a written evaluation more likely provides a better opportunity for all directors to evaluate the CEO in an objective, fair, and unbiased way. Moreover, having a written record that can be reviewed and summarized generally contributes to a more orderly process.

Responsibility for Process and Evaluation Timetable

As mentioned earlier, the CEO evaluation process usually is "owned" by the compensation committee, the corporate governance committee, or the full board. In a "Corporate Governance Survey" of Fortune 1000 companies by Buck Consultants released in 2003, the compensation committee had full approval authority for the CEO evaluation in 48% of the responding companies and recommending approval authority in 40% of the responding companies. In only 4% of the responding companies did the compensation committee have no authority in the CEO evaluation process.

While, as noted before, the CEO evaluation is handled differently by different boards, some have devised an approval authority flow:

- A "lead director" (same person who gives the feedback to the CEO) is appointed by the board.
- All outside directors complete the CEO evaluation form.
- The CEO also completes the self-assessment form.
- These forms are then provided to the chairs of the compensation and corporate governance committees.
- The committee chairs agree on some points and "agree to disagree" on other points.
- The CEO evaluation is then discussed in executive session at the next compensation and/or corporate governance committee meetings.
- A final review of the evaluation is made, and the full board (excluding the CEO) finalizes the evaluations at the same meeting.
- An appointment is made with the CEO (usually sometime after the meeting).
- The chair of the compensation or corporate governance committee (singly or jointly) typically gives the feedback. It is important that this meeting is conducted in person, as body language and facial expressions convey significant meaning in these types of discussions.
- The evaluation is then used, in conjunction with financial results, to award the CEO his or her bonus at the next board meeting.
- The work papers associated with the evaluation are destroyed. This includes notes taken at the board meeting (standard practice at most companies).

The lead director is key to this process, as he or she is the link between the CEO and the evaluation committee and/or full board. In addition, having a lead director allows for utmost confidentiality and integrity of the process.

Evaluation Criteria

In determining the criteria to be used for evaluating the CEO, directors should focus on the following questions:

- Is our CEO the best for our company—at this time and this place? Why?
- Are there gaps in expectations, goals, and commitments? If so, is the CEO addressing them?
- Does the CEO understand the gaps in expectations, goals, and commitments, and respond to them?
- Has the board specifically discussed the performance measurement criteria with the CEO?
- What does the CEO have to do to succeed? Is he or she doing it?
- Is a strong succession plan in place? Do we pay enough attention to succession issues?
- Are the proper strategies in place?
- What two or three strategies can most affect the company, such as price increases, changes in the product mix, adding value to products?
- Are things getting better or worse?
- Where is the new top line growth in the company going to come from?
- Does the CEO develop, attract, retain, and motivate an effective management team?
- Is there high-quality, cost-effective management of operations?

Generally, most directors prefer that a portion of the CEO's annual bonus be based on qualitative and/or nonfinancial criteria. For example, criteria that some boards prefer as nonfinancial goals but which should be taken into account in determining the annual bonus are leadership development and succession planning. Simply put, how well is the CEO grooming his or her successor, and how much talent is there in the pipeline? As with most qualitative criteria, it is sometimes difficult to accurately measure this performance, but the collective subjective assessments by all participating directors generally can provide a fairly accurate picture.

The following should be taken into account in designing an evaluation form:

- Type of evaluation:
  - Self evaluation
  - Peer evaluation (board only)

- 360-degree evaluation (board, certain executive officers, rank-and-file employees, and shareholders)
- Rating system:
  - Letter grades (e.g., A through F) with comments
  - Number grades (e.g., 1 through 5; 1 through 10) with comments
  - No ratings with comments
- Measurement criteria:
  - Qualitative
  - Quantitative financial
  - Quantitative nonfinancial
- Linkage between evaluation process and bonus decision

It is recommended that a combination self-evaluation and board evaluation be completed. The self-evaluation will allow the CEO to focus on his or her performance and may uncover facts and accomplishments that have not come to the attention of the board. The 360-degree approach generally takes six to eight weeks to complete the process, may be counterproductive, and does not necessarily lead to an improved or different rating than a board evaluation. However, a review of the leadership survey that covers those constituencies may be used as input to a CEO evaluation. This leadership survey might capture actions and activity that the board does not see directly, such as nurturing positive relationships with senior executives. One caveat is leadership surveys typically work well in organizations where the culture is healthy, trust is deep, and the CEO invites this type of feedback.

Use of a rating scale of 1 to 6 is recommended, with identifying characteristics for each number (e.g., "always exceeds expectations," "meets expectations," "below expectations"). Use of letter grades (A, A−, B+, etc.) can have a negative connation associated with doing poorly in school, and accordingly is not recommended. Using a rating scale can also require that the board answer each question with comments. Directors should be encouraged to comment on each criterion; however, a rating focuses the director and can be tabulated and summarized. See Exhibit 3.2 for a sample CEO evaluation form, and Exhibit 3.3 for a sample evaluation form from The Conference Board.

The next step is to weight these criteria. It should be made clear to the CEO that certain criteria may be more important than others. Several sections of the evaluation may have equal weight. In any event, it is imperative that the criteria and the weighting of the criteria be clearly understood at the beginning of the performance period. Exhibit 3.4 provides a summary of the CEO evaluation process, and Exhibit 3.5 provides sample questions to include in the evaluation.

Exhibit 3.2   Illustrative CEO Evaluation Form

Section	Major Topics and Description	Weight	Rating*
1.	Strategic Planning	10	
	• Ensures the development of a long-term strategy.		
	• Establishes objectives and plans that meet the needs of shareholders, customers, employees, and all other corporate stakeholders, and ensures consistent and timely progress toward strategic objectives.		
	• Obtains and allocates resources consistent with strategic objectives. Reports regularly to the board on progress toward strategic plan milestones.		
2.	Leadership	10	
	• Develops and communicates a clear and consistent vision of the company's goals and values.		
	• Ensures that this vision is well understood, widely supported, and effectively implemented within the organization.		
	• Fosters a corporate culture that encourages, recognizes, and rewards leadership, excellence, and innovation.		
	• Ensures a culture that promotes ethical practice, individual integrity, and cooperation to build shareholder value.		
3.	Financial Results	15	
	• Establishes and achieves appropriate annual and longer-term financial performance goals.		
	• Ensures the development and maintenance of appropriate systems to protect the company's assets and assure effective control of operations.		
4.	Management of Operations	4	
	• Ensures high-quality, cost-effective management of the day-to-day business affairs of the company.		

Exhibit 3.2 Continued

Section	Major Topics and Description	Weight	Rating*
	• Promotes continuous improvement of the quality, value, and competitiveness of the company's products and business systems.		
	• Encourages and rewards creative solutions to business and management solutions.		
5.	Management Development	10	
	• Develops, attracts, retains, and motivates an effective and unified senior management team.		
	• Ensures that programs for management development and succession planning have the required resources and direction to grow the future leaders of the company.		
6.	Human Resources	6	
	• Ensures the development of effective programs for the recruitment, training, compensation, retention, and motivation of employees.		
	• Ensures that adequate human resources are available to meet the needs of the company.		
	• Establishes and monitors programs to promote workplace diversity.		
	• Provides for appropriate recognition of the achievements of individuals and groups.		
7.	Communications	7	
	• Serves as chief spokesperson for the company, communicating effectively with shareholders, prospective investors, employees, customers, suppliers, and consumers.		
	• Effectively represents the company in relationships with industry, the government, and the financial community, including major investor groups and financial services firms.		

(*continues*)

Exhibit 3.2   Continued

Section	Major Topics and Description	Weight	Rating*
8.	Board Relations	10	
	• Works closely with the board to keep directors informed on the state of business on critical issues relating to the company.		
	• Works closely with the board to keep the directors informed on the company's programs toward the achievement of operating plan and strategic plan milestones.		
	• Provides effective support for board operations, including board materials, and advisory services.		

* Note: The numeric ranking system is:

1. Substantially Below Expectations
2. Slightly Below Expectations and Progressing Toward Meeting Expectations
3. Meets Expectations
4. Well Above Expectations
5. Clearly Exceeds Expectations in the Most Important Aspects of Section
6. Substantially Exceeds Expectations in All Aspects of Section

Exhibit 3.3   The Conference Board Sample CEO Evaluation Form

Process:

- Evaluation sheet distributed (date) to active independent board members
- Completed evaluation sheets returned to xxx by (date)
- Xxx will summarize input and pass on anonymously to yyy
- Yyy will circulate to the board and preview with zzz, adding his own feedback
- Active independent board members discuss evaluation with zzz at (date) board meeting

Evaluation:

Your name: _____(will be removed by xxx)

Please return to xxx prior to (date)

Section A: Primary Responsibilities of the CEO

Consider the factors listed below when forming your evaluation. Provide relevant examples when possible.

Exhibit 3.3 Continued

1. Development of the primary strategy and objectives of the company

- Appropriateness given the external environment
- Clarity and consistency of the strategy
- Process that encourages effective strategic planning

Grade (check one) ☐ Outstanding ☐ Good ☐ Needs Improvement

Comments/examples:

_____
_____
_____

2. Tone and structure of how the company operates

- Appropriateness of organizational structure to the primary strategy
- Alignment of management with the strategy
- Clearly communicated with a process for identifying and measuring progress toward the strategy
- Timely adjustments in strategy when necessary
- Fosters a culture of ethical behavior that includes effective compliance programs, strong auditing, and financial controls

Grade (check one) ☐ Outstanding ☐ Good ☐ Needs Improvement

Comments/examples:

_____
_____
_____

3. Leadership and development of the management team

- Succession planning in place at higher levels that includes an effective plan for developing candidates for the long term
- Turnover of management
- Energy of management team
- Motivates and inspires employees to realize the company's vision
- Effective role model for the organization

Grade (check one) ☐ Outstanding ☐ Good ☐ Needs Improvement

Comments/examples:

_____
_____
_____

4. Relationship with the board

- Keeps the board fully informed of important aspects of the company
- Practices and encourages open, honest, and timely communication

(*continues*)

Exhibit 3.3 Continued

- Effective presentations
- Ability to raise and explain key issues
- Ability to draw on past experiences in issues facing the corporation

Grade (check one) ☐ Outstanding ☐ Good ☐ Needs Improvement

Comments/examples:

_____
_____
_____

Section B: Performance to (company) values

The CEO should set the tone by role modeling (company) values. Please consider the CEO's strengths, areas for development, and the factors listed below. Provide relevant examples when possible.

1. Results orientation

- Sets challenging and competitive goals
- Focuses on output
- Assumes responsibility
- Constructively confronts and solves problems
- Executes flawlessly

Grade (check one) ☐ Outstanding ☐ Good ☐ Needs Improvement

Comments/examples:

_____
_____
_____

2. Risk taking

- Fosters innovation and creative thinking
- Embraces change and challenges the status quo
- Listens to all ideas and viewpoints

Grade (check one) ☐ Outstanding ☐ Good ☐ Needs Improvement

Comments/examples:

_____
_____
_____

3. Discipline

- Conducts business with uncompromising integrity and professionalism
- Makes and meets commitments
- Properly plans, funds, and staffs projects
- Learns from our successes and mistakes

Exhibit 3.3   Continued

Grade (check one) ☐ Outstanding ☐ Good ☐ Needs Improvement

Comments/examples:

_____
_____
_____

4. Quality

• Strives to achieve the highest standards of excellence
• Does the right things right
• Continuously learns, develops, and improves

Grade (check one) ☐ Outstanding ☐ Good ☐ Needs Improvement

Comments/examples:

_____
_____
_____

5. Customer orientation

• Listens and responds to our customers, suppliers, and stakeholders
• Clearly communicates mutual intentions and expectations
• Delivers innovative and competitive products and services

Grade (check one) ☐ Outstanding ☐ Good ☐ Needs Improvement

Comments/examples:

_____
_____
_____

6. Great place to work

• Style: open and direct
• Works as a member of a team with respect and trust for each other
• Recognizes and rewards accomplishments
• Manages performance fairly and firmly
• Makes (company) an asset to our communities worldwide

Grade (check one) ☐ Outstanding ☐ Good ☐ Needs Improvement

Comments/examples:

_____
_____
_____

(*continues*)

Exhibit 3.3   Continued

Section C: Overall summary

1. Greatest strength as a CEO

Comments/examples:

_____
_____
_____

2. Major highlights and lowlights of the past 12 months

Comments/examples:

_____
_____
_____

3. Words of advice to the CEO

Comments/examples:

_____
_____
_____

4. Overall performance

Grade (check one) ☐ Outstanding ☐ Good ☐ Needs Improvement

Comments/examples:

_____
_____
_____

_____

Linking the Evaluation to CEO Incentive Compensation

The last and very important part of the evaluation process is to link the evaluation process to the CEO's pay package. It is important to ensure that CEO pay is in line with corporate performance. For example, care should be taken to avoid large stock grants, bonus payments, salary increases, and other perceived compensation windfalls when there is an employee layoff, stock slump, or earnings drop.

Historically, the CEO evaluation process has been delinked from the CEO bonus decision. The bonus is usually determined using quantitative financial criteria such as EPS growth, or EBITDA. As mentioned previously, the CEO evaluation form generally is more qualitative than quantitative, and with nonfinancial criteria,

Exhibit 3.4 CEO Evaluation Process Checklist

These questions are designed to help boards assess their CEO evaluation process and determine if any improvements are necessary.

Questions
1. Does the CEO have a current, written position description that is clear and comprehensive? This job description can be based on traits and characteristics of the position.
2. Does the CEO have an employment agreement that, among other items, includes severance benefits?
3. Has the board established a written policy statement covering the policy statement, a formal CEO goal setting and appraisal process?
4. Has the board formed an effective and independent compensation committee and corporate governance committee? Do these committees have charters?
5. Do both the CEO and board members perceive the executive evaluation process as constructive and objective?
6. Does the CEO receive clear and useful feedback on the board's expectations and evaluation of his or her performance?
7. Do all members of the board have sufficient input into establishing the CEO's goals and evaluating performance?
    a. How is this input obtained:
        i. Via a written questionnaire?
        ii. Conversations with the board chair?
        iii. Interviews conducted by an independent third party who summarizes findings?
        iv. Other means?
8. Does the executive evaluation committee make a summary report of its work to the full board so all members can be confident that an effective evaluation process is in place, and so they are aware of the CEO's current goals?
9. Do all board members understand and honor the confidential nature of any personnel evaluation, including executive appraisal?
10. Are the CEO's performance goals both quantitative and qualitative, and do they reflect all important aspects of the organization's mission, strategic vision, and major priorities, not only financial and business objectives?
    a. Qualitative factors such as the CEO's ability to develop the leadership pipeline, and a continuously learning organization should be included.
11. Is the CEO performance evaluation effectively linked to executive compensation in a way that rewards the CEO for effective performance?
12. If challenged by shareholders, employees, the public, media, or governmental agencies, can members of the board clearly articulate a policy and rationale for the CEO's compensation and benefits package?

Exhibit 3.5   CEO Question Reference Guide

Suggested areas for investigation and performance traits with related questions in six major areas of CEO expertise: strategy, leadership, organizational issues, building and maintaining relationships, functional knowledge, and integrity and ethics.

Part I. Strategy

A. Company's business model: Knowledge of how and where an organization makes its profits and its revenues in relationship to its suppliers and customers.

  1. How well does the CEO understand the business model and critical success factors?
  2. Is the CEO able to come up to speed quickly with a business model that he or she may not have had previous exposure to?
  3. Does this individual appreciate the interrelationship of suppliers, value creation, and customer needs?

B. Corporate strategy formulation: Knowledge of alternative strategies and knowledge of the strengths and weaknesses of different strategy alternatives. Knowledge of a company's customer base and trends within differing customer segments that may offer strategic opportunities.

  1. How strategic is the CEO in his or her thought processes? Do the questions he or she asks reflect appreciation of the importance of clear strategic thinking?
  2. Have you observed incidents in which the CEO has strongly influenced or made a significant contribution to strategic direction or its determination in a company or board setting?
  3. Does the CEO respond to critical questions to investigate the depth of management's analysis and thinking on strategic alternatives?

C. Competition: Knowledge of key competitors (their strategies, core competencies, leadership) as well as knowledge of potential competitors who might enter an industry due to shifts in the market or technology.

  1. How externally focused and knowledgeable is the CEO regarding existing and potential competitors within the company's competitive universe?
  2. Does the CEO add value to a board discussion of competitive threats to a company?
  3. Does the CEO have previous exposure to companies that are or may become competitors?

D. Global markets: Understanding existing and potential international markets for the company and fundamental knowledge about national economies and government relations in those markets.

  1. Does the CEO have a multinational frame of reference based on experience and/or interest?
  2. Does the CEO have knowledge of and/or experience in regions of the world in which the company is operating or wishes to expand into?
  3. How sensitive is the CEO to cultural differences and beliefs, and are there illustrative specific examples?

Exhibit 3.5 Continued

Part II. Leadership

A. Senior executive coaching: Skills in coaching senior executives and helping them set goals for self-development and personal growth.

   1. Does the CEO have a record of accomplishment of successful coaching and mentorship?
   2. Do you have information regarding the CEO's reputation with subordinates?
   3. Does the CEO ask questions in a board setting that display an interest in succession and people development?

B. Senior executive development: Ability to transfer knowledge about a business, suggests learning experiences, and provides meaningful feedback to senior executives about their behavior.

   1. Do you believe the CEO can establish a strong advisory and trusting relationship with senior management? Are there any examples?
   2. Would the CEO be willing to counsel a senior executive regarding inappropriate personal behaviors that are negatively affecting the CEO's effectiveness?
   3. Has a member of the board sought out the CEO for advice? Frequently?

Part III. Organizational Issues

A. Strategy implementation: Understanding how strategic plans need to be implemented through organizational systems with appropriate deployment of resources. Demonstrate an understanding of initiatives that build on a company's core competencies.

   1. How astute is the CEO in understanding the need to bring along people to initiate and execute strategies?
   2. Does the CEO follow up in subsequent board meetings to ensure that proposed and agreed-upon strategies were tried and/or implemented?
   3. Is the CEO realistic and practical regarding the company's capability to actually implement strategic proposals and new ways of doing business?

B. Change management: Knowledge of basic change processes, such as communications strategies, tactics to overcome resistance, dedicated change management teams, and the use of benchmarks.

   1. Has the CEO led significant organizational change?
   2. How sophisticated is the CEO's understanding of the inherent obstacles to change?
   3. Does the CEO hold senior management accountable for implementing required organizational change?

C. Group effectiveness: Understanding of information about how groups best do knowledge sharing and how the board can effectively get information to assist in key strategic decisions.

   1. Are you aware of the CEO's exposure and/or appreciation of the need for a knowledge-sharing mentality in a learning-oriented company?

(continues)

Exhibit 3.5   Continued

---

2. Does the CEO work well with senior management and the board for the best interest of the company?
3. Does the CEO's ego get in the way of his or her effectiveness with others?

D. Organizational design: Understanding of alternative organizational designs, their strengths
and weaknesses, and how they affect and relate to business strategy.

1. Have you observed the CEO's knowledge and experience with alternative organizational structures?
2. Does the CEO share appropriate insights regarding organizational alternatives that
display experience and knowledge of these considerations in a board setting?
3. Are you aware if the CEO has learned from a significant mistake in organizational
design?

Part IV. Building and Maintaining Relationships

A. Governments: Understanding of how to deal with governmental entities in terms of regulatory approval and financial management.

1. Have you observed or do you know about the CEO's record of accomplishment in
working effectively with governmental agencies?
2. Any reason to be concerned about the CEO's reputation with governmental agencies
that have oversight or interest in the company's business?

B. Investors, financial analysts, and the media: Knowledge about communicating effectively
with investor groups, analysts, and media representatives.

1. Have you observed the CEO's communications ability in public forums such as with
analysts, media, or other external constituencies?
2. Does the CEO alienate or turn people off by his or her communication style? Does
he or she win people over with persuasive and sincere communications?

C. Communities and the environment: Knowledge of key communities in which the company has its headquarters and major operations. Understanding of legal and social issues
concerning the environmental impact of the company's operations.

1. How sensitive is the CEO to interest groups or community groups that require
attention?
2. Does the CEO consider community service an integral part of a senior executive's
role in a significant leadership position?

Part V. Functional Knowledge

A. Finance: Understanding of alternative sources of capital and acquisitions, mergers, and
divestitures.

1. Is the CEO comfortable with financial and capital analysis and external reporting requirements to be an effective director?
2. Has the CEO raised capital for his or her own enterprise and/or does he or she appreciate the intricacies of this process?
3. Is the CEO well known and respected in the capital markets?

Exhibit 3.5 Continued

B. Audit: Comprehension of financial statements and auditing procedures.

1. Is the CEO familiar with generally accepted accounting principles and appropriate standards for public company financial reporting?

C. Technical expertise: Knowledge of the key core competencies in the organization with respect to how they are obtained and managed.

1. Does the CEO understand the core organizational competencies required for an organization to be successful?

D. Legal issues: Understanding of the particular legal issues that the organization faces in its business, from both a business and regulatory perspective.

1. Does the CEO have significant experience with legal requirements of his or her own business or of a company on whose board he or she serves?
2. Are there any legal difficulties that the CEO has been affected by that might lead to embarrassment or difficulty for the company?

E. Human resources: Understanding of the critical talent issues of the organization and, if relevant, understanding of labor relations.

1. To your knowledge, does the CEO value the need for outstanding talent? Are there particular initiatives that the CEO has implemented or insisted on in a board role?
2. Has the CEO ever been involved in a particularly contentious labor dispute or been subject to criticism for his or her treatment of people?

F. Information technology: Particular focus on the impact of enterprise information systems and the Internet on the company from the point of view of internal management and with regard to the capability of these systems to provide effective interfaces with customers and suppliers.

1. How knowledgeable is the CEO in the areas of information technology utilization in the company?
2. Does the CEO appreciate the need for technology to achieve competitive strategic advantage?
3. How comfortable is the CEO in critically evaluating the need for significant capital investment in information systems and other technological improvements?

G. Marketing: Understanding of and information about the company's markets and the ability to structure the organization to interface effectively with its markets.

1. Does the CEO bring strong general management appreciation of the role of marketing to the success of the overall enterprise?
2. How comfortable is the CEO in evaluating marketing initiatives?
3. Does the CEO add value to board discussions regarding marketing programs and expenditures?

(*continues*)

Exhibit 3.5   Continued

Part VI. Integrity and Ethics

A. Ethical responsibilities: Ability to identify and raise key ethical issues concerning the activities of the company and of senior management as they affect the business community and society.

  1. Are you aware of any issues in the CEO's background, experience, or behavior that indicate anything less than the highest standards of personal integrity?
  2. Is integrity and ethical behavior a strong personal value of the CEO?
  3. To your knowledge, has the CEO had to deal with unethical situations?

such as leadership, communications, board relations, and management development. Companies are beginning to link these two evaluation processes.

Qualitative criteria should be used in the CEO evaluation process. Unfortunately, for public companies, Section 162(m) of the Internal Revenue Code (Code), which caps the deduction of non-performance-based compensation paid to top executives at $1 million, requires quantitative—not qualitative—performance goals. Thus, many public companies avoid using qualitative CEO evaluations as a performance metric for the annual cash bonus. It is preferable to use qualitative goals to determine the size of equity-based incentive compensation grants (e.g., stock options or stock appreciation rights) that still are subject to other time-based or performance-based conditions. Thus, if the grant satisfies the Code Section 162(m) performance requirements (such as an at-the-money stock option or stock appreciation right) and the other Code Section 162(m) requirements, the underlying compensation should be fully deductible under Code Section 162(m).

Another method that some companies might use to incorporate qualitative performance goals into an arrangement that qualifies for deductibility under Code Section 162(m) involves using a concept known as "negative discretion." This is done by "oversizing" the incentive compensation target and then reducing that amount based on the achievement of the qualitative goals. For example, assume that a CEO has an annual bonus target of 100% of base salary based on achieving specified EBITDA goals. The compensation committee would like to pay an additional 50% of base salary if 100% of the qualitative goals are achieved, and perhaps 20% if between 75% and 100% are achieved. The compensation committee then sets the annual bonus target at 150%, still based on achieving the EBITDA goals. Assuming the EBITDA goals were achieved, the committee then determines whether the qualitative goals were achieved, and to what degree. If all of the qualitative goals were achieved, then the bonus is not reduced. If only 80% of the qualitative goals were achieved, then the bonus is reduced by 20%. If less than 75% of the qualitative goals were achieved, then the bonus is reduced by 33⅓%.

Chapter 4

Director Compensation

Generally, members of boards of directors who are not employees or major share-holders are paid for their services as directors. For purposes of this chapter, the assumption is that only outside/independent directors are paid director compensation and that employee-directors and/or major shareholder-directors are paid nothing with respect to their director services.

In the past, directors fees tended to be meaningful but relatively modest amounts, primarily due to the limited amount of time that directors devoted to such service. For example, for many years the estimated annual service time for a director was thought to be approximately 100 hours. Thus, assuming $250 per hour, the annual total amount that would be paid to a director would be $25,000; at $500 per hour, it would be $50,000 per year. Again, these are meaningful compensation amounts but relatively small when compared to the annual compensation of many actively employed directors. For those directors who were retired from their life careers, directors fees usually represented an ancillary "stipend" for board service that the retiree director relished for its prestige and honor, not for its pay. Of course, there were some directors who served on five, six, or even 10 boards, and the aggregate of that compensation made for quite a tidy sum. Generally, however, directors—whether they were current chief executive officers (CEOs), retired CEOs, investors, law firm partners, professors, physicians, and/or politicians—did not serve on a board for the compensation.

Much has happened to change the nature of board service in the 21st century. In the post-Enron era, new federal and state legislation, new Securities and Exchange Commission (SEC) regulations, new stock exchange listing rules, a new sense of public outrage toward perceived corporate excesses, and a new fear of shareholder litigation have caused directors to work harder, longer, and—more importantly—more carefully than ever before. It would not be unusual for some directors at public companies to now devote 200 to 300 service hours a year to a single board.

In addition, directors are being limited in the number of boards on which they may serve. Service on too many boards is negatively perceived by the public and the investment community—the view is that the director is stretched too thin for effective performance. Moreover, the increased annual time commitment required for board service in today's environment will for most directors serve as a practical limit against serving on multiple boards. Accordingly, it is expected that directors likely will serve on no more than four boards, with a more typical number being two or three.

The combination of the reduction in the number of boards on which a director can serve, the increase in hours devoted to board service, the new emphasis on training and expertise, and the aura of increased accountability has logically indicated that changes in director compensation are in order. Accordingly, in recent years, director fees have been substantially increasing. Recent surveys report that director fees have increased in the range of 25% to 45% from 2001 to 2003. While these surveys examined different company or industry groups, and thus produced different results, there is no question that compensation for board service is and will continue to increase until these new workload requirements and service arrangements level out.

In most cases, boards rely on the compensation committee to review director compensation and recommend appropriate compensation levels applicable to all directors. In some cases, review and setting of director compensation is a joint effort between the compensation committee and the corporate governance committee. In almost every case, however, the ultimate committee recommendation is presented to the full board for discussion and approval. Typically, director compensation is reviewed every two or three years, although more frequent review may be the rule while the structure of director compensation is under wholesale reconfiguration.

ELEMENTS OF DIRECTOR COMPENSATION

Generally, most directors receive elements of both cash-based and equity-based compensation, such as stock options, restricted stock, and/or restricted stock units (RSUs). The impact of the changes in the accounting for director equity-based compensation is discussed later in this chapter. In addition, in the past, directors often had additional benefits and perquisites, such as pension or deferred compensation arrangements, health and life insurance coverage, and/or company-paid charitable contributions made at the direction of the director. However, these programs have fallen out of favor with shareholders and the public, and most companies have phased out and discontinued these programs.

The most typical elements of director compensation include:

- Board member annual retainer, usually paid in cash, equity, or a combination of both
- Board chair annual retainer, usually paid in cash, but sometimes paid in both cash and equity

- Board member in-person meeting fee, usually paid in cash
- Board member telephonic meeting fee, usually paid in cash, but sometimes ignored, particularly if the telephonic meeting was short and informal, and/or no minutes were recorded
- Board chair in-person meeting fee, usually paid in cash
- Committee member annual retainer, usually paid in cash
- Committee chair annual retainer, usually paid in cash
- Committee member in-person meeting fee, usually paid in cash
- Committee member telephonic meeting fee, usually paid in cash but sometimes ignored, particularly if the telephonic meeting was short and informal, and/or no minutes were recorded
- Committee chair in-person meeting fee, usually paid in cash
- Special one-time initial (or sign-on/sign-up) fee, usually paid in equity
- Lead director special fees, paid in equity and/or cash
- Other special project or per diem fees, usually paid in cash

In addition, expenses incurred by the directors for board service (e.g., travel, office services, continuing director education) are normally reimbursed by the company.

The preceding elements of director compensation are neither uniform nor consistent from industry to industry nor from company to company. For example, some companies may pay a high annual retainer and small (or no) meeting fees. Other companies may pay a small (or no) annual retainer and high meeting fees. Some companies pay no additional compensation for committee service, while others pay additional compensation (both as an annual retainer and meeting fees) for committee service. Some companies provide new directors a "sign-on" or "sign-up" equity grant (formerly, this tended to be in the form of stock options) as an inducement to join the board.

As is the case with executive compensation, the equity compensation practices for outside directors historically were guided in large part by accounting considerations. Because almost all companies used Accounting Principles Bulletin Opinion No. 25 (APB 25) as their equity-based compensation accounting standard, equity-based compensation for directors usually was in the form of "at-the-money" stock options (i.e., stock options with an exercise price equal to the fair market value of the stock on the date of grant). Common practice, along with the accounting interpretation provided in FASB Interpretation No. 44 (FIN 44), treated at-the-money stock options granted to directors as resulting in no compensation expense. Some companies did use stock, stock units, restricted stock, or RSUs in lieu of or in addition to stock options; but this, of course, resulted in a compensation charge under APB 25. However, almost no company granted stock appreciation rights (SARs), as this type of equity-based compensation produced "variable accounting" under APB 25 and FASB Interpretation No. 28 (see Chapter 8 for more detail). Most companies granted equity-based compensation with some vesting requirements that varied from company to company. Some companies imposed a vesting schedule of only one year, while others imposed three-, four-, or five-year pro-rata vesting schedules. And, of course, some companies imposed no vesting restrictions on directors' equity awards.

Because of the anticipated equity-based accounting rules that will require a compensation charge for stock option grants, many companies will rethink their director equity compensation programs. While some companies may continue to use at-the-money director stock options (or SARs payable only in stock), based on the notion that such awards are purely performance based, others are likely to switch to "full-value" stock awards, deferred stock units, restricted stock or RSUs, based on the notion that the equity award is in lieu of cash and does contain a performance upside/downside element. It is also expected that discounted stock options/SARs may be used by some companies for director equity-based compensation. These "in-the-money" awards were not used in the past due to the accounting charge required under APB 25, but under the expected accounting rules they could find favor in appropriate circumstances.

Traditionally, it has been customary for equity-based compensation for directors to vest immediately upon a change in control (similar to the accelerated vesting of equity-based compensation granted to executives and other employees). While this acceleration feature could present a potential conflict of interest (tempting a director to unduly favor a proposal that would accelerate the vesting of his or her awards), most companies reasoned that the accelerated vesting provision of director equity grants was not meaningful enough to negatively impact a director's decision regarding a change in control. However, given the hard focus on director independence in the post-Enron era, this reasoning may need to be revisited.

Many companies have or are contemplating implementing some type of program that requires executives to either maintain specified company stock ownership levels and/or prevents executives from selling compensatory shares received through option exercise, vesting of restricted stock, or delivery of shares underlying RSUs. Similarly, some companies have imposed these programs with respect to director equity-based compensation. In some instances, new directors are required to buy and hold a specified number of shares or dollar amount of company stock. While in the past this program often included a company-provided loan arrangement, such loan arrangements are now prohibited by Section 402 of the Sarbanes-Oxley Act of 2002. Therefore, these "mandatory purchase" arrangements will be less popular and certainly will not have a company loan feature. In other instances, directors are required to hold all or substantially all of their compensatory shares of company stock until they leave the board. However, this kind of program may seem too onerous and might impair director recruiting activities. Generally, some minimum level of company share ownership is desired for all directors, but the appropriate level is largely dependent on the type and dollar amount of the director compensation program.

Director equity-based compensation generally is granted under a company stock or incentive compensation plan. Under old SEC rules regarding the exemption of equity-based compensation from short-swing profit liability under Section 16(b) of the Securities Exchange Act of 1934, only "disinterested" directors (as then defined) were eligible to grant exempt awards to Section 16 insiders. To preserve the "disinterested" status of directors for this purpose, they could only receive equity awards pursuant to a formula plan that did not allow any discretion about the timing or amount of such awards to the directors. Therefore, companies commonly maintained separate formula plans for awards to outside directors. This rule, however, was changed in 1996 by eliminating the concept of "disinterested" director status. It was replaced by a different concept of director independence embodied in the definition of a "non-employee" director, as discussed more fully in Chapter 1, which does not depend on the source or manner of making equity awards to such director. Thus, equity-based compensation may now be granted to both employees and directors under the same plan. Nevertheless, whether director awards are made from a separate plan or under the company's employee equity plan, many institutional investors prefer to see grants to outside directors made pursuant to an established formula, program, or policy, in order to avoid any implication that directors might be making grants to themselves on a discretionary basis. This makes good sense from a corporate governance perspective. See Chapter 6 for a more detailed discussion of the Section 16 short-swing profit rules.

Finally, there has been discussion whether director cash-based arrangements should be tied to performance goals, such as earnings targets or growth, similar to an executive annual bonus or long-term cash compensation program. While there may be a few examples of companies that have done this, most companies avoid this type of director compensation arrangement due to the inherent conflicts it engenders. Simply put, these kinds of arrangements are best suited for management, who run the day-to-day business of the company and, therefore, have more direct effect on the attainment of particular financial performance measures. It is more appropriate that long-term stock price movements be the primary performance measure to impact director compensation.

DISCLOSURE

Compensation arrangements for directors of public companies must be disclosed. This disclosure typically is found in a company's annual proxy statement, but it could be found in a special proxy statement, or in a Form 10-K, S-1, or S-4. The SEC rules require a description of all standard director compensation arrangements (stating dollar amounts or otherwise) pursuant to which directors of the company are compensated for any services provided as a director, including any additional amounts payable for committee participation or special assignments. In addition, the rules require a description of any other arrangements pursuant to which any director is paid for any service provided as a director, stating the amount paid and the name of the director. This description applies to any arrangement (including consulting contracts) entered into in consideration of the director's service on the board, and the material terms of any such arrangement must be disclosed.

Currently, this disclosure is in the form of a narrative description. However, during the late 1990s, the SEC proposed "tabularizing" director compensation disclosure, similar to the way it now requires tabularized disclosure of executive compensation, but these proposals never were finalized. So, for the moment, narrative disclosure of director compensation is still the rule. However, companies should be aware that the SEC has indicated its intention to review and update its rules on executive compensation disclosure. Thus, there is a possibility that the proposed rules regarding a tabular presentation of director compensation, as well as changes in other aspects of director compensation disclosure, may be forthcoming in the not so distant future.

In addition, if the company is presenting a new compensation plan for shareholder approval, the SEC requires that a "New Plan Benefit Table" be included in the proxy statement. This table must disclose the aggregate of the proposed benefits or amounts to be paid or granted under the new plan to the "current directors who are not executive officers as a group."

NEW TRENDS IN DIRECTOR COMPENSATION

As mentioned previously, director compensation is undergoing two fundamental changes. First, the overall level of director compensation is increasing due to the additional workload and the fact—to some degree—that directors can no longer serve on many boards at the same time. Second, recent changes in accounting rules regarding equity-based compensation are impacting the type and form of equity awards companies use to compensate directors. Together, these changes are causing most boards to reexamine the director compensation structure and levels. This reexamination is likely to be done on an annual basis, at least until patterns stabilize and it makes sense to get back to a more typical review schedule of every two to three years.

Certain specific trends are unmistakable. One is the payment of additional fees to audit committee chairs and/or members that are over and above what other committee chairs and/or members receive. Another is the payment of additional amounts to nonexecutive board chairs or lead directors. Also, as mentioned previously, a third likely trend is the replacement of stock option grants with full-value equity awards.

Of perhaps a less universal nature is the emerging practice of "bundling" all director compensation (i.e., annual retainers, meeting fees, committee fees) into a single amount that applies to all directors. The rationale for this is that it simplifies the fee structure and administration. The drawback is that this "one-size-fits-all" approach presumes that all directors provide equal service to the company, which in many circumstances is not the case. Payment of this universal fee usually is in a combination of cash and equity. Thus, for example, a company may have a fixed annual fee of $150,000 of which $75,000 is paid in cash and $75,000 is paid in equity. The equity portion may be allocated between restricted stock/RSUs and stock options/SARs, or it may be paid all in restricted stock/RSUs or all in stock options/SARs. Since all equity-based compensation will result in a compensation charge, this leaves room for design creativity in determining whether the grant should be a full-value award (such as restricted stock/RSUs) or an appreciation award (such as options/SARs) and, in either case, whether it should be fully vested as of the grant date or subject to vesting (by continued service or other performance measures).

A variation of bundling is to provide a variety of fee levels, based on the position or positions of each individual director. For example, a board might pay a base retainer to all directors, plus varying supplemental retainers to directors who serve as (i) board chair or lead director, (ii) chair of the audit committee, (iii) chair of any other committee, and/or (iv) member of the audit committee. The layering of these different fees for service will result in individual directors being paid different amounts, but it has the advantage of allocating the overall director compensation budget on the basis of work and responsibility.

For those companies that do not favor a fixed-fee approach, the trend may be to substantially increase board and committee meeting fees and to maintain or slightly increase annual retainers. The rationale here is that the compensation is paid for actual service—service in a board position that requires meetings once a month should be compensated at a higher level than a position that entails meetings held once a quarter.

Whatever approach is followed, because the audit committee has assumed at least the appearance of heightened importance and public scrutiny, the fees relating to service on the audit committee most likely will become and continue to be higher than for service on other committees. Moreover, as compensation committee service continues to attract public focus and require greater expertise, fees relating to service on the compensation committee may similarly be higher than fees for service on the governance/nominating and other board committees.

Finally, the practice of making an initial equity grant, in a meaningful amount, to induce new directors to join the board probably will increase, since many people who might otherwise have considered board service may be dissuaded by the increased workload and perceived level of exposure. The initial sign-up award most likely will be in the form of restricted stock/RSUs, and with some kind of vesting requirement.

Ultimately, the decisions as to director compensation (both as to types and levels) will vary from company to company, based on company size, industry, culture, and simply the makeup of the board itself. How the board divides its labors will be a major consideration. Some companies may strive to balance the work so that service is equally shared among all independent directors, while others may have one or two independent directors who shoulder the lion's share. Since there is no magic formula, many companies and boards will perform selected benchmarking studies to help design and construct an appropriate director compensation program. However, in that context, care should be taken not to allow the benchmarking exercise to lead to the exploding compensation phenomenon observed in the recent past with respect to executive compensation, where companies pegged compensation in each year to the 75th percentile of market. As long as the benchmarking is used to discern market trends in director program design, and rational discipline is applied to the overall compensation levels, this type of market survey approach can be a useful tool.

CONDUCTING A DIRECTOR COMPENSATION STUDY

Conducting a director compensation study is very similar to conducting an executive compensation study. One useful resource is published surveys produced by compensation consulting firms, executive search firms, and corporate-advisory organizations such as the National Association of Corporate Directors, the Investors Responsibility Research Center, and The Conference Board. A second useful exercise is to observe the director programs at a peer group of companies that would serve well for comparison (usually due to size and/or industry). The information from these two sources would then be compared to the company's current board practices.

A wide range of discretion can be applied in selecting appropriate peer companies in a director compensation study, due to the similarities in the nature of director service for public companies across different industries, revenue ranges, and stock exchanges. Because not all companies pay the same types of director compensation, a minimum of 15 companies, preferably 20 to 30, should be selected in order to provide a useful comparator group. For example, if only 10 peer companies are used, and only half pay committee chair annual retainers, the data may not be statistically reliable. However, if 30 or more companies are selected, the incidence of those that pay committee chair annual retainers is likely to be higher and provide a better base for comparison. While increasing the number of peer companies to 50 would produce even more "hits" on a particular type of compensation used, the statistical relevance of the difference between groups of 30 or 50 companies is not likely to be as meaningful as the difference between groups of 10 and 30 companies.

The study should break down the components of director compensation into various types, and measure the level of each type. In addition, the study should determine total director compensation paid in the aggregate to all directors, and determine a per-director annual compensation level. For purposes of comparison, an assumption as to the number of board meetings and committee meetings is necessary. For example, it is typical to assume that a board will meet four times per year, and each committee will meet six times, per year. A study may be more complicated if the subject company has more committees than the typical three oversight committees (compensation, audit, and governance/nominating) for which it intends to pay special remuneration.

The following is an example of applying these assumptions at Company # 1 of a peer group of 15 companies:

Assumptions:

- Full board meets four times per year
- Compensation committee meets six times per year
- Audit committee meets six times per year
- Corporate governance committee meets six times per year
- There are no telephonic meetings

Fees:

- Cash annual board retainer of $20,000 per year
- $2,000 for each board meeting
- $1,500 for each committee meeting
- Additional audit committee member retainer of $5,000 per year
- Additional audit committee chair retainer of $10,000 per year
- 2,000 RSUs per year, valued at $35,000

Results:

- Each director receives:
  - $20,000 as a cash annual retainer
  - $35,000 as an equity annual retainer
  - $8,000 for attendance at board meetings

  for a total of $63,000.

- Each committee member receives:
  - $63,000 as a board member
  - $9,000 for committee meetings

  for a total of $72,000.

- Each audit committee member receives:
  - $63,000 as a board member
  - $9,000 for committee meetings
  - $5,000 as an audit committee member cash annual retainer

  for a total of $77,000.

- The audit committee chair receives:
  - $63,000 as a board member
  - $9,000 for committee meetings
  - $10,000 as an audit committee chair cash annual retainer

  for a total of $82,000.

These assumptions are similarly applied to the other 14 peer companies. Next, a model is built to show each data point for each component of director compensation, whether or not such component is used at the peer company or the subject company, using the previously stated assumptions and then combining all components to determine a relativistic total compensation figure for each company. See Exhibit 4.1 for a director compensation benchmarking study template.

These models should be reviewed both quantitatively and qualitatively. For example, a company may want to know what should be the level of sign-on/sign-up grants. The median may be $100,000, but if only two companies out of 30 pay such grants, then two conclusions could be reached. First is that most companies do not use this type of director compensation. Second is that this compensation—while it may not have been paid as a sign-on grant—may have been paid in another form (e.g., higher annual equity grants). Therefore, it would be necessary to examine other types and totals. In other words, director compensation studies do not typically allow an "apples-to-apples" comparison. Accordingly, boards must examine not only what the numbers are, but also what the numbers actually mean. Only after a complete review and proper consideration of the data, and perhaps after consultation with outside advisors, can the compensation committee make optimal use of such a study in preparing recommendations of the types and levels of director compensation appropriate for the company.

Exhibit 4.1 Director Compensation Benchmarking Study Template

Company	(1) Board Cash Annual Retainer	(2) Board Equity Annual Retainer	(3) Board In-Person Meeting Fee	(4) Board Teleph. Meeting Fee	(5) Board Chair Annual Retainer	(6) Board Chair Meeting Fee	(7) Lead Director Annual Retainer	(8) Lead Director Meeting Fee
Co. #1								
Co. #2								
. . . .								
Co. #15								
Minimum								
25th Percentile								
Median								
75th Percentile								
Maximum								
Average								
Subject Co.								Continued...

Company	(9) Chair Audit Cmte Cash Annual Retainer	(10) Chair Audit Cmte Meeting Fees	(11) Chair Comp Cmte Cash Annual Retainer	(12) Chair Comp Cmte Meeting Fees	(13) Chair Gov Cmte Cash Annual Retainer	(14) Chair Gov Cmte Meeting Fees	(15) Other	(16) Other
Co. #1								
Co. #2								
. . . .								
Co. #15								
Minimum								
25th Percentile								
Median								
75th Percentile								
Maximum								
Average								
Subject Co.								Continued...

(continues)

Exhibit 4.1 Continued

Company	(17) Cash Annual Retainer	(18) Comp Cmte Audit Cmte Meeting Fees	(19) Cash Annual Retainer	(20) Gov Comte Comp Cmte Meeting Fees	(21) Cash Annual Retainer	(22) Gov Cmte Meeting Fees	(23) Other	(24) Other
Co. #1								Continued…
Co. #2								
…								
Co. #15								
Minimum								
25th Percentile								
Median								
75th Percentile								
Maximum								
Average								
Subject Co.								

Company	(25) Total Board Chair	(26) Total Lead Director	(27) Total Board Member	(28) Total Chair Audit Cmte	(29) Total Chair Comp Cmte	(30) Total Chair Gov Cmte	(31) Total Member Audit Cmte	(32) Total Member Comp Cmte	(33) Total Member Gov Cmte
Co. #1									
Co. #2									
…									
Co. #15									
Minimum									
25th Percentile									
Median									
75th Percentile									
Maximum									
Average									
Subject Co.									

Part Two

Legal and Regulatory Framework

Chapter 5

Corporate Governance

This chapter discusses matters of corporate governance that should be of particular interest to compensation committees. The chapter begins with a discussion of the fiduciary duties of good faith, care, and loyalty owed by corporate directors to the corporation on whose board they serve. The next section addresses practical applications of director fiduciary duty rules for the compensation committee in specific contexts. The section "SRO Corporate Governance Rules and 'Best Practice' Recommendations" covers the 2003 New York Stock Exchange (NYSE) and Nasdaq corporate governance rules and "best-practices" recommendations published by various business interest groups, including The Conference Board Commission on Public Trust and Private Enterprise, The Business Roundtable, the National Association of Corporate Directors (NACD), and the Teachers Insurance and Annuity Association-College Retirement Equities Fund (TIAA-CREF). The chapter concludes with a discussion of certain state law provisions that permit the delegation beyond the compensation committee of authority to make equity grants.

FIDUCIARY DUTIES OF DIRECTORS

A corporate director stands in a fiduciary relationship to the corporation he or she serves and, as such, has certain duties to the corporation. A fiduciary duty claim brought against a director of a corporation is governed by the law of the state in which the corporation is incorporated. For purposes of this chapter, it is assumed that the applicable state's business corporation statute is based on the Revised Model Business Corporation Act developed by the Committee on Corporate Laws of the Section of Business Law of the American Bar Association (the "Model Act"). This chapter will also refer to the corporation law of the State of Delaware. While Delaware's business code does not follow the Model Act, it is the jurisdiction widely recognized as having the most fully developed body of corporation law.

Model Act §8.30 specifically imposes three duties on a director:

A director shall discharge his duties as a director, including his duties as a member of a committee:

(a) In good faith;

(b) With the care an ordinarily prudent person in a like position would exercise under similar circumstances; and

(c) In a manner the director reasonably believes to be in the best interests of the corporation.[1]

Delaware has no statute that sets out the standard of conduct for corporate directors. However, through its reported decisions, the Supreme Court of Delaware has recognized a similar "triad" of fiduciary duties consisting of good faith, due care, and loyalty.[2]

Duty of Good Faith

The duty of good faith[3] is not susceptible to concise definition.[4] It is a broad principle that applies to all aspects of the conduct of corporate fiduciaries.[5] Courts

---

[1]*See 2 ABA Model Bus. Corp. Act Ann.* (3d ed. 2000 & Supp. 2002) § 8.30 (the "*ABA Model Bus. Corp. Act Ann.*").

[2]*McMullin v. Beran,* 765 A.2d 910, 917 (Del. 2000); *Malone v. Brincat,* 722 A.2d 5, 10 (Del. 1998).

[3]Some courts characterize good faith as a stand-alone fiduciary duty and others treat it as subsumed within the duty of loyalty. *Compare, e.g., Emerald Partners v. Berlin,* 787 A.2d 85 (Del. 2001) with *Orman v. Cullman,* 794 A.2d 5 (Del. Ch. 2002). However, these two viewpoints can be reconciled by considering whether the duty of loyalty is limited to self-interest and self-dealing, or is construed more expansively to extend to other types of misconduct. Under the narrow view of the duty of loyalty, good faith is treated as a separate fiduciary duty in order to encompass and proscribe bad faith conduct that does not necessarily serve the personal interests of the fiduciary. Under a more expansive view of the duty of loyalty, good faith becomes subsumed within loyalty on the theory that an officer or director cannot simultaneously act in bad faith and be loyal to the corporation. Determining which is the better view is of limited practical value because both views ultimately lead to proscribing the same types of conduct as violations of fiduciary duty. Considered from this perspective, whether one views the duty of loyalty narrowly (thus recognizing good faith as a stand-alone duty) or expansively (thus subsuming good faith) becomes little more than an exercise in labeling.

[4]*See, e.g., Guth v. Loft,* 5 A.2d 503, 510 (Del. 1939) ("The occasions for the determination of honesty, good faith and loyal conduct are many and varied, and no hard and fast rule can be formulated."). This reluctance to adopt a hard and fast rule defining good faith is also evident in other contexts.

[5]*See 2 ABA Model Bus. Corp. Act Ann.* § 8.31 Official cmt. at 8-200 ("The expectation that

have held that "[b]y 'bad faith' is meant a transaction that is authorized for some purpose *other than* a genuine attempt to advance corporate welfare or is *known to constitute* a violation of applicable positive law."[6] Similarly, the Official Comments to the Model Act provide, "[c]onduct involving knowingly illegal conduct that exposes the corporation to harm will constitute action not in good faith, and belief that decisions made (in connection with such conduct) were in the best interests of the corporation will be subject to challenge as well."[7] According to the American Law Institute, "a director or officer violates the duty to perform his or her functions in good faith if he or she knowingly causes the corporation to disobey the law."[8]

Another perspective on the duty of good faith is provided by the following Official Comment to the Model Act:

> Where conduct has not been found deficient on other grounds, decision-making outside the bounds of reasonable judgment—an abuse of discretion perhaps explicable on no other basis—can give rise to an inference of bad faith. That form of conduct (characterized by the court as 'constructive fraud' or 'reckless indifference' or 'deliberate disregard' in the relatively few case precedents) giving rise to an inference of bad faith will also raise a serious question whether the director could have reasonably believed that the best interests of the corporation would be served.[9]

a director's conduct will be in good faith is an overarching element of his or her baseline duties.").

Under Delaware law, the duty of good faith is getting increased attention from courts in the context of determining whether the level of oversight provided by a director (an element of a director's duty of care) is so woefully inadequate as to amount to conduct not in good faith. *See In re Caremark Int'l Inc. Derivative Litig.*, 698 A.2d 959 (Del. Ch. 1996); and *McCall v. Scott*, 239 F.3d 808 (6th Cir. 2001), *amended*, 250 F.3d 997 (6th Cir. 2001). In *McCall*, a decision involving Delaware law, the defendant directors sought to dismiss claims against them on the grounds that the claims were precluded by a director exculpation clause contained in the corporation's certificate of incorporation. By its terms, the exculpation clause did not apply to acts or omissions not in good faith. In the course of determining that the plaintiffs' claims were not precluded by the exculpation clause, the Sixth Circuit held that the plaintiffs had adequately "alleged a conscious disregard of known risks, which conduct, if proven, cannot have been undertaken in good faith." *Id.* at 1001.

[6]*Gagliardi v. TriFoods Int'l, Inc.*, 683 A.2d 1049, 1051 n.2 (Del. Ch. 1996) (citing *Miller v. AT&T*, 507 F.2d 759 [3d Cir. 1974]).

[7]2 *ABA Model Bus. Corp. Act Ann.* § 8.31 Official cmt. at 8-200 to 8-201.

[8]*ALI Principles*, §4.01(a), cmt. d.

[9]2 *ABA Model Bus. Corp. Act Ann.* § 8.31 Official cmt. at 8-201.

Thus, if a "decision is so beyond the bounds of reasonable judgment that it seems essentially inexplicable on any [other] ground," courts may infer bad faith.[10]

Duty of Loyalty

In the leading case of *Guth v. Loft, Inc.*, the Delaware Supreme Court held that the rule requiring undivided and unselfish loyalty from a director to the corporation "demands that there shall be no conflict between duty and self-interest."[11] A basic principle of Delaware corporate law is that directors are subject to the fundamental fiduciary duty of loyalty and may not derive any personal benefit through self-dealing.[12]

However, for corporate fiduciaries, the mere existence of a conflict of interest does not automatically lead to liability for a breach of fiduciary duty. Having a conflict of interest is not something someone is "guilty of"; it is simply a state of affairs. In fact, it has been acknowledged that "a corporation and its shareholders may secure major benefits from a transaction despite the presence of a corporate fiduciary's conflicting interest."[13] Consistent with this view, the Model Act provides a statutory safe harbor for certain director conflict-of-interest transactions.[14]

Duty of Care and the Business Judgment Rule

When corporate directors exercise discretionary authority by making a business decision on behalf of the corporation, they must do so with due care. However, to understand the duty of care, one must begin with an understanding of the business judgment rule. The Delaware Supreme Court has articulated the business judgment rule as follows:

> The business judgment rule has been well formulated by *Aronson* and other cases. *See, e.g., Aronson*, 473 A.2d at 812 ("It is a presumption that in making a business decision the directors . . . acted on an informed basis, in good faith and in the honest belief that the action taken was in the best interests of the corporation.").

---

[10]*See J & S Packaging Profit Sharing Plan v. Rexene Corp. (In re Rexene Corp. Shareholders Litig.)*, No. 10897, 1991 WL 77529, at *4 (Del. Ch. May 8, 1991), *aff'd sub nom. Eichorn v. Rexene Corp.*, 604 A.2d 416 (Del. 1991) (quoting *West Point Pepperell, Inc. v. J.P. Stevens & Co. [In re J.P. Stevens & Co. Shareholders Litig.]*, 542 A.2d 770, 780 [Del. Ch. 1988]).

[11]*Guth v. Loft, Inc.*, 5 A.2d 503, 510 (Del. 1939).

[12]*See Anadarko Petroleum Corp. v. Panhandle E. Corp.*, 545 A.2d 1171 (Del. 1988); *Guth v. Loft, Inc.*, 5 A.2d 503 (Del. 1939).

[13]2 *ABA Model Bus. Corp. Act Ann.*, ch. 8, subch. F, Introductory cmt. at 8-372.

[14]2 *ABA Model Bus. Corp. Act Ann.*, § 8.60-8.63.

Thus, directors' decisions will be respected by courts unless the directors are interested or lack independence relative to the decision, do not act in good faith, act in a manner that cannot be attributed to a rational business purpose or reach their decision by a grossly negligent process that includes the failure to consider all material facts reasonably available.[15]

When a plaintiff challenging a director's decision succeeds in rebutting the presumption of the business judgment rule, the judicial deference to director decision-making afforded by the rule disappears and the burden shifts to the defendant director to prove the entire fairness of the challenged decision.[16]

A director's breach of one of the other two components of the fiduciary duty triad, good faith or loyalty, will render the business judgment rule inapplicable. Accordingly, taking all components of the triad into account, the business judgment rule will protect a business decision of a corporate director *unless* (i) the duty of loyalty is implicated, (ii) the duty of good faith is implicated, (iii) the decision cannot be attributed to any rational business purpose, or (iv) the director fails to satisfy his or her duty of care with respect to the process by which he or she reaches the decision.

Thus, the business judgment rule focuses the duty-of-care analysis of a business decision primarily on the *process* by which the decision was reached (e.g., whether all material information reasonably available was taken into consideration), as opposed to the *substance* of the decision itself (e.g., whether a reasonably careful or risk-free course of action was selected).[17] In other words, where the business judgment rule is applicable, the duty of care may be characterized as simply a duty to exercise informed business judgment.

Under Delaware law, the adequacy of the decision-making process is measured by concepts of gross negligence.[18] Some states, however, have applied concepts of ordinary negligence in application of the fiduciary duty of care. In light of the "ordinarily prudent person" language of the standard of care set forth in Model Act § 8.30,[19] it is likely that a court undertaking a business judgment rule analysis

---

[15]*Brehm v. Eisner*, 746 A.2d 244, 264 n.66 (Del. 2000).

[16]*See Emerald Partners v. Berlin*, 787 A.2d 85, 91 (Del. 2001); *McMullin v. Beran*, 765 A.2d 910, 917 (Del. 2000); and *Croton River Club, Inc. v. Half Moon Bay Homeowners Ass'n (In re Croton River Club, Inc.)*, 52 F.3d 41, 44 (2d Cir. 1995).

[17]*See Brehm*, 746 A.2d at 264 ("Courts do not measure, weigh or quantify directors' judgments. We do not even decide if they are reasonable in this context. Due care in the decision-making context is process due care only.").

[18]*See, e.g., Aronson v. Lewis*, 473 A.2d 805, 812 (Del. 1984) ("While the Delaware cases use a variety of terms to describe the applicable standard of care, our analysis satisfies us that under the business judgment rule director liability is predicated upon concepts of gross negligence."), *overruled on other grounds, Brehm*, 746 A.2d 244.

[19]2 *ABA Model Bus. Corp. Act Ann.* § 8.30, Official cmt. at 8-167.

under a Model Act state would measure the adequacy of the decision-making process by concepts of ordinary negligence.

Even if a director makes a business decision (that does not implicate the duty of loyalty or the duty of good faith) in a manner that satisfies the duty of care due process, the business judgment rule will not protect a decision that cannot be attributed to any rational business purpose.[20] Put another way, irrationality is the outer limit of the business judgment rule. However, the limited substantive review of a business decision contemplated by this outer limit of the business judgment rule (i.e., is the decision "irrational") may really be a way of inferring bad faith, and thus may have little or no significance independent of the good faith element of the business judgment rule.[21]

In summary, the business judgment rule protects the business decisions of corporate directors who act in good faith, on an informed basis, and without a conflict of interest so long as the decisions can be attributed to a rational business purpose. Nevertheless, as indicated previously, there are limits on the degree of judicial deference afforded to the business judgments of corporate directors.

Board Oversight Duties

The role of a corporate director includes two principal functions: a decision-making function and an oversight function.[22] The decision-making function generally involves action taken at a particular point in time, while the oversight function generally involves ongoing monitoring of the corporation's business and affairs over a period of time.[23]

Proper discharge of the board's oversight responsibility has two principal components: (i) a duty to monitor by undertaking reasonable efforts to remain attentive to and informed of the corporation's business and affairs; and (ii) a duty to

---

[20]*Brehm*, 746 A.2d at 264 (citing *Sinclair Oil Corp. v. Levien*, 280 A.2d 717, 720 (Del. 1971)).

[21]*See, e.g., Parnes v. Bally Entm't Corp.*, 722 A.2d 1243, 1246 (Del. 1999) ("The presumptive validity of a business judgment is rebutted in those rare cases where the decision under attack is 'so far beyond the bounds of reasonable judgment that it seems essentially inexplicable on any ground other than bad faith.'") (quoting *West Point Pepperell, Inc. v. J.P. Stevens & Co. [In re J.P. Stevens & Co.]*, 542 A.2d 770, 780-81 [Del. Ch. 1988]); *In re RJR Nabisco, Inc. Shareholders Litig.*, No. 10389, 1989 WL 7036, at *22 n.13 (Del. Ch. Jan. 31, 1989) (stating that the limited substantive review contemplated in the business judgment rule [i.e., whether the decision is irrational or egregious or so beyond reason]) is really a way of inferring bad faith).

[22]2 ABA *Model Bus. Corp. Act Ann.* (3d ed. 2000 & Supp. 2002) § 8.31 Official cmt. at 8-204.

[23]*Id.*

inquire when indications of potential problems, or "red flags," arise. As explained by the drafters of the Model Act, the board's oversight function:

> refers to concern with the corporation's information and reporting systems and not to proactive inquiry searching out system inadequacies or noncompliance. While directors typically give attention to future plans and trends as well as current activities, they should not be expected to anticipate the problems which the corporation may face except in those circumstances where something has occurred to make it obvious to the board that the corporation should be addressing a particular problem. The standard of care associated with the oversight function involves gaining assurances from management and advisers that systems believed appropriate have been established coupled with ongoing monitoring of the systems in place, such as those concerned with legal compliance or internal controls—followed up with a proactive response when alerted to the need for inquiry.[24]

Duty to Monitor

The duty of a board of directors to monitor corporate affairs is well established.[25] The failure to discharge this duty, where found actionable, typically has been characterized by the courts in terms of abdication or sustained inattention, not a brief distraction or temporary interruption.[26] The American Law Institute (ALI) notes "[c]ourts have generally recognized the dangers inherent in making *post hoc* judgments about the care exercised by directors and officers and have allowed them considerable leeway."[27] Nevertheless, according to the ALI, sustained patterns of inattention to obligations by directors or officers or unreasonable blindness to problems that later cause substantial harm will create exposure to liability.[28]

When directors do remain actively engaged and attentive to corporate affairs, courts have been more reluctant to hold them liable for breach of the duty to monitor notwithstanding their failure to detect and prevent misconduct occurring within the corporation.[29]

---

[24]2 *ABA Model Bus. Corp. Act Ann.* § 8.30 Official cmt. at 8-169.

[25]*See* American Law Institute, *Principles of Corporate Governance: Analysis & Recommendations* § 3.02 cmt. d (1994) (the "ALI Principles") ("A significant aspect of oversight by the board is continuing attention to the conduct of the corporation's business.").

[26]2 *ABA Model Bus. Corp. Act Ann.* § 8.31 Official cmt. at 8-204.

[27]ALI Principles § 4.01(a) cmt. h.

[28]Cases illustrative of directors found liable for breaching the duty to monitor include *Francis v. United Jersey Bank,* 432 A.2d 814 (N.J. 1981), and *Hoye v. Meek,* 795 F.2d 893 (10th Cir. 1986).

[29]Notable Delaware cases illustrative of this include *Graham v. Allis-Chalmers Manufacturing Co.,* 188 A.2d 125 (Del. 1963), and *In re Caremark International Inc. Derivative Litigation,* 698 A.2d 959 (Del. Ch. 1996).

In summary, courts have generally been reluctant to impose liability on directors for failing adequately to monitor corporate affairs absent some form of sustained inattention or abdication of duty. Courts have acknowledged that actively engaged boards will not always be able to detect and prevent misconduct occurring within the corporation. Thus, as long as reasonable efforts are undertaken to remain attentive to and informed of the corporation's business and affairs, directors generally will be found to have discharged their duty to monitor, even if loss-creating activities go unnoticed.

Duty to Inquire

The second prong of the duty of oversight is the duty to inquire when, in the course of monitoring corporate affairs, red flags arise indicating a potential problem that merits more in-depth attention. As stated by the drafters of the Model Act:

> embedded in the oversight function is the need to inquire when suspicions are aroused. This duty is not a component of ongoing oversight, and does not entail proactive vigilance, but arises when, and only when, particular facts and circumstances of material concern (e.g., evidence of embezzlement at a high level or the discovery of significant inventory shortages) suddenly surface.[30]

Thus, in addition to remaining informed generally of corporate affairs through ongoing monitoring, directors must exercise reasonable care to recognize and inquire about circumstances that awaken suspicion. The circumstances surrounding a duty of inquiry can affect the manner and scope of inquiry that is appropriate.[31]

Director Exculpation

Since 1986, nearly every state has adopted a statute permitting a corporation to include in its charter a provision limiting the personal liability of the corporation's directors for monetary damages to the corporation or its shareholders for breaches of fiduciary duty as a director, within certain public policy limits. These so-called "exculpation" statutes go a long way toward providing protection of directors, but the shield from liability is not absolute. All such exculpation statutes carve out certain types of liability for which the directors cannot be exculpated. In the Model Act and in Delaware those limitations include liability: (i) for any breach of the director's duty of loyalty to the corporation, (ii) for acts or omissions not in good faith or that involve intentional misconduct or a knowing violation of law, (iii) for

---

[30] *2 ABA Model Bus. Corp. Act Ann.* § 8.31 Official cmt. at 8-204 to 8-205.
[31] Two recent cases illustrating the duty of inquiry are *McCall v. Scott,* 239 F.3d 808 (6th Cir.), *amended,* 250 F.3d 997 (6th Cir. 2001) and *In re Abbott Laboratories Derivative Shareholders Litigation,* 325 F.3d 795 (7th Cir. 2003).

approving unlawful distributions under state law, or (iv) for any transaction from which the director derived an improper personal benefit.

The carve out for "acts or omissions not in good faith or that involve intentional misconduct or a knowing violation of law" leaves room for a finding of liability in breaches of the duty of oversight. In this regard, it is noteworthy that the *Caremark* court characterized its test for liability in the oversight context (i.e., "sustained or systematic failure of a director to exercise reasonable oversight") as conduct that lacks good faith. Accordingly, a failure to monitor that amounts to sustained inattention or abdication is not likely to be protected by a customary director exculpation provision.

A breach of the duty to inquire may be similarly vulnerable. As discussed previously, when "red flags" arise in the course of monitoring corporate affairs, directors have an affirmative duty to respond to those red flags by making further inquiry. Under many states' laws, a negligent failure to recognize and respond to red flags may constitute a breach of this duty. However, when a director exculpation provision applies (such as that in the Model Act or the Delaware code), a director's failure to respond to red flags must amount to conduct "not in good faith" or must involve "intentional misconduct" or "a knowing violation of law" in order to establish liability. Where, as under two leading cases regarding the duty to inquire (*McCall* and *Abbott*), a failure to respond to red flags amounts to a "conscious disregard of known risks," this would constitute conduct not in good faith and, therefore, would not be protected by such a director exculpation provision.

Practical Applications of Fiduciary Duty Rules for the Compensation Committee in Specific Contexts

The Increasing Focus on "Good Faith" in Making Compensation Decisions

When directors of a corporation make business decisions on behalf of the corporation, they must satisfy their fiduciary duty of care.[32] Likewise, members of the compensation committee must satisfy a duty of care when making compensation decisions. Recent decisions in the Delaware Supreme Court may be broadening the focus to include a greater emphasis on the duty of good faith, as well.

As discussed in the previous section, a doctrine known as the business judgment rule focuses the duty-of-care analysis of a business decision on the process by which the decision was reached (e.g., whether all material information reasonably available was taken into consideration), as opposed to the substance of the decision itself. Where the business judgment rule applies, the duty of care may be characterized as a duty to exercise informed business judgment. However, even if

---

[32]As always, directors must also satisfy their fiduciary duties of good faith and loyalty.

a director makes a business decision in a manner that satisfies the duty-of-care due process test, the business judgment rule will not protect a decision that cannot be attributed to any rational business purpose.

Moreover, when directors know they are making material decisions without adequate information and without adequate deliberation, their conduct may be considered to lack good faith. The recent case of *In re Walt Disney Co. Derivative Litigation*[33] should be of particular interest to directors serving on the compensation committee. In that case, the plaintiffs alleged that Disney's directors breached their fiduciary duties when they blindly approved an employment agreement with Michael Ovitz, and then, again without any review or deliberation, ignored Michael Eisner's dealings with Ovitz regarding his nonfault termination, resulting in an award to Ovitz (allegedly exceeding $140 million) after barely one year of employment. As alleged, Eisner, Disney's chief executive officer (CEO), decided unilaterally to hire Ovitz, Eisner's close friend for over 25 years, as Disney's president. The *Disney* court summarized the facts alleged in the complaint as follows:

> No draft employment agreements were presented to the compensation committee or to the Disney board for review before the September 26, 1995 meetings. The compensation committee met for less than an hour on September 26, 1995, and spent most of its time on two other topics, including the compensation of director Russell for helping secure Ovitz's employment. With respect to the employment agreement itself, the committee received only a summary of its terms and conditions. No questions were asked about the employment agreement. No time was taken to review the documents for approval. Instead, the committee approved the hiring of Ovitz and directed Eisner, Ovitz's close friend, to carry out the negotiations with regard to certain still unresolved and significant details.
>
> The [board] met immediately after the committee did. Less than one and one-half pages of the fifteen pages of [board] minutes were devoted to discussions of Ovitz's hiring as Disney's new president. Actually, most of that time appears to have been spent discussing compensation for director Russell. No presentations were made to the [board] regarding the terms of the draft agreement. No questions were raised, at least so far as the minutes reflect. At the end of the meeting, the [board] authorized Ovitz's hiring as Disney's president. No further review or approval of the employment agreement occurred. Throughout both meetings, no expert consultant was present to advise the compensation committee or the [board]. Notably, the [board] approved Ovitz's hiring even though the employment agreement was still a "work in progress." The [board] simply passed off the details to Ovitz and his good friend, Eisner.[34]

---

[33]825 A.2d 275 (Del. Ch. 2003).
[34]*Id.* at 287 (footnote omitted).

The complaint alleged facts depicting even less involvement by the Disney board in the decision to grant Ovitz a nonfault termination, which, in turn, triggered significant financial benefits to Ovitz. That decision allegedly was made by Eisner and one other director without ever consulting the board. Once the board was made aware of the decision, the directors allegedly did nothing to question it, explore alternatives, or evaluate the implications of the nonfault termination.

Denying the directors' motion to dismiss the claims, the *Disney* court concluded:

> These facts, if true, do more than portray directors who, in a negligent or grossly negligent manner, merely failed to inform themselves or to deliberate adequately about an issue of material importance to their corporation. Instead, the facts alleged in the new complaint suggest that the defendant directors *consciously and intentionally disregarded their responsibilities*, adopting a "we don't care about the risks" attitude concerning a material corporate decision. Knowing or deliberate indifference by a director to his or her duty to act faithfully and with appropriate care is conduct, in my opinion, that may not have been taken honestly and in good faith to advance the best interests of the company. Put differently, all of the alleged facts, if true, imply that the defendant directors *knew* that they were making material decisions without adequate information and without adequate deliberation, and that they simply did not care if the decisions caused the corporation and its stockholders to suffer injury or loss. Viewed in this light, plaintiffs' new complaint sufficiently alleges a breach of the directors' obligation to act honestly and in good faith in the corporation's best interests for a Court to conclude, if the facts are true, that the defendant directors' conduct fell outside the protection of the business judgment rule.[35]

The court also concluded that the plaintiffs' claims fell outside the protection of the director exculpation provision in Disney's charter because the claims were based on alleged actions that are either "not in good faith" or "involve intentional misconduct."[36]

Thus, the lesson for compensation committees from *Disney* is that blind reliance on the business judgment rule is not warranted, especially in matters as fundamental to the committee's charge as considering and approving the terms of management compensation and severance. Moreover, if the committee's action in approving such an arrangement is deemed to lack good faith, the director exculpation provision in the company's charter is not likely to be an effective shield to liability for personal damages for claimed harm resulting to the company or its shareholders.

---

[35]*Id.* at 289 (emphasis in original) (citation omitted).
[36]*Id.* at 290.

Public Disclosure of Compensation and Philosophy

As a committee of the board of directors of a public company, the compensation committee is called upon to address the shareholders directly, in the form of an annual report on the committee's compensation policies applicable to the company's executive officers. This report appears in the proxy statement for meetings at which directors are elected and/or in the company's annual report on Form 10-K. Specific discussion is required of the compensation committee's basis for the CEO's compensation, including the factors and criteria upon which the CEO's compensation was based, and the relationship of the company's performance to the CEO's compensation.[37]

Whenever corporate fiduciaries communicate publicly or directly with shareholders, they must do so honestly, candidly, and completely in all material respects.[38] This standard of disclosure arises out of the more general fiduciary duties of good faith, care, and loyalty.

A leading case for this proposition is *Malone v. Brincat*,[39] in which the Delaware Supreme Court found an implied duty of accurate and honest disclosure whenever directors communicate publicly on behalf of the corporation, stating:

> Whenever directors communicate publicly or directly with shareholders about the corporation's affairs, with or without a request for shareholder action, directors have a fiduciary duty to shareholders to exercise due care, good faith and loyalty. It follows *a fortiori* that when directors communicate publicly or directly with shareholders about corporate matters the *sine qua non* of directors' fiduciary duty to shareholders is honesty.[40]

However, *Malone* and its progeny are directly addressing disclosures that have a direct impact on the financial condition of the company and may not bear as

---

[37]For more information on the nature of this required report, see Item 402(k) of Regulation S-K of the Securities and Exchange Commission, which is discussed in Chapter 6 and included in full in Appendix A.

[38]*See, e.g., Malone v. Brincat*, 722 A.2d 5 (Del. 1998); *Marhart, Inc. v. CalMat Co.*, No. 11,820, 1992 WL 82365, at *3 (Del. Ch. Apr. 22, 1992) ("fiduciaries who undertake the responsibility of informing stockholders about corporate affairs . . . [are] required to do so honestly"); *Freedman v. Rest. Assocs. Indus., Inc.*, No. 9212, 1990 WL 135923, at *5 (Del. Ch. Sept. 21, 1990) (holding that where management chooses to disclose certain information, the information must be stated honestly and candidly); and *Kelly v. Bell*, 254 A.2d 62, 71 (Del. Ch. 1969) ("[o]f course directors owe a duty to honestly disclose all material facts when they undertake to give out statements about the business to stockholders"), *aff'd*, 266 A.2d 878 (Del. 1970).

[39]722 A.2d 5 (Del. 1998).

[40]*Malone*, 722 A.2d at 10.

directly on disclosures of policy such as the compensation committee's proxy report, where "honesty" is less of an issue than clarity and completeness. This distinction is perhaps illustrated in the SEC's position that the compensation committee's annual report to shareholders is not subject to the liabilities of Section 18 of the Securities Exchange Act of 1934 (Exchange Act), which subjects a person to civil liability for misleading statements made in a document filed with the SEC.[41] Certainly, this does not excuse the compensation committee from being forthright, thoughtful, and honest in its report. However, the scrutiny applied to the report may not be quite as intense as for disclosure of a more factual nature that could affect the financial condition of the company.

Change-in-Control Considerations

Compensation committees should be particularly mindful of the increased scrutiny that may be accorded their decisions about executive compensation or employment/severance agreements in anticipation of a "hostile" change in control of the company (such as a tender offer or unsolicited merger proposal).

Directors faced with a takeover attempt are inherently endowed with competing interests. On the one hand, they must, as always, act in the best interests of the corporation and its shareholders, complying with the familiar duties of care, loyalty, and good faith. On the other hand, a change in control of the corporation often portends a change in management, including directors, thus feeding the directors' (particularly management directors') self-interest in preserving their positions with the company. Recognizing this inherent conflict, the Delaware judiciary introduced a notion of heightened scrutiny for board decisions made in defensive situations. Under this so-called "Unocal" standard,[42] the business judgment rule will not apply to protect the board's defensive action unless (i) the directors can show that they had reasonable grounds for believing that a danger to corporate policy and effectiveness existed because of another person's stock ownership, and (ii) any defensive measure taken is reasonable in relation to the threat posed.

Once in a defensive situation, the *Unocal* standard would apply, for example, to decisions to approve change-in-control severance agreements for management or to approve generous executive compensation packages, both of which can have a deterrent effect to the acquiror. Having a majority of independent directors making the decision materially enhances the board's ability to satisfy the *Unocal* standard.

Whether or not in a defensive situation, when considering employment, severance, or retirement agreements for management, the compensation committee

---

[41]Item 402(a)(9) of Regulation S-K of the Securities and Exchange Commission; Section 18 of the Securities Exchange Act of 1934.
[42]*Unocal Corp. v. Mesa Petroleum Co.*, 493 A.2d 946 (Del. 1985).

should insist on reviewing numerical illustrations of the effect of the proposed benefits under various scenarios. An understanding of the magnitude of the arrangement is a baseline for the committee's ability to form a reasonable belief that it is in the best interest of shareholders. For example, while it is not uncommon to see agreements with full change-in-control tax gross-up protection for executive officers, or a "free-walk" period following a change in control during which the executive can resign without provocation and receive a full severance benefit, the committee should fully understand the practical effects and hypothetical costs of such provisions before approving them. To appreciate the potential cost of such provisions, it is necessary to understand the nature and operation of the so-called "golden parachute" excise tax. For a more technical discussion of these tax rules, see Chapter 7.

SRO CORPORATE GOVERNANCE RULES AND "BEST PRACTICE" RECOMMENDATIONS

NYSE and Nasdaq Rules

On November 4, 2003, the SEC approved significant changes to the listing standards of the NYSE and Nasdaq that are intended to enhance corporate governance and bolster investor confidence following a number of well-publicized corporate failures among U.S. public companies.[43] These listing standards changes are the culmination of nearly two years of deliberations among the SEC, the NYSE, and Nasdaq (including a public comment period) that resulted in at least six separate rulemaking proposals and 16 amendments.

These listing standards supplement, rather than replace, the corporate governance reforms adopted by the SEC pursuant to the Sarbanes-Oxley Act of 2002. Both the NYSE and Nasdaq generally conformed their listing standards to the audit committee composition requirements, compliance dates, and transition periods under the SEC's Exchange Act Rule 10A-3, which was adopted pursuant to Section

---

[43]Self-Regulatory Organizations; New York Stock Exchange, Inc. and National Association of Securities Dealers, Inc.; Order Approving Proposed Rule Changes (SR-NYSE-2002-33 and SR-NASD-2002-141) and Amendments No. 1 thereto; Order Approving Proposed Rule Changes (SR-NASD-2002-77, SR-NASD-2002-80, SR-NASD-2002-138, and SR-NASD-2002-139) and Amendments No. 1 to SR-NASD-2002-80 and SR-NASD-2002-139; and Notice of Filing and Order Granting Accelerated Approval of Amendment Nos. 2 and 3 to SR-NYSE-2002-33, Amendment Nos. 2, 3, 4, and 5 to SR-NASD-2002-141, Amendment Nos. 2 and 3 to SR-NASD-2002-80, Amendment Nos. 1, 2, and 3 to SR-NASD-2002-138, and Amendment No. 2 to SR-NASD-2002-139, Relating to Corporate Governance, www.sec.gov/rules/sro/34-48745.htm (Nov. 4, 2003).

301 of the Sarbanes-Oxley Act. In addition, the NYSE and Nasdaq each modified its rules in certain respects to conform to the standards proposed by the other.

Without going into detail here about all aspects of these new corporate governance listing standards, Exhibit 5.1 gives a brief overview and comparison of the NYSE and Nasdaq rules.

Exhibit 5.1 NYSE and Nasdaq Corporate Governance Rules

	NYSE Standards	Nasdaq Standards
Composition of Board of Directors	Must have a majority of independent directors.	Must have a majority of independent directors and identify them in the proxy statement.
Definition of Director Independence	Board must affirmatively determine that the director has no material relationship with the company.	Board must affirmatively determine that the director has no relationships that would interfere with the exercise of independent judgment.
	The following persons *cannot* be considered independent:	The following persons *cannot* be considered independent:
	• A director who is or was in the last three years an employee of the company, or whose immediate family member is or was in the last three years an executive officer of the company.	• A director who is or was in the last three years an employee of the company or an affiliate.
	• A director who, or whose immediate family member, received in the last three years more than $100,000 per year in direct compensation from the company.	• A director who, or whose family member, accepted in the last three years payments in excess of $60,000 from the company or an affiliate.
	• A director who is or was in the last three years affiliated with or employed by, or whose immediately family member is or was in the last three years affiliated with or employed in a professional capacity by, a present or former internal or external auditor of the company.	• A director with any family member who is or was in the last three years an executive officer of the company or an affiliate.
		• A director who is, or has a family member who is, a partner, controlling shareholder, or executive officer of any organization to which the company made, or from which the company received,

(continues)

Exhibit 5.1   Continued

	NYSE Standards	Nasdaq Standards
Definition of Director Independence (*continued*)	• A director who, or whose immediate family member, is or was in the last three years employed as an executive officer of another company where any of the listed company's present executives serve on the compensation committee of the other company. • A director who is an executive officer or employee of, or whose immediate family member is an executive officer of, another company that makes payments to or receives payments from the company for property or services in an amount that in any single fiscal year exceeds the greater of $1 million or 2% of the other company's consolidated gross revenues, is not independent until three years after falling below such threshold.	payments for property or services in the last three years, that exceeded the greater of $200,000 or 5% of the recipient's consolidated gross revenues for the year in which the payments were made. • A director who is, or who has a family member who is, employed as an executive officer of another entity where at any time during the current or past three years any of the executive officers of the listed company served on the compensation committee of such other entity. • A director who is, or whose family member is, a current partner of the company's outside auditor, or was a partner or employee of the company's outside auditor who worked on the company's audit at any time during any of the past three years.
Nonmanagement Director Executive Sessions	Nonmanagement directors (which may include directors who do not qualify as "independent") must meet in regularly scheduled executive sessions without management present. An executive session of only "independent" directors should be held at least once a year.	Independent directors must regularly meet in executive sessions at which only they are present (Nasdaq "contemplates" that these meetings will be held at least twice a year). A nominating committee comprised solely of independent directors or a majority of the independent directors must select, or recommend for the board's selection, director nominees.
Nominating/ Corporate Governance Committee	Company must have a nominating/corporate governance committee composed entirely of independent directors. The committee must have and publish a written charter.	The company must certify that it has adopted a formal written charter or board resolution addressing the nominations process.

Exhibit 5.1   Continued

	NYSE Standards	Nasdaq Standards
Compensation Committee	Must be composed entirely of independent directors. The committee must adopt and publish a written charter. The charter must be included on the company's Web site, and the Form 10-K must state that the charter is available on the Web site and in print to any shareholder who requests it.	CEO compensation must be determined, or recommended to the board for determination, either by a compensation committee comprised solely of independent directors or a majority of the independent directors, and the CEO may not be present during voting or deliberations. Compensation of all other executive officers must be determined in the same manner, except that the CEO may be present. If the compensation committee has at least three members, one nonindependent director (who is not an officer or employee or a family member of an officer or employee) may serve on the committee (for no more than two years) if the board, under exceptional and limited circumstances, determines it is in the company's and the shareholders' best interests. The nature of such nonindependent director's relationship with the company and the reasons for the board's determination must be disclosed in the next annual proxy statement or in its Form 10-K if a proxy statement is not filed.
Audit Committee Member Qualifications	*Independence.* Company must have an audit committee with a minimum of three members, who each satisfy the independence requirements under both the NYSE and Exchange Act Rule 10A-3(b)(11).	*Independence.* Company must have an audit committee consisting of at least three directors who each satisfy the independence requirements under Nasdaq and Exchange Act Rule 10A-3(b)(11) *and* have not participated in the preparation of

(continues)

Exhibit 5.1   Continued

	NYSE Standards	Nasdaq Standards
Audit Committee Member Qualifications (*continued*)	*Financial Literacy.* Each member of the audit committee must be financially literate or must become financially literate within a reasonable period of time after appointment to the committee. At least one member also must have accounting or related financial management expertise.	the financial statements of the company or any current subsidiary of the company at any time during the past three years. *Financial Literacy.* Members must be able to read and understand financial statements. The company must certify that at least one audit committee member is financially sophisticated (as defined).
Audit Committee Charter and Internal Audit Function	Audit committee must adopt and publish a written charter. The company must also establish an internal audit function, which may be outsourced to a firm other than its independent auditor. The company must include the audit committee charter on its Web site, and the Form 10-K must state that the information is available on the Web site and in print to any shareholder who requests it.	Audit committee must adopt a written charter. The company must conduct an appropriate review of all related-party transactions (as defined in Item 404 of Regulation S-K) on an ongoing basis, and all such transactions shall be approved by the audit committee or another independent body of the board of directors.
Shareholder Approval of Equity Compensation Plans	See Chapter 6 for a discussion of these rules.	See Chapter 6 for a discussion of these rules.
Corporate Governance Guidelines	Company must adopt and disclose corporate governance guidelines.	No requirement.
Codes of Business Conduct and Ethics	Company must adopt and disclose a code of business conduct and ethics for directors, officers, and employees. Only the board of directors or a board committee may waive provisions of the code for executive officers or directors, and such waivers must be promptly disclosed to the company's shareholders.	Company must have a publicly available code of conduct that complies with the definition of a Code of Ethics under the Sarbanes-Oxley Act and which is applicable to all directors, executive officers, and employees. Only the board of directors may grant waivers of compliance with the code for

Exhibit 5.1 Continued

	NYSE Standards	Nasdaq Standards
Codes of Business Conduct and Ethics (*continued*)		executive officers and directors, and all such waivers, as well as the reason for the waiver, must be disclosed on a Form 8-K within five days.
Certifications	CEOs of listed companies must certify to the NYSE each year that, as of the date of the certification, he or she is not aware of any violation by the listed company of the NYSE corporate governance listing standards.	No requirement.
Enforcement	NYSE may issue public reprimand letters, suspend trading, or delist a company for violations of listing standards.	Nasdaq may deny relisting to a company based upon a corporate governance violation that occurred while that company's appeal of the delisting was pending. A material misrepresentation or omission by an issuer to Nasdaq may form the basis for delisting.

Business Groups Weigh In with "Best Practices" Recommendations Regarding Executive Compensation

The Conference Board Report

The Conference Board's 12-member Commission on Public Trust and Private Enterprise was formed in 2002 to address the circumstances that led to the well-publicized corporate scandals of 2001 and 2002 and the resulting decline of confidence in corporations, their leaders, and America's capital markets. The first of the Commission's three reports, entitled "Executive Compensation: Principles, Recommendations and Specific Best Practice Suggestions," was published in September 2002.[44] The Commission first identified certain factors related to executive compensation that it believed contributed to the corporate implosion, including overuse of fixed-price stock options in the face of a sustained bull market, an imbalance between unprecedented levels of executive compensation and the relationship to

---

[44]www.conference-board.org/PDF_free/756.pdf

long-term company performance, lack of independent and vigorous oversight by compensation committees, and the lack of downside risk in compensation vehicles. The report sets out seven principles that are intended to guide compensation committees to restore good corporate governance, followed in each instance with specific practice suggestions. This report, along with those that follow, is suggested reading for all directors who serve on compensation committees.

Breeden Report on MCI: "Restoring Trust"

Next out of the box was the so-called Breeden Report.[45] This report arose out of the bankruptcy of WorldCom in 2002, which followed accusations of accounting fraud and executive malfeasance by former CEO Bernie Ebbers. The court appointed Richard Breeden (who is a former chairman of the SEC) to serve as corporate monitor to investigate corporate practices at WorldCom and issue a report of recommendation. Published in August 2003, the Breeden Report contains 78 detailed recommendations dealing with board governance. All of these were accepted unanimously by the new MCI board. Of the 78 specific recommendations, nine relate to executive compensation practices, five to director compensation, and nine to the compensation committee itself.

While the Breeden Report is specific to MCI, generally speaking, its recommendations are ultraconservative positions when compared to historical practices. Some of the more noteworthy recommendations are mandatory 10-year term limits for directors, separating the chairman and CEO positions, a requirement to change accounting firms every 10 years, an absolute prohibition on granting stock options, and the requirement that compensation limits be housed in the corporate charter or bylaws. Some of the other recommendations may be useful for consideration. In any event, the Breeden Report is interesting reading for its creativity if not for practical guidance.

Business Roundtable Report

The Business Roundtable is an association of CEOs of leading U.S. corporations with a combined workforce of 10 million employees and over $3.7 trillion in annual revenues. It is recognized as an authoritative voice on matters affecting U.S. business corporations, and as such has an interest in improving corporate governance practices. In November 2003, The Business Roundtable published its "Report on Executive Compensation: Principles and Commentary," containing and discussing a list of six corporate governance principles relating to executive compensation. Short and to the point, they are as follows, with commentary on each principle contained in the longer report:[46]

---

[45]www.nysd.uscourts.gov/rulings/02cv4963_082603.pdf
[46]www.businessroundtable.org/pdf/ExecutiveCompensationPrinciples.pdf

1. Executive compensation should be closely aligned with the long-term interests of shareholders and with corporate goals and strategies. It should include significant performance-based criteria related to long-term shareholder value and should reflect upside potential and downside risk.
2. Compensation of the CEO and other top executives should be determined by a compensation committee composed entirely of independent directors, either as a committee or together with the other independent directors based on the committee's recommendations.
3. The compensation committee should understand all aspects of the compensation package and should review the maximum payout under that package, including all benefits. The compensation committee should understand the maximum payout under multiple scenarios, including retirement, termination with or without cause, and severance in connection with business combinations on sale of the business.
4. Compensation committees should require executives to build and maintain significant continuing equity investment in the corporation.
5. The compensation committee should have independent, experienced expertise available to provide advice on new executive compensation packages or significant changes in existing packages.
6. Corporations should provide complete, accurate, understandable, and timely disclosure to shareholders concerning all significant elements of executive compensation and executive compensation packages.

NACD Report

Shortly on the heels of The Business Roundtable report, the National Association of Corporate Directors (NACD) Blue Ribbon Commission published in December 2003 its report on executive compensation and the role of the compensation committee.[47] Primary issues addressed in the NACD report include (i) identifying and addressing key challenges for the compensation committee, such as establishing a healthy dynamic on the committee that encourages constructive skepticism, finding better ways to measure and reward performance, and understanding the complexity and true cost of executive pay; (ii) development of a sound compensation philosophy; and (iii) focus on the composition, duties, and support of the compensation committee.

Institutional Shareholder Services Report

Institutional Shareholder Services (ISS) maintains that, while independent directors bear much of the responsibility to ensure good corporate governance, shareholders

---

[47]A summary of the NACD report can be found, and a copy may be ordered, at www.nacdonline.org

also should play a critical role in the governance process. ISS issues proxy voting and corporate governance guidelines to institutional investors and corporations. In January 2004, ISS published its report on "ISS Domestic Corporate Governance Policy: 2004 Updates." The report discusses ISS's current and new policy positions on a number of corporate governance issues and addresses the rationale behind its evolving policies with respect to particular issues. There are over 15 corporate governance issues identified and discussed in the 2004 report, including board independence, "overboarded" directors, mandatory holding periods for equity awards, performance-based stock options, SERP provisions, the definition of independent directors, and equity-based compensation plans. Given the increased focus on shareholders' interests, compensation committee members should find this report instructive for anticipating reactions of institutional shareholders with respect to corporate governance and executive compensation issues.

TIAA-CREF Policy Statement

The fourth edition of the policy statement on corporate governance by TIAA-CREF[48] reflects its policies and guidelines in light of recent changes in the corporate governance and equity compensation arena. The statement discusses TIAA-CREF's policies and guidelines with respect to the following aspects of corporate governance: (i) the board of directors, (ii) shareholders' rights and responsibilities, (iii) executive compensation, (iv) the role of independent advisors, (v) governance of companies domiciled outside the United States, (vi) social responsibility issues, and (vii) guidelines for assessing compensation plans.

DELEGATION OF AUTHORITY TO MAKE EQUITY GRANTS

Source of Authority to Grant Shares

Under most states' laws, the ability to approve the issuance of stock (and therefore the ability to grant rights to acquire stock) is housed in the board of directors. The board can, and typically does, delegate this authority, in part, by designating the compensation committee as administrator of the company's equity compensation plans, and giving the compensation committee delegated authority to approve and grant equity awards under such plans.

The following subsection discusses issues relating to further delegation by the compensation committee—both downward to one or more officers and, more rarely, upward to the independent directors as a group.

---

[48]www.tiaa-cref.org/pubs/html/governance_policy/index.html

Downward Delegation

State Law Delegation Authority

Acknowledging the need in today's business environment to make equity awards more frequently than the compensation committee is likely to meet, Delaware recently enacted Section 157(c) of the Delaware General Corporation Law (DGCL), making it expressly permissible for the board of directors to delegate to one or more officers of the company (even officers who are not directors) the authority, within designated parameters, to grant "rights and options" with respect to company stock. Such grants can be made to officers and employees of the company, but not to consultants or nonemployee directors, and the designated officers cannot make grants to themselves. Other states have similar laws.

There is some question as to whether DGCL Section 157(c) extends to the grant of restricted stock, which is not technically a "right or option" but rather an outright grant of stock—although some conjecture that restricted stock is a right to "buy" stock through the provision of services over the vesting period.

In light of this uncertainty, a more conservative and comprehensive method of complete delegation is to have the board, pursuant to DGCL Section 141(c)(2), or the corresponding provision of other states' corporation codes, designate an inside director, such as the CEO (in his or her capacity as a director), as a single-member committee of the board for purposes of making grants of all types of incentive awards under the company's incentive plan (including, for example, options, stock appreciation rights, performance shares, restricted stock, and other equity-based awards) within designated parameters. Under this type of delegated authority (in contrast to delegated authority under DGCL 157(c)), the single-member board committee could also make grants to consultants.

Practical Advice

The board's delegating resolutions should require the special committee to regularly *report* all such grants to the compensation committee, but not require further ratification or approval. It is important for tax, accounting, and securities reasons to be able to pinpoint the grant date as the date of the special committee's action, which is possible only where there is a *complete* delegation of grant authority (i.e., subject to prescribed guidelines but with no subsequent ratification required).

Such specific delegation of grant authority to an officer or to a single board member should be viewed as a pragmatic business practice in keeping with sound corporate governance principles. This is evidenced by Delaware's enactment in 2001 of DGCL Section 157(c), discussed previously, which strikes a proper balance between (i) a company's need for flexibility, for example, to make time-sensitive special inducement awards or routine awards to rank-and-file employees, and (ii) appropriate board oversight imbedded in the delegation parameters. The single-member board committee approach is even more conservative than that permitted under DGCL Section 157(c), in that it maintains the granting authority within the confines of the board.

Precise limitations built into the delegation resolutions—limiting the number, price, and other terms of awards that can be granted by the special committee—further safeguard against allegations of lax corporate governance. In furtherance of this, it is recommended that the board or the compensation committee adopt a form of award agreement(s) to be used by the special committee pursuant to its delegated authority.

While the special committee holding delegated authority could distribute the awards within the delegation parameters however it wants—theoretically even granting all the shares to one person—as a practical matter, such committee should take a more thoughtful approach to the allocation to assure that the available shares are distributed fairly and appropriately to the eligible grantees.

Section 16 Issues

The delegated authority should specifically *exclude* grants to persons who are directors or executive officers of the company as of the date of grant. In order to provide a ready exemption from the short-swing profit recovery rules of Section 16(b) of the Exchange Act, grants to such persons should be made either by the full board or by a committee that consists solely of two or more "non-employee" directors, as defined in Rule 16b-3 (i.e., typically the compensation committee). For this purpose, the *grant date* is the relevant focus for determining a grantee's status as a Section 16 insider—the fact that a person may later become a Section 16 insider will not affect the original exemption for the grant of the award.

The delegating resolutions could specifically preauthorize the delivery or withholding of company stock to pay the exercise price of an option or the tax liability associated with an award. That is appropriate, in that such preapproval secures the Rule 16b-3(e) exemption for such transaction (a disposition of shares to the issuer) for a person who, while not a Section 16 insider at the date of grant, becomes a Section 16 insider before the time of exercise or vesting of the award.

Internal Revenue Code Section 162(m) Issues

As discussed in more detail in Chapter 7, Section 162(m) of the Internal Revenue Code (Code) limits the company's income tax deduction to $1 million of compensation paid to any one of its "covered employees" in a given year, except for compensation that qualifies as "performance-based" under such tax provision. To be performance-based, an award generally must (among other things) be approved in advance by a committee of the board consisting solely of two or more directors who are "outside" directors, as defined in the Code Section 162(m) regulations (which would not include the CEO).

In contrast to the Section 16 issue discussed earlier, it is the time that the taxable event occurs (i.e., the *exercise date* in the case of a nonqualified option, or the *vesting date* in the case of a performance-based restricted stock award)—as opposed to the grant date—that is the relevant focus for purposes of determining a grantee's status as a "covered employee" because that is the time the company seeks to take the tax deduction. Because it is not possible to know at the date of grant whether a person will later become a "covered employee" during the life of the award, it is recommended that the special committee avoid making grants to any employees who are reasonably expected to become a "covered employee" during the term of the award. It would be better to have the compensation committee make awards to those grantees, in anticipation of preserving the full tax deduction.

Amendment to Incentive Plans

Oftentimes, a company's equity incentive plan gives the compensation committee sole authority to make grants under the plan. To permit the desired delegation of authority to a special committee (such as the CEO), it may be necessary to effect a plan amendment. Depending on the terms of the plan, such amendment may or may not require shareholder approval. However, absent a plan provision requiring shareholder approval, such an amendment most likely would not constitute a "material revision or amendment" of the plan that would require shareholder approval under the new NYSE or Nasdaq shareholder approval rules. Such an amendment is not among (or even similar to) the listed plan revisions that would in all cases be deemed material, specifically: (i) a material increase in benefits to participants (Nasdaq only), (ii) a material increase in the number of shares available under the plan, (iii) an expansion of the types of awards that may be granted under the plan, (iv) a material expansion in the class of persons eligible to participate in the plan, (v) a material extension of the term of the plan, (vi) a material change to the method of determining the strike price of options under the plan, or (vii) the deletion or limitation of any provision prohibiting the repricing of options.

Compensation Committee Charter

The charter of the compensation committee may need to be amended to reference the delegation of grant authority to a person or entity other than the compensation committee. The new NYSE corporate governance rules require the compensation committee charter to address "the Committee's purpose and responsibilities—which, at a minimum, must be to have direct responsibility to . . . make recommendations to the board with respect to non-CEO compensation . . ." (NYSE

Rule 303A.05(b)(i)(B)). The NYSE's "Frequently Asked Questions" indicate that the term *non-CEO* compensation in this regard means compensation of Section 16 officers other than the CEO. Compensation for employees who are not Section 16 officers may, but need not be, set by the compensation committee. Therefore, it would not be inconsistent with NYSE corporate governance rules to permit someone other than the compensation committee to make equity awards to nonexecutive officers.

Upward Delegation

Compensation committees are under far more scrutiny for their decisions in today's environment than ever before. An interesting reaction of some compensation committees is an inclination to share the spotlight by making recommendations for compensation decisions to the full board, or at least to the larger group of independent directors, as much as possible. This raises interesting issues, including (i) whether such delegation is permitted by NYSE and Nasdaq rules; (ii) whether awards approved by the independent directors, as a group, can qualify as deductible "performance-based" compensation under Code Section 162(m); and (iii) how such delegation affects public disclosure of the decision-making process. These are discussed in turn next.

NYSE Rules

Under NYSE rules, there are certain aspects of CEO compensation that *cannot* be delegated to any group other than the compensation committee (or a committee performing similar functions):

- The review and approval of corporate goals and objectives relevant to CEO compensation
- The evaluation of the CEO's performance in light of those goals and objectives

Therefore, any award to the CEO that entails the setting of goals and objectives and evaluation of performance against such goals and objectives (such as a cash incentive bonus intended to be exempt from the Code Section 162(m) deduction limit or a performance-based restricted stock unit award) *must* be made by the compensation committee alone, and not by the larger group of independent directors.

NYSE rules would allow the ultimate level of pay to the CEO (based on the compensation committee's performance evaluation) to be set by the larger group of independent directors in concert with the compensation committee. However, performance-based awards to the CEO will in most cases be intended to qualify for a full tax deduction under Code Section 162(m), and therefore must by definition be *objectively determinable* (i.e., leaving no discretion to determine what the actual award level will be if the goals are attained—other than discretion to pay less than the formula amount). In that case, there would be little aspect of such an award that could (under NYSE rules) be relegated to the independent directors as a group (i.e., only a decision to pay the CEO *less* than the amount resulting from the formulaic performance award).

Nasdaq Rules

Under Nasdaq rules, the compensation of the CEO and other executive officers may be set by a compensation committee comprised solely of independent directors or by a majority of the independent directors. Therefore, such upward delegation should not be an issue for a Nasdaq company.

Code Section 162(m) Deductibility

Awards approved by the independent directors as a group could qualify for the "performance-based" compensation exception under Code Section 162(m) only if all of the independent directors meet the definition of "outside" directors under Code Section 162(m). The test for "outside" directors is similar, but not identical, to the test for "independent" directors under the NYSE/Nasdaq rules and "non-employee" directors under Section 16 rules.

Public Disclosure Issues

If the independent directors, as a group, are, by having ultimate approval authority for executive compensation decisions, performing the essential function of the compensation committee, the compensation committee report would need to be made over the names of all such directors. Alternatively, if one concludes that the independent directors are not, by virtue of merely acting on recommendations made by the compensation committee, serving the essential function of the compensation committee, then if the board or the independent directors modify or reject in any material way any action or recommendation made by the compensation committee with respect to such decisions, the compensation committee report must so indicate and explain the reasons for their actions and be made over the names of all such directors. In short, such "passing of the buck" may lead to some interesting and unintended disclosures.

Chapter 6

Securities Issues

This chapter discusses certain specific securities issues that should be of particular interest to compensation committees of public companies. The first section contains a discussion of special rules regarding insider trading, including (i) the reporting system and short-swing profit liability provisions of Section 16 of the Securities Exchange Act of 1934 (Exchange Act), (ii) the prohibition against trading on "inside information," (iii) the prohibition against insider trades during pension fund blackout periods, and (iv) sales of restricted and control stock under Rule 144 of the Securities Act of 1933 (Securities Act). The next section addresses recent NYSE and Nasdaq rules regarding shareholder approval of equity compensation plans. The following two sections cover public disclosure of equity compensation plans and compensation of and transactions with directors and officers. The chapter concludes by highlighting the effect of certain other provisions of the Sarbanes-Oxley Act of 2002 on executive compensation, including the prohibition on loans to directors and executive officers (Section 402) and the requirement to disgorge profits from equity awards upon certain financial restatements (Section 304).

SPECIAL RULES AFFECTING INSIDER TRADING

Section 16 of the Exchange Act

Background

Section 16 of the Exchange Act was adopted in response to perceived abuses by corporate insiders thought to be trading on material nonpublic information. Section 16 operates without regard to the insider's awareness or use of material nonpublic information, achieving its intended deterrent effect by (i) requiring certain officers, all directors, and all shareholders beneficially owning more than 10% of the issuer's equity securities (collectively, "Reporting Persons") to file reports indicating their present beneficial ownership of the issuer's equity securities and reporting all subsequent changes in such beneficial ownership, and (ii) allowing the issuer's shareholders to sue on behalf of the issuer to recapture all "short-swing" profits realized by a Reporting Person from any nonexempt purchase and sale (or sale and purchase) of the issuer's equity securities within any six-month period.

An officer will be considered a Reporting Person if he or she performs policy-making functions within the issuer—including the chief executive officer (CEO), president, principal accounting officer, principal financial officer, and officers in charge of significant subsidiaries, business units, or divisions. The board should designate its Section 16 officers each year, based on the changing roles and responsibilities of the issuer's officers. In addition to permitting private actions to require a Reporting Person to disgorge any short-swing profit, the securities laws also permit the SEC to seek court orders imposing civil monetary penalties of up to $500,000 for each violation of federal securities law. In addition, all late Section 16 reports (and/or the failure to file a report) must be disclosed in the issuer's Form 10-K and proxy statement, identifying the late filer by name and number of late transactions.

Reporting Requirements

Initial Report—Form 3   Each Reporting Person is required to file with the SEC an "Initial Statement of Beneficial Ownership of Securities" on Form 3 within 10 days after becoming a director, executive officer, or 10% shareholder. The Form 3 establishes the Reporting Person's baseline securities ownership position for reporting purposes. A Form 3 must be filed even if the director or officer does not own shares of company stock.

Subsequent Reports—Form 4   A Reporting Person must keep the information on file with the SEC up to date by filing reports on Form 4 ("Statement of Changes in Beneficial Ownership of Securities") and Form 5 ("Annual Statement of Changes in Beneficial Ownership of Securities"). A Form 4 must be filed electronically with the SEC no later than the second business day following the day on which the transaction has been executed that results in a change in the Reporting Person's "beneficial ownership" (discussed in the following section) of issuer equity securities, unless the transaction falls into one of two narrow exceptions for which a slightly longer Form 4 filing period is permitted, or unless an exemption is available that allows for deferred reporting on Form 5. There are two narrow exceptions for delayed Form 4 filings: (i) transactions that meet the conditions set forth in Rule 10b5-1(c) (discussed later in this chapter) are eligible for slightly delayed reporting on Form 4, as long as the Reporting Person does not select the date of execution; and (ii) "discretionary transactions" in employee benefit plans also are eligible for slightly delayed Form 4 reporting as long as the Reporting Person does not select the date of execution. Discretionary transactions are defined specifically in Rule 16b-3 and are limited to transactions pursuant to an employee benefit plan that result in either an intra-plan transfer involving an issuer securities fund or a volitional cash distribution from an issuer securities fund.

Annual Reports—Form 5; Alternative Written Statement   A Form 5 must be filed with the SEC annually on or before the 45th day after the end of the issuer's fiscal year for any person who was a Reporting Person at any time during the year, *unless* (i) such person had no transactions in the issuer's securities during the fiscal year, or (ii) all holdings and transactions required to be reported for the fiscal year have already been reported on Form 3 or Form 4. If a Reporting Person is not required to file a Form 5 for any year for either of these reasons, he or she should provide a written representation to the issuer that no Form 5 is required. Otherwise, the issuer may be forced to disclose that such person failed to file a Form 5 for that year in its annual meeting proxy statement. Only a small number of transactions, such as gifts and *de minimis* purchases, are eligible for reporting on Form 5.

Determining Beneficial Ownership

The "beneficial ownership" reported on Forms 3, 4, and 5 has a special meaning under Section 16, and may often be different from simple record ownership. For purposes of the Section 16(a) reporting requirements, a Reporting Person is regarded as the beneficial owner of securities if such person, directly or indirectly, through any contract, arrangement, understanding, relationship, or otherwise, has or shares a direct or indirect "pecuniary interest" therein (essentially an opportunity to profit from a transaction in the securities). For instance, such person will be deemed to have an indirect pecuniary interest in shares held by a family member who shares the same household (this is in addition to the family member's own direct pecuniary interest). Such person may also be regarded as the beneficial owner of securities owned by a partnership or corporation if such person is a member of the partnership or a shareholder in the corporation.

The rules relating to beneficial ownership are complicated. This is particularly true because the SEC has adopted one set of rules for reporting beneficial ownership under Section 16(a), as described previously, and a different set of rules governing beneficial ownership of securities for purposes of reporting the officers' and directors' beneficial ownership of shares in registration statements filed by the issuer with the SEC and in the issuer's proxy statements.

Derivative Securities

A Reporting Person must also report such person's beneficial ownership of all types of "derivative securities." Included among "derivative securities" are puts, calls, options, warrants, stock appreciation rights, or other securities convertible into, exchangeable for, or that otherwise derive value from the issuer's common or preferred stock. Such derivative securities and underlying equity securities are considered part of the same class of equity security, and, if not exempt, the acquisition or disposition of a derivative security must be reported and can be matched with a disposition or acquisition of an identical derivative security or underlying equity security within six months to establish liability under Section 16(b). Exercises, exchanges, and conversions of derivative securities for or into underlying equity securities are also reportable events. A Reporting Person is required to report the acquisition or disposition of a derivative security on a Form 4 by the close of business on the second business day following the day on which the acquisition or disposition occurs. In addition, the exercise, exchange, or conversion of a derivative security must be reported on a Form 4 by the close of business on the second business day after such event.

Short-Swing Profit Liability

As indicated previously, nonexempt purchases and sales (or sales and purchases) of issuer equity securities by a Reporting Person occurring within any six-month period in which a profit is realized result in "short-swing profits" that may be recovered by the issuer or a shareholder acting on its behalf. Most securities granted to officers or directors by an issuer, while reportable under Section 16(a), would be exempt from short-swing profit liability under Rule 16b-3 if the grant is approved by a *fully independent* compensation committee or by the full board of directors or, more rarely, is approved or ratified by the shareholders. The most common nonexempt transactions that are subject to short-swing liability include open market purchases and sales (including broker-assisted cashless exercises of stock options, where shares are sold into the market to cover the exercise price or to satisfy the optionee's tax withholding obligation) and "Discretionary Transactions" (as defined under Rule 16b-3) under employee benefit plans.

For purposes of Section 16, short-swing profit is generally calculated to provide the maximum recoverable amount. The measure of damages is the profit derived from any nonexempt purchase and sale or any nonexempt sale and purchase within the six-month, short-swing period, without regard to any set-offs for losses or any first-in or first-out rules. This approach is sometimes referred to as the "lowest price in, highest price out" rule.

Insiders also may be liable for the receipt of short-swing profits in transactions involving the purchase or sale of derivative securities, such as options to purchase company common stock. As noted earlier, most derivative securities granted by the issuer would be exempt from Section 16(b) short-swing liability under Rule 16b-3 if the awards are properly granted by a fully independent compensation committee or the full board. Third-party derivatives written on company securities are not eligible for this exemption, however. For the purpose of determining liability, transactions involving derivative securities may be matched against transactions involving the underlying securities (i.e., the stock itself) because ownership of the derivative securities constitutes "beneficial ownership" of the underlying securities for purposes of Section 16. For example, the purchase of a call option on the issuer's stock and the sale of either the option or the shares of underlying stock within six months could result in short-swing profit liability.

The imposition of liability under Section 16(b) is not dependent upon proving the intent to violate that provision. Any profit (by a purchase and subsequent sale within six months at a higher price) or avoidance of loss (by a sale and subsequent purchase within six months at a lower price) whatsoever that falls within the mechanical test of Section 16(b) is recoverable, regardless of intentions and whether the sale or purchase was made on the basis of any inside information. Recall that:

- Only *nonexempt* transactions are subject to short-swing profit liability.
- Filing reports on Forms 3, 4, or 5 does not protect a Reporting Person from short-swing profit liability.
- Purchases and sales do not have to relate to the same shares for liability to arise.

Experience indicates that in the event of a violation of the short-swing profit provisions, it is *very likely* that an action will be brought, mainly because Form 4 and 5 reports will bring every violation to the attention of shareholders, particularly those professional shareholders and their attorneys who vigorously pursue Section 16(b) claims.

Rule 10b-5 of the Exchange Act

General

A second type of trading-related liability occurs when an insider (including not just Reporting Persons for Section 16 purposes, but also any employee or other person, whether or not employed by the issuer, who acquires material nonpublic information) trades in the issuer's common stock while in possession of material nonpublic information. Rule 10b-5 prohibits such persons from trading upon undisclosed material information to their advantage, and also prohibits them from providing such information to any other person (a practice known as "tipping").

Penalties

Insider trading is a serious offense, vigorously pursued by the SEC, that may result in imprisonment, criminal fines and civil money penalties, as well as civil liability to a potentially large class of plaintiffs for damages bearing no relation to the insider's or tippee's profit. In addition, an insider trading violation constitutes a violation of one of the antifraud provisions for which an insider may be barred from serving as a corporate officer or director. Therefore, if a director, officer, or employee has material nonpublic information, such person should not disclose that information (except through public dissemination) or trade in securities of the issuer until the information has been effectively disclosed to and digested by the investing public. Because a director, officer, or employee will likely be unable to disclose the information (as disclosure may be against the issuer's interest and could constitute a violation of a fiduciary duty to the issuer), the safest course is to refrain from trading when any such person is in possession of material undisclosed information.

Trading Policies

Because of the seriousness of the offense, it is common for issuers to adopt an insider trading policy that requires directors, executive officers, and certain other designated individuals who desire to buy or sell the issuer's common stock to obtain preclearance from one of several compliance officers (usually the general counsel and/or one or more attorneys in the issuer's legal department) before engaging in any transaction in the issuer's securities. Typically, individuals covered by the policy will be prohibited from trading in issuer securities during quarterly blackout periods related to the compilation and public disclosure of quarterly earnings information and during event-specific blackout periods. In this manner, independent safeguards will exist to ensure that persons likely to be in possession of material nonpublic information are unable to knowingly or unknowingly buy or sell stock while there exists material nonpublic information about the issuer. Such a policy will also help the issuer and its "controlling persons" avoid liability that arises from insider trading by a director, officer, or employee of the issuer.

Having mentioned the risks of insider trading, it is also possible to identify circumstances in which information has been sufficiently disseminated to permit an insider to trade. The proper time when insiders may trade depends both on how thoroughly and how quickly inside information is disseminated by the news services and the press after public disclosure. Insiders should, as a general rule, always wait until a release has appeared in the press before making a purchase or sale and should further refrain from trading following dissemination until the public has had an opportunity to evaluate the information thoroughly. The waiting period depends on the circumstances, but it is typical to require that insiders must wait until the second business day after release before commencing any trading. Furthermore, trading even at that time is prohibited if the person is aware of additional undisclosed material information that was not the subject of the release. In addition, officers of the issuer will continually be faced with the very sensitive question of when and to what extent the officers inform the board of directors of corporate developments. Insufficient and untimely delivery of information to the board could result in numerous problems, including subjecting the directors to allegations of insider trading violations since the SEC will likely presume that the board members are aware of all material nonpublic information relating to the issuer.

Rule 10b5-1

Rule 10b5-1 under the Exchange Act provides an affirmative defense to shield an insider from liability for insider trading if certain conditions are satisfied. Rule 10b5-1 provides that a person (such as a corporate insider) may, during a time that he or she is *not* in possession of material nonpublic information, enter into a binding contract, arrangement, or plan (a "preestablished trading program") for effecting subsequent sales or purchases of the issuer's stock, even if the person *is* in possession of material nonpublic information at the time of the sale or purchase. Such preestablished trading programs must (i) specify the amount of securities to be purchased or sold and the price at which and the date on which such sales or purchases are to take place, or (ii) include a written formula or algorithm or a computer program for determining the amount of securities to be purchased or sold and the price at which and the date on which such sales or purchases are to take place, or (iii) otherwise prohibit such persons from exercising any subsequent influence over how, when, or whether to effect purchases or sales (provided that any person who *is* permitted to exercise such influence must not have been aware of material nonpublic information when doing so). It is also a requirement of the rule that the purchase or sale actually occurs pursuant to the preestablished trading program and not in a manner that altered or deviated from such program. In addition, the insider cannot make hedging transactions or positions with respect to the securities traded pursuant to the preestablished trading program. The insider may change or terminate a preestablished trading program at any time that he or she is not in possession of material nonpublic information.

Note that Rule 10b5-1 does not shield an insider from short-swing profit liability or reporting obligations under Section 16, and that trading pursuant to a preestablished trading program under Rule 10b5-1 does not necessarily mean that the trade is exempt under Section 16(b). In fact, it is most likely the preestablished trading program would involve nonexempt sales on the open market. If a Section 16 insider entered into such a preestablished trading program that called for annual or more frequent sales in the market, that person could never make a nonexempt purchase without incurring short-swing profit liability under Section 16(b). Therefore, officers and directors should be ever thoughtful in designing a preestablished trading program under Rule 10b5-1.

Insider Trades during Pension Fund Blackout Periods— Disgorgement of Profits

Background

Section 306 of the Sarbanes-Oxley Act is divided into two related but distinct parts. Section 306(a) prohibits a director or executive officer of a public company from trading in issuer equity securities during a blackout period during which pension plan participants are unable to effect transactions involving company stock. Section

306(b) of the Sarbanes-Oxley Act requires a 30-day advance notice to plan participants and beneficiaries of a more broadly defined set of blackout periods. The discussion in this chapter is limited to the provisions of Section 306(a), as Section 306(b) has no direct effect on stock trading by directors and executive officers.

Generally, during a pension fund blackout period, plan participants can contribute to their accounts, but cannot switch their account funds between investment options. This effectively locks them into their existing investment choices for a period of time, which can be worrisome when an unforeseen event, such as a sudden stock price decline, occurs during that period of time.

Enron and other highly publicized cases demonstrated the catastrophic consequences that can befall employees who have invested substantially all of their retirement savings in their employer's equity securities when the market price of such securities falls sharply. There have been allegations that, at a time when rank-and-file employees were precluded from selling their employer's equity securities held in their individual pension plan accounts, corporate executives were exercising and cashing out employee stock options and selling other securities acquired through the company's equity compensation plans.

Section 306(a) is intended to address the apparent unfairness of an issuer's directors and executive officers being able to sell their equity securities when the issuer's nonexecutive employees cannot. It does this by prohibiting directors and executive officers from trading in equity securities of the issuer when a substantial number of the issuer's employees are subject to a blackout period under their individual pension plan accounts.

Regulation BTR

In 2002, the SEC adopted Regulation BTR (Blackout Trading Restriction) to implement the statutory trading prohibitions of Section 306(a). By using many of the same concepts that have been developed under Section 16 of the Exchange Act, Regulation BTR provides a broad scope to the trading prohibition of Section 306(a), takes advantage of a well-established body of rules and interpretations concerning the trading activities of corporate insiders, and facilitates enforcement of Section 306(a) by generally allowing reference to Section 16 trading reports (i.e., Forms 3, 4, and 5 discussed previously).

Regulation BTR prohibits a director or executive officer of an issuer from purchasing, selling, or otherwise acquiring or transferring any equity security of the issuer during a pension plan blackout period, if the equity security was acquired in connection with the director's or executive officer's service or employment as a director or executive officer. Therefore, the scope of the trading prohibition is limited to:

- An acquisition of equity securities during a blackout period if the acquisition is in connection with service or employment as a director or executive officer.

- A disposition of equity securities during a blackout period if the disposition involves equity securities acquired in connection with service or employment as a director or executive officer.

The Section 306(a) trading prohibition is limited to equity securities that a director or executive officer acquires in connection with his or her service or employment as a director or executive officer. Therefore, it does not completely preclude a director or executive officer from trading in equity securities of the issuer during a blackout period. This raises the difficulty of determining whether a particular transaction during a blackout period, such as a sale on the open market, involves equity securities that are subject to Section 306(a) or equity securities that are not so subject. To avoid this problem, Regulation BTR establishes an irrebuttable presumption that *any* equity securities sold or otherwise transferred during a blackout period were acquired in connection with service or employment, to the extent that the director or executive officer holds such securities, without regard to the actual source of the securities disposed of. However, to avoid an overly broad application of the presumption, in a given blackout period, equity securities held by a director or executive officer that were acquired in connection with service or employment could only count once against a disposition transaction during that blackout period.

Generally, equity securities acquired by an individual before he or she became a director or executive officer would not be subject to Section 306(a). This would exclude from the trading prohibition any equity securities acquired under a plan or arrangement while the individual was an employee, but not a director or executive officer, of the issuer. However, shares acquired in a director or executive officer capacity before January 26, 2003 (the effective date of Section 306) or before the company becomes a public "issuer" would be subject to the trading prohibition.

Transactional Exemptions

Similar to several familiar Section 16 transactional exemptions, Regulation BTR exempts from the trading restriction of Section 306(a):

- Acquisitions of equity securities under broad-based dividend or interest reinvestment plans
- Purchases or sales of equity securities pursuant to valid Rule 10b5-1(c) programs, as long as the advance election was not made or modified during the blackout period or at a time the director or executive officer was aware of the impending blackout
- Purchases or sales of equity securities pursuant to certain "tax-conditioned" plans, other than discretionary transactions (such terms are defined similarly to the Rule 16b-3 definitions of such terms)
- Increases or decreases in the number of equity securities held as a result of a stock split or stock dividend applying equally to all equity securities of that class

There is not, however, a complete parallel between the transactional exemptions under Regulation BTR and those available under Section 16. For example, there is no exemption under Regulation BTR for preapproved transactions directly with the issuer, as in Rule 16b-3(d) and Rule 16b-3(e).

Blackout Period Defined

Section 306(a) defines the term "blackout period" to mean any period of more than three consecutive business days during which the ability of not fewer than 50% of the participants or beneficiaries under all individual account plans maintained by the issuer to purchase, sell, or otherwise acquire or transfer an interest in any equity security of such issuer held in such an "individual account plan" is temporarily suspended by the issuer or by a fiduciary of the plan.

A blackout period does not include (i) a regularly scheduled trading suspension that is incorporated into the plan and timely disclosed to employees before becoming participants or as a subsequent plan amendment, or (ii) any suspension that is imposed solely in connection with persons becoming participants or beneficiaries in such plan by reason of a corporate merger, acquisition, divestiture, or similar transaction involving the plan or plan sponsor.

Common administrative reasons for imposing blackout periods include changes in investment alternatives, changes in record keepers for the plan or other service providers, and mergers, acquisitions, or spin off transactions that affect the coverage group of plan participants. For example, in the case of a change in record keepers, plan activities might be suspended to provide time for reconciliation of participant accounts and conversion of accounts to the new record keeper's system. Some blackout periods, however, are not within the control of the plan administrator, such as those caused by computer failure.

Individual Account Plan

In general, an "individual account plan" is a pension plan in which an individual account is maintained for each participant, which provides benefits based solely on the amounts contributed to the account (either by the participant or the issuer, through forfeitures or otherwise) and any earnings or losses thereon. For example, typical individual account plans would include 401(k) plans, profit-sharing and savings plans, stock bonus plans, and money purchase pension plans. Defined-benefit pension plans are not likely to be individual account plans.

Notice Requirement

Section 306(a) requires a company to timely notify its directors and executive officers, as well as the SEC, of the existence of a blackout period during which they would be prohibited from trading in issuer equity securities.

Remedies for Noncompliance; Disgorgement of Profits

Section 306(a) contains two distinct remedies. First, a violation is subject to a possible SEC enforcement action. This would include possible civil injunctive actions, cease-and-desist proceedings, civil penalties, and all other remedies available to the SEC to redress violations of the Exchange Act. Under appropriate circumstances, a director or executive officer also could be subject to possible criminal liability.

In addition, where a director or executive officer realizes a profit from a prohibited transaction during a blackout period, the issuer, or a shareholder on the issuer's behalf, may bring an action to recover the profit. This remedy reflects a standard of strict liability (regardless of the intent of the director or executive officer in entering into the transaction) that is similar to the standard under Section 16(b) of the Exchange Act.

As under Section 16(b) of the Exchange Act, the concept of realized profit would mean that the director or executive officer received a direct or indirect pecuniary benefit from the prohibited transaction. The SEC acknowledged the potential complexity of determining whether a transaction has resulted in the realization of recoverable profits, especially in the case of a purchase or other acquisition of equity securities during a blackout period. Therefore, Regulation BTR provides a straightforward standard:

- Where a transaction involves a purchase, sale, or other acquisition or transfer (other than a grant, exercise, conversion, or termination of a derivative security) of a regularly traded equity security, recoverable profit is measured by comparing the difference between the amount paid or received for the equity security on the date of the transaction during the blackout period and the average market price of the equity security calculated over the first three trading days after the ending date of the blackout period.

- For any other transaction, profit is to be measured in a manner consistent with the objective of identifying the amount of any gain realized or loss avoided as a result of the transaction taking place during the blackout period rather than taking place outside of the blackout period.

For example, assume that during a blackout period, a director acquired, for $10 per share, in connection with service as a director, 1,000 shares of issuer stock. The average price of the issuer stock over the first three trading days after the blackout period was $12. The recoverable profit is $2 per share, or $2,000. If the average price of the issuer stock over the first three trading days after the blackout period had been less than $10, there would have been no recoverable profit, but the director would still be subject to potential sanctions, including SEC enforcement action.

Similarly, assume that during a blackout period, a director sold 1,000 shares of option-acquired stock for $20 per share. The average price of the issuer stock over the first three trading days after the blackout period was $12. The recoverable profit is $8 per share, or $8,000. If the average price of the issuer stock over the first three trading days after the blackout period had been more than $20, there would have been no recoverable profit, but the director would still be subject to potential sanctions, including SEC enforcement action.

Practical Considerations

As a practical matter, temporary pension plan blackout periods that will trigger a need to halt insider trading under Section 306(a) should be infrequent. Moreover, there are many exemptions that will keep the rule from being a complete bar to trading, and appropriately so. Still, the new Section 306(a) trading restrictions add another layer of complexity to the maze of rules that make insider trading in issuer securities a challenge of timing and judgment.

Sales of Restricted and Control Stock under Rule 144

Background

A fundamental premise of the Securities Act is that securities may not be sold without registration unless an exemption from the registration requirements of the Securities Act is available for the transaction. This rule applies both to original issuances of common stock by the issuer and to trading on the secondary level by the issuer's shareholders.

With respect to secondary trading, registration or an exemption from registration is necessary for (i) every sale of "restricted securities" (i.e., securities received in an unregistered private placement or an equivalent transaction) by any shareholder, and (ii) every sale by an "affiliate" of any common stock of the issuer, whether or not the common stock was previously registered under the Securities Act. Shares of common stock that were purchased by affiliates in the open market or pursuant to a registered offering by the issuer and that are not "restricted securities" are referred to as "control securities" (referring to ownership by the affiliate, who is presumed to "control" the issuer). The distinction between restricted securities and control securities is important in determining which conditions of Rule 144 apply to a particular sales transaction.

The term "affiliate" refers to persons controlling, controlled by, or under common control with the issuer and presumptively includes executive officers, directors, greater than 10% shareholders, and the immediate relatives of all of the foregoing. Depending upon the factual circumstances, however, certain of these persons may not actually have the ability to control the issuer and, therefore, may not be affiliates in all cases. Conversely, persons outside of these categories nevertheless may have control capabilities and, therefore, may be deemed affiliates in certain instances.

Rule 144

Because of the expense of a registration and in view of serious potential liabilities, it is important to assure that any sales made by an affiliate come within an applicable registration exemption. Although other exemptions may be available in some limited circumstances, the most commonly used exemption is a sale in a brokers' transaction under Rule 144. Rule 144 permits affiliates to sell common stock, whether characterized as "restricted securities" or "control securities," of the issuer if each of the following conditions is met:

1. The affiliate must have owned any "restricted securities" (as described earlier) for at least one year prior to resale.
2. The amount of common stock that an affiliate may sell during any three-month period may not exceed the greater of (i) 1% of the outstanding common stock or (ii) the average weekly trading volume of the common stock for the four-week period prior to the date of the sale.
3. The issuer must have been subject to the reporting requirements of the Exchange Act for at least 90 days and must have filed all required reports during the 12 months preceding the sale.
4. The common stock must be sold in a "brokers' transaction" (a transaction where the activity of the selling broker is limited) or in a transaction with a "market maker" in the common stock.
5. A notice of sale on Form 144 must be filed at the time of the sale, unless sales in the three-month period of the sale involve 500 or fewer shares and an aggregate sales price of less than $10,000. The affiliate must mail Form 144, if required, to the SEC contemporaneously with placing an order to sell common stock with the affiliate's broker. This form is usually provided by the brokerage firm when an affiliate places a sell order.

If for any reason a sale does not comply with the Rule 144 requirements, the broker may insist that the transaction be broken at the affiliate's expense. The affiliate should make sure that any broker used is experienced in Rule 144 trades.

The Rule 144 conditions may be disregarded in certain limited circumstances. A shareholder who is not an affiliate of the issuer at the time of the sale and has not been an affiliate during the preceding three months may sell or otherwise dispose of restricted securities under Rule 144(k) without complying with the conditions noted previously, provided he or she has held such securities for at least two years. Gifts of restricted securities that satisfy the two-year holding period to charitable or other similar types of institutions, or to adult family members not living with the donor and not dependent upon the donor generally, may be sold immediately under Rule 144(k) by the donees, provided the donees are not affiliates of the issuer at the time of the sale of the stock and were not affiliates for the three months preceding the date of sale.

NYSE/NASDAQ RULES: APPROVAL OF EQUITY COMPENSATION PLANS

Background

Effective June 30, 2003, the SEC approved new NYSE and Nasdaq rules that significantly broaden shareholder approval requirements for equity-based compensation plans, including material revisions to such plans, subject to certain limited exceptions described later.[1] Among other things, the new rules eliminate exceptions formerly available for broadly based plans and certain *de minimis* equity grants. In addition, the NYSE rule prohibits brokers holding shares on behalf of customers from voting such shares on equity compensation plan matters without specific voting instructions from the customers.

Because the final NYSE and Nasdaq rules are significantly similar, the following discussion applies to both the NYSE and the Nasdaq rules, except as otherwise noted.

Equity Compensation Plans Defined

The NYSE rule defines "equity-compensation plan" as a plan or other arrangement that provides for the delivery of equity securities (either newly issued or treasury shares) to any employee, director, or other service provider as compensation for services (including compensatory grants of options or other equity securities that are not made under a plan). The Nasdaq rule requires shareholder approval when a stock option or stock purchase or other equity compensation plan or arrangement is to be established or materially amended pursuant to which options or stock may be acquired by officers, directors, employees, or consultants. Neither the NYSE rule nor the Nasdaq rule permits companies to avoid the shareholder approval requirements by funding options with repurchased or treasury shares.

Under the NYSE and Nasdaq rules, the following plans or arrangements are excluded from the shareholder approval requirement:

- Plans that are made available to shareholders generally (such as dividend reinvestment plans or plans involving the distribution of shares or purchase rights to all shareholders).
- Plans that merely allow employees, directors, and other service providers to purchase shares on the open market or from the company at fair market value

[1]Self-Regulatory Organizations; New York Stock Exchange, Inc. and National Association of Securities Dealers, Inc.; Order Approving NYSE and Nasdaq Proposed Rule Changes and Nasdaq Amendment No. 1 and Notice of Filing and Order Granting Accelerated Approval to NYSE Amendments No. 1 and 2 and Nasdaq Amendments No. 2 and 3 Thereto Relating to Equity Compensation Plans, www.sec.gov/rules/sro/34-48108.htm (June 30, 2003).

(regardless of whether shares are delivered immediately or on a deferred basis or whether payments for shares are made directly or through deferral of compensation).

- Arrangements under which employees receive cash-only payments based on the value of the company's stock (such as phantom stock payable in cash).

Exceptions to Shareholder Approval Requirement

In addition to excluded plans as just described, the following arrangements are exempt from the NYSE and Nasdaq shareholder approval requirements, provided they are made with the approval of the company's compensation committee or a majority of the company's independent directors.

Employment Inducement Awards

Shareholder approval is not required for the grant of options or other equity-based compensation as a material inducement to a person being hired, or being rehired after a *bona fide* period of employment interruption (including grants to new employees in connection with a merger or acquisition), by a company or any of its subsidiaries. Promptly following the grant of an inducement award, a company must disclose the material terms of the award in a press release.

Plans or Arrangements Relating to a Merger or Acquisition

Shareholder approval is not required for:

- Options and other awards that are made or adopted to convert, replace, or adjust outstanding options or other equity compensation awards of another company in connection with the acquisition of that other company.
- Shares available under preexisting plans[2] of a company acquired in a merger or acquisition by a listed company that are used for certain post-transaction grants, provided: (i) the plan originally was approved by the shareholders of the target company; (ii) the number of shares available for grants is adjusted to reflect the transaction; (iii) the time during which those shares are available is not extended; and (iv) the options or other awards are not granted to individuals who were employed by the acquiring company or its subsidiaries at the time the merger or acquisition was consummated.[3]

---

[2]For purposes of this exemption, a plan adopted by the acquired company in contemplation of a merger or acquisition transaction would not be considered "preexisting."

[3]Any additional shares available for issuance under a plan or arrangement acquired in connection with a merger or acquisition would be counted by the NYSE or Nasdaq, as applicable, in determining whether the transaction involved the issuance of 20% or more of the company's outstanding common stock, thus triggering the shareholder approval requirements under NYSE Listed Company Manual Section 312.03(c) and Nasdaq Rule 4350(i)(1)(C).

Plans Intended to Meet the Requirements of Sections 401(a) or 423 of the Internal Revenue Code and Parallel Excess Plans.[4]

Shareholder approval is not required for these plans, as such plans are regulated by the Internal Revenue Code (Code) and Treasury Department regulations.

NYSE listed companies must notify the NYSE in writing when relying on one of the foregoing exceptions to the shareholder approval requirement.[5]

Material Revisions/Amendments

Material revisions/amendments to equity-compensation plans and arrangements require shareholder approval. The NYSE and Nasdaq rules provide that a material revision/amendment includes, but is not limited to:

- A material increase in the number of shares available under the plan (other than solely to reflect a reorganization, stock split, merger, spinoff, or similar transaction)
- An expansion of the types of awards available under the plan
- A material expansion of the class of employees, directors, or other service providers eligible to participate
- A material extension of the term of the plan

---

[4]The NYSE rule uses the term *parallel excess plan*, and the Nasdaq rule uses the term *parallel nonqualified plan*, both of which are defined to mean a plan that is a "pension plan" within the meaning of the Employee Retirement Income Security Act of 1974 that is designed to work in parallel with a plan intended to be qualified under Code Section 401(a) to provide benefits that exceed the limits set forth in Code Section 402(g) (the section that limits an employee's annual pretax contributions to a 401(k) plan), Code Section 401(a)(17) (the section that limits the amount of an employee's compensation that can be taken into account for plan purposes), and/or Code Section 415 (the section that limits the contributions and benefits under qualified plans), and/or any successor or similar limitations that may be enacted. A plan will not be considered a parallel excess plan or a parallel nonqualified plan unless: (1) it covers all or substantially all employees of an employer who are participants in the related qualified plan whose annual compensation is in excess of the limit of Code Section 401(a)(17) (or any successor or similar limits that may be enacted); (2) its terms are substantially the same as the qualified plan that it parallels except for the elimination of the limits described in the preceding sentence and the limitation described in clause (3); and (3) no participant receives employer equity contributions under the plan in excess of 25% of the participant's cash compensation.

[5]The SEC's release indicates that Nasdaq is considering whether to impose a disclosure requirement when a Nasdaq listed company relies upon any of these exceptions to the shareholder approval requirements.

In addition, the NYSE rule states that a material revision includes any material change to the method of determining the strike price of options under the plan and any deletion or limitation of any provision prohibiting repricing of options. Similarly, the Nasdaq rule provides that a material amendment would include any material increase in benefits to participants, including any reduction in the exercise price of outstanding options or the price at which shares or options to purchase shares may be offered.

Under the NYSE rule, if a plan has an "evergreen" provision that provides for automatic increases in the number of shares available under the plan, or the plan provides for automatic formula grants (in either case, a "formula plan"),[6] each increase or grant is considered a revision requiring shareholder approval unless the plan has a term of not more than 10 years. Under the Nasdaq rule, a formula plan cannot have a term in excess of 10 years unless shareholder approval is obtained every 10 years.

If a plan has no limit on the number of shares available and is not a formula plan (a "discretionary plan"), then under both the NYSE and Nasdaq rules, each grant under the plan is considered a material revision/amendment requiring separate shareholder approval regardless of whether the plan has a term of not more than 10 years. As a practical matter, very few plans were "discretionary" plans even before these new shareholder approval requirements came into effect.

Option Repricings

In addition to treating a repricing as a material revision/amendment requiring shareholder approval, the NYSE rule provides that a plan that does not contain a provision specifically permitting the repricing of options will be considered to prohibit repricing.[7] Moreover, according to the NYSE rule, any actual repricing of options will be considered a material revision of a plan even if the plan itself is not revised.

The Nasdaq rule treats repricings as material amendments requiring shareholder approval.

[6]The NYSE rule provides examples of formula plans, which include annual grants to directors of restricted stock having a certain dollar value, and company "matching contributions" whereby stock is credited to a participant's account based upon the amount of compensation a participant elects to defer. The Nasdaq rule describes formula plans as providing for automatic grants pursuant to a dollar-based formula, such as annual grants based on a certain dollar value, or company matching contributions based upon compensation a participant elects to defer.

[7]A "repricing" is defined in the NYSE rule to include any of the following or any other action that has the same effect: (i) lowering the strike price of an option after it is granted; (ii) any other action that is treated as a repricing under GAAP; or (iii) canceling an underwater option in exchange for another option, restricted stock, or other equity, unless in connection with a merger, acquisition, spin-off, or similar transaction.

Effective Date

As a general rule, under both the NYSE and Nasdaq rules, plans that were adopted before June 30, 2003 are grandfathered and will not require shareholder approval unless and until they are materially revised or amended. Equity compensation plans and arrangements adopted (or materially revised or amended) on or after June 30, 2003 are subject to the new rules regarding shareholder approval. Certain transition rules applied to evergreen and formula plans, but those transition periods expired on June 30, 2004 or earlier.

Limitation on Broker Voting

Under amended NYSE Rule 452, brokers holding shares for the accounts of customers are no longer permitted to vote those shares with respect to equity compensation plan matters unless the beneficial owner of the shares (i.e., the customer) has given the broker specific voting instructions.[8] This change has significantly raised the bar for obtaining the requisite shareholder vote to approve equity compensation plans.

SEC RULES REGARDING DISCLOSURE OF EQUITY COMPENSATION PLANS

Background

Item 201(d) of Regulation S-K, adopted by the SEC in 2002, requires enhanced disclosure regarding a company's equity compensation plans. The disclosure must appear in the company's annual report on Form 10-K every year, and must also be included in the proxy statement in years in which the company is submitting any compensation plan proposal, including a plan amendment, for shareholder approval.[9] The disclosure is designed to reveal the potential dilutive effect of a company's equity compensation plans on shareholder value and to afford shareholders a clearer understanding of all equity-based compensation paid by the company. The full text of Item 201(d) is reproduced in Appendix A.

[8]The SEC noted that existing rules of the National Association of Securities Dealers, Inc. prohibit discretionary voting by broker-dealers without explicit instructions from the beneficial owner.

[9]For any year in which the company is required to provide the disclosure in both the Form 10-K and proxy statement, the Form 10-K disclosure may consist of an incorporation by reference to the proxy statement disclosure, if the proxy statement involves the election of directors and is filed not more than 120 days after the end of the fiscal year covered by the Form 10-K. The disclosure is not required in prospectuses filed under the Securities Act.

Content and Form of the Disclosure

The rules require disclosure relating to equity compensation plans in effect as of the end of the company's last completed fiscal year. An equity compensation plan is one that provides for the award of the company's securities or the grant of options, warrants, or rights to purchase the company's securities to any person. The disclosure is required for all arrangements under which equity compensation may be issued, including arrangements for nonemployees, such as directors, consultants, advisors, vendors, customers, suppliers, or lenders, and for individual arrangements even if not pursuant to a broader plan. The disclosure is not required for plans that are intended to meet the qualification requirement of Code Section 401(a) or arrangements that provide for the issuance of rights to all security holders of the issuer on a pro rata basis (such as a dividend reinvestment plan).

Tabular Plan Disclosure

The rules require disclosure in tabular form of all employee stock options and other rights to acquire securities of the company under all equity compensation plans and arrangements of the company. The table must include the number and weighted-average exercise price of outstanding options, warrants, and rights, and the number of securities available for future issuance under the company's existing equity compensation plans. The disclosure must be given separately for plans that have already been approved by shareholders and for plans that have not been approved by shareholders. Exhibit 6.1 is an example of how the table should look.

Certain information that does not readily fit into the table should be disclosed in a footnote. For example, any "evergreen" formula that automatically increases the number of securities available for issuance under a plan should be described in a footnote to the table. In addition, with respect to any individual options, warrants, or rights assumed in connection with a merger or other acquisition transaction where no future options may be granted under the plan, the information required by table columns (a) and (b) should be disclosed in a footnote. If the assumed plan is ongoing, however, it should be disclosed as a nonshareholder approved plan (unless the shareholders have separately approved it) in columns (a) and (c). To the extent that the number of securities remaining available for future issuance set forth in table column (c) includes securities available for issuance other than upon the exercise of an option, warrant, or right, the company must describe such other securities in a footnote.

Narrative Plan Descriptions

In addition to the table shown in Exhibit 6.1, the rules also provide that the material features of each nonshareholder approved plan must be described briefly in narrative form. If the company's financial statements contain such a narrative description,

Exhibit 6.1 Equity Compensation Plan Information

	(a)	(b)	(c)
Plan category	Number of securities to be issued upon exercise of outstanding options, warrants, and rights	Weighted-average exercise price of outstanding options, warrants, and rights	Number of securities remaining available for future issuance under equity compensation plans (excluding securities reflected in column (a))
Equity compensation plans approved by security holders			
Equity compensation plans not approved by security holders			
Total			

this requirement may be satisfied by cross-referencing the appropriate financial statement disclosure.

Plan Filing Requirements

A company must file with the SEC a copy of each nonshareholder approved plan in which any employee participates, unless immaterial in amount or significance. If a particular nonshareholder approved plan is not set forth in a formal written document, the company must file a written description of the plan. Any nonshareholder approved plan assumed in connection with a merger, consolidation, or other acquisition transaction is subject to this filing requirement if the company is able to make additional grants or awards of its equity securities under the plan.

Disclosure Tips

Restricted Stock and Restricted Stock Units

Restricted stock should not be included in the table in either column (a) or column (c), because these shares, once issued, are already reflected as outstanding in a company's financial statements. Restricted stock units, however, represent an obligation to issue shares in the future, and therefore shares subject to restricted stock units should be included in column (a) of the table, with an explanatory footnote.

Employee Stock Purchase Plans

Shares authorized for future issuance under an employee stock purchase plan should be included in column (c) of the table, but outstanding purchase rights that are accruing during a purchase period may be disregarded and need not be transferred to column (a) and (b). Because employee stock purchase plans are generally perceived favorably, companies may want to show in a footnote how many of the shares in column (c) are reserved under an employee stock purchase plan.

Directors' Deferred Compensation Plans

Deferred compensation plans for directors typically allow directors to defer all or a portion of their retainers and/or meeting fees and provide for future payouts in cash or in shares of company stock. Outstanding awards of company stock under such a plan should be shown in column (a), but would not be included in the weighted average price calculation in column (b). If the plan has an overall share limit, the number of remaining shares available for issuance under the plan should be included in column (c), but if the plan is limited only by the amount of compensation payable from time to time to participating directors, a footnote describing how the plan works should be appended to column (c).

401(k) Plans

Shares issuable pursuant to a qualified Code Section 401(k) plan do not need to be disclosed in the table.

Options Assumed in a Merger

Options assumed in a merger, where no future options may be granted under a plan of the acquired company, do not need to be included in column (a), but should be disclosed in a footnote that would include the weighted-average exercise price. If the company retains the ability to grant future awards under an acquired company's plan, then the assumed options must be shown in column (a) and the remaining shares shown in column (c). In addition, the assumed plan will be considered non-shareholder approved (and subject to the narrative description requirement) unless the company's shareholders have separately approved the assumption of the plan.

Expired Plans

Any outstanding grants should be reflected in column (a), even if the plan under which the grants were made has expired.

DISCLOSURE OF COMPENSATION OF AND TRANSACTIONS WITH MANAGEMENT

Background

In an attempt to make compensation disclosure clearer, more comprehensive, and more useful to shareholders, the SEC in 1992 adopted extensive revisions to its rules governing disclosure of executive officer and director compensation in proxy and information statements, registration statements and periodic reports under the Exchange Act, and registration statements under the Securities Act. The rules are encompassed in SEC Regulation S-K, which states the requirements applicable to the content of the nonfinancial portions of registration statements filed under the Securities Act and registration statements and periodic reports filed under the Exchange Act. Similar rules for small business issuers are found in Regulation S-B.

The full texts of Items 401, 402, 403, 404, 405, and 601(b)(10) of Regulation S-K are reproduced in Appendix A. All compensation committee members should be conversant with these rules, as they are the primary disclosure rules for executive compensation. Brief summaries of those sections follow.

Item 401: Directors, Executive Officers, Promoters, and Control Persons

Item 401 of Regulation S-K requires disclosure of certain personal and background information about the company's directors and executive officers, including their age, family relationships, business experience, legal proceedings, and other information that would likely be relevant to shareholders in assessing such persons' ability to serve the company.

Item 402: Executive Compensation

Item 402 of Regulation S-K is designed to furnish shareholders with a comprehensive presentation of the nature and extent of an issuer's executive compensation. It does so by (i) consolidating the requisite disclosure in a series of tables setting forth each compensatory element for a particular fiscal year; (ii) requiring a report by the compensation committee articulating the basis for its compensation decisions, including the relationship to corporate performance; and (iii) requiring a line graph comparing total shareholder returns of the company against those of a broad market index and peer group.

The disclosures focus on the compensation of five or more individuals referred to as the "named executive officers." This group consists of (i) all individuals serving as CEO or acting in a similar capacity during the last completed fiscal year, regardless of compensation level, (ii) the company's four most highly compensated executive officers other than the CEO who were serving as executive officers at the end of the last fiscal year; and (iii) up to two additional former executive officers whose reportable salary and bonus would place them in the group of four highest paid executive officers if they had remained in an executive officer capacity at year end.

The Summary Compensation Table is generally regarded as the linchpin of the executive compensation disclosure scheme. This tabular, three-year summary provides an easily understood overview of a company's executive compensation in a single location within the proxy statement and enables shareholders to identify trends in a company's compensation of its top executives and to compare such trends with those disclosed by other companies.

In addition to the Summary Compensation Table, the rules include several tables providing more detailed information concerning grants, exercises and value of outstanding stock options, long-term incentive plans, and other information. Finally, Item 402 provides the rules for the Compensation Committee report (discussed previously in Chapter 1).

Item 403: Security Ownership of Certain Beneficial Owners and Management

Item 403 of Regulation S-K requires disclosure of beneficial ownership of company securities held by (i) any persons known by the company to own more than 5% of any class of the company's voting securities, and (ii) each director and director nominee, each of the named executive officers, and the directors and executive officers of the company as a group. The required disclosure includes the total number of shares beneficially owned and the percent of the class so owned. Beneficial ownership for this purpose includes securities that a person has a right to acquire within 60 days, such as securities underlying vested stock options (and stock options that will vest within 60 days). This item also requires a description of any known arrangements that may result in a change in control of the company.

Item 404: Certain Relationships and Related Transactions

Item 404 of Regulation S-K requires disclosure of transactions involving amounts in excess of $60,000 between the company and any director or director nominee, executive officer, 5% shareholder, or any member of the immediate family of any such persons. This item also requires disclosure of certain business relationships involving a director or director nominee and an entity that has certain specified relationships with the company. For example, disclosure is required where a director or a director nominee is an executive officer of, or beneficially owns more than 10% of, any business or professional entity that has made payments to the company in excess of 5% of the company's or the other entity's gross revenues for the last fiscal year. In addition, disclosure is required of indebtedness of a director or director nominee, executive officer, and certain other specified entities to the company in excess of $60,000.

Item 405: Compliance with Section 16(a) of the Exchange Act

Item 405 of Regulation S-K requires disclosure of any of the company's Section 16 Reporting Persons who failed to file a Form 3, 4, or 5 on a timely basis during the most recent fiscal year or prior fiscal years. The disclosure must include the number of late reports, the number of transactions that were not reported on a timely basis, and any known failure to file a form.

Item 601(b)(10): Material Contracts

Item 601(b)(10) of Regulation S-K sets forth criteria for identifying the company's material contracts that must be filed as exhibits to the company's public filings. Compensation committees should note that material contracts that must be filed include any management contract or any compensatory plan, contract, or arrangement in which any director or any named executive officer of the company participates, and any other management contract or compensatory plan in which any other executive officer participates, unless it is immaterial in amount or significance.

SELECTED SARBANES-OXLEY PROVISIONS RELATING TO EXECUTIVE COMPENSATION

Section 402: Prohibition on Loans to Directors and Executive Officers

Background

Section 402 of the Sarbanes-Oxley Act introduced a sweeping prohibition of personal loans by a public company to its directors and executive officers. The broad language used in Section 402 has raised many questions regarding the intended scope of the prohibition, and it is unclear when or if the SEC will offer interpretive guidance. In the meantime, public companies should carefully review anything that could be viewed as an extension of, or arrangements for an extension of, credit with its directors and executive officers.

Section 402 prohibits a public company from directly or indirectly extending, maintaining, arranging, or renewing a personal loan to or for a director or executive officer. Specifically, it amended Section 13 of the Exchange Act by adding a new Section 13(k):

> It shall be unlawful for any issuer . . . directly or indirectly, including through any subsidiary, to extend or maintain credit, to arrange for the extension of credit, or to renew an extension of credit, in the form of a personal loan to or for any director or executive officer (or equivalent thereof) of that issuer. An extension of credit maintained by the issuer on [July 30, 2002] shall not be subject to the provisions of this subsection, provided that there is no material modification to any term of any such extension of credit or any renewal of any such extension of credit on or after [July 30, 2002].

The Section 402 prohibition extends only to the extension or arrangement of credit that takes the form of a personal loan, but the act does not define the relevant terms. Because the SEC and the Board of Governors of the Federal Reserve System have broadly interpreted the concepts of arranging and extending credit in other contexts, the Section 402 prohibition could be interpreted to apply to a wide variety of transactions that are not commonly considered loans.

Certainly, public companies are prohibited under Section 402 from directly lending or cosigning or otherwise guaranteeing or providing security for an insider's personal loan. However, other common practices may or may not be prohibited, including such things as selecting a lending institution for an insider, making salary advances, awarding bonuses that are repayable in certain circumstances, using company funds to advance an insider's tax withholding obligations, and even advancement of litigation expenses.

Cashless Exercise Programs

One of the more common areas of concern that flared up in the immediate aftermath of the passage of Section 402, but seems to have subsided somewhat in the ensuing months, is the issue of whether certain broker-assisted cashless stock option exercises would violate the loan prohibition.

Many stock option arrangements provide for the exercise of an option through a broker-assisted cashless exercise. In a typical arrangement, the broker, upon receipt of exercise instructions, will sell a sufficient number of shares to remit the exercise price and applicable tax withholding amounts to the company, with the remaining shares or sales proceeds being delivered to the optionee (less applicable commissions). If the broker pays the company the exercise price on the date of exercise but does not receive the proceeds of the stock sale until the settlement date (typically on the third following business day, or T+3), the company may be considered to have "arranged for" the broker's margin loan to the insider, particularly if the company required or encouraged the optionee to use that particular broker to effect the cashless exercise. Or, if the company releases the shares to the broker upon exercise but does not receive payment until the T+3 settlement date, the company may be considered to have provided a short-term loan of the shares to or for the insider, although this is certainly not an unassailable theory. In either event, a potential Section 402 problem exists. There are arguments to be made (some based on legal theory, others on policy grounds) that most broker-assisted cashless exercises are not prohibited by the Sarbanes-Oxley Act, but there is as yet no binding authority or guidance from the SEC or Congress.

In light of this uncertainty, many companies have instructed their directors and executive officers not to engage in any form of broker-assisted cashless exercise of options until further guidance is provided or until "safe" cashless exercise structures have been identified and become widely accepted. As an alternative, companies may consider encouraging their directors and executive officers to pay the option exercise price and withholding tax obligation by surrendering to the company shares of company stock they have owned for at least six months, to the extent that the company's stock option documents presently permit this method of exercise. In addition, Section 402 does not prohibit the exercise of an option for cash, even where the director or executive officer obtained financing for such exercise (without company involvement).

Penalties for Violation of Section 402

The prohibitions of Section 402 apply to the issuer, rather than to the individual directors and executive officers. However, a director or executive officer could be subject to a state law derivative action to recover proceeds of illegal loans, and aiding and abetting claims may be possible. The issuer could be subject to civil or criminal sanctions under the Exchange Act, including administrative and civil remedies. For example, the SEC could seek injunctive remedies or monetary penalties of up to $500,000 under Section 21 of the Exchange Act, or could issue a cease-and-desist order or impose a temporary freeze on "extraordinary payments" during investigation under Section 21C of the Exchange Act. The Department of Justice could institute a criminal proceeding under Section 32 of the Exchange Act for willful violations and/or impose criminal fines of up to $25,000,000 for corporate violations of the Exchange Act. It is unlikely that a right to a private civil action would be implied under the Exchange Act for Section 402 violations.

Section 304: Forfeiture of Bonuses and Profits Triggered by Restatements of Financial Reports

Background

Section 304 of the Sarbanes-Oxley Act provides that if "misconduct" results in material noncompliance with SEC financial reporting requirements, and as a result of such noncompliance the company is required to restate its financial statements, then the CEO and CFO must disgorge both:

- Any bonuses or other incentive-based or equity-based compensation that he or she received during the 12-month period following the first public issuance or filing (whichever is earlier) of a financial document embodying such financial reporting requirement.
- Profits on the sale of company securities during such 12-month period.

While Section 304 has not yet received as much publicity as some of the other executive compensation provisions of the Sarbanes-Oxley Act (such as the prohibition of loans to insiders and the shortened Section 16 reporting rules), public companies should take special notice of the breadth of its potential application and its required penalties.

Events Triggering Disgorgement

Section 304's disgorgement requirement is triggered when a public company is required to prepare an accounting restatement due to material noncompliance with SEC financial reporting requirements as a result of misconduct. Unfortunately, Section 304 does not define several key terms critical to the application of this provision. While the Sarbanes-Oxley Act grants the SEC authority to adopt exemptions from Section 304 for certain persons, it does not require the SEC to adopt regulations that implement or interpret Section 304. Thus, it is not clear when or whether the SEC will provide interpretive guidance on the scope of these terms.

Key Terms Lack Definition

As with many other areas, it is impossible to know with certainty how this provision of the Sarbanes-Oxley Act will be applied. Among the terms that lack definition are:

- *Required.* First, the circumstances under which a company will be deemed to have been *required* to prepare an accounting restatement are unclear. For example, a restatement might be prepared voluntarily upon the advice of a new accounting firm, or pursuant to comments and suggestions from the SEC in connection with a securities offering. In many cases, the decision whether to prepare a restatement may be a judgment call by the company, driven by the interpretation of accounting principles, rather than any mandate or clear-cut requirement. Until the SEC provides guidance, it may be reasonable to assume that a restatement is *required* when the company's accounting firm cannot complete its interim review or deliver its audit opinion unless the restatement is made.
- *Misconduct.* Whatever the source of the "requirement" that financial statements be restated, Section 304's disgorgement provisions only apply when the require-

ment to restate arises from *misconduct* that results in material noncompliance with SEC financial reporting requirements. The Sarbanes-Oxley Act does not define "misconduct" or describe the necessary link between the misconduct and the restatement requirement. While Section 304's disgorgement provisions apply only to CEOs and CFOs, there is no specific requirement that such officers be the actual source of the misconduct. However, it is consistent with the general theme of the Sarbanes-Oxley Act that the ultimate responsibility for the integrity of a company's financial reporting rests with the CEO and the CFO.

• *Result.* Presumably the determination of whether a financial restatement was required *as a result of* misconduct would be a matter of proof in an enforcement action, much as causation is a required element of an action based on negligence. The Sarbanes-Oxley Act does not assign a presumption of causation.

Compensation to Be Disgorged

Disgorgement under Section 304 applies to any bonus or other incentive-based or equity-based compensation received by the CEO or CFO from the issuer during the 12 months following the first public issuance or filing of the tainted financial document. It is not clear whether this includes compensation received from affiliates of the issuer. It also is not clear whether the issuance of an earnings press release, for example, would start the 12-month clock running. While an earnings press release is not itself subject to financial reporting requirements, it typically contains selected information that will subsequently be included in a financial document embodying a financial reporting requirement, such as Form 10-Q or 10-K. Just as the events that trigger the disgorgement obligations are ill-defined, several key terms relating to what must be disgorged are also open to question. For example:

• *Received.* It is unclear what compensation will be deemed to have been *received* by the executives during the applicable 12-month period. Certainly, cash bonuses paid during the period would be "received" and subject to disgorgement. However, awards subject to multiyear vesting could be deemed "received" either upon grant or upon vesting or upon exercise or settlement. It is possible that the SEC or the courts could take the position, for example, that options *granted* during the 12-month period are tainted, and any profits obtained upon their future exercise must be disgorged, even if the exercise occurred outside the 12-month period. It is also unclear how the "receipt" requirement would be applied to cash bonuses or other awards accrued during the 12-month period but paid or payable on a later date under a deferral arrangement.

• *Profits.* Section 304 requires disgorgement of profits from the executive's sale of company equity securities during the 12-month period. However, in order to calculate profit from the sale of securities, it is necessary to compare the sale price to a purchase price of a matching acquisition. Section 304 gives no guidance as to the time period for the matching acquisition. Note that unlike Section 306(a) of the Sarbanes-Oxley Act relating to insider trading during pension fund blackout periods (as discussed earlier), the securities related to a possible disgorgement under Section 304 are not limited to securities acquired by the executive in connection with the performance of service to the company. It also is unclear whether avoidance-of-loss principles will apply (as in Section 16 short-swing profit rules) such that a matching acquisition may either precede or follow the sale to produce a recoverable profit.

Salary Is Not at Risk

The compensation that must be reimbursed is limited to bonuses or other incentive-based or equity-based compensation. Therefore, Section 304 may have the anomalous consequence of encouraging CEOs and CFOs to insist that a greater percentage of their pay be in the form of salary. This cuts against recent corporate governance initiatives to create more of a link between executive compensation and performance.

Enforcement

Unlike the disgorgement provisions of Section 306(a) of the Sarbanes-Oxley Act and Section 16(b) of the Exchange Act, there are no enforcement procedures set forth in Section 304. It is unclear whether enforcement will be limited to SEC action or whether Section 304 is intended to create a new private right of action.

Section 306(a): Insider Trades during Pension Fund Blackout Periods—Disgorgement of Profits

See the section "Special Rules Affecting Insider Trading" in this chapter for a discussion of this provision of the Sarbanes-Oxley Act.

Chapter 7

Tax, ERISA and Labor Laws, Regulations, and Rules

This chapter provides general overview of the applicable laws, rules, regulations, and other legal or rule-making authority with respect to tax, ERISA, and labor issues with which compensation committee members will need to be familiar. It does not present all rules and issues that compensation committees will face, but those common issues that arise when dealing with executive employment and compensation arrangements.

TAX LAW AND REGULATION

Overview

This section provides a fundamental working knowledge of the relevant U.S. federal tax laws and regulations that most compensation committees will encounter in discharging their committee duties. However, compensation committee members will need to recognize that tax issues generally arise under the following tax regimes:

- U.S. federal tax law
- State tax law
- Local tax law
- International tax laws

Of course, most tax issues presented to compensation committees concern U.S. federal tax law, but other taxing authorities also need to be taken into account. Thus, in many cases it will be necessary for compensation committees to consult their tax advisors for all tax effects (and in some cases, appropriate local counsel). Basically, the issues encountered by compensation committee members generally concern the following questions:

- Will the payment or benefit be deductible by the company?
- Will the payment be treated as ordinary income or as capital gain?
- What are the company's withholding and FICA obligations?
- If the payment is deferred, is there constructive receipt?
- Is there a tax penalty, and if so, what could it be?
- Will the arrangement impact an executive's estate planning?

As mentioned previously, in most cases, compensation committees surely will need to engage tax counsel to help analyze and work through these issues.

Organizations Responsible for Federal Tax

First and foremost, Congress is responsible for the laws of the Internal Revenue Code (IRC or Code). Legislative history with respect to the enactment of the various sections of the IRC may become relevant. Indeed, language and concepts from the legislative history very often become part of the administrative regulations promulgated under the statute.

The Treasury Department is responsible for the promulgation of the regulations interpreting the tax law. These regulations generally are first proposed—and sometimes amended (Proposed Regulations). Then, after notice and comment, the Proposed Regulations are reissued as final regulations (Regulations). In some cases, the Treasury Department may issue temporary regulations to address transition issues or those that require immediate guidance.

The Internal Revenue Service (IRS or Service) usually is the author of or main contributor to the Regulations. The IRS, however, has its own set of guidance and standards that shows the IRS's position with respect to certain issues. The IRS issues Revenue Rulings that generally address a specific issue or set of issues and which are applicable to all taxpayers. Similarly, the IRS may issue a Revenue Procedure that is also applicable to all taxpayers but explains the IRS's position by "process," not through "ruling." In some cases, there is a fine line substantively between Revenue Rulings and Revenue Procedures, as both have the effect of influencing taxpayer behavior. The IRS also issues Private Letter Rulings (PLRs) that address a specific set of facts with respect to a specific taxpayer who has requested such a ruling; while PLRs have no precedential power, they are helpful in gauging the IRS's thinking. Similar to PLRs are Technical Advice Memoranda (TAMs) that typically are written by IRS national officials to IRS field agents. As with PLRs, they are limited to their specific issues and facts and have no precedential power. As part of the IRS's examinations of specific issues, the IRS's General Counsel may issue General Counsel Memoranda (GCMs) analyzing the legal issues in detail.

Finally, U.S. tax law ultimately is decided by U.S. federal courts. Most cases are first litigated in U.S. Tax Court, which is a national court system resolving only tax law cases. Most disputes are first brought to Tax Court because the taxpayer is not obligated to pay the disputed amount. If, however, the taxpayer is willing to pay the disputed amount before trial, then the case may be brought to a U.S. District Court (presumably, the taxpayer has decided that this court would be better for the taxpayer than Tax Court). A decision rendered in either the Tax Court and the District Court may be appealed to the applicable U.S. Circuit Court of Appeals. A decision rendered in a Circuit Court may be appealed to the U.S. Supreme Court. A decision by the U.S. Supreme Court is, of course, final and nonappealable.

Relevant Tax Code Sections

The following sections of the U.S. federal tax code are the most relevant to compensation committee members:

- 55-59
- 61
- 83
- 101(a)
- 105(h)
- 132
- 162(a)
- 162(m)
- 280G and 4999
- 401 and 402
- 404
- 415
- 421-424
- 451
- 1032
- 2001, 2501, 2601
- 3101
- 3401
- 7702 and 7702A
- 7872

Again, as stated earlier, the preceding list is not exhaustive, so compensation committees may be faced with issues arising from other sections of the tax code.

IRC Sections 55–59: Alternative Minimum Tax

IRC Sections 55 through 59 contain the laws on the alternative minimum tax (AMT). Congress originally created the AMT in the Tax Reform Act of 1986 to ensure that wealthy taxpayers pay some tax. This is accomplished by eliminating many of the deductions that may be taken by individuals under the "standard" income tax calculation process and by including other "income" that would otherwise not be subject to income tax. Of particular importance to executives is Section 56(b)(3), which requires that compensation attributable to the exercise of incentive stock options (see IRC Section 421-424) be included as income under AMT; otherwise, these options are not normally taxed until the underlying stock is sold.

IRC Section 61: Taxation of Split-Dollar Life Insurance, Other

Section 61 generally defines "gross income," which includes "compensation for services, including fees, commissions, fringe benefits, and similar items." Thus, it contains some rules applicable to what (and how) certain executive compensation is taxed (e.g., personal use of corporate-owned or corporate-provided aircraft). In addition, recently released Regulations under Section 61 provide one of the two tax treatments applied to split-dollar life insurance arrangements (the other treatment is found under Section 7872). Section 61 treatment is applied to split-dollar life insurance arrangements where the company (not the executive or his or her trust) is the owner of the policy. This generally is known as the "economic benefit" treatment. Under this treatment, the value of one-year term life insurance is deemed the economic benefit under the split-dollar life insurance arrangement, and the value of such insurance, based on either the actual cost of the term life insurance or the rates contained in a table issued by the IRS, is included in an employee's annual compensation. In addition, any other "economic benefit" (such as policy dividends paid to the executive or increases in the policy's cash value over the amount required to be paid back to the company) is also included in an employee's annual compensation and subject to tax.

IRC Section 83: Taxation of Property Transferred in Connection with the Performance of Services

When property (e.g., stock) is transferred to an employee in connection with the performance of services, Section 83 is the Code section containing rules as to how and when the compensation will be taxed. Section 83 was enacted in 1969. The Regulations were released in 1976.

Section 83(a) generally provides that property transferred in connection with the performance of services will be taxed at the first time such property is transferable or is no longer subject to a substantial risk of forfeiture. The amount to be taxed is the fair market value (FMV) of the property at such time, less any amount paid for the property by the employee or other service provider.

Section 83(b) provides an "election" to have the FMV of the property subject to the transfer taxed at the time of transfer, even if the property is still subject to restrictions on transfer and/or a substantial risk of forfeiture. This election "closes out" the compensatory element to the transfer. Future appreciation in the FMV of the property (if any) would then be taxed as capital gain. This election, of course, requires the employee or other service provider to pay taxes before the compensation associated with the transferred property is paid. It should be noted that these paid taxes would not be recoverable if the property depreciates.

Section 83(e) generally provides that options that have a "readily ascertainable FMV" will be treated as property under Section 83, and options that do not have a "readily ascertainable FMV" will not be treated as property under Section 83. A "readily ascertainable FMV" is not defined by the Code, but it is defined (to some extent) by the Regulations. It means that the option is actively traded on an established exchange, or that the option can be valued based on a list of factors. At the moment, compensatory options generally do not have a "readily ascertainable FMV" on the date of grant. Thus, most compensatory options are not covered by Section 83 on the date of grant. However, the Regulations provide that an option without a readily ascertainable FMV on the date of grant will be taxed under Section 83 when the option is exercised or otherwise disposed of in an arm's-length transaction. The value to be taxed will be the FMV as determined under Section 83 methodology; in other words, the spread in the option, or if the option is sold, then the sale price.

Section 83(h) generally provides that a company may take a corresponding deduction for the value of the property transferred when the employee or other service provider is taxed on the compensation. However, the company must file a Form W-2 or Form 1099, as applicable, to qualify for the deduction.

The Regulations provide that dividends or other income paid with respect to stock that has not yet been taxed under Section 83 will be treated as first being paid to the company and then paid by the company to the employee or other service provider as compensation. The Regulations also provide that if a shareholder transfers property to an employee or other service provider in connection with the performance of services, it will be treated as first being a transfer from the shareholder to the company, and then transferred from the company to the employee or other service provider. The Regulations also provide definitions and examples of what is meant by the terms "transfer," "property," "fair market value," and "substantial risk of forfeiture."

IRC Section 101(a): Life Insurance Death Benefits

Section 101(a) generally provides that life insurance death benefits are not taxable to the recipient of such benefits. But it also provides that a life insurance policy that is transferred for valuable consideration, whether by assignment or otherwise, will have some or all of the death benefits taxed. However, this will not apply if the transfer is to the insured, to a partner of the insured, to a partnership in which the insured is a partner, or to a corporation in which the insured is a shareholder or officer.

IRC Section 105(h): Executive Medical Benefits

Section 105(h) imposes income tax on certain highly compensated employees who participate in a self-insured medical expense reimbursement plan that violates the discrimination rules contained in Section 105(h).

IRC Section 132: Certain Fringe Benefits

Section 132 contains the rules regarding whether certain fringe benefits (generally certain travel and security-related perquisites) will be included in the employee's gross income.

IRC Section 162(a): Reasonable Compensation

Section 162(a) provides that there is a deduction for all ordinary and necessary business expenses, including a "reasonable allowance for salaries or other compensation for personal services actually rendered." The Regulations provide, among other things, that "the test of deductibility in the case of compensation payments is whether they are reasonable and are in fact payments purely for services." This creates what is now known as the "amount" test where the question to be answered is whether the amount of the compensation is reasonable (i.e., not excessive), and the "intent" test where the question to be answered is whether the parties intended that the payments be compensation for actual services.

While Section 162(a) has been the subject of much litigation, IRS challenges have been confined to compensation at private companies, not public companies. Presumably, the IRS believes there are enough checks and balances at public companies to prevent the payment of excessive compensation (both now and even before the enactment of Section 162(m), discussed later in this section). However, there may come a time when the IRS, for whatever reason, might challenge the reasonableness of compensation paid to executives at a public company, and compensation committee members of public companies should be aware of this possibility no matter how remote.

Compensation committee members of private companies, however, need to be acutely aware of Section 162(a) and the various "issues" associated with it:

• Disguised dividends (i.e., payment of compensation that otherwise should have been paid as dividends)

- Phantom income (i.e., payment of compensation that in substance should be treated as a gift)
- Contingent compensation arrangements (i.e., payment of compensation based on questionable contingencies the nonpayment of which might otherwise increase a company's taxable earnings)

Most disputes involve the application of the amount test—not the intent test—since the amount test is an objective test and the intent test generally is regarded as a subjective test. Moreover, most disputes almost always involve cash compensation, not stock-based compensation, but there may come a time when stock-based compensation at private companies similarly will be examined.

Courts have developed various approaches for testing reasonable compensation based on a myriad of factors. For example, there is a "5-factor" test (9th Circuit in the *Elliotts, Inc. v. Commissioner* case), a "7-factor" test (7th Circuit in the *Edwin's, Inc. v. Commissioner* case), a "9-factor" test (6th Circuit in the *Mayson Manufacturing Company v. Commissioner* case), and even a "21-factor" test (Tax Court in the *Foos v. Commissioner* case). Some of the factors usually considered by courts are:

- Employee's qualifications
- Nature, extent, and scope of employee's work
- Employee's work and salary scale
- Prevailing rates of compensation in the industry
- Size and complexity of the business
- Ratio of compensation to income of the business
- Contingent nature of the salary agreement
- General economic conditions
- Compensation paid in prior years
- Date of determination of the compensation
- Existence of action by the board of directors
- Comparison of compensation with distributions to shareholders
- Whether compensation is paid in proportion to the stock interest of employees of closely held corporations
- Time contributed to the business

Note that generally no one factor is controlling. The IRS has developed its own "12-factor" test, which was published in a former version of the Internal Revenue Manual (IRM) at 4233.232.2(3):

1. Nature of duties
2. Background and experience
3. Knowledge of the business
4. Size of the business
5. Individual's contribution to profit making
6. Time devoted
7. Economic conditions in general and locally
8. Character and amount of responsibility
9. Time of year when compensation is determined
10. Relationship of stockholder-officer's compensation to stockholdings
11. Whether alleged compensation is in reality—in whole or in part—payment for a business or assets acquired
12. The amount paid by similar size businesses in the same area to equally qualified employees for similar services

This "12-factor" test apparently has been amplified and/or replaced as of May 1999 by new IRM 4.3.1.5–2.5.2.2, which list eight steps to test the reasonableness of officers' salaries in the context of partnerships and S corporations:

1. Determine total compensation paid or accrued to principal officers
2. Determine if and to what extent each principal officer's compensation is unreasonable
3. The examiner should take into account the "IRS 12-factor" test
4. Be alert to closely held multiple corporate situations
5. Determine that accruals payable to controlling shareholders are paid within the prescribed limit
6. Determine if executives have received substantial bonuses under the guise that the proceeds would be used by the recipient to make significant political contributions
7. Be aware of excessive compensation to S corporation officer/shareholders with respect to IRC Section 1375
8. Be aware of inadequate salaries paid to officer/shareholders who receive substantial nontaxable distributions

Current judicial trend has been to apply an "independent investor" test. This test generally examines whether an independent investor would approve the compensation paid, based on the actual return on equity and taking into account all the facts and circumstances. Thus, this test for excessive compensation is whether the compensation would unacceptably decrease the corporation's rate of return on equity for a substantial independent shareholder who is not actively engaged in the business. The proper base against which the rate of return is often measured is the initial investment in the corporation plus any additional capital contributions and any appreciation in the value of the stock. In using the independent investor test, many courts have thus rejected the "automatic dividend" theory; however, lack of payment of dividends may arouse IRS and judicial scrutiny. Courts are mixed as to how much weight to assign to the independent investor test.

Finally, as stated previously, public company compensation committees most likely will not be faced with a Section 162(a) issue. However, a recent Tax Court case (*Square D Company v. Commissioner*) applied Section 162(a) principles to an analysis of whether golden parachute payments under Section 280G (discussed later in this section) qualified as reasonable compensation.

IRC Section 162(m): The $1 Million Cap on Executive Compensation

In response to criticism involving what was perceived as excessive executive compensation in the early 1990s, Congress enacted Section 162(m) to "cap" the amount of compensation that could be deducted by a public company paid to its top five executives. Section 162(m) was enacted in 1993. The Proposed Regulations were released in 1993, and the Regulations were released in 1995.

Terminology used in the application of Section 162(m) includes:

- Publicly held corporation
- Applicable employee remuneration
- Covered employee
- Performance-based compensation
- Outside director

For whatever reason, the drafters of Section 162(m) repeatedly chose to use the word *remuneration* instead of the word *compensation*; however, for all intents and purposes, they are synonymous, and the statute's use of the word *remuneration* should not be a distraction.

Section 162(m)(1) provides that in the case of any "publicly held corporation," no deduction will be allowed for "applicable employee remuneration" with respect to any "covered employee" to the extent that the amount of such remuneration for the taxable year with respect to such employee exceeds $1 million. The $1 million cap is not indexed. Thus, due to inflation, the cap effectively is reduced every year and most likely becomes applicable to more executives.

Section 162(m)(2) defines "publicly held corporation" as any corporation issuing any class of equity securities required to be registered under Section 12 of the Securities Exchange Act of 1934 (Exchange Act). A corporation is not considered publicly held if the registration of its securities is voluntary. Determination is based solely on whether, as of the last day of the corporation's taxable year, it is subject to the reporting obligations of Section 12 of the Exchange Act.

Section 162(m)(3) defines "covered employee" as any employee of the corporation who, as of the close of the taxable year, is the CEO of the corporation (or an individual acting in such capacity), or whose total compensation for the taxable year is required to be reported to shareholders under the Exchange Act by reason of such employee being among the four highest compensated officers for the taxable year (other than the CEO). Thus, covered employees generally are the "named executive officers" listed in the Summary Compensation Table found in a company's annual proxy statement or Form 10-K. Additionally, it is interesting to note that termination of employment of an employee immediately before the close of the taxable year results in that employee not being treated as a covered employee. Thus, for example, a company might want an executive who is a covered employee and who plans to retire at the end of the company's tax year to instead retire immediately before the close of the company's tax year.

Section 162(m)(4) provides that "applicable employee remuneration" means—with respect to any covered employee—the aggregate amount allowable as a deduction under the IRC for such taxable year (determined without regard to Section 162(m)) for remuneration for services performed by such employee (whether or not during the tax year). "Remuneration" generally means cash and property. Excluded from the definition of "applicable employee remuneration" are:

- Commissions based on individual performance
- Any payment referred to in IRC Section 3121(a)(5)(A) through IRC Section 3121(a)(5)(D) (which generally relates to payments from qualified pension plans)
- Any benefit provided to or for the benefit of an employee if at the time such benefit is provided it is reasonable to believe that the employee will be able to exclude such benefit from his or her gross income
- "Performance-based compensation"

Section 162(m)(4)(C) provides the rules relating to "performance-based compensation." It means remuneration payable solely on account of the attainment of one or more performance goals, but only if:

- The performance goals are determined by a compensation committee of the board of directors of the corporation, which is comprised solely of two or more "outside directors."
- The material terms under which the remuneration is to be paid, including the performance goals, are disclosed to shareholders and approved by a majority of the vote in a separate shareholder vote before the payment of such remuneration.
- Before any payment of such remuneration, the compensation committee certifies that the performance goals and any other material terms were in fact satisfied.

Thus, it is a three-step test for compensation to qualify as performance-based. First, compensation committee members must satisfy the "outside director" requirement. The term "outside director" is not defined by Section 162(m), but is defined in the Regulations. A director qualifies as an outside director if:

- He or she is not a current employee of the corporation.
- If he or she is a former employee of the corporation, he or she is not receiving compensation for prior services (other than benefits under a tax-qualified retirement plan) during the taxable year.
- He or she has never been an officer of the corporation.
- He or she does not receive remuneration from the corporation, either directly or indirectly, in any capacity other than as a director.

"Remuneration received" includes remuneration paid:

- Directly or indirectly to a director personally or to an entity in which the director has a more than 50% beneficial ownership interest
- To an entity in which the director has a 5% to 50% beneficial ownership interest (other than *de minimis* remuneration)
- To an entity by which the director is employed or self-employed other than as a director (other than *de minimis* remuneration)

"*De minimis* remuneration" is defined as remuneration received by the entity that is less than 5% of the gross revenue of such entity, so long as the remuneration received does not exceed $60,000 if paid (i) to an entity that the director has a 5% to 50% beneficial ownership interest or, (ii) for personal services if the director is employed or self-employed by the entity.

Second, performance goals must be both "preestablished" and "objective." Goals are "preestablished" if they are established in writing by the compensation committee not later than 90 days after the performance period begins or within the first 25% of the performance period if such period is shorter than one year. The outcome must be substantially uncertain at the time the goal is established. Goals are "objective" if a third party having knowledge of the relevant facts could determine whether the goal is met. Increasing the amount of compensation over the compensation levels set by the preestablished performance goals (usually referred to as "positive discretion") is not permitted. However, a compensation committee may unilaterally reduce, with or without reason, the amount of compensation below the compensation levels set by the preestablished performance goals (usually referred to as "negative discretion"), assuming this can be done under the terms and conditions of the arrangement. Acceleration of payment must be discounted to reasonably reflect the time value of money. Restricted stock that vests based solely on service will not qualify as performance-based compensation. Stock options and stock appreciation rights that are granted with an exercise price at or above current stock FMV on the date of grant generally will qualify as performance-based compensation.

Third, shareholder approval is valid only if the following material terms are disclosed as part of the voting process:

- Those employees who are eligible to receive compensation
- A description of the business criteria on which the performance goal is based
- The maximum amount of compensation that can be paid to any employee
- Any other material terms of a performance goal as required under the same standards applicable under the Exchange Act

If the compensation committee can change the targets under a performance goal, shareholder reapproval is required every five years. Since most plans today have a menu of performance metrics (e.g., earnings, revenue growth, stock price, total shareholder return, return on assets, return on equity, etc.), compensation committees need to ensure that the plans they administer are reapproved by shareholders every five years.

Finally, the compensation committee must make sure that it certifies in writing that the performance goals (and all other material terms and conditions) were met.

The Regulations provide an exemption for privately held companies that become publicly held companies. In such a situation, compensation paid by a publicly held corporation pursuant to a compensation plan or agreement that existed during the period in which the corporation was not publicly held is exempt from Section 162(m). However, if the privately held corporation becomes publicly held through an IPO, then the previous exemption applies only if the prospectus accompanying the IPO discloses information concerning those plans or arrangements that satisfy all applicable securities laws then in effect. The exemption applies until the earliest of the following four occurrences:

- The expiration of the plan or agreement
- A material modification of the plan or agreement (a material modification occurs when the plan or agreement is amended to increase the amount of compensation payable to the employee)
- The issuance of all employer stock and other compensation that has been allocated under the plan
- The first meeting of shareholders at which directors are to be elected that occurs after the close of the third calendar year following the calendar year in which the

IPO occurs, or in the case of a privately held corporation that becomes publicly held without an IPO, the first calendar year following the calendar year in which the corporation becomes publicly held

There are two methods to qualify compensation as performance-based compensation for corporations created by a spin-off transaction. Under a "prior establishment and approval" method, where the compensation qualified as performance-based compensation prior to the spin-off date, the compensation remains qualified if the compensation committee (comprised of two or more outside directors) of the spin-off company certifies that the performance goals have been met. Under a "transition period exemption" method, where all requisite elements of performance-based compensation are met other than the shareholder-approval requirement, the compensation will be qualified until the first regularly scheduled meeting of the spin-off's shareholders that occurs more than 12 months after the date the corporation becomes a publicly held corporation.

The $1 million cap is reduced by the amount (if any) that would have been included in the compensation of the covered employee for the taxable year but, because of the golden parachute tax rules, was disallowed as an excess parachute payment under IRC Section 280G (discussed next).

Example: Executive X receives $1,500,000, of which none is exempt from Section 162(m). Of the $1,500,000, $600,000 is an excess parachute payment (and thus the $600,000 becomes nondeductible under Section 280G). Thus, the corporation can deduct only $400,000 ($1,000,000 minus the already nondeductible $600,000) of the $1,500,000 payment.

IRC Sections 280G and 4999: Golden Parachutes

In the early 1980s, there was public outcry regarding some very large (at the time) golden parachutes made to certain executives. Accordingly, this public outcry was translated into tax law that generally eliminated a tax deduction for a company that paid golden parachutes and applied a 20% penalty tax on the executive who received a golden parachute. Sections 280G and 4999 were enacted in 1984. The Proposed Regulations were first released in 1989, and then "reproposed" in 2002. The Regulations were released in 2003. It is important to note that unlike IRC Section 162(m), Section 280G applies to both public and private corporations.

The term *golden parachutes* generally refers to either severance-related payments or transaction-bonus payments made to executives, usually—but not necessarily—contingent on or in connection with a change in control of the company. The Regulations provide that a payment is treated as being contingent on a change in control if the payment would not, in fact, have been made had no change in control occurred, even if the payment is also conditioned on the occurrence of another event. Additionally, a payment generally is treated as one that would not, in fact, have been made in the absence of the change in control unless it was substantially certain, at the time of the change, that the payment would have been made whether or not the change occurred.

The key definitions and terms used in applying Sections 280G and 499 are:

- Parachute payments
- Excess parachute payments
- Base amount
- Base period
- Disqualified individual
- Annual includible compensation for the base period
- Reasonable compensation
- Change in control or ownership
- Safe harbor amount (Note that while this is not a term used under Section 280G, it is a term used by most practitioners in the golden parachute area, and thus is included.)

Section 280G(a) provides that a company will lose a tax deduction for all "excess parachute payments." Section 280G(b)(1) defines an "excess parachute payment" as an amount equal to the excess of any "parachute payment" over the portion of the "base amount" allocated to such payment. Section 4999 imposes a 20% excise (penalty) tax on the recipient of any "excess parachute payment." Section 4999 also requires that a company must withhold in many cases an amount equal to the excise tax imposed.

Section 280G(b)(2) provides that a "parachute payment" is a payment in the nature of compensation to or for a "disqualified individual" if such payment is contingent on a "change in control or ownership" and the aggregate present value of the payments in the nature of compensation to or for the disqualified individual equals or exceeds 300% of the "base amount."

Section 280G does not define what a "change in control or ownership" is. The Regulations provide that a de facto change in control occurs if a person or group acquires either more than 50% of the voting stock of a corporation or one-third of the assets of the corporation. The Regulations presume that a change in control occurs if a person or group acquires 20% or more of a corporation's voting stock or if there is a change in the majority of directors of the corporation; however, this presumption may be rebutted by establishing that there has been no transfer of power to control the management and policies of the company.

Section 280G(b)(3) provides that the "base amount" is the "disqualified individual's annualized includible compensation for the base period." Section 280G(c) provides that a "disqualified individual" is an employee or independent contractor of the corporation, and who is also an officer, shareholder, or highly compensated individual of the company. The Regulations provide that a highly compensated individual is a "highly compensated employee" as defined by IRC Section 414(q) under the pension laws (which currently is an employee earning $90,000 a year or more). In addition, a disqualified individual only includes a shareholder who owns stock of a corporation with a fair market value that exceeds 1% of the fair market value of the outstanding shares of all classes of the corporation's stock. Section 280G(d)(1) provides that the "annualized includible compensation for the base period" is the average compensation that was payable by the corporation undergoing the change in control or ownership and was includible in the gross income of the disqualified individual for taxable years in the "base period." Section 280G(d)(2) provides that the "base period" is the period consisting of the most recent five taxable years ending before the date on which the change in control or ownership occurs. The Regulations provide that the base period may be less than five years if the disqualified individual did not work for the company for all five years.

Simply put, determining whether there is a loss of deduction and penalty tax under Sections 280G and 4999 is a two-step test. The first step is to test whether all payments that could be characterized as parachute payments equal or exceed 300% of the base amount. This is why many arrangements have come to use "299%" as the "magic" threshold level; however, sometimes in these arrangements this threshold level is erroneously applied to current compensation or current cash compensation and not—as it should be—to the base amount (which usually is less than the current annual compensation). Practitioners usually will determine this threshold, called the "safe harbor amount," as 300% of the base amount less $1. The second step is to test whether the parachute payments exceed the safe harbor amount (even by $1), and if they do, then all parachute payments above the base amount (i.e., everything over 100% of the base amount, not 300% of the base amount) are called "excess parachute payments." It is only the excess parachute payment that is used to calculate the lost tax deduction and penalty tax.

Finally, Section 280G(b)(4) provides that parachute payments do not include any payments that the taxpayer establishes by clear and convincing evidence are reasonable compensation for personal services, whether rendered before or after the change in control. Reasonable compensation rendered after the change in control is completely disregarded. However, reasonable compensation rendered before the change in control is included in the parachute calculations and then used to reduce the excess parachute payments after first being applied to the base amount.

Example 1:   CEO has a base amount of $1,000,000. Thus, the safe harbor amount is $2,999,999 ($1,000,000 × 300% − $1). There is a change in control and CEO receives $10 million as a transaction bonus. Assume none of the $10 million can be shown by clear and convincing evidence to be reasonable compensation. This is the only payment made in the nature of compensation and in connection with the change in control. The full $10 million is a parachute payment (because the payment exceeded the safe harbor amount of $2,999,999). $9 million is the excess parachute payment. The company loses $9 million as a tax deduction, and CEO must pay $1.8 million ($9,000,000 × 20%) as penalty tax.

Example 2:   Same as Example 1, but CEO receives $3 million as a transaction bonus. The full $3 million is a parachute payment (because the payment still exceeded the safe harbor amount of $2,999,999). $2 million is the excess parachute payment. The company loses $2 million as a tax deduction, and CEO must pay $400,000 as penalty tax.

Example 3:   Same as Example 2, but company and CEO agree that CEO will forego $1 of the $3 million payment. Thus, CEO receives $2,999,999 as a transaction bonus. The $2,999,999 payment is *not* a parachute payment since it did not exceed the safe harbor amount. Since the payment is not a parachute payment, there are no excess parachute payments, and thus no loss of deduction and no penalty tax.

The following shows the step-by-step process involved in applying the golden parachute rules:

1. Determine if a change in control or ownership has occurred under the Regulations. If not, then Section 280G does not apply and no further steps are required.
2. Identify all individuals who qualify as a disqualified individual.
3. Determine the base period for each disqualified individual.
4. Calculate the base amount for each disqualified individual.
5. Calculate the potential parachute payments that will be or have been made to each disqualified individual. This would include cash payments, stock-based compensation payments, accelerated payment of existing cash-based awards (e.g., retention programs), accelerated vesting of equity-based compensation, accelerated vesting/payment of deferred compensation, triggering of pension "enhancers" (e.g., additional years and service), continued welfare benefits, and so forth. These amounts are each present-valued as of the change-in-control date, and then totaled.
6. Test the total amount against the safe harbor amount. If the total amount does not exceed the safe harbor amount, then the payments are not parachute payments and no further steps are required. If the total amount exceeds the safe harbor amount, then determine whether the parachute payments and/or the excess parachute payments may be reduced by various techniques (such as treating some of the payments as reasonable compensation).

7. Calculate tax gross-up amounts for the penalty tax amounts (if required by agreement), or identify and calculate what amounts and actual payments will be reduced (if required by agreement).

Finally, while not a part of Section 280G per se, the following market practices regarding Section 280G are noted:

- Full reduction of parachute payments to the safe harbor amount
- Mandatory reduction only if the executive is in a better after-tax position from the reduction
- Full tax gross-up (i.e., reimbursement of the excise tax, and then continued reimbursement of all excise, income, employment, and other taxes resulting from payment of the reimbursements)
- Partial tax gross-up (e.g., the company pays only the first excise tax, not the resulting tax impositions due to the reimbursement of the first excise tax; or a "corridor" is established so that no tax gross-up is paid if the parachute payments do not exceed a specific percentage or dollar amount above the safe harbor amount; or the company agrees to pay a percentage of a full tax gross-up, such as 50%)
- Nothing (usually referred to as the "let the chips fall where they may" approach)

IRC Section 401 and 402: Qualified Pension Plans

Sections 401 and 402 generally contain many of the rules necessary to qualify a pension plan for special tax treatment. Section 401(a)(17) is the section that limits the amount of annual compensation taken into account for purposes of computing a pension benefit; for 2004, this amount is $205,000, and increased in $5,000 increments thereafter based on cost-of-living adjustments (COLA). Section 402(g) is the section that limits annual elective deferrals to certain pension plans (notably 401(k) plans); for 2004, this amount is $13,000, for 2005, this amount is $14,000, for 2006, this amount is $15,000, and this amount will be increased in $500 increments thereafter based on COLA.

IRC Section 404: Tax Deduction for Bonuses and Deferred Compensation

Section 404(a) provides the rules associated with when a company may take a deduction for contributions made under a stock bonus, pension, profit-sharing, or annuity plan. Under 404(a)(5), the general rule for most executive plans is that the company may take a deduction for the year relating to the year when the compensation is taken into income by the executive. Under the Regulations for Section 404(b), a bonus paid within 2½ months of the year for which it was earned will not be treated as deferred compensation, and will relate to the year in which it was earned for purposes of deductibility.

IRC Section 415: Limitations on Benefits from and Contributions to Pension Plans

Section 415(b) generally provides that annual benefits under a defined-benefit pension plan will be capped. For 2004, this amount is $165,000, and this amount will be increased in $5,000 increments thereafter based on COLA. Section 415(c) generally provides that annual contributions to a defined-contribution pension plan will be capped. For 2004, this amount is $41,000, and this amount will be increased in $1,000 increments thereafter based on COLA.

IRC Sections 421–424: Incentive Stock Options and Employee Stock Purchase Plans

Sections 421 through 424 provide the rules relating to "incentive stock options" (ISOs) and Employee Stock Purchase Plans (ESPPs).

Section 421 provides the general rule that if an award of stock or stock options qualifies as an ISO or an ESPP option under the applicable arrangement, then the taxable event will occur when the stock is sold, and the applicable tax rate will be the current long-term capital gain rate.

Section 422 provides the rules for ISOs. Generally, these rules are:

- Optionees must be employees of the company (or parent or subsidiary).
- The stock underlying the option must be held for at least more than two years from the date of grant *and* more than one year from the date of exercise.
- The option must be granted under a plan that was approved by shareholders within one year of the adoption of the plan.
- Options granted under the plan must be granted within 10 years of the earlier of the adoption of the plan or shareholder approval.
- The option term cannot exceed 10 years.
- The option must be nontransferable (other than by the laws of descent and distribution).
- The option must have an exercise price at or above the stock FMV on the date of grant.
- The option must have a post-employment exercise period not longer than 90 days (one year if termination is due to a disability as defined under IRC Section 22(e)).
- Only options with an aggregate value of up to $100,000 (based on the stock FMV on the date of grant) may become exercisable in any calendar year (options that vest and which exceed this $100,000 limit lose their qualification as ISOs).
- If the optionee owns more than 10% of the stock, then the exercise price must be at least 110% of the stock FMV and the option term cannot exceed five years.

Section 423 provides the rules for ESPPs. While the arrangement is referred to as a "purchase plan," it operates very much as an option arrangement, and the law refers to these vehicles as "options." Generally, the rules are:

- Optionees must be employees of the company (or parent or subsidiary) and cannot own 5% or more of the stock.
- All employees (with some exceptions) must be able to participate in the plan.
- The stock underlying the option must be held for at least more than two years from the date of grant *and* more than one year from the date of exercise.
- The option must be granted under a plan that was approved by shareholders within one year of the adoption of the plan.
- The option term cannot exceed five years.
- The option must be nontransferable (other than by the laws of descent and distribution).
- The option must have an exercise price at least equal to 85% of the stock FMV on the date of grant or the date of exercise.
- The option must have a post-employment exercise period not longer than 90 days (one year if termination is due to a disability as defined under IRC Section 22(e)).
- Only options with an aggregate value of up to $25,000 (based on the stock FMV on the date of grant) may be granted to any individual in any calendar year.

Section 424 provides a variety of rules applicable to ISOs and ESPPs. Section 424(a) and the Regulations provide that in the context of a corporate reorganization or liquidation, ISOs substituted or converted into options on a surviving company's stock (a "rollover") will continue to qualify as ISOs provided that the rollover passes the spread test and the ratio test, and that the optionee does not receive additional and/or more favorable benefits under the new ISO. The spread test is satisfied if the spread in the pre-rollover option equals the spread in the post-rollover option. The ratio test is satisfied if the ratio used to convert the pre-rollover ISO shares into post-rollover ISO shares is the inverse of the ratio used to convert the pre-rollover exercise price into the post-rollover exercise price. The additional/more favorable benefit test is a facts-and-circumstances test, but one example offered by the Regulations is that additional exercise methods (e.g., allowing a stock-for-stock exercise in addition to cash exercise) would be treated as an additional/more favorable benefit.

Section 424 also provides that an ISO that is modified, extended, or renewed results in the deemed new grant of an option. The concern here is that if there is existing spread in the option, the deemed new option will not qualify as an ISO since the exercise price was below stock FMV on the date of grant. However, accelerating the vesting date of an existing ISO will not result in a deemed new grant.

IRC Section 451: Constructive Receipt

Section 451 provides the general rules relating to what is known as "constructive receipt." The concept of constructive receipt is that a taxpayer may not turn his, her, or its back on taxable income (usually through a deferral arrangement) to avoid taxation. Thus, while the payment is not actually received by the taxpayer, it still is constructively received (and thus taxable).

Section 451(a) provides a basic rule that any item of gross income will be included in the gross income of the taxpayer for the taxable year in which it was received unless under the taxpayer's method of accounting used in computing taxable income such amount is properly accounted for as of a different period. It is the Regulations that essentially explain what is meant by constructive receipt. Regulation Section 1.451-2(a) provides that income, although not actually reduced to a taxpayer's possession, is constructively received by the taxpayer in the taxable year in which it is credited to the taxpayer's account, set apart for the taxpayer, or otherwise made available so that the taxpayer may either draw upon it at any time, or could have drawn upon it during the taxable year if notice of intention to withdraw had been given. However, income is not constructively received if the taxpayer's control of its receipt is subject to substantial limitations or restrictions. It is this concept of substantial limitation or restrictions upon which many deferred compensation arrangements build.

Section 132 of the Tax Reform Act of 1978 has prohibited the IRS from issuing Revenue Rulings in this area. Instead, the IRS has issued several Revenue Procedures to explain the minimum requirements it considers necessary in a deferred compensation arrangement before it will offer a favorable ruling through a Private Letter Ruling. Revenue Procedures 71-19 and 92-65 provide that:

- The election to defer compensation must be made before the beginning of the period of service for which the compensation is payable, regardless of the existence of forfeiture provisions in the plan.

- If any elections, other than the initial election referred to previously, may be made by an employee subsequent to the beginning of the service period, then the plan must set forth substantial forfeiture provisions that must remain in effect throughout the entire period of the deferral. A substantial forfeiture provision will not be considered to exist unless its conditions impose upon the employee a significant limitation or duty that will require a meaningful effort on the part of the employee to fulfill and there is a definite possibility that the event that will cause the forfeiture could occur.

- New plans may allow new participants 30 days after adoption of the plan to make elections with respect to compensation earned after such election.
- New participants to an existing plan may have 30 days after becoming a participant of the plan to make elections with respect to compensation earned after such election.
- The plan may allow for earlier payout in the event of an "unforeseeable emergency."
- The plan must provide that participants have the status of unsecured creditors.

In addition, since many deferred compensation arrangements were funded using a "rabbi trust" (called such because the first Private Letter Ruling to address whether this kind of trust resulted in constructive receipt concerned a trust created by a congregation for its rabbi), the IRS issued Revenue Procedure 92-64 at the same time it issued Revenue Procedure 92-65. This Revenue Procedure presented a "model rabbi trust" that needed to be followed if a taxpayer was requesting a Private Letter Ruling as to whether the trust caused constructive receipt. A rabbi trust generally is a "grantor trust" (within the meaning of IRC Sections 671–679) established by the company that holds company assets for payment of the deferred compensation benefit; however, if there is a bankruptcy or insolvency, the trustee must then hold the trust's assets for the benefit of the company's general unsecured creditors.

There are differing views with respect to whether the IRS's position on deferred compensation would be upheld by the courts. First is the issue of how far in advance the election to defer must be made. Most companies provide that salary deferral be made in the year before the salary is earned. Some companies, however, allow that bonus deferrals can be made just before the bonus is calculated and paid. Another example of a questionable technique is something called a "haircut," where the amount of deferred compensation will be reduced if the taxpayer elects an earlier payout. Some believe that a substantial haircut tracks the language of the Regulations since it results in a substantial limitation or restriction. For example, assume that Executive X has $1 million in a deferred compensation account, and can elect an earlier payout but will forfeit 10% (or $100,000) of the deferred amount. Not only is there no consensus on whether 10% (or even a smaller percentage) is enough to trigger the "substantial limitation or restriction" requirement, there is even a question as to whether at least $900,000 is constructively received. Another issue is whether an election once made may be changed (e.g., Executive X made a deferral election on 1/1/05 to defer $1 million until 1/1/15, and then on 1/1/10, Executive X changes the payout date to 1/1/14). Based on the Tax Court case of *Martin v. Commissioner*, there is a position that a change made at least a year before payout is permissible.

Finally, for several years, Congress has contemplated legislation that would repeal Section 132 of the Tax Reform Act of 1978 and enact specific rules with respect to deferred compensation. For example, the new legislation might: (i) tax deferred compensation protected by offshore rabbi trusts when the assets are moved offshore; (ii) require a minimum delay (e.g., six months) before an executive may receive his or her deferred compensation after a termination of employment; (iii) allow subsequent changes in distribution timing but only if the change defers receipt of the compensation for at least another five years; and (iv) require that distributions made within one year of a change in control be treated as "excess parachute payments" under IRC Section 280G. The proposed legislation also anticipates further rulemaking by the IRS. Accordingly, it is essential for compensation committees to consult tax counsel with regard to any aspect of deferred compensation planning.

IRC Section 1032: Exchange of Stock for Property

Section 1032 generally provides that no gain or loss is recognized by a corporation if the corporation receives cash or property in exchange for stock of the corporation. The Regulations issued in 2000 provide that there must be an "immediate transfer" of the stock and that it cannot be held for any period of time. This rule impacts transfers of company stock to subsidiaries through the use of rabbi trusts.

IRC Sections 2001 et seq., 2501 et seq., and 2601 et seq.: Gift and Estate Planning

While an executive's personal estate planning generally is not an area of concern for the compensation committee, there may be instances where the design of a compensation program is affected by the executive's estate plan. In many cases, this will involve transfers of life insurance, options or other equity-based compensation, or deferred compensation to family trusts or other similar entities. The issue for most compensation committees will be whether the company is negatively impacted by structuring a certain program a certain way for the benefit of the executive.

Generally, compensation committees should be aware of the sections of the tax code that relate to estate-planning issues. Sections 2001 through 2210 provide the rules with respect to federal estate tax. Sections 2501 through 2524 provide the rules with respect to gift tax. Sections 2601 through 2664 provide the rules for generation-skipping transfers. Finally, Sections 2701 through 2704 provide special valuation rules.

IRC Sections 3101 et seq.: FICA Tax

Sections 3101 through 3128 contain the rules relating to the tax imposed under the Federal Insurance Contributions Act (i.e., Social Security and Medicare taxes). Of note is Section 3121, which generally defines "wages." In addition, Section 3121(v) provides that deferred compensation generally will be subject to FICA tax at the later of when the services are performed or when there is no substantial risk of forfeiture of the rights to such amount. Finally, it is noted that there is still an issue whether compensation attributable to ISOs or ESPPs (in whole or in part) should be treated as "wages" and subject to FICA tax.

IRC Sections 3401 et seq.: Withholding

Sections 3401 through 3406 contain the rules relating to the company's obligation to withhold on wages. Of note is Section 3401(a), which generally defines "wages." This definition is very close but not identical to the definition of "wages" under FICA. In addition, it is noted that there is still an issue whether compensation attributable to ISOs or ESPPs (in whole or in part) should be treated as "wages" and subject to withholding.

IRC Sections 7702 and 7702A: Definition of Life Insurance

Section 7702 provides the definition of a life insurance contract, and requires that the contract pass either a "cash value accumulation" test, or meet a guideline premium requirement and fall within the "cash value corridor." Section 7702A generally provides that a life insurance contract will fail to be treated as a life insurance contract—and instead will be treated as a "modified endowment contract"—if it fails to pass the "seven-pay test," which generally measures how much of the investment is used to buy life insurance. A modified endowment contract does not receive the tax advantages that a life insurance contract receives.

IRC Section 7872: Below-Market Loans and Split-Dollar

Section 7872 was enacted under the Tax Reform Act of 1986, generally to address interest-free loans. In the employer-employee context, Section 7872 requires that an interest-free loan or even a below-market loan be treated as compensation. The amount of "imputed" compensation is the amount of interest that the employee would otherwise have had to pay if the loan had an interest rate equal to the "applicable federal rate," which is an interest rate published monthly by the IRS. Section 7872 does differentiate between "term" loans and "demand" loans, and does provide a *de minimis* exemption of $10,000 for employer-employee loans.

Recent Regulations have applied Section 7872 to split-dollar life insurance arrangements where the owner of the policy is the executive (or a related trust). In this situation, the amount of the premium paid by the company is treated as an interest-free loan to the executive. This new Regulation has dramatically altered market practices with respect to using this kind of split-dollar life insurance (usually called "equity split dollar"), and companies will need to determine whether applying Section 7872 is cost-effective and does not violate the federal securities law prohibiting a company from making personal loans to executives.

ERISA LAW AND RULES

Overview

The Employee Retirement Income Security Act of 1974 ("ERISA") was Congress's attempt at federalizing pension law in the United States. It accomplished this by creating a comprehensive set of laws relating to pensions and other employee benefit arrangements, and by creating a "preemption" law that caused ERISA to override most other laws.

While ERISA generally applies to broad-based rank-and-file benefit plans, there are aspects of the law that compensation committee members will need to know. Essentially, the issue usually involves whether the executive arrangement is subject to ERISA, or whether it is exempt (in whole or in part) from ERISA. Thus, the definitions of the following terms are critical to the analysis:

- Employee benefit plan.
- Pension-benefit plan.
- Welfare-benefit plan.
- Excess benefit plan.
- Top-hat plan.

In addition, most executive plans are concerned only with the first five "Parts" under Subtitle B of Title I of ERISA:

- Part 1, dealing with disclosure and reporting.
- Part 2, dealing with participation and vesting.
- Part 3, dealing with funding requirements.
- Part 4, dealing with fiduciary responsibility.
- Part 5, dealing with administration and enforcement.

ERISA Section 3(3) defines "employee benefit plan" or "plan" as an employee welfare benefit plan, or an employee pension benefit plan, or a plan that is both an employee welfare benefit plan and an employee pension benefit plan.

ERISA Section 3(1) defines "employee welfare benefit plan" and "welfare plan" as any plan, fund, or program that was heretofore or is hereafter established or maintained by an employer or by an employee organization, or by both, to the extent that such plan, fund, or program was established or is maintained for the purpose of providing for its participants or their beneficiaries, through the purchase of insurance or otherwise, (A) medical, surgical, or hospital care or benefits, or benefits in the event of sickness, accident, disability, death, or unemployment, or vacation benefits, apprenticeship or other training programs, or day care centers, scholarship funds, or prepaid legal services, or (B) any benefit described in section 186(c) of this title (other than pensions on retirement or death, and insurance to provide such pensions).

ERISA Section 3(2) defines "employee pension benefit plan" and "pension plan" as any plan, fund, or program that was heretofore or is hereafter established or maintained by an employer or by an employee organization, or by both, to the extent that by its express terms or as a result of surrounding circumstances, such plan, fund, or program provides retirement income to employees, or results in a deferral of income by employees for periods extending to the termination of covered employment or beyond, regardless of the method of calculating the contributions made to the plan, the method of calculating the benefits under the plan, or the method of distributing benefits from the plan.

The preceding three definitions are a starting point for any ERISA analysis, because in some cases, a compensation arrangement (such as an equity-based plan), either by its own terms or operationally, may fall within the definition of an ERISA employee benefit plan. Moreover, an executive severance plan will need to be analyzed as to whether it properly is characterized as a pension plan or as a welfare plan. In addition, there is case law that defines what is meant by the word *plan*; thus, some arrangements may be outside of ERISA because they do not rise to the level of an ERISA plan. Finally, all plans are subject to the "Fort Halifax" test, as described by the U.S. Supreme Court in the case *Fort Halifax Packing v. Coyne*, which generally means that there must be ongoing administration of the arrangement for it to be subject to ERISA.

ERISA Section 3(36) defines "excess benefit plan" as a plan maintained by an employer solely for the purpose of providing benefits for certain employees in excess of the limitations on contributions and benefits imposed by IRC Section 415, without regard to whether the plan is funded. To the extent that a separable part of a plan (as determined by the Secretary of Labor) maintained by an employer is maintained for such purpose, that part shall be treated as a separate plan that is an excess benefit plan. ERISA Section 4(b)(5) provides that Title I of ERISA does not apply to any employee benefit plan that meets the definition of an excess benefit plan. Thus, excess benefit plans are not subject to the reporting and disclosure requirements of Part 1 of Subtitle B of Title I of ERISA, the participation and vesting requirements of Part 2, the funding requirements of Part 3, the fiduciary responsibility requirements of Part 4, and the administration and enforcement requirements of Part 5. It should be noted that while excess benefit plans are allowed to uncap the benefit and contribution limits contained in IRC Section 415, it does not expressly provide for uncapping the compensation limit contained in IRC Section 401(a)(17). Thus, a plan that uncaps both the Section 415 and 401(a)(17) limits may actually be a top-hat plan and not an excess benefit plan.

The term "top-hat plan" is not defined in ERISA. Nor is it explicitly defined in the Regulations, although Regulation Section 2520.104-23 essentially provides such definition. It generally refers to a plan that is unfunded and is maintained by an employer primarily for the purpose of providing deferred compensation for a select group of management or highly compensated employees. These executive benefit programs are referred to as "top-hat plans" for obvious reasons.

Unlike an excess benefit plan, which is exempt from ERISA, top-hat plans are subject to some, but not all, of ERISA's requirements. For example, top-hat plans are subject to the reporting and disclosure requirements under Part 1 and the enforcement and administration requirements of Part 5. However, top-hat plans are exempt from the participation and vesting requirements of Part 2, the funding requirements of Part 3, and the fiduciary responsibility requirements of Part 4.

With respect to the reporting and disclosure requirements of Part 1, Regulation Section 2520.104-23 provides an "alternative method of compliance for pension plans for certain selected employees." An employer may satisfy all Part 1 reporting and disclosure requirements with respect to all of its top-hat plans by filing with the Department of Labor (DOL) within 120 days after the adoption of the plans a statement that contains:

- The name and address of the employer
- The IRS employer identification number
- A declaration that the employer maintains the plans primarily for the purpose of providing deferred compensation for a select group of management or highly compensated employees
- A statement of the number of such plans and the number of employees in each
- A copy of the plan or plans

This filing (commonly referred to by practitioners as the "top-hat plan one-pager") is all a company needs to do to relieve itself of ERISA's Part 1 burdens. Compensation committees should check with their legal or HR departments to make sure that these one-pagers have been filed.

Issues arising under top-hat plans often involve whether or not the plan is "unfunded" and whether the plan is for management or highly compensated employees. Various case law on these issues provide some clarification, but overall, each situation is a facts-and-circumstances test and will need to be specifically analyzed.

LABOR LAWS AND REGULATIONS

Overview

Compensation committees generally have little concern with labor laws, since most of such laws are with respect to rank-and-file employees and not executives. However, issues concerning executives usually arise with respect to:

- Over age 40 discrimination under the Age Discrimination in Employment Act of 1967 (ADEA), as amended by the Older Workers Benefit Protection Act of 1991 (OWBPA).
- Sex, race, religion, color, or national origin discrimination under Title VII of the Civil Rights Act of 1964, as amended by the Civil Rights Acts of 1972 and 1991.
- Disability discrimination under the Americans with Disabilities Act of 1990.
- Equal Pay Act.
- Fair Labor Standards Act.
- Family and Medical Leave Act.
- Various similar statutes under state and local laws.

Generally, the issue is whether the executive has—or could have—a claim under any of the preceding laws. If the executive has a claim (e.g., a sex discrimination claim), then it usually becomes a matter for the company and its legal department and not for the compensation committee. However, if the executive is willing to waive any and all claims, then the compensation committee needs to know the applicable rules involving waivers and releases, as discussed in the following section.

ADEA Law

Section 631(a) provides that the prohibitions against age discrimination are limited to individuals who are at least 40 years of age.

Section 631(c) provides that compulsory retirement of any employee who has attained 65 years of age, and who for the two-year period immediately before retirement is employed in a bona fide executive or a high policymaking position, is permissible, but only if such employee is entitled to an immediate nonforfeitable annual retirement benefit from a pension, profit-sharing, savings, or deferred compensation plan, or any combination of such plans, of the employer of such employee, which equals, in the aggregate, at least $44,000.

Since most executives are age 40 or over, ADEA is the starting point for all discrimination claims by executives. Presumably, compensation committees become involved in executive discrimination claims only as part of the severance process. In determining the ultimate value of the severance package, a waiver and release of all employment-related claims (and many times, any and all claims) by the terminated executive is required before any severance will be paid. Section 626 contains the rules relating to waiver and release of age discrimination claims. Since severance agreements do not separate out various discrimination claims and other claims that are being waived, the Section 626 requirements are therefore applied across the board.

Section 626(f) provides the an individual may not waive any right or claim under ADEA unless the waiver is knowing and voluntary. Generally, the waiver will not be considered knowing and voluntary unless at a minimum:

- The waiver is part of an agreement between the individual and the employer that is written in a manner calculated to be understood by such individual, or by the average individual eligible to participate.
- The waiver specifically refers to rights or claims arising under ADEA.
- The individual does not waive rights or claims that may arise after the date the waiver is executed.
- The individual waives rights or claims only in exchange for consideration in addition to anything of value to which the individual already is entitled.
- The individual is advised in writing to consult with an attorney prior to executing the agreement.
- The individual is given a period of at least 21 days within which to consider the agreement; or if a waiver is requested in connection with an exit incentive or other employment termination program offered to a group or class of employees, the individual is given a period of at least 45 days within which to consider the agreement.
- The agreement provides that for a period of at least seven days following the execution of such agreement, the individual may revoke the agreement, and the agreement shall not become effective or enforceable until the revocation period has expired.
- If a waiver is requested in connection with an exit incentive or other employment termination program offered to a group or class of employees, the employer (at the commencement of the applicable 45-day period mentioned previously) informs the individual in writing in a manner calculated to be understood by the average individual eligible to participate, as to any class, unit, or group of individuals covered by such program, any eligibility factors for such program, and any time limits applicable to such program; and the job titles and ages of all individuals eligible or selected for the program, and the ages of all individuals in the same job classification or organizational unit who are not eligible or selected for the program.

Chapter 8

Accounting Rules

This chapter provides a fundamental working knowledge of the relevant accounting principles, standards, and issues that most compensation committee members will encounter in discharging their committee duties. It is not intended to be complete; rather, it attempts to familiarize the compensation committee member with the accounting regulatory and organizational framework and the various relevant accounting pronouncements and their origins. Specific application and examples of these rules are contained in Part Three of this book.

Accounting issues for compensation committees generally will involve the value of compensation expense and the timing of such expense. Major changes in equity-based compensation accounting standards both in the United States and internationally are causing compensation committees to compare the attributes and detriments of equity-based compensation with cash-based compensation. While stock options may no longer have the allure that they once had (since there usually was no impact on the P&L), equity-based compensation still retains some advantages over cash-based arrangements. For example, a grant of stock generally is valued as of the date of grant and expensed over the service period, and subsequent appreciation in the stock price (and thus increases in the value of the grant) is disregarded. A grant of cash, however, is valued by the amount paid.

This chapter first discusses the various organizations responsible for enacting and applying accounting standards. This is followed by selected accounting standards that compensation committees may need to know (even though some of these standards have been modified or eliminated by new standards).

ORGANIZATIONS RESPONSIBLE FOR ACCOUNTING STANDARDS (PAST AND PRESENT)

Accounting standards that now comprise United States generally accepted accounting principles (US GAAP) originally were promulgated by the American Institute of Certified Public Accountants (AICPA), a national trade organization for accountants that traces its beginnings back to 1887. Following the creation of the Securities and Exchange Commission (SEC) in 1934, the SEC also became involved in the process relating to creation of US GAAP standards.

In 1939, the AICPA, with SEC encouragement, established the Committee on Accounting Procedure (CAP). From 1939 to 1959, the CAP issued 51 Accounting Research Bulletins (ARBs), of which ARB 43 was a compilation of the prior 42 ARBs. The general purpose of the ARBs was to address specific accounting issues that arose from time to time. Although it has been said that ARB 43 created US GAAP, the ARBs did not, in fact, create a comprehensive set of accounting rules.

In 1959, the AICPA replaced CAP with the Accounting Principles Board (APB). The APB issued a total of 31 Opinions and 4 Statements. For all intents and purposes, US GAAP was created through these Opinions and Statements. However, some felt that the APB, partly due to the fact that it was a part of the AICPA (i.e., a trade association), was not as effective as it should be, since the rulemaking body was part of the trade association representing those who would be affected by these rules. Thus, in 1971, the Wheat Commission (chaired by former SEC Commissioner Francis M. Wheat) examined whether the APB was the best accounting rulemaking structure. The Wheat Commission concluded that the APB should be replaced, and recommended that an independent organization be entrusted with the responsibility of setting U.S. accounting standards.

Following these recommendations, the Financial Accounting Standards Board (FASB) was established in 1974. So far, the FASB has issued 150 Statements of Financial Accounting Standards (FAS), 46 FASB Interpretations (FIN), and various Technical Bulletins and Statements of Concepts. In 1984, the FASB created the Emerging Issues Task Force (EITF), whose membership consists of the FASB Director of Research and Technical Activities (EITF chairman) and various individuals from public accounting firms, large companies, and certain relevant associations (e.g., the Financial Executives Institute, the Institute of Management Accountants). The EITF releases interpretations (or what is referred to as a "consensus") on specific issues under US GAAP. In addition, the FASB staff also releases from time to time its interpretations on specific issues through FASB Staff Bulletins.

The AICPA thus no longer sets accounting standards. It still does contribute to the process, however, through issuance of its own Statements of Positions (SOPs), very few of which would impact compensation committees. In addition, the SEC, while it has delegated accounting standards setting to the FASB, does issue Staff Accounting Bulletins (SABs), very few of which—for the most part—directly impact compensation committee members.

Outside the United States, the International Accounting Standards Committee (IASC), formed in 1973, was the organization involved in setting worldwide accounting standards. The IASC issued 41 International Accounting Standards (IASs), which are similar in concept to FAS pronouncements issued by the FASB, and 33 Standing Interpretations Committees (SICs), which are similar in concept to FIN pronouncements issued by the FASB. In 2001, the IASC was replaced by the International Accounting Standards Board (IASB). The IASB so far has issued two International Financial Reporting Standards (IFRSs), which are similar to—and a replacement for—an IAS, and will also be issuing International Financial Reporting Interpretations Committees (IFRICs), which are similar to—and a replacement for—an SIC. Compensation committee members should be aware of a concept called "convergence" through which the FASB and the IASB are attempting to reconcile and essentially merge accounting standards so that US GAAP is fundamentally the same as international GAAP.

Finally, because financial statements of state and local governments are so different from private and public businesses, the Governmental Accounting Standards Board (GASB) was created in 1984 to set the accounting standards for state and local governments; however, it is unlikely that compensation committee members will need to know anything more about the GASB other than its existence.

ACCOUNTING STANDARDS THAT COMPENSATION COMMITTEE MEMBERS MAY NEED TO KNOW

While a company's audit committee, independent auditors, and financial departments will be the key players addressing accounting issues and will be primarily involved in all aspects of the compensation committee decisions impacting the financial statements, the following list contains most of the major relevant accounting standards that compensation committees will face in discussing and addressing the financial impact of compensation committee decisions:

- ARB 43
- APB Opinion No. 12 (APB 12)
- APB Opinion No. 15 (APB 15)
- APB Opinion No. 16 (APB 16)
- APB Opinion No. 25 (APB 25)
- FASB Statement of Financial Accounting Standards No. 5 (FAS 5)
- FASB Statement of Financial Accounting Standards No. 87 (FAS 87)
- FASB Statement of Financial Accounting Standards No. 88 (FAS 88)
- FASB Statement of Financial Accounting Standards No. 106 (FAS 106)
- FASB Statement of Financial Accounting Standards No. 123, including the Exposure Draft amending FAS 123 (FAS 123)
- FASB Statement of Financial Accounting Standards No. 128 (FAS 128)
- FASB Statement of Financial Accounting Standards No. 132 (FAS 132)

- FASB Statement of Financial Accounting Standards No. 141 (FAS 141)
- FASB Statement of Financial Accounting Standards No. 142 (FAS 142)
- FASB Statement of Financial Accounting Standards No. 148 (FAS 148)
- FASB Interpretation No. 28 (FIN 28)
- FASB Interpretation No. 31 (FIN 31)
- FASB Interpretation No. 38 (FIN 38)
- FASB Interpretation No. 44 (FIN 44)
- Emerging Issues Task Force Issue No. 84-13 (EITF 84-13)
- Emerging Issues Task Force Issue No. 84-18 (EITF 84-18)
- Emerging Issues Task Force Issue No. 84-34 (EITF 84-34)
- Emerging Issues Task Force Issue No. 85-1 (EITF 85-1)
- Emerging Issues Task Force Issue No. 85-45 (EITF 85-45)
- Emerging Issues Task Force Issue No. 86-27 (EITF 86-27)
- Emerging Issues Task Force Issue No. 87-6 (EITF 87-6)
- Emerging Issues Task Force Issue No. 87-23 (EITF 87-23)
- Emerging Issues Task Force Issue No. 87-33 (EITF 87-33)
- Emerging Issues Task Force Issue No. 88-6 (EITF 88-6)
- Emerging Issues Task Force Issue No. 90-7 (EITF 90-7)
- Emerging Issues Task Force Issue No. 90-9 (EITF 90-9)
- Emerging Issues Task Force Issue No. 94-6 (EITF 94-6)
- Emerging Issues Task Force Issue No. 95-16 (EITF 95-16)
- Emerging Issues Task Force Issue No. 96-18 (EITF 96-18)
- Emerging Issues Task Force Issue No. 97-5 (EITF 97-5)
- Emerging Issues Task Force Issue No. 97-14 (EITF 97-14)
- Emerging Issues Task Force Issue No. 00-12 (EITF 00-12)
- Emerging Issues Task Force Issue No. 00-23 (EITF 00-23)
- Emerging Issues Task Force Issue No. 02-8 (EITF 02-8)
- International Financial Reporting Standard 2 (IFRS 2)
- SEC Staff Accounting Bulletin No. 1 (Topic 4E) (SAB 1)
- SEC Staff Accounting Bulletin No. 79 (Topic 5T) (SAB 79)
- SEC Staff Accounting Bulletin No. 83 (Topic 4D) (SAB 83)

It should be noted that many of the preceding standards will no longer have any applicability to future financial reporting (e.g., it appears that APB 25 will soon be obsoleted); however, for historical perspective and to help explain past practices, most relevant accounting standards impacting executive compensation are included.

ARB 43, Chapter 13B: Compensation Involved in Stock Option and Stock Purchase Plans (1953)

ARB 43 generally was a compilation of the previous 42 ARBs. Chapter 13B was the first pronouncement with respect to equity-based compensation. Generally, it provided that market value was to be used in determining expense. For purposes of options, grant-date spread (i.e., the difference between the exercise or strike price of the option and the grant-date value of the underlying stock, if positive) was considered market value.

APB 12: Omnibus Opinion (Deferred Compensation Contracts) (1967)

This was the accounting standard used to measure deferred compensation costs. Generally, APB 12 requires the accrual of an employer's obligation under an individual deferred compensation arrangement pursuant to the terms of the arrangement; this meant that the obligation would be measured by the life expectancy of the employee using "best estimates." This vagueness caused inconsistent application and eventually led to an amendment in 1990 contained in FAS 106 (discussed later in this section).

APB 15: Earnings Per Share (1969)

Earnings per share (EPS) generally is calculated by dividing total earnings of the company by the number of outstanding shares. This accounting standard was important because it took into account the impact of stock options and similar instruments (called "common stock equivalents") in computing "fully diluted" EPS. This is accomplished by using a concept called the "treasury stock method," which presumes that all options (vested and unvested) are exercised as of the EPS calculation date, and the proceeds presumed to be received from the company due to such fictional exercise are used to buy shares on the open market at the current fair market value (FMV) of a share of the company's common stock ("stock FMV"). Thus, for example, if a company had 3,000,000 shares outstanding and 100,000 outstanding stock options with an exercise price of $10 when the stock FMV was $16, then the EPS denominator would be 3,037,500 shares computed as follows:

1. $100,000 option shares x $10 exercise price = $1,000,000 presumed proceeds
2. $1,000,000 / $16 = 62,500 "fictional" additional shares
3. 3,000,000 outstanding shares + 100,000 "exercised" shares − 62,500 "repurchased" shares = 3,037,500.

APB 16: Business Combinations (1970)

APB 16 was the accounting standard that established two types of accounting for transactions. The first was "purchase accounting," where the transaction was treated as a purchase of one company by another. This resulted in the creation of the intangible asset called "goodwill," which was amortized as an expense over a specific time period and reduced a company's earnings. The second was "pooling-of-interest accounting," where the two companies were treated for accounting purposes as always having been one company. This eliminated goodwill, and thus a going-forward company's earnings were not negatively impacted. While the rules involving pooling-of-interest accounting were strict, and many companies were forced to use purchase accounting, many companies specifically (and sometimes aggressively) structured their business combinations to fit the preferred pooling-of-interest accounting. In 2001, APB 16 was replaced by FAS 141 (discussed later in this section), which eliminated pooling-of-interest accounting.

APB 25: Accounting for Stock Issued to Employees (1972)

Prior to the revision of FAS 123 (discussed later), APB 25 has been the accounting standard most companies use to expense equity-based compensation. Similar to ARB 43, the overarching principle is to value the stock award (i.e., a restricted stock award or a stock option) on the date of grant, and then to expense that amount over the service period. Thus, for example, a grant of restricted stock with a total FMV of $1,000 on the date of grant, which vests 25% per year, would result in a compensation expense of $250 expensed over the next four years.

With respect to stock options, APB 25 acknowledged that stock options indeed have a value, but essentially conceded that valuation was too problematic. It should be remembered that the Black-Scholes valuation methodology first appeared in 1974, and for that matter, it took almost 20 years before it was applied to compensatory stock options. Accordingly, APB 25 created the concept of intrinsic value, which simply meant the difference between the FMV of the stock award and any purchase price (i.e., spread). Thus, a stock award of FMV $100 where the grantee paid $10 would have an intrinsic value of $90. Similarly, a stock option with an exercise price of $10 granted when the stock FMV was $100 would also have an intrinsic value of $90. However, a stock option with an exercise price of $100 granted when the stock FMV was $100 would have an intrinsic value of $0.

This, perhaps, is what is most misunderstood about APB 25. Many believe that APB 25 provides that stock options have no value. In reality, however, the rule is that a "fixed" stock option granted with an exercise price equal to or greater than the stock FMV on the date of grant results in $0 compensation expense, and a "fixed" stock option with an exercise price less than the stock FMV on the date of grant (i.e., a discounted stock option) results in a compensation charge equal to the intrinsic value on the date of grant.

The concept of "fixed" equity-based awards and "variable" equity-based awards is another confusing issue relating to equity-based compensation. These terms sometimes are thrown about as "fixed-plan accounting" versus "variable-plan accounting," which generally referred to older style nondiscretionary stock plans where all the terms and conditions (e.g., vesting schedule, option term, termination of employment, etc.) were "fixed" in the plan document, and where the award agreement merely listed the number of shares and the exercise price. Usually, these concepts were simply referred to as "fixed accounting" and "variable accounting." However, as stock plans changed over the years, and provided more and more for a variety of terms and conditions, it became possible for some awards granted under the plan to be "fixed" and some awards granted under the same plan to be "variable"; thus, "fixed-award accounting" and "variable-award accounting" are the preferred terms. Essentially, a fixed award is an award where the number of shares and the purchase/exercise price are known on the date of grant (this point in time is referred to as the "measurement date" in APB 25). An award is treated as fixed even if there is a vesting schedule, so long as the vesting schedule is time-based and not performance-based. If the number of shares is not known on the date of grant, then there is no measurement date until the number of shares becomes known (e.g., in a performance-based award, the measurement date occurs when the performance goals are achieved and the equity-based award vests or becomes payable). If an award is "variable," then the intrinsic value is measured each reporting period and is "marked-to-market" (i.e., if a stock award, then the stock FMV on the recording date is used; if an option, then the option's spread on the recording date is used) and then recorded based in accordance with FAS 5 (discussed later). Obviously, variable accounting generally eliminates the accounting advantages of granting equity-based awards under APB 25 if, in fact, the stock FMV increases after the date of grant.

Using a concept known as the "ultimate vest," some companies used plans called TARSAPs (for Time Accelerated Restricted Stock Award Plans) or PASOPs (for Performance Accelerated Stock Option Plans) where the vesting of the stock award or stock option would occur at the end of the award's life—usually near the 10th anniversary of the date of grant—but would vest earlier if certain preestablished performance goals were achieved. The SEC examined this issue, and over the years, the "ultimate" cliff vest date has been reduced from 10 years to approximately seven years. Basically, the issue was whether the ultimate cliff vest date was illusory, and if it were, then the award would be subject to variable accounting.

APB 25 applied only to employee compensatory plans and not to employee "noncompensatory" plans, an example of which was an employee stock purchase plan that met the qualifications of Internal Revenue Code (Code) Section 423 (discussed in Chapter 7). While APB 25 did not explicitly allow non-employee directors to be treated as employees, these rules were extended to non-employee directors who received stock option grants. Finally, APB 25 provided that if an option term was extended, then a new measurement date occurred, and if there was spread in the option on this new measurement date, then such intrinsic value would be recorded as a compensation expense; in substance, such amendment would be treated as a cancellation of the existing stock option and a grant of a new option.

FAS 5: Accounting for Contingencies (1975)

FAS 5 established the accounting principle that estimated expense from a loss contingency will be recorded if and when it is probable that an asset has been impaired or a liability has been incurred, and provided that the amount of loss can be reasonably estimated. This principle has been applied to determining when a performance cash-based or equity-based award will be recorded as an expense. The result is that a performance cash-based or equity-based award will not be expensed until it is probable that the contingency (i.e., the performance goal) will be achieved. At that point, the value of the award is measured (actual dollar amount if a cash award or dollar amount based on fair market value of the underlying stock at the time of measurement if an equity-based award) and expensed.

FAS 87: Employers' Accounting for Pensions (1985)

FAS 87 generally applies to expensing and disclosure of broad-based employee defined-benefit and defined-contribution pension plans. A fundamental objective of FAS 87 is to recognize the compensation cost of an employee's pension benefits over that employee's approximate service period. FAS 87 continues past practices of delaying the recognition of certain events, reporting net cost, and offsetting liabilities and assets. Compensation committees may need to consider FAS 87 if they become involved with new or existing pension plans.

FAS 88: Employers' Accounting for Settlements and Curtailments of Defined-Benefit Pension Plans and for Termination Benefits (1985)

FAS 88 established the accounting standards for an employer's accounting for settlement of defined-benefit pension obligations, for curtailment of a defined-benefit pension plan, and for termination benefits, and is closely related to FAS 87. Compensation committees may need to consider FAS 88 in the context of any executive's termination of employment.

FAS 106: Employers' Accounting for Postretirement Benefits Other than Pensions (1990)

FAS 106 establishes the accounting standards for an employer's accounting for post-retirement benefits other than pension benefits (which commonly are referred to by the acronym "OPEB" for "Other Postretirement Employee Benefits" or sometimes "Other Post Employment Benefits"). Prior to FAS 106, OPEBs were accounted for when paid (similar to the "pay-as-you-go" standard under the federal

Social Security system). Instead, FAS 106 required recognition of the accrued obligation. Generally, the standards under FAS 106 are similar to the standards under FAS 87. FAS 106, however, amended APB 12 to explicitly require that an employer's obligation under deferred compensation arrangements be accrued following the terms of the individual contract over the required service periods to the date the employee is fully eligible for the benefits. This eliminated the vagueness of the "best estimates" provision contained in APB 12.

Other significant aspects of FAS 106 are:

- In estimating future costs, anticipated plan changes may be considered in certain circumstances.
- Benefit/years-of-service actuarial method is mandated; actuarial valuation of obligation must be as of a date within three months of year end, while current year expense shall be based on beginning of year assumptions.
- Employer must estimate its health care cost trend rate and assume current Medicare law continues.
- The discount rate selected should reflect current rates of return available on high-quality bonds.
- Prior service cost is amortized over the future service period of active employees.
- Delayed recognition of actuarial gains and losses is permitted; if unrecognized amount exceeds 10% of assets or obligation, minimum amortization of the excess amount over average remaining service of active employees is required.
- The obligation or asset upon adopting FAS 106 is either expensed or amortized over the remaining service life of active employees (or 20 years if longer); if amortized and total expense is less than cash payments, additional amortization is required.
- The annual expense for a multiemployer plan is generally the contribution called for that period.
- Balance sheet reflects the difference between cumulative amounts expensed and amounts funded (no minimum liability rules).
- The full liability net of any plan assets should be recorded at the date of a purchase business combination.

FAS 123: Accounting for Stock-Based Compensation (1995, Revised 2004 and Retitled "Share-Based Payment")

When it was released in 1995, FAS 123 was a controversial accounting standard that originally was to require mandatory expensing of all equity-based compensation (including options) using stock FMV to value stock awards and a recognized option-pricing model (basically, the Black-Scholes option-pricing model) to value options.

However, due to political pressures from both the business community and Congress, the FASB decided that companies could elect to adopt FAS 123 or continue to expense equity-based compensation under APB 25. The only new requirement applicable to all companies was that if a company elected to continue to expense under APB 25, then the financial statements must contain pro forma disclosure of what the equity-based compensation expense would have been if the company had adopted FAS 123. In addition, if a company elected to use FAS 123, it could never later change back to use APB 25.

In the late 1990s and early 2000s, any company that decided to adopt FAS 123 and that granted stock options would thus have its earnings reduced, even if the stock option's exercise price was at or above stock FMV on the date of grant. Accordingly, prior to 2002, very few companies adopted FAS 123.

The important aspect of FAS 123 was that the valuation of a stock option did not take into account vesting, forfeitability, nontransferability, and performance conditions. Thus, a 10-year option that vested 25% per year based only on continued employment was valued the same as a 10-year option that only vested if EPS growth targets were achieved. In the FASB's view, this "leveled the playing field" between performance-based awards and time-based awards. In reality, it caused companies not to adopt FAS 123 and also not to use performance-based awards.

In addition, FAS 123 did not contain rules on vesting, but some rules relating to vesting were provided in EITF 96-18 (discussed later), which was released shortly after FAS 123 was issued. Essentially, for employee compensatory awards, the amount of expense would be expensed over the service period. Thus, for example, assume that two awards, one a time-based award and the other a performance-based award, were made at the same time. The value of a time-based award that vested 25% per year would be expensed over four years. The value of a performance-based award where the performance goals were achieved at the end of the fourth year would similarly be expensed (through restatement or otherwise and in accordance with FAS 5) over the same four years.

In March 2004, the FASB released a proposal to amend FAS 123 (these FASB proposals generally are referred to as "Exposure Drafts"). As stated in the summary of the Exposure Draft, the amendments to FAS 123 address the accounting for transactions in which an enterprise exchanges its valuable equity instruments for employee services and transactions in which an enterprise incurs liabilities that are based on the fair value of the enterprise's equity instruments or that may be settled by the issuance of those equity instruments in exchange for employee services. The Exposure Draft does not change the accounting for (i) business transactions, (ii) similar transactions involving parties other than employees, or (iii) employee stock ownership plans (which are subject to AICPA Statement of Position 93-6, *Employers' Accounting for Employee Stock Ownership Plans*).

The objective of the accounting required by FAS 123 as amended by the Exposure Draft is to recognize in an entity's financial statements the cost of employee services received in exchange for valuable equity instruments issued, and liabilities incurred, to employees in share-based payment transactions. Key provisions of the Exposure Draft are:

- For public entities, the cost of employee services received in exchange for equity instruments would be measured based on the grant-date fair value of those instruments (with limited exceptions). That cost would be recognized over the requisite service period (often the vesting period). Generally, no compensation cost would be recognized for equity instruments that do not vest.

- For public entities, the cost of employee services received in exchange for liabilities would be measured initially at the fair value of liabilities and would be remeasured subsequently at each reporting date through settlement date. The pro rata change in fair value during the requisite service period would be recognized over that period, and the change in fair value after the requisite service period is complete would be recognized in the financial statements in the period of change.

- The grant-date fair value of employee share options and similar instruments would be estimated using option-pricing models adjusted for the unique characteristics of those options and instruments (unless observable market prices for the same or similar options are available).

- The Exposure Draft requires the use of "tranche expensing" (see description and example in FIN 28 section).

- If an equity award is modified subsequent to the grant date, incremental compensation cost would be recognized in an amount equal to the excess of the fair value of the modified award over the fair value of the original award immediately prior to the modification.

- Employee share purchase plans would not be considered compensatory if the terms of those plans were no more favorable than those available to all holders of the same class of shares, and substantially all eligible employees could participate on an equitable basis.

- Excess tax benefits—defined as the realized tax benefit related to the amount (caused by changes in the fair value of the entity's shares after the grant date) of deductible compensation cost reported on an employer's tax return for an individual employee's equity instruments in excess of the compensation cost for those instruments recognized for financial reporting purposes—would be recognized as an addition to paid-in capital. Cash retained as a result of those excess tax benefits would be presented in the statement of cash flows as financing cash inflows. The write-off of deferred tax assets relating to unrealized tax benefits associated with recognized compensation cost would be reported as income tax expense.

- The Exposure Draft allows nonpublic entities to elect to measure compensation cost of awards of equity share options and similar instruments at intrinsic value through the date of settlement. That election also would apply to awards of liability instruments. The Exposure Draft also requires that public entities measure compensation cost of awards of equity share options and similar instruments at intrinsic value through the date of settlement if it is not reasonably possible to estimate their grant-date fair value.

- The notes to financial statements of both public and nonpublic entities would disclose the information that users of financial information need to understand the nature of share-based payment transactions and the effects of those transactions on the financial statements.

Finally, from a practical standpoint, the revised FAS 123 will substantially alter compensation committees' design and use of equity-based compensation, notably:

- More use of "full-value awards" (e.g., restricted stock and restricted stock units) over stock options and stock appreciation rights
- More use of stock appreciation rights payable in stock
- Less use of broad-based equity-based compensation programs
- Less use of performance goals based on stock price
- Less use of reload options
- More use of shorter options terms
- More use of discounted stock options and stock appreciation rights
- More use of cliff vesting or staggered vesting rather than pro rata graded vesting

FAS 128: Earnings Per Share (1997)

FAS 128 replaced APB 15 as the accounting standard for EPS. The concept of "primary EPS" was replaced with "basic EPS," and "fully diluted EPS" was replaced by "diluted EPS." Essentially, the concept of converting common-stock equivalents into additional fictional shares using the treasury stock method was retained.

FAS 132: Employers' Disclosures about Pensions and Other Postretirement Benefits (1998, Revised 2003)

This statement was revised in 2003 to address concerns that users of financial statements did not receive sufficient pension information. The statement replaces the disclosure provisions of FAS 87, 88, and 106. The statement applies to defined benefit plans and other retirement benefits and requires that the following information be provided annually:

- A breakdown of plan assets held in equity securities, debt securities, real estate, and other assets
- A description of the plan's investment strategies, policies, and target investment allocations
- Projections of the expected future benefit payment for the next five years
- The accumulated benefit obligation
- Estimated contributions for the next year
- Measurement dates
- A table of the key assumptions that the plan uses to determine its benefit obligation, net periodic benefit cost, and assumed health care cost trend rates.

In addition, companies must report pension and other postretirement benefit costs quarterly. Domestic retirement plans must provide the preceding information, except estimated future benefit payments, for fiscal years ending after December 15, 2003. Estimated future benefit payments must be reported for years ending after June 15, 2004. Foreign plans and nonpublic entities must provide the information for years ending after June 15, 2004. The quarterly information is required for quarters beginning after December 15, 2003, for all plans.

FAS 141: Business Combinations (2001)

FAS 141 replaced APB 16 as the accounting standard for business combinations. The most important aspect of FAS 141 is that it eliminated pooling-of-interest accounting.

FAS 142: Goodwill and Other Intangible Assets (2001)

In conjunction with the adoption of FAS 141, the concept of amortizing goodwill as an expense under a purchase-accounting transaction and disregarding goodwill as an expense under a pooling-of-interest accounting transaction was replaced by the FAS 142 concept that goodwill will be expensed as it becomes impaired. While this did not provide the advantages of pooling-of-interest accounting, it helped to some degree reduce the disadvantages of using APB 16 purchase accounting. The concepts of how and when goodwill actually becomes impaired and when the expense must be recorded is still being discussed.

FAS 148: Accounting for Equity-Based Compensation—Transition and Disclosure—an Amendment of FASB Statement No. 123 (2002)

Under the original FAS 123, a company that adopted FAS 123 was not required to restate prior years' financial statements but would record equity-based compensation expense on a going-forward basis (this was called the "prospective only" approach). In 2002, as more and more companies began to adopt FAS 123, some companies wanted to restate prior years' financial statements to avoid the appearance that the company had a large decrease in earnings (i.e., companies wanted to "ramp up" the presentation of equity-based expenses due to the adoption of FAS 123). FAS 128 amended original FAS 123 to provide that companies could transition over from APB 25 to FAS 123 under three transition scenarios. The first was simply to restate all prior years as if the company had always been under FAS 123. The second was to expense new awards and prior awards that were unvested on the adoption date. The third was to use the prospective only approach as contained in FAS 123, but which would now only be available to companies that adopted FAS 123 on or prior to their fiscal years ending on or before December 15, 2003.

FIN 28: Accounting for Stock Appreciation Rights and Other Variable Stock Option or Award Plans (1978)

FIN 28 established the principle that stock appreciation rights (SARs) and other equity-based compensation awards payable in cash should be treated more as a cash-based award than as an equity-based award. This led to the principle of variable accounting for SARs, phantom stock, etc., which required that the value or spread of the award be "marked-to-market" each recording period and taken as a compensation expense. It also introduced the concept of "tranche expensing" that for the first time distinguished between cliff vesting (i.e., 100% of the stock award vests on one single date) and graded vested (i.e., various percentages of the stock award vest on various dates). FIN 28 required that tranche expensing be applied to all SARs. The application of tranche expensing results in compensation expense being front-loaded so that more of the total expense is recorded up front than equally over the service period. This resulted in "accelerated vesting" and is best presented by the following example:

Example: Award is 100 shares of restricted stock each with a per-share FMV of $10 (total FMV = $1,000) on date of grant.

	Traditional Vesting under APB 25		Accelerated Vesting under FIN 28	
Vesting:	4-Year Cliff	25% per Year	4-Year Cliff	25% per Year*
End of Year 1	$ 250.00	$ 250.00	$ 250.00	$ 520.83
End of Year 2	$ 250.00	$ 250.00	$ 250.00	$ 270.83
End of Year 3	$ 250.00	$ 250.00	$ 250.00	$ 145.84
End of Year 4	$ 250.00	$ 250.00	$ 250.00	$ 62.50
TOTAL	$1,000.00	$1,000.00	$1,000.00	$1,000.00

*Accelerated vesting at 25% per year using the tranche-vesting method as shown next.

100 share grant vesting 25% per year is treated as 4 separate grants of 25 shares each, with each tranche cliff vesting at the end of Year 1, 2, 3, and 4, respectively:

	End of Year 1	End of Year 2	End of Year 3	End of Year 4
Tranche 1	$250.00	$ 0.00	$ 0.00	$ 0.00
Tranche 2	$125.00	$125.00	$ 0.00	$ 0.00
Tranche 3	$ 83.33	$ 83.33	$ 83.34	$ 0.00
Tranche 4	$ 62.50	$ 62.50	$ 62.50	$62.50
TOTAL	$520.83	$270.83	$145.84	$62.50

FIN 31: Treatment of Stock Compensation Plans in EPS Calculations (1980)

Funds used in applying the treasury stock method are the sum of the cash to be received upon exercise, the currently measurable compensation to be charged to expense in the future, and any tax benefit to be credited to capital. The interpretation also provides guidance on how to treat variable plans, combination plans, or plans payable in cash or in stock.

FIN 38: Determining the Measurement Date for Stock Option, Purchase, and Award Plans Involving Junior Stock (1984)

FIN 38 addressed a situation involving the accounting for a class of stock known as "junior stock." Junior stock was a special class of stock issued to executives that was convertible to a company's common stock if certain performance goals were achieved. Because of a variety of restrictions and limitation of other rights, junior stock was expensed at a fraction of the stock FMV. FIN 38 applied variable accounting and required valuation and recording of the expense at the time the performance goals were achieved and with the value equal to the common stock. Essentially, FIN 38 shut down the use of junior stock.

FIN 44: Accounting for Certain Transactions Involving Stock Compensation (2000)

Within a few years following the issuance of the original FAS 123, the FASB decided to review APB 25 under what was known as the "maintenance and repairs" project. Essentially, the FASB examined specific practices that it felt exceeded the authority of APB 25. Some of these practices and a description of the changes were:

- *Repricing:* Any direct or indirect cancellation of an outstanding "underwater" option (i.e., an option where the exercise price is greater than the current stock FMV) and a grant of a new "repriced" option would result in variable accounting for the new repriced option.

- *Employees:* APB 25 only applies to common-law employees and a company's non-employee directors.
- *Business combinations:* Rollover of options in business combinations may result in compensation expense using FAS 123 valuation methodologies.
- *Accelerated vesting:* Discretionary accelerated vesting may cause additional compensation expense based on facts and circumstances.
- *Withholding:* Companies may only withhold the statutory minimum with respect to equity-based awards.
- *Puts and calls:* Stock (including stock received after the exercise of an option) must be held at least six months before it is cashed out by the issuer, or else it will be treated as a variable award.
- *ESPP:* An employee stock purchase plan that qualifies under Code Section 423 will continue to be treated as a "noncompensatory" plan.
- *Reloads:* A stock option with a reload feature as of the date of grant will be a fixed award; an existing stock option that is subsequently amended to provide a reload feature will be a variable award; the grant of the reload stock option itself will be treated as a new grant.

FIN 44 superseded EITF 87-33 and EITF 90-9.

EITF 84-13: Purchase of Stock Options and Stock Appreciation Rights in a Leveraged Buyout (1984)

This EITF reached the consensus that a target company must record as compensation expense the amount it pays to acquire options and rights.

EITF 84-18: Stock Option Pyramiding (1984)

When an employee exercises an option by exchanging shares, unless the employee has held the shares for at least six months (i.e., the shares are mature), the option award is, in substance, a variable plan (or a stock appreciation right) requiring compensation charges. EITF 84-18 is the source of the "six-month mature share" rule applied to stock-for-stock cashless exercise programs.

EITF 84-34: Permanent Discount Restricted Stock Purchase Plan (1984)

In these plans, the company has a right of first refusal to repurchase the shares at the current market price less the original discount. Although no consensus was reached, most EITF members believe the plan is compensatory. Most of those believe compensation is fixed at the grant date. Others believe variable accounting is appropriate if buyback is likely or the employer must repurchase the stock (such as when the employee has a put).

EITF 85-1: Classifying Notes Received for Capital Stock (1985)

The EITF reached a consensus that when an enterprise receives a note rather than cash as a contribution to equity, reporting the note as an asset is generally inappropriate, except in very limited circumstances when there is substantial evidence of ability and intent to pay within a reasonably short period of time. The SEC (see SAB 1, discussed later) requires that public companies report such notes receivable as a deduction of shareholder's equity unless collected in cash prior to the issuance of the financial statements.

EITF 85-45: Business Combinations: Settlement of Stock Options and Awards (1985)

If a target company settles stock options voluntarily, at the direction of the acquiring company, or as part of the plan of acquisition, the target must recognize compensation expense. No consensus was reached on the issue of how the target should account for reimbursement from the acquiring company for the settlement cost.

EITF 86-27: Measurement of Excess Contributions to a Defined Contribution Plan (1986)

An employer terminates a plan and contributes the excess assets to an ESOP that purchases stock. The amount in excess of the annual contribution is not allocated to participants. The unallocated shares should be reported as treasury stock. Compensation expense should be recognized at the allocation date at the then current market price; any difference from the purchase price is reflected in equity. Dividends used to purchase more stock should be charged to treasury stock rather than retained earnings. Dividends paid to participants on unallocated shares should be charged to compensation expense. The sponsor should report its own debt securities owned by the ESOP as both an asset and debt. Unallocated shares will not be outstanding shares for earnings-per-share purposes.

EITF 87-6: Adjustments Related to Stock Compensation Plans (1987)

The EITF addressed four separate issues:

EITF 87-6A. "Changes to Stock Option Plans Arising from the Tax Reform Act of 1986": Minor technical changes linked to the 1986 act would not create a new measurement date if the aggregate effect on the value of the option is *de minimis* from the perspective of the employee. Changes to the option beyond the minimum necessary for disqualification would presumptively lead to a new measurement date. Because eliminating or changing a sequential exercise requirement may give the employee an economic benefit, such a change may not be *de minimis*.

EITF 87-6B. "Stock Option Plan with Tax-Offset Cash Bonus": Plans with tax-offset cash bonuses must be accounted for as variable plans. However, for grants outstanding before April 7, 1987 that were granted with tax-offset cash bonuses or that are modified before that date to add a tax-offset cash bonus in connection with the employer's disqualification of the option and that meet certain other requirements, split accounting treatment (option and bonus accounted for separately, with option treated as a fixed plan) is appropriate.

EITF 87-6C. "Use of Stock Option Shares to Cover Tax Withholding": An option plan that allows the use of option shares to meet tax withholding requirements may be considered a fixed plan. Compensation expense must be recorded for all shares used to satisfy withholding if the fair value of the shares withheld exceeds the required tax withholding.

EITF 87-6D. "Phantom Stock-for-Stock Exercise": An employee presents mature shares (see EITF 84-18) to satisfy the exercise price. The enterprise allows the employee to retain the shares presented and issues a certificate for the net shares. This plan remains a fixed plan.

EITF 87-23: Book Value Stock Purchase Plans (1987)

This consensus addresses private company plans that set the purchase price based on a formula such as book value or earnings and provide for a repurchase upon termination or a determinable date using the same formula. If the employee makes a substantive investment that will be at risk for a reasonable period of time, no compensation expense should be recorded for changes in the formula. Variable plan accounting must be used between the grant date and the exercise date for options to purchase restricted stock based on the formula price; no substantive investment is at risk prior to exercise. Formula stock option plans for public companies are variable plans, although fixed plan accounting is permitted for grants prior to January 28, 1988 that had been previously accounted for as fixed plans.

EITF 87-33: Stock Compensation Issues Related to Market Decline (1987)

The EITF addressed five separate issues:

1. If the exercise price of an option is reduced, or an option is cancelled in exchange for the issuance of a new option that contains identical terms except for a reduced exercise price, (1) any originally measured compensation is not reversed; any unamortized amount should continue being amortized, and (2) a new measurement date occurs; compensation is measured using the current market price and the new exercise price. Any compensation in excess of the original amount measured should be amortized over the remaining vesting period.

2. If an option is repurchased in contemplation of the issuance of a new option containing identical terms to the remaining terms of the old option, the guidance in 1. should be applied. The cash paid represents additional compensation that should be expensed.
3. The conclusions in 1. and 2. also apply to restricted stock awards.
4. A new option is granted for a proportionately fewer number of shares at a lower exercise price, with a stipulation that each share acquired under the new grant cancels a proportionate number of shares under the original grant and vice versa. These awards are variable plans because the number of shares and the exercise price is not known. Compensation is measured as the amount by which the market price exceeds the exercise price under the new grant. No additional compensation is recognized after the point that the employee will receive more value under the original grant.
5. If an option contains a tandem stock indemnification right, the right should be accounted for separately only if the individual is subject to the SEC's six-month insider trading restrictions and the right is effective for six months. Under this approach, during the six months following exercise, compensation should be measured as the decrease in the market price from the exercise date. If the two criteria are not met, the entire arrangement (option plus right) is accounted for as a variable plan.

EITF 88-6: Book Value Stock Plans in an Initial Public Offering (1988)

A book value stock purchase plan of a public company is a performance plan; variable plan accounting must be used (see EITF 87-23).

Book value options in an IPO: For book value stock options that do not change after the IPO, the company should continue variable plan accounting and expense any increase in book value due to the IPO. For book value stock options that convert to market value options, compensation expense should be recognized for the difference between market value and book value at the date of the IPO. Because the conversion to a market value option establishes a new measurement date, no further compensation cost would be recognized.

Book value stock in an IPO: If the stock retains its book value buyback provisions after the IPO, no compensation is recognized as a result of the IPO. However, compensation expense should be recognized for subsequent changes in book value. If the restrictions lapse so that the book value stock converts to market value stock, no compensation expense is recognized at the date of the IPO or in future periods. In either case, if the shares were issued within one year of or in contemplation of the IPO, compensation expense must be recognized for the increases in book value since the issuance date.

EITF 90-7: Accounting for a Reload Stock Option (1990)

A reload stock option automatically awards additional options at the then current market price whenever existing options are exercised by tendering owned shares. These plans should be accounted for as fixed plans provided that shares tendered are mature as defined in EITF 84-18 and that the total number of shares that can be issued net of shares tendered is limited to the shares in the original grant.

EITF 90-9: Changes to Fixed Employee Stock Option Plans as a Result of Equity Restructuring (1990)

As a result of a restructuring in the form of a spinoff or a large, special, nonrecurring dividend, an employer changes outstanding options to offset the effects of the resulting dilution. Any consideration paid should be expensed. Other changes do not result in a new measurement date if (1) the aggregate intrinsic value does not increase, (2) the ratio of the option price to the market price of the shares is not reduced, and (3) the vesting and other provisions do not change.

EITF 94-6: Accounting for a Buyout of Compensatory Stock Options (1994)

This EITF requires that a buyout of a stock option will result in a compensation expense equal to the amount paid for the option.

EITF 95-16 Accounting for Stock Compensation Arrangements with Employer Loan Features under APB 25 (1995)

EITF 95-16 examined the situation where a stock option is exercised using a nonrecourse note with the employer. The conclusion was that use of the nonrecourse note was similar in substance to the use of an option, because if the stock price decreased below the value of the note, then there would not be reason to repay the note. Thus, repayment would be similar to exercising the option. If the term of the note was longer than the original term of the option, then the option's term was extended and a new measurement date occurred.

EITF 96-18: Accounting for Equity Instruments that Are Issued to Other than Employees for Acquiring, or in Conjunction with Selling, Goods or Services (1996)

Original FAS 123 did not address vesting. EITF 96-18 addressed vesting generally for independent contractors. However, many of the principles were believed to be applicable to employee stock options.

EITF 97-5: Accounting for Delayed Receipt of Option Shares Upon Exercise under APB Opinion No. 25 (1997)

This EITF addressed a compensation technique where unrealized gain in a stock option was, in substance, converted into a deferred compensation account. All or a portion of the account would then be invested in employer stock; any amount not invested in employer stock would be invested in other securities and vehicles for purposes of diversification. EITF 97-5 concluded that the conversion to a deferred compensation payable only in employer stock was a nonevent; however, if the account was diversified, then the award became variable since the number of shares delivered under the option was not known on the date of grant.

EITF 97-14: Accounting for Deferred Compensation Arrangements Where Amounts Earned Are Held in a Rabbi Trust and Invested (1997)

The EITF analyzed whether employer stock held by a rabbi trust should be treated as fixed or variable. EITF 97-14 concluded in part that the stock should be treated as fixed. This is the authority used to support fixed accounting for restricted stock units payable only in stock.

EITF 00-12: Accounting by an Investor for Stock-Based Compensation Granted to Employees of an Equity Method Investee (2000)

Both the investor and the investee companies are to recognize compensation cost (in the same amount and over the same vesting period) equal to the "fair value" of the stock compensation as ultimately measured on the award's vesting date (in accordance with FAS 123 and EITF 96-18), with a corresponding credit to each company's capital account. Further, there are no net changes to the asset or equity accounts on the balance sheets of the investor and the investee companies, and the income statements and balance sheets of other investor companies (if any) are not affected by the recognition of the stock compensation cost.

EITF 00-23: Issues Related to the Accounting for Stock Compensation under APB 25 and FIN 44 (2000)

Almost immediately after the release of FIN 44 in March 2000, the EITF (prodded by the SEC) began examining a list of fact patterns and issues relating to repricings, reloads, modifications, puts and calls, and many of the same issues that FIN 44 was to address and settle. This EITF is divided into some 50 separate issues, some of which are further divided into subissues. It is now virtually impossible to apply APB 25 without FIN 44, and it is equally impossible to apply FIN 44 without EITF 00-23. Since many fact patterns and examples are presented in EITF 00-23, compensation committee members should, when analyzing an APB 25/FIN 44 issue, first ask whether EITF addresses the specific issue.

EITF 02-8: Accounting for Options Granted to Employees in Unrestricted, Publicly Traded Shares of an Unrelated Entity (2002)

This EITF requires that a company that grants its employees options not on company stock but on shares of an unrelated entity should account for such grants in accordance with the guidance provided in FAS 133, *Accounting for Derivative Instruments and Hedging Activities.*

IFRS 2: Share-Based Payments (2004)

As promised, the IASB released its international standard that generally requires options to be expensed when granted prior to the FASB's release of its Exposure Draft that amended FAS 123. IFRS 2 is effective for periods beginning on or after January 1, 2005. It applies to grants of shares, share options, or other equity instruments that were granted after November 7, 2002 and had not yet vested at the effective date of the IFRS. It applies retrospectively to liabilities arising from share-based payment transactions existing at the date effective as of January 1, 2005. It uses a "fair value" approach to value the compensatory aspect of the option, and requires the six input assumptions of stock price, exercise price, volatility, option term, dividend yield, and risk-free interest rate of the Black-Scholes option-pricing model. However, IFRS 2 explicitly allows the use of other option-pricing models, and allows the valuation to take into account early exercise or variations of the other inputs over the option's life. Stock appreciation settled only in stock will be accounted for as an option. Compensation expense is not recognized if service or performance conditions are not met, but will be recognized (and not reversed) if a "market" condition (essentially a performance condition using stock price as the measure) is not met. Compensation expense similarly will not be reversed if underwater options expire unexercised.

The main requirements of IFRS 2 are:

- An entity must recognize share-based payment transactions in its financial statements, including transactions with employees or other parties to be settled in cash, other assets, or equity instruments of the entity. There are no exceptions to IFRS 2, other than for transactions to which other IFRS rules apply.
- In principle, transactions in which goods or services are received as consideration for equity instruments of the entity should be measured at the fair value of the goods or services received, unless that fair value cannot be estimated reliably. If the entity cannot estimate reliably the fair value of the goods or services received, the entity is required to measure the transaction by reference to the fair value of the equity instruments granted.
- For transactions with employees and others providing similar services, the entity is required to measure the fair value of the equity instruments granted, because

it is typically not possible to estimate reliably the fair value of employee services received. The fair value of the equity instruments granted is measured at grant date.

- For transactions with other parties (i.e., other than employees and those providing similar services), there is a rebuttable presumption that the fair value of the goods or services received can be estimated reliably. That fair value is measured at the date the entity obtains the goods or the counterparty renders service. In rare cases, if the presumption is rebutted, the transaction is measured by reference to the fair value of the equity instruments granted, measured at the date the entity obtains the goods or the counterparty renders service.

- For goods or services measured by reference to the fair value of the equity instruments granted, IFRS 2 specifies that, in general, vesting conditions are not taken into account when estimating the fair value of the shares or options at the relevant measurement date (as specified previously). Instead, vesting conditions are taken into account by adjusting the number of equity instruments included in the measurement of the transaction amount so that, ultimately, the amount recognized for goods or services received as consideration for the equity instruments granted is based on the number of equity instruments that eventually vest.

- The fair value of equity instruments granted must be based on market prices, if available, and to take into account the terms and conditions upon which those equity instruments were granted. In the absence of market prices, fair value is estimated, using a valuation technique to estimate what the price of those equity instruments would have been on the measurement date in an arm's length transaction between knowledgeable, willing parties.

- IFRS 2 also sets out requirements if the terms and conditions of an option or share grant are modified (e.g., an option is repriced) or if a grant is cancelled, repurchased, or replaced with another grant of equity instruments.

- For cash-settled share-based payment transactions, an entity must measure the goods or services acquired and the liability incurred at the fair value of the liability. Until the liability is settled, the entity is required to remeasure the fair value of the liability at each reporting date and at the date of settlement, with any changes in value recognized in profit or loss for the period.

- IFRS 2 also sets out requirements for share-based payment transactions in which the terms of the arrangement provide either the entity or the supplier of goods or services with a choice of whether the entity settles the transaction in cash or by issuing equity instruments.

- IFRS 2 prescribes various disclosure requirements to enable users of financial statements to understand:

  (a) The nature and extent of share-based payment arrangements that existed during the period

(b) How the fair value of the goods or services received, or the fair value of the equity instruments granted, during the period was determined

(c) The effect of share-based payment transactions on the entity's profit or loss for the period and on its financial position

• Before the issue of IFRS 2, there was no existing International Financial Reporting Standard on the recognition or measurement of share-based payment. The requirements in IFRS 2 replace the disclosure requirements in IAS 19, *Employee Benefits* that deal with equity compensation benefits.

As with IFRS 1, the IASB has released IFRS 2 as three separate booklets: the first booklet contains the mandatory requirements of IFRS 2; the second booklet contains the IASB's Basis for Conclusions, which sets out the IASB's reasoning behind the requirements in IFRS 2; and the third booklet consists of implementation guidance, including various illustrative examples.

There are differences between IFRS 2 and the Exposure Draft amending FAS 123, including the accounting for nonpublic enterprises, income tax effects, and certain modifications. The scope of IFRS 2 includes accounting for all share-based payment arrangements, regardless of whether the counterparty is an employee. All of those arrangements generally will be accounted for using the modified grant-date method that the Exposure Draft requires for share-based payment transactions with employees. However, for transactions with parties other than employees, in which it is not possible to reliably estimate the fair value of goods or services received, IFRS 2 requires that the fair value of those goods or services be measured by reference to the fair value of the equity instruments granted, measured at the date those goods or services are received. In contrast, EITF 96-18 requires that grants of share options and other equity instruments to nonemployees be measured at the earlier of (a) the date at which a commitment for performance by the counterparty to earn the equity instruments is reached, or (b) the date at which the counterparty's performance is complete. For many grants, the measurement date under EITF 96-18 may be different from the measurement date prescribed by IFRS 2.

SAB 1 (Topic 4E): Receivables from Sale of Stock

Deferred compensation or receivables arising from the issuance of stock or options to employees should be presented in the balance sheet as a deduction from stockholders' equity.

SAB 79 (Topic 5T): Accounting for Expenses or Liabilities Paid by Principal Stockholder(s)

When a principal stockholder pays an expense for a registrant, the registrant should reflect the expense and a corresponding capital contribution, unless the stockholder's action is caused by a relationship or obligation completely unrelated to his position as a stockholder or the registrant clearly does not benefit from the transaction.

SAB 83 (Topic 4D): Cheap Stock

If stock or options have been issued below the IPO price within one year of filing an IPO registration statement or in contemplation of the IPO, the stock or options should be considered outstanding for all periods presented for the purposes of computing earnings per share. The SEC staff will permit the use of the treasury stock method to determine the dilutive effect of options. Registrants must also consider whether compensation expense should be recognized for these awards.

Part Three

Practical Applications

Chapter 9

Executive Employment and Severance Arrangements

This chapter discusses executive employment and severance arrangements. It begins by underscoring the compensation committee's obligation to evaluate and understand the material aspects of an executive employment agreement before approving it. The chapter then addresses the basic components common to most executive employment agreements and key issues that routinely arise. The final section explores special issues relating to changes in control and the additional severance benefits that are often provided in that context.

INTRODUCTION

The current emphasis on corporate governance best practices brings an invigorated focus on the compensation packages of executive officers and the depth of analysis that goes into approving those packages. Executive employment agreements reflect and integrate the compensation and employment philosophies of the compensation committee. As such, they may be viewed as the most visible and comprehensive embodiment of the work of the committee.

The rights of the parties reflected in any particular employment agreement will vary depending upon a number of factors, including the particular industry involved, the overall business climate, the historical approach of the employer to such agreements, the position of the executive, the relative bargaining strength of the parties, and the employment package offered by the executive's previous employer (a portion of which may have been surrendered in the move to the current employer). Nevertheless, the basic structural components—such as duration, title and reporting relationships, duties, base pay and incentive opportunities, benefits, termination events, effects of termination including severance benefits, restrictive covenants, and dispute resolution—are generally common to most executive employment agreements. As reflected in the following discussion, these components should be viewed in relation to each other when evaluating the employment agreement and the overall compensation package.

An employment agreement generally serves a number of purposes:

- It defines the executive's position and duties, base compensation, place of employment, fringe benefits, and other provisions benefiting the executive during his or her employment.
- It determines in advance what the executive will receive if he or she terminates employment under a variety of circumstances (death, disability, retirement, termination with or without cause, or voluntary termination with or without good reason).
- It can include special or enhanced severance provisions that apply in the context of a change in control.
- It can serve as a repository for any restrictions on the executive's postemployment activities (e.g., noncompetition covenants, nonsolicitation of customers, clients, or employees, and covenants not to disclose confidential information or trade secrets).
- It provides a convenient method for obtaining a release of employment-related claims when termination of employment occurs.

Many of these functions could be covered separately (such as in restrictive covenants agreements, severance pay plans, or special change-in-control agreements), but an employment agreement provides a convenient vehicle to house all of these functions, especially in the case of the company's chief executive officer (CEO) and most senior executives. Whether a public company uses employment agreements is generally a matter of the company's individual custom or culture.

THE IMPORTANCE OF HOMEWORK

Some of the well-publicized executive terminations of recent years are instructive not merely as examples of the heights of corporate excess, but also because of the lessons to be learned from ensuing litigation and publicity. A case in point is the arrangement between Disney and Michael Ovitz, in which Ovitz received approximately $140 million in severance after working for the company for only 14 months. Disney shareholders brought suit, alleging that Disney's board of directors had spent less than an hour reviewing the terms of the employment agreement.[1] The plaintiffs alleged that the board breached its fiduciary duties by failing to evaluate the agreement or to comprehend the payout to Ovitz in the event of his

---

[1]*In re Walt Disney Co. Derivative Litigation,* 825 A.2d 275 (Del. Ch. 2003).

termination. For a fuller discussion of the *Disney* case in the context of a breach of fiduciary duty, see Chapter 5.

A more recent illustration of the same point is the April 2004 settlement of the *Cendant* shareholder lawsuit brought in Delaware Chancery Court. The complaint alleged that the directors breached their fiduciary duties in approving an amendment to the CEO's employment agreement that would have provided, among other things, an uncapped annual bonus stated as a percentage of the company's pre-tax earnings, $100 million of life insurance for life, and severance benefits that could have exceeded $140 million. According to the complaint, the board failed to analyze the potential cost or financial impact to Cendant of the new agreement, did not seek or consider advice from outside advisors, and did not involve any member of the compensation committee in the negotiation of the agreement.

Aside from highlighting the need to avoid unwanted publicity, what has become clear from these and similar cases is the committee's obligation to pay attention to, analyze, and fully understand the material aspects of an executive's employment agreement and severance benefits. These are matters that cannot be viewed in a vacuum. A thoughtful review requires an understanding of the various elements of the employer's entire compensation program (such as SERP formulas, deferred compensation programs, equity incentives, welfare plans, and the like) and the interplay of tax and accounting rules that may be implicated based on specific facts and circumstances contemplated in the agreement.

In order to meet this charge, the committee should fully review, discuss, and consider the terms of proposed executive agreements, taking the full amount of time necessary to seek the input of outside experts, in-house compensation specialists, and other board members, to the extent indicated. It may not be possible to give full consideration in one meeting, depending on how much information and analysis is provided ahead of time. While the committee's analysis will depend on the specific agreement involved, at a minimum it should include consideration of the structural components of the arrangement (e.g., duration, compensation levels, termination provisions, severance protection, etc.), the pros and cons of alternative provisions, and the appropriateness of the agreement in light of industry and company standards and the company's business prospects.

STRUCTURAL COMPONENTS OF EMPLOYMENT AGREEMENTS

The following is a discussion of various structural components that are found in almost all employment agreements.

Term of Agreement and Severance Period

As with most aspects of executive employment agreements, there is no standard "term" of employment. A recent study of S&P 500 companies indicated that employment terms of three years have been prevalent.[2] However, the study also found evidence of some significantly longer employment terms for senior executives, ranging from five to seven years. Ironically, one effect of the increased public scrutiny of employment arrangements may be to cause executives to feel less secure about the future, inducing them to seek greater contractual commitments regarding the term of employment.

The term of an employment agreement is of distinct relevance where severance benefits are tied to the length of the remaining term of the agreement, such as a provision providing a continuation of salary and benefits for the duration of the original term of agreement despite the employer's earlier termination of the executive without cause or the executive's resignation for "good reason." However, the agreement term is less important where the severance is expressed as a stated multiple of salary and/or bonus and a continuation of certain benefits for a number of years equal to that multiple, as is the more typical arrangement.

Whatever the term of the original agreement, the compensation committee should consider whether the term will be renewable, and if so, the manner in which it can be renewed. At one end of the continuum is a continually rolling employment period, in which an additional day is tacked on at the conclusion of each day of active employment. As a result, the employment term remains constant, regardless of how much time has elapsed since the date of the original agreement. When severance is payable for the remainder of the term, this has the effect of making the severance period coextensive with the rolling employment term.

Another variation involves automatic renewals for additional specified terms (typically one year at a time) unless notice of termination is given before the next renewal date. Under this type of "evergreen" agreement, the committee should determine the time period for giving notice of nonrenewal (typically, notice of nonrenewal must be given 90 or 180 days before the next renewal date), and determine the severance rights of the executive, if any, in the event that notice of nonrenewal is given and the agreement is allowed to expire.

Further along the continuum, as favored in some of the business groups' "best-practices" reports described in Chapter 5, is a fixed term of employment that expires on a specified date. This arrangement gives the committee an opportunity to take a fresh look every few years at the entire arrangement and opens the door to renegotiate terms to more adequately reflect the evolved relationship of the parties and the then-current business environment.

Finally, some employment agreements have no stated term, other than the length of any notice period for termination. The severance benefits simply vary depending on the reason for the termination. This structure is uncommon for senior

---

[2]See Paul Hodgson, *Golden Parachutes and Cushion Landings, Termination Payments and Policy in the S&P 500* (February 2003) (citing Board Analyst).

executives of public companies, but it may be appropriate for employment agreements that extend further down the executive ranks.

Title and Duties

Virtually all employment agreements include provisions regarding the executive's title, reporting relationships, and duties. In some agreements, the executive's duties are described in only general terms, while in others, the specific duties of the executive are spelled out. Similarly, some agreements specify the executive's right (or obligation) to serve as a director of the employer or its affiliates, and the time commitment of the executive (e.g., substantially all working time, or full business time and attention, etc.), while other agreements are less precise regarding these matters. In agreements that specify the executive's time commitment, it is common to include additional provisions allowing the executive to devote time to nonbusiness-related matters, such as charitable or community activities.

These provisions should not be viewed merely as a recitation of the executive's status with the company. The agreement's description of the executive's title, reporting relationships, and duties can be the basis for a determination of the severance benefits to which the executive is entitled. For example, where an element of the "cause" definition is the executive's failure to perform his or her duties, the description of those duties can be pivotal. Similarly, where one of the elements of "good reason" for the executive's resignation (thus triggering favorable severance benefits) includes a diminution of his or her position, authority, duties, or responsibilities, the specificity of the agreement in this regard may be determinative.

The "duties" provision of the agreement can also impact employer decisions in other contexts. For example, if the executive is unable to work due to injury or illness, a finding of disability may rest on the extent to which the executive can continue to perform his or her assigned duties. In addition, depending upon the level of the executive and the business of the employer, the executive's noncompetition covenants may be prescribed by the nature of his or her duties for the employer.

Base Salary and Incentive Compensation

The agreement provisions relating to base salary and bonus are often straightforward, with a recitation of the amount and timing of the payments to be made. This is a reflection of the committee's work in setting the levels of compensation and in choosing appropriate performance criteria for incentive opportunities.

The committee should consider the coordination between provisions in the employment agreement relating to incentive compensation and the terms of any separate incentive programs in effect. In particular, in instances in which the employment agreement provides for specific terms of equity awards, the committee should confirm that the prescribed terms are consistent with or otherwise allowable under the separate plan or program providing the source of such awards.

Executive Benefits

For the most part, the stand-alone benefit programs of an employer will operate independently of any individually negotiated employment agreements. It is typical to recite in the agreement that the executive and his or her eligible dependents may participate in the benefit plans, practices, policies, and programs (including welfare benefits and fringe benefits) provided by the employer to the extent applicable generally to peer executives at the company (as defined in the employment agreement). Since the agreement will likely become a matter of public record (filed as an exhibit to the employer's SEC reports), some executives and employers elect not to spell out specific perquisites to be provided, such as club dues, car allowance, company airplane usage, and similar benefits that would probably be provided by the employer regardless of whether they are spelled out in the agreement.

Events of Termination

Employment agreements almost always specify a number of ways in which the employment can be terminated early by either party and the consequences of such termination. The agreement typically addresses terminations by reason of the executive's death, disability, retirement, resignation with or without "good reason," and termination by the employer with or without "cause." The reason for the termination generally determines the amount of the severance benefit, if any. Generally, there is symmetry in the severance benefit where, on the one hand, the executive is fired without cause or quits for good reason (both of which result in the maximum severance benefit), and, on the other hand, where the executive is fired for cause or quits without good reason (both of which result in minimum or no severance benefit). It is common to provide no special severance benefit in the case of the executive's death, disability, or retirement, but rather to provide that the executive or his or her estate will be entitled to receive whatever death, disability, or retirement benefits apply under the separate plans, programs, practices, and policies that are applicable to the executive on the date of termination.

Because of the significance of the reason for the termination in determining the severance benefits, certain key definitions merit special attention.

Cause. Historically, the definition of *cause* in executive employment contracts has been very tightly drawn, so that only the most egregious acts or misdeeds would trigger the employer's right to dismiss the executive for cause. The stated justification for using a very tight definition for top executives is that, at that level, the executive generally has negotiated the minimum level of compensation and benefits he or she is willing to receive in exchange for agreeing to join the company and has the bargaining power to require that such benefits not be taken away at the discretion of the company absent egregious and willful malfeasance on the part of the executive. In other words, unsatisfactory performance results are simply part of the risk the company takes when hiring the executive.

However, in the wake of the corporate scandals of the early 2000s, there is a tendency to loosen the *cause* definition somewhat, so that an executive who engages in intentional misconduct or knowingly violates the employer's code of ethics, for example, can be terminated without triggering generous severance benefits. The goal is to achieve the proper balance between giving the executive reasonable assurance that he or she will be entitled to the benefit of his or her bargain, and not fettering the employer's ability, in good faith, to dismiss an executive on grounds of misconduct without paying a windfall severance.

Generally speaking, the definition of *cause* in an executive's employment agreement would not include the executive's failure, after reasonable efforts, to meet performance expectations. Such definition also typically affords reasonable due-process protection to the executive in the sense that it requires a full board review and an opportunity for the executive to present his or her case. Following such hearing, the affirmative vote of a majority (or a designated super-majority) of the board or the independent directors is typically required to sustain the "for cause" determination.

Exhibit 9.1 contains a sampling of the types of conduct or circumstances that might constitute cause, with those in the left column being of a formulation more favorable to the executive, and those in the right column providing more flexibility for the employer.

Good Reason. Most executive employment agreements contain provisions allowing the executive to terminate employment for a defined "good reason," in which case the executive will typically receive full severance benefits. This is sometimes referred to a "constructive termination." As in the case of "cause" definitions, "good reason" definitions historically have tended to be written so that it is quite easy for the executive to identify circumstances that justify resignation with full severance. However, there is an emergence of agreements that are not quite so generous in this area.

Exhibit 9.2 contains a sampling of the types of events or circumstances that might constitute good reason for resignation, with those in the left column being of a formulation more favorable to the executive, and those in the right column being somewhat mitigating in favor of the employer.

Good reason should specifically exclude the executive's death, disability, or retirement, as those events are dealt with under other sections of the agreement. The agreement should provide ground rules for determining whether "good reason" has occurred. For example, in some contracts, the executive's determination is

Exhibit 9.1   Conduct Constituting "Cause"

Wording More Favorable to Executive	Wording Providing More Flexibility to Employer
Conviction of a felony [which may result in a term of imprisonment] or a crime involving moral turpitude	Commission of (or indictment for) a crime, typically a felony or a crime involving moral turpitude
[Adjudication of] fraud, embezzlement, theft, or other dishonest act against the employer	Willful engaging by executive in illegal conduct or gross misconduct that is materially and demonstrably injurious to the company
	Abuse of alcohol or drugs
	Any act that constitutes, on the part of the executive, fraud, dishonesty, breach of fiduciary duty, misappropriation, embezzlement, or gross misfeasance of duty
	Executive's willful disregard of published employer policies and procedures or codes of ethics
	Conduct by executive in his or her office with the company that is grossly inappropriate and demonstrably likely to lead to material injury to the company
	Insubordination and failure to follow direction (rare in top-level executive contracts)

conclusive. In most cases, the employer has an opportunity to cure any claimed event of good reason (other than the "free walk" provision discussed later), and in some cases, the board's good faith determination of cure is binding.

The "free walk" good reason trigger, if any, typically is a relatively short period beginning on the first anniversary of a change in control, during which the executive may resign without any reason and still trigger the maximum severance benefits. Arguably, this benefits shareholders by encouraging the executive to assist in the completion of the transaction and to continue to render constructive service during a reasonable transition period following the change in control, without the need to prove that some other element of "good reason" has been triggered. For example, it avoids the need to argue that the change in control has resulted in a diminution of the executive's position or authority, which is almost always a subjective analysis, prone to disagreement. As a practical matter, a "free walk" provision gives the executive a certain amount of leverage to negotiate a new

Exhibit 9.2 Events or Circumstances Constituting "Good Reason" for Resignation

Wording More Favorable to Executive	Wording More Favorable to Employer
Without the written consent of the executive, the assignment to the executive of duties inconsistent in any [material] respect with the executive's position (including status, offices, titles, and reporting requirements), authority, duties, or responsibilities as in effect on [the effective date of the agreement], excluding an isolated, insubstantial, and inadvertent action not taken in bad faith and which is remedied by the employer promptly after receipt of notice thereof given by the executive	Same as on left, but with the following proviso: provided, however, the fact that the executive's employment after a change in control shall be with a nonpublicly traded subsidiary of an entity resulting from or surviving the change in control, if that is the case, shall not of itself be deemed a material diminution in the executive's position, authority, duties, or responsibilities
A reduction in the executive's base salary	Same as on left
Failure by the employer (a) to continue in effect any compensation plan in which the executive participates that is material to total compensation, unless an equitable arrangement has been made with respect to such plan, or (b) to continue the executive's participation therein on a basis not materially less favorable, both in terms of the amount of benefits provided and the level of the executive's participation relative to other participants	Same as on left, but with the following added: excluding an isolated, insubstantial, and inadvertent action not taken in bad faith and which is remedied by the employer promptly after receipt of notice thereof given by the executive
Requiring the executive, without his or her consent, to be based at any office or location other than in [city] or to travel on employer business to a substantially greater extent than required immediately prior to the [effective date of the agreement]	Requiring the executive, without his or her consent, to be based at any office or location other than in [designated area], except in connection with a relocation of the company's headquarters
Failure by the employer to require a successor to assume the agreement	No comparable provision
Any termination by the executive for any reason or no reason during a designated window period following a change in control (typically, the 30-day period beginning on the first anniversary of a change in control)	No comparable provision

employment agreement with the acquiror. While this provision is not universally embraced, a 2001 survey of 150 leading companies by Executive Compensation Advisory Services[3] (the *ECAS Survey*) showed that 45% of the surveyed companies had at least one executive agreement with this feature or a similar "single-trigger" feature, which represented a 33% increase over its survey for the prior year. The *ECAS Survey* confirmed that the predominant single-trigger "window" is the 30-day period following the first anniversary of the change in control.

Disability. In considering the appropriate definition of "disability" for purposes of an employment agreement, the committee should bear in mind the consequences of such a determination. If the agreement provides no severance other than benefits under an applicable disability insurance plan, then it probably makes sense to tie the agreement definition to the plan definition in such a way that the executive is most likely to be eligible for such plan benefits. If the employment agreement does provide additional severance benefits in the case of disability, the provision should be drafted in a way to assure that the disability carrier will be the primary payer.

Severance

Severance benefits are often closely tied to the compensation and benefits provided during the active employment phase. The level of benefits should depend upon a number of factors, including the industry involved, the overall business climate, the historical approach of the employer to severance benefits, and the relative bargaining strength of the parties.

The *ECAS Survey* provides a good source for quick analysis of the prevalence and trends with respect to the most typical features of management change-in-control arrangements. However, the *ECAS Survey* is based on 2001 information, and there is little doubt that the landscape is becoming increasingly conservative in the area of executive compensation. Moreover, the *ECAS Survey* focuses on change-in-control agreements and related severance benefits. Generally speaking, it is common to provide somewhat enhanced severance benefits in a change-in-control situation. Nevertheless, the *ECAS Survey* showed that a majority of executive change-in-control agreements in the survey expressed severance as a multiple of "pay," with no perceived correlation between the multiple (e.g., 2x, 3x, etc.) and the type of pay to which it applies. According to the survey, the severance multiple typically applies only to salary and bonus. A significant majority of the executive change-in-control agreements reported in the *ECAS Survey* used a 3x multiple of pay to calculate change-in-control severance in contracts for the top five executive officers.

---

[3]*2001 Guide to Change in Control* (McGowan, ed., Executive Compensation Advisory Services, 3rd ed. 2001).

Restrictive Covenants

Executive employment agreements typically include restrictive covenants imposing prohibitions on competing, soliciting customers or employees, and disclosing confidential information. Employers' natural inclination is to negotiate provisions that are as broad as possible so as to protect the employer's business interests. However, restrictive covenants are governed by state law, and it is imperative to consider which state's law will apply and the requirements such law imposes for the restriction to be enforced.

Many states are generally reluctant to enforce noncompetition restrictions except to the extent that the time and geographic scope of the restrictions are reasonably necessary to protect the employer's business interests and the restrictions will not unduly interfere with the executive's ability to earn a living. In designing a noncompetition restriction, therefore, it is necessary to consider the executive's position in the company, his or her ability to compete with the employer, and the particular interests of the employer that must be protected from competition. It is critical to consider the effect under state law if the restrictions are found to be overly broad or otherwise unenforceable. Some states do not allow "blue penciling" to reign in an over broad restriction, and some will invalidate *other* restrictive covenants if the noncompetition covenant fails. In these states, it may be prudent to omit a noncompetition covenant in favor of covenants not to solicit protected employees and customers. As a practical matter, those two nonsolicitation covenants, together with a confidentiality covenant, provide most of the protection a company needs, and they are more likely to be enforceable than a traditional noncompetition covenant. The committee should resist relying on a "standard" form of restrictive covenants, as the law of the state in which the executive provides services is most likely to govern the enforceability of such covenants, and state laws vary widely in this area.

CHANGE-IN-CONTROL ARRANGEMENTS

Beginning with the rash of "hostile" takeover activity in the 1980s, and evolving through the "friendly" strategic business combinations of the 1990s, protecting management against a change in control has been at the center of focus for boards of directors. Whenever faced with the consideration of a business combination transaction, whether in a defensive or aggressive posture, executives inevitably experience a strong sense of personal uncertainty as to their own future if the combination occurs. The primary function of change-in-control protections for senior management is to offset these pressures—providing retention incentives, in the case of companies that are probable merger targets, and in the case of companies seeking strategic alliances, making it possible for executives to stay focused on negotiating and completing such transactions without undue personal distraction. This helps protect and enhance shareholder value by keeping the management team pulling together during the important phases of negotiation and implementation and also during the critical transition period after closing.

Change-in-control protection can come in the form of a broad-based plan or policy, but for senior management it is more typically housed in individual agreements—either as a stand-alone agreement that springs into effect once a change in control has occurred, or as an element of the executive's employment agreement in the form of an enhanced severance benefit where the termination of employment is closely related to a change in control.

As discussed in Chapter 5, a board's decision to adopt change-in-control protections is usually analyzed under the business judgment rule, protecting the board's decision as long as reasonable consideration is applied and there is no conflicting interest. However, if change-in-control protections are instituted during a pending or threatened takeover contest, the board's action may be analyzed under stricter scrutiny. Under this so-called "Unocal" standard,[4] the business judgment rule will not apply to protect the board's defensive action unless (i) the directors can show that they had reasonable grounds for believing that a danger to corporate policy and effectiveness existed because of another person's stock ownership, and (ii) any defensive measure taken is reasonable in relation to the threat posed.

Whether or not in a defensive situation, when considering change-in-control arrangements for management, the board or compensation committee should insist on reviewing numerical illustrations of the effect of the proposed benefits under various scenarios. In order to appreciate the potential cost of such provisions, it is necessary to understand the nature and operation of the so-called "golden parachute" excise tax. For a more technical discussion of these tax rules, see Chapter 7.

Very simply, the golden parachute rules are a manifestation of the government's social policy, as articulated in the mid 1980s, that executives should not enjoy a substantial windfall upon a change in control. The parachute rules are designed to discourage such windfalls by (i) imposing a stiff (20%) excise tax on excess "parachute payments," and (ii) denying the employer's compensation deduction for such amounts.

Any payment or benefit that is paid to a "disqualified individual" (which generally would include employees who are officers, or who own more than 1% of the fair market value of the company's outstanding stock, or who are highly compensated) in connection with a change in control of the company could be a parachute payment. If the total parachute payments to the person equal or exceed *three* times his or her "base amount" (which generally is the person's average taxable compensation from the employer over the last five years), then there is an "excess parachute payment" equal to the amount by which the total parachute payments exceed

[4]*Unocal Corp. v. Mesa Petroleum Co.*, 493 A.2d 946 (Del. 1985).

one times the base amount. The employee would owe a 20% excise tax on the excess parachute payment, and the company would lose its compensation deduction for the excess parachute payment. The excise tax is in addition to any applicable income tax.

It is impossible to calculate parachute payments with specificity in advance of an actual change in control because much depends on facts not yet known, such as the stock price and interest rates in effect at the time of the change in control and the executive's base amount. However, to satisfy its duties of care and good faith in considering the proposed arrangement, the board (or compensation committee) should model the potential costs in advance, based on hypothetical assumptions.

There are several approaches for dealing in a contract with the possible imposition of the excise tax. On a continuum from the most to least favorable to the executive, they might include:

(i) A full or partial gross-up payment by the employer to cover the amount of the excise tax, plus any income and excise taxes associated with the gross-up payment. Depending on the tax bracket of the executive, and due to the compounding effect of the taxes, as a rule of thumb, it can cost the company 2.5 to 3 times the amount of the original excise tax to accomplish a full gross-up. The company continues to lose its tax deduction on the excess parachute payment (which itself is increased by the amount of the gross-up payment).

(ii) A gross-up payment by the employer, *but only if* the after-tax benefit to the executive is at least $xxxx (this should be a meaningful amount to the executive, such as $50,000 or $100,000). If the after-tax benefit would be less, there would typically be a cutback of parachute payments to the extent necessary to avoid the imposition of the excise tax (i.e., limited to 2.99 times the executive's base amount).

(iii) A comparison of the after-tax benefit to the executive of (A) the total parachute payments after he or she pays the excise tax and income taxes thereon, to (B) a cutback of parachute payments to the extent necessary to avoid the imposition of the excise tax (i.e., limited to 2.99 times the executive's base amount). The employee would be paid whichever amount yields the more favorable result to the executive.

(iv) A cutback of parachute payments to the extent necessary to avoid the imposition of the excise tax (i.e., limited to 2.99 times the executive's base amount).

(v) Remain silent. It is possible for the executive to be worse off paying the excise tax than having his or her benefits limited to the extent necessary to avoid the imposition of the excise tax.

Although disproportionately expensive to the employer, many companies have adopted a "gross-up" provision. The *ECAS Survey* referenced earlier shows that 78% of the study companies with individual change-in-control agreements for management provided an excise tax gross-up for one or more executives. However, because of the high marginal cost of grossing up parachute payments if they are only slightly over the 299% safe harbor amount, it often makes sense to provide that a cutback, rather than the gross-up, applies if the parachute payments do not exceed a certain threshold amount (i.e., to follow the approach described in clause (ii)).

Definition of Change in Control

Most change-in-control agreements are so-called "double trigger" arrangements, meaning that the occurrence of a change in control is the first of two events that must occur in order to trigger benefits to the executive. The second of such events is a termination of employment (either termination by the employer without "cause" or resignation by the executive for "good reason").

More rarely, benefits are triggered by the mere occurrence of a change in control, which is referred to as a "single-trigger" arrangement.

In either case, the definition of change in control is paramount. A well-drafted definition will usually include some or all of the following elements:

(i)   A "hostile" change in the composition of a majority of the board (typically following a successful proxy contest).

(ii) A third party acquires a significant percentage (typically 20% to 35%) of the outstanding common stock or voting power of the employer (with certain exceptions).

(iii) Consummation of a merger or similar business transaction involving the employer, or a sale of substantially all of the stock or assets of the employer, or the acquisition by the employer of stock or assets of another corporation, unless, immediately after the transaction, some or all of the following conditions are met:

    (A) The employer's shareholders continue to hold more than a designated percentage (typically 50% to 60%) of the common stock and voting power of the surviving entity, in substantially the same proportion as before such transaction.

    (B) No person (other than the employer or the surviving entity or its parent) holds in excess of a designated percentage (typically matches the percentage in (ii)) of the common stock or voting power of the surviving entity.

    (C) At least a majority of the surviving corporation's board consists of individuals who were incumbent directors of the employer at the time such transaction was approved.

(iv) The shareholders of the employer approve a complete liquidation or dissolution of the company.

Paragraphs (i) and (iv) of the preceding definition are quite standard, generally uncontroversial, and not very likely to be the activating trigger of a change in control. Paragraph (ii) (the "Stock Acquisition Trigger") and paragraph (iii) (the "Transaction Trigger") are standard provisions in concept, but vary from company to company as to the applicable percentages employed (i.e., in the case of the Stock Acquisition Trigger, the percentage of common stock that a third party must acquire in order to trigger a change in control, and in the case of the Transaction Trigger, the percentage of continuity of ownership and voting control that must be retained after the transaction in order not to trigger a change in control).

The Stock Acquisition Trigger

Based on the *ECAS Survey*, the percentages of common stock and voting power that a third party must acquire in order to trigger a change in control under this element of the definition ranged from 10% to 80%, with 20% being the predominant percentage. This is not surprising since, as a practical matter, ownership of a 20% block of common stock is likely to command the ability to significantly influence board policy, regardless of the absence of legal ability to vote the board out of office. The lower the percentage used, the more likely it is that a change in control will be deemed to have occurred.

There should be exceptions to the Stock Acquisition Trigger that keep it from being activated in unwarranted circumstances. For example, the following acquisitions typically should be excluded as a change-in-control event under this element of the definition:

(A) An acquisition directly from the employer
(B) An acquisition by the employer or its subsidiaries
(C) An acquisition by any employer-sponsored employee benefit plan (or related trust)
(D) An acquisition that would not trigger a change in control under the Transaction Trigger (as discussed next)

Thus, for example, if the employer were to intentionally place a large block of stock with an investor by issuing new shares, that should not trigger a change in control.

The Transaction Trigger

This is the element of the definition that is probably most likely to be triggered in today's business environment. However, not all business combinations should trigger a change in control. The issue is whether the transaction should justifiably engender management's sense of job insecurity. For example, a merger, such as a change-of-domicile merger, that does not result in any change of the employer's shareholder base or board of directors should clearly not affect job security and should not constitute a change in control. However, a transaction in which the shareholder base is materially changed, particularly if the board of the resulting entity is comprised of a majority of new directors, could well portend employment changes at the highest ranks, thereby underscoring the need for the change-in-control protections. Striking an appropriate balance between these two extremes requires thoughtful consideration. For example, if the Transaction Trigger were set at 50% or less continuity-of-ownership, a 45% to 55% "merger of equals" (where the employer represented the 55% side) would not trigger the definition. This may not be an ideal result, since the executives of the employer would still face considerable job insecurity in the face of such a "merger of equals." Based on this, it is not uncommon to see the Transaction Trigger set at 60% or more, so as to be more likely to include an actual "merger of equals" transaction. However, the board may feel that it is not desirable to trigger enhanced severance incentives in the case of a merger of equals, in which case the Transaction Trigger may be set at 50% or less. According to the *ECAS Survey,* the most common Transaction Trigger continuity-of-ownership percentage used by companies in the study was 50% or 51%, with several using a percentage as high as 70%. The higher the continuity-of-ownership percentage, the more likely it is that a given transaction will result in a change in control.

Some companies have attempted to address these concerns by giving the board of directors discretion to determine whether or not a particular transaction will be considered a change in control. This can put the board in an untenable position, however, where the acquiror asserts pressure on the board to conclude that the transaction does not constitute a change in control and thereby eliminate the severance protection. In any event, the ability of the board to make this subjective decision substantially dilutes the primary purpose of the change-in-control arrangement— to engender confidence in management that they will be protected.

Chapter 10

Incentive Compensation

Most executive compensation arrangements consist of annual base salary, short-term incentives (e.g., annual bonus), long-term incentives (e.g., stock options), retirement arrangements, welfare benefits, and perquisites. This chapter provides a general overview of the design of short-term and long-term incentive arrangements and the specifics of these arrangements (other than arrangements that involve the grant of equity-based compensation, which is discussed in Chapter 11). The chapter also presents topics, ideas, and issues that compensation committees need to know, review, and address with respect to these arrangements. In addition, market practices associated with these arrangements will be noted. Finally, while not an incentive arrangement per se, retention-only plans are also discussed.

The following items will be covered:

- Useful definitions when discussing incentive arrangements
- General comparison of using cash-based or equity-based incentive compensation
- Typical plan and award types and features
- Shareholder approval
- Retention-only plans

USEFUL DEFINITIONS

The following is a list of useful definitions that will be helpful in discussing these incentive arrangements. Note that these definitions are neither universal nor absolute, but generally are part of the executive compensation "lexicon" and will be used for purposes of this chapter:

- *Award:* A compensatory grant under a plan.
- *Award agreement* or *award letter:* A written document between the awardee and the company memorializing the terms and conditions of the award (including the terms and conditions that are already a part of the overlying plan).

- *Awardee:* A person or entity who has received an award.
- *Cash-based arrangement:* An arrangement where the compensation is determined solely based on a specified dollar amount and does not in any way take into account a specified number of company shares (e.g., an annual bonus program that awards a percentage of base salary).
- *Equity-based arrangement* or *stock-based arrangement:* An arrangement where the compensation is determined solely based on a specific number of company shares, and does not in any way take into account a specified dollar amount (e.g., a grant of stock appreciation rights payable in cash, a grant of restricted stock units payable in stock).
- *Holding period:* The time period over which nonforfeitable compensation will be held before the payout date (note: while not entirely accurate, some may use the term *holding period* but actually should use the term *vesting period* if the compensation is subject to forfeiture).
- *Hybrid arrangement:* An arrangement that is both a cash-based arrangement and an equity-based arrangement.
- *Long-term:* A time period longer than one year.
- *Mid-term:* A time period generally between one and three years ("mid-term" is not used very often by practitioners, and most often is used interchangeably with "long-term").
- *Omnibus plan* or *master plan:* A plan or program that is used to make grants of all types of compensatory awards or used to create other incentive compensation plans or programs (see *subplans*).
- *Payout date:* The date that the compensation is paid (if cash) or delivered (if property).
- *Performance-based compensation:* Generally refers to compensation where payout only occurs if a performance goal is reached (e.g., a stock option where the exercise price is at or above the stock price on the date of grant is performance-based compensation, while restricted stock that vests only if there is continued employment is not performance-based compensation); it is also used to refer to compensation that meets the requirements of Internal Revenue Code (Code) Section 162(m).
- *Performance measure* or *performance metric:* The measure used to rate performance.
- *Performance goal* or *performance target* or *performance objective:* A definable and measurable level of performance.
- *Performance vested:* Vesting that occurs only if a performance goal is reached.
- *Plan* or *program:* A written document detailing the compensation arrangement.
- *Plan life:* The time period during which awards may be made under the plan (in many cases, the plan life is 10 years).

- *Plan period:* The time period consisting of both the performance period (if applicable) and/or the vesting period (if applicable) and/or the restricted period (if applicable).

- *Performance period* or *performance cycle:* The time period over which performance is measured.

- *Short-term:* A time period equal to or less than one year.

- *Subplan* or *subprogram:* A plan or program the terms and conditions of which are subject to an omnibus plan.

- *Time-vesting:* Vesting that occurs only if there is continued employment/service by the awardee.

- *Vest:* Generally when the compensation becomes nonforfeitable; however, in the case of certain awards (e.g., stock options or stock appreciation rights), when the award may be exercised, but may be subject to forfeiture or accelerated expiration if there is a termination of employment.

- *Vesting period* or *restricted period* or *restriction period:* The time period over which continued employment is required, and if this requirement is not met, the compensation is forfeited.

CASH VS. EQUITY

There is no "right" answer to the question of whether to use cash or equity as the basis of an incentive plan. Each has its own attributes and detriments. With changes to the equity-based accounting rules, equity-based compensation may be losing its "edge" over cash-based compensation since both will now be treated as an expense. However, nonperformance-based equity-based compensation (e.g., time-vested restricted stock or restricted stock units) may result in a lower and more manageable expense charge since the valuation date is the date of grant, not the payout date. This, though, is dependent on how the accounting profession applies the new standards under FAS 123 and IFRS 2 (as discussed in Chapter 8).

The main difference between equity-based compensation and cash-based compensation is that the performance measure for equity-based compensation simply is the price of the stock. As a performance measure, stock price is easily understood by the awardee and easily accessible if the company is publicly traded. It also (at least on the surface) directly aligns the interests of the awardee with the interests of shareholders. For an equity-based incentive program at a private company, the stock most likely will need to be valued on a fairly regular basis (usually once a year, or perhaps even each quarter) if the company wants to imitate a public company stock incentive program and maintain a "line of sight" to the value of the enterprise. If it does not (usually because the "exit strategy" is a sale or IPO), then the awardee does not need a continuing line of sight since the focus is on the "end of the tunnel" when the sale or IPO occurs.

With the recent executive compensation scandals and controversies, most of which focused on the use of "plain vanilla" stock options, the current thinking is that companies need to focus on performance measures other than stock price. Thus, the list of performance measures presented in this chapter should be reviewed by compensation committees and their senior executives to see if (and which of) these measures are the proper business drivers.

Finally, it is noted that there are such things as "hybrid" or "combination" incentive plans that are both cash-based and equity-based. This is not to be confused with a cash-based plan that pays out in stock (e.g., an annual bonus plan that pays 50% in cash and 50% in fully vested company stock), or an equity-based plan that pays out in cash (e.g., a stock appreciation right that pays in cash). A hybrid plan is a plan where the compensation delivered is determined by the price of the stock and some other performance measure. For example, a hybrid plan could be a plan where there is a three-year performance period requiring a performance goal based on increases in EPS growth that pays out 50% in cash and 50% in restricted stock at the end of the performance period, and where the restricted stock cliff vests at the end of a two-year vesting period that begins at the end of the three-year performance period. Thus, while the plan period is five years, for the first three years it is essentially a cash-based plan, and for the last two years it is essentially an equity-based plan.

TYPICAL PLAN FEATURES AND DESIGNS

Incentive plans come in all shapes and sizes, and, similar as to whether to use cash or equity, there is no "right" plan. Simply put, one size does not fit all. Compensation committees will need to examine all elements of incentive compensation plans and decide what plan features and design are best for their companies.

The following are the incentive compensation plan features and design that compensation committees generally will need to consider:

- Type of awards and type of plan
- Purpose of plan
- Administration of plan
- Eligibility and participation
- Award levels
- Performance periods
- Performance measures
- Performance goals

- What happens if a participant's employment is terminated due to:
  - Death
  - Disability
  - Retirement
  - For "Cause"
  - Without "Cause"
  - For "Good Reason"
  - Without "Good Reason"
- What happens on a change in control
- Payout in cash or stock or both
- Other miscellaneous issues

Types of Awards and Types of Plans

When speaking of a "type" of incentive plan, the first type to consider is whether the plan is a "specific" or a "general" plan. A specific type of plan usually is an arrangement where the delivery of compensation is limited to a specific type of award. Types of awards include:

- Incentive stock options (these are the options qualified under Code Section 422)
- Nonqualified stock options (these are options that are not intended to qualify as incentive stock options)
- Stock appreciation rights (which may be payable in cash or stock or both)
- Stock
- Restricted stock
- Stock units (which may be payable in cash or stock or both)
- Restricted stock units (which may be payable in cash or stock or both)
- Performance shares
- Performance units (which may be payable in cash or stock or both)
- Cash
- Property (other than company stock)

Thus, a plan may be a "Stock Option Plan," which only provides for the grant of stock options, a "Performance Unit Plan," which only provides for the grant of performance units, or an "Executive Annual Cash Bonus Plan," which only provides for the grant of annual cash bonuses. The point is that all these plans are limited in design and function.

A plan type may be further defined by the performance period. Thus, a plan may be the "2005 Annual Incentive Plan," which would correspond to the company's fiscal year 2005, or it may be the "2005–2007 Performance Unit Plan," which would provide for a grant of performance units over a performance period from the beginning of the company's fiscal year 2005 and ending at the end of the company's fiscal year 2007. These types of specific plans are limited in design and function.

Moreover, a specific type of cash-based plan may provide the performance measure to be used to determine compensation. For example, an "EVA Plan" is a long-term cash-based arrangement that uses "economic value added" as a performance measure (and which typically has a feature where the compensation is "banked" and subject to loss or reduction if future performance is poor). Alternatively, the plan may be an "EPS Growth Plan," where cash or stock compensation is paid if EPS growth targets are achieved.

Overall, a "specific" plan, being limited in scope and function, does not allow a compensation committee (or whatever committee is administering the plan) a wide degree of discretion in setting the terms and conditions of the awards. This may have utility in some situations, but usually it "paints" compensation committees "into a corner." Accordingly, these types of plans are being phased out at many companies, particularly at publicly held companies. This is because, for example, too many times a company has had only a stock option plan and found that it needed to grant restricted stock but couldn't unless the plan was amended and approved by shareholders.

If a plan is not a "specific" plan, then it starts to migrate over to a "general" plan, which may combine several different types of awards (e.g., stock options and stock appreciation rights), or—as is becoming the trend—combining all award types (even cash-based awards) under the moniker of an "omnibus" plan or simply as the "XYZ Company Incentive Compensation Plan."

While some companies still prefer to have a specific plan document for each compensation program, most companies are using "omnibus" plans that provide wide flexibility and discretion in devising and implementing compensation programs and where the only other relevant document is the award agreement. As noted earlier, this is probably the arrangement that most public companies will use in the future, since shareholder approval is secured for all programs in one fell swoop (subject to shareholder reapproval in five years), and thus new subplans and other programs will not require shareholder approval. In addition, due to the new shareholder-approval rules at the various stock exchanges, it is likely that the omnibus plan will be extremely general and very discretionary in nature; in other words, the plan will contain only the terms and conditions with which shareholders and their various advising services will be concerned. It is likely that there will be more subplans or "operating guidelines" associated with these omnibus plans, since many of the typical terms and conditions may be left out of the master plan. Thus, awardees would receive a copy of the master plan (which would contain some, but not many, terms and conditions associated with the award), a copy of the subplan (which would contain most of the specifics associated with the particular compensation program), and a copy of the award agreement (which, most likely, would be simply a one- or two-page document, and would contain terms and conditions specific to that particular award and awardee).

Plan Purpose

It is usually important to establish the purpose of the incentive plan to the executives. Essentially, this is a communication issue for HR or Finance. If the executives don't understand what the incentive plan is all about, they may not be able to see the objectives. Most plan documents contain a section (usually the first or second section) that details or at least outlines the purpose of the program. For public companies, this purpose section of the plan is also an opportunity for the company and the compensation committee to communicate to shareholders and potential investors. It essentially is up to the committee to determine how extensive this description of the purpose should be, and whether it is primarily directed to management, shareholders, investors, or the public in general.

Administration of the Plan

A person or a committee will need to administer the plan. For public companies, the committee will need to satisfy the outside director requirements of IRC Section 162(m), the non-employee director requirements of Rule 16b-3 under federal securities law, and the independent director rules under the various stock exchanges. The committee usually is the compensation committee, but it also could be a subcommittee of the compensation committee or could be the entire board of directors or all independent directors. The committee should have wide authority in administering and interpreting the terms and conditions of the plan, and the determination of the committee should be final and binding on all awardees. The committee should be able to delegate some of its responsibilities and hire outside advisors. Committee members should be indemnified (other than for bad faith or gross negligence). It is also important that the committee understands its duties, responsibilities, and obligations under federal law and applicable state law (primarily the state's corporation law).

Eligibility and Participation

While "eligibility" and "participation" may appear to be (and for that matter may be) the same thing, there can be a difference. This difference is that while all employees may be eligible to participate in the plan, only some employees do in fact become participants. Of course, the plan may be a broad-based annual cash bonus plan where all employees are eligible to participate and indeed are all participants. Alternatively, the plan may be a three-year cash-based plan where executives above a specific salary grade are automatic participants and other employees are selected by the committee in its sole discretion to be participants. Essentially, this will be driven by the purpose of the plan. Sometimes, employees will be divided into groups or "tiers" of employees, which determines who will participate in the plan. For example, employees in Tiers 1, 2, 3, and 4 will be participants in the company's annual bonus plan, but only employees in Tiers 1 and 2 will be participants in the company's long-term incentive plan.

In addition, the plan may or may not allow new hires to become participants in an existing compensation plan or ongoing program. For example, assume a company has overlapping three-year performance period EPS-growth programs, and a new CEO is hired in the middle of the fiscal year. The plan should allow the new CEO to "cycle into" the company's overlapping performance cycles so that he or she would receive $\frac{1}{6}$ of the award for the performance period that is $2\frac{1}{2}$ years through, $\frac{1}{2}$ of the award for the performance cycle that is $1\frac{1}{2}$ years through, and $\frac{5}{6}$ of the award for the performance cycle that is only six months through.

Award Levels

Award levels may be specified in the plan (e.g., a percentage of base salary), determined through the use of a "bonus pool" where percentages of the pool are allocated to participants, or simply left to the sole discretion of the committee in creating specific award levels with respect to a specific subplan (e.g., under the XYZ Company Executive Annual Bonus Plan, the 2005 subplan determined award levels as a percentage of actual base salaries, while the 2006 subplan determined award levels based on salary grade). Award levels may be set at a single level; in other words, if the performance goal is met, the employee will receive $100,000. Or, it may be expressed as a "minimum" or "threshold" level, a target level, and a maximum or "stretch" level. For example, an awardee with a base salary of $200,000 may have a target award level expressed as 50% of base salary, with a minimum at 75% of award level and maximum at 125%; thus, this awardee has a threshold award level of $75,000, a target award level at $100,000, and a maximum award level at $125,000. Note that the minimum, target, and maximum award levels are tied to a minimum, target, and maximum performance goal, respectively, and that the variance between the award levels may or may not have a correlation to the variance between the performance goal levels. Thus, using the preceding example, the 75% minimum award level may be tied to a minimum performance goal equal to 95% of the target performance goal, and the maximum award level may be tied to 150% of the target performance goal.

Plan Performance and Restricted Periods

Performance periods may be specified in the plan or left to the sole discretion of the committee to determine specific performance periods with respect to a specific subplan (e.g., under the XYZ Company Omnibus Plan, which allows committee discretion in setting performance periods, the company created the XYZ Company Annual Bonus Plan with a performance period of one year, the XYZ Company 2004–2006 Long-Term Incentive Plan with a performance period of three years, and the XYZ Company Retention Plan with a vesting period of two years). Performance periods, for the most part, should be established in direct coordination with the company's business plan.

Performance Measures

The following are common performance measures (other than stock price) that some companies might use (and in some cases a description of the measure):

- Revenue: Typically, this would relate to a target revenue amount, or revenue growth; may include all revenue or may carve out certain types of revenue (e.g., investment income), or may apply only to certain types of revenue (e.g., North American revenue).
- Sales: Same as revenue, but normally exclude nonsales revenue.
- Pretax income before allocation of corporate overhead and bonus.
- Budget.
- Cash flow: Simply, the cash that a company takes in (cash inflow) and pays out (cash outflow).
- Earnings per share: Measures a company's performance; calculated by dividing net profit by number of common shares outstanding (Basic EPS), or includes "common-stock equivalents" like stock options and warrants (Diluted EPS).
- Net income.
- Division, group, or corporate financial goals.
- Dividends.
- Total shareholder return (this is the return based on increases in stock price plus dividend payments).
- Return on shareholders' equity: This is a measure of profitability; ROE = net profit after taxes/stockholders' equity.
- Return on assets: This is a measure of profitability and efficiency (i.e., how a company generates profits from assets); ROA = net profit after taxes/total assets.

- Return on investment: Similar to ROE; measures how efficiently the financial resources available to a company are used; ROI = annual profit/average amount invested.
- Internal rate of return: A present-value-based measure used for determining the compounded annual rate of return on investments held for a time period of one year or more.
- Attainment of strategic and operational initiatives.
- Market share.
- Operating margin: This is equal to the ratio of operating income to sales revenue.
- Gross profits.
- EBIT: Earnings before interest and taxes. Also known as "operating profit," as it is income from a company's ordinary business activities.
- EBITDA: Earnings before interest, taxes, depreciation, and amortization; used by many to measure cash flow.
- EVA: Economic value-added models; this is a measure of the superiority of the return a company is able to realize on invested capital above the baseline return expected by the investment community. The formula to calculate EVA is EVA = NOPAT − (C × K(c)) where NOPAT is Net Operating Profit After Taxes, C is the amount of capital a company plans to invest in a project, and K(c) is the cost of capital.
- Comparisons with various stock market indices.
- Increase in number of customers.
- Reduction in costs.
- Mortgage loans.
- Bringing assets to market.
- Resolution of administrative or judicial proceedings or disputes.
- Funds from operations.

While some arrangements will focus on only one performance measure, it is not uncommon for companies to use two, three, or more performance measures to calculate payout. Typically, the use of two performance measures (e.g., revenue and EBITDA) may be presented using a matrix as shown in Exhibit 10.1. Overall, as with determining performance periods, the determination of which performance measure to use must be based on the company's business plan.

Performance Goals

Performance may be specified in the plan (e.g., a 10% annual growth in EPS) or left to the sole discretion of the committee in creating specific award levels with respect

Exhibit 10.1   Example of Multiple Performance Measures

	$180m	50%	60%	70%	80%	90%	100%
	$170m	40%	50%	60%	70%	80%	90%
R	$160m	30%	40%	50%	60%	70%	80%
E	$150m	20%	30%	40%	50%	60%	70%
V	$140m	10%	20%	30%	40%	50%	60%
E							
N	$130m	0%	10%	20%	30%	40%	50%
U	$120m	0%	0%	10%	20%	30%	40%
E	$110m	0%	0%	0%	10%	20%	30%
	$100m	0%	0%	0%	0%	10%	20%
	EBITDA	**$30m**	**$35m**	**$40m**	**$50m**	**$65m**	**$70m**

to a specific subplan (e.g., under the XYZ Company Executive Annual Bonus Plan, the performance goal is a 10% annual growth in EPS). As shown in Exhibit 10.1, a program may use more than one performance measure and thus more than one performance goal. While two or three measures are not uncommon, the use of more than three performance measures is unusual. Since the purpose of the performance measure is to focus the employee on the measure and achieving the measure's performance level, introducing a myriad of measures may confuse the "line of sight" needed to properly motivate and incent most employees.

While some plans use an "all or nothing" approach to achieving a performance goal (e.g., minimum award is paid if 90% of the goal is achieved, target if 100% of the goal is achieved, and maximum if 150% of the goal is achieved), many plans will use interpolation to award amounts that fall in between the specific performance goals.

The matrix in Exhibit 10.1 shows how a company would pay out using two performance measures.

Thus, an awardee with a salary of $200,000 who has an award target level of 50% of salary would receive $100,000 (or 100% of award target level) if revenue at the end of the performance period equaled $180 million and EBITDA at the end of the performance period equaled $70 million, or $50,000 if revenue equaled $130 million and EBITDA equaled $70 million. The plan design shown in Exhibit 10.1 might provide that the percentages only reflect achievements of the specific goals; thus, revenue of $149 million and EBITDA of $39 million would result in an award level of 20%. However, if interpolation were applied, the award level would be 28.8%. Exhibit 10.1 shows a maximum award level of 100% of goal; it could, of course, show award levels exceeding 100% of goal.

Indexing of the performance goal is also used by some companies, on the theory that a company's performance must be compared with the performance of its competitors to determine true performance. While the actual application can be complex, there is a purity in the concept of using relative performance comparisons, and to determine true underperformance or overperformance with respect to a defined market.

Termination of Employment

The consequences of the various types of termination of employment can range from total forfeiture of any award to full payment of the award. The applicable standard will be determined by the committee on either an employee-by-employee or group-by-group basis. In some cases, an employment agreement may control the consequence. The following list shows the various terminations and some comments:

- *Death.* Since this termination is an "act of God," neither the company nor the employee is "at fault." Complete forfeiture is typical, but this should take into account whether there is adequate company-provided life insurance (either paid in whole or in part by the company). However, there is an argument that the employee works for some portion of the performance period, and thus is entitled to a pro rata award, either based on target at time of termination or actual payout as if the employee had not died. Market practice appears to be leaning toward a pro rata award.

- *Disability.* Similar to death, this is a termination where neither the company nor the employee is at fault. Complete forfeiture is typical, but this should take into account whether there are company-provided disability benefits (either paid in whole or in part by the employee). The pro rata argument similarly exists, and market practice appears to be leaning that way.

- *Retirement.* Retirement is not always addressed in these programs, and in those cases it usually is treated as a termination without Good Reason. However, if such is the case, an employee may decide to postpone retirement until a performance cycle ends, if the award is meaningful. Astute companies generally provide for a pro rata award for an employee who retires prior to the end of a performance period.

- *For Cause.* A termination of the employee's employment by the company for Cause (whether defined in the plan, in the award letter or agreement, in an employment agreement, or under common-law principles) almost always results in complete forfeiture of the award. Note that "Cause" generally means that the employee engaged in some type of egregious behavior and generally does not mean poor individual performance. However, there seems to be a trend where the award may be forfeited (either in whole or in part) for a termination due to poor performance.

- *Without Cause.* A termination of the employee's employment by the company without Cause may result in total forfeiture, complete payment, or a pro rata payment. Factors considered are the salary grade of the employee, the number of days the employee was employed in the performance period, provisions in an employment agreement, and so forth. From the employee's perspective, the argument generally is that the company has taken away the employee's opportunity to earn the compensation, through no fault of the employee. From the company's perspective, the argument is that the compensation was never guaranteed and that the employee's employment was "at will," meaning that it could be terminated at any time for any reason or for no reason. However, companies must keep an eye on local law to make sure that the incentive compensation will not be treated as earned wages, which the employee has a legal right to receive. Another issue is when a termination of employment occurs after the end of the performance period. From the employee's perspective, the argument is that the termination of employment after the end of the performance period but before payout (usually within 2½ months of the end of the performance period) "robs" the employee of the compensation. However, many companies require that the employee be employed as of the payout date, not just through the entire performance period. Here again, if the employee has been told what the compensation is, and then is fired, there is a concern that it may be earned wages and subject to receipt under state law. Finally, as noted previously, some companies have applied a concept that falls somewhere between "Cause" and "Without Cause"—a termination due to poor performance. In such a case, the employee generally forfeits 100% of the award, but in some cases may be entitled to a portion of the award.

- *For Good Reason.* The term "Good Reason" usually means that the company has "constructively" (but not actually) terminated the employee's employment without Cause. For example, the company may relocate the employee to a desolate working location, reduce the employee's compensation, or assign duties that are materially inconsistent with the employee's title and position. Thus, as a constructive termination, the same logic and standards applicable to a termination without Cause would exist, and it is a matter of prior company practice and/or company culture whether a Good Reason termination will be treated as a termination without Cause.

- *Without Good Reason.* A termination without Good Reason simply means that the employee quit his or her job, and almost always, there is a complete forfeiture of the compensation, unless the compensation has been earned but deferred.

Change in Control

Some plans may contain specific terms and conditions relating to a change in control. If so, the plan usually contains a definition of change in control (although not always). Typically, a plan may require that all outstanding awards vest or are paid out at target (or sometimes at maximum) if there is a change in control. Sometimes, the plan may contain provisions relating to Code Section 280G golden parachutes, either providing for a tax gross-up or a reduction in the award if it would be treated by the IRS as an excess parachute payment. Alternatively, the plan may provide complete committee discretion, which may be exercised on the date of grant and contained in individual award agreements, or when there is a change in control. If committees do exercise discretion after the date of grant, the consequences of award modification need to be taken into account.

Payout in Cash or Stock or Both

Generally, payout is not a determining factor as to whether a plan is a cash-based arrangement or an equity-based arrangement. Simply put, using either cash or stock is a matter of what "currency" the company should use to pay out the compensation. Additionally, design of the award may determine whether the payout is in cash or stock; for example, a stock appreciation right may pay out only in stock so as to receive "favorable" accounting treatment.

SHAREHOLDER APPROVAL

If the company is publicly traded, then IRC Section 162(m) will apply and may limit the amount of deductible compensation paid to the company's top executives. Thus, for publicly traded companies, all incentive plans will need to be approved by shareholders to be exempt from Code Section 162(m). This means that shareholders will approve a single performance metric or a laundry list of performance metrics. In addition, the maximum compensation payable to any single participant must be disclosed. If the plan is an "omnibus" type plan, it may be necessary to break out the various types of cash compensation that may be paid. For example, the plan may state that the maximum amount of compensation (measured by a dollar amount) that may be paid is $2,000,000 for any arrangement where the performance period is short term, and $10,000,000 for any arrangement where the performance period is long term. Moreover, plans that have a laundry list of performance metrics will need to be reapproved by shareholders every five years. Finally, if a plan is materially amended or revised, shareholders will need to approve the amendment or revision.

RETENTION-ONLY PLANS

Retention-only plans were very popular in the late 1990s when M&A activity was peaking. The rationale for these plans was that the management team (whether consisting of the most senior executives or all of management) was a valuable asset of the company, and the preservation of that team was necessary to preserve and increase the value of the company. Generally, the design of these arrangements was fairly straightforward: the executive would receive a cash amount over a specified period of time. The time period usually was between one and two years, and the cash amount would be a percentage or multiple of base salary. For example, the CEO might receive a cash payment of 2x base salary at the end of a two-year period, and an EVP might receive 1x base salary at the end of such two-year period. Some arrangements (generally based on the notion that the payment of the retention award was too far off in the future), might pay a portion of the award over the retention period; for example, participants in a two-year program might receive 30% at the end of the first year, another 30% at the end of the 18-month period, and the remaining 40% at the end of the two years. Because retention-only plans were nonperformance-based, they generally were negatively perceived by shareholders. Accordingly, compensation committees should adequately and properly analyze these programs before implementation.

Chapter 11

Equity-Based Compensation

The beginning of this chapter describes some of the most common forms of equity-based compensation vehicles, with a focus on their tax and accounting consequences, Section 16 reporting and liability issues, an overview of principal advantages and disadvantages, and predictions of future trends. The next section covers special topical considerations related to direct and indirect stock option repricings, and the final section discusses trends in stock ownership and retention guidelines.

EQUITY-BASED INCENTIVE AWARDS

There is no doubt that equity will continue to play an essential role in the compensation of executives of public companies. While stock options have been the gold standard of employee compensation for the last two decades, the mandatory expensing of stock options (expected to begin in 2005 or 2006) will eliminate the compelling P&L advantage of "plain vanilla" stock options over other types of equity awards. This expectation has already led to a much broader use of other types of equity-based incentives—in particular, those that focus on the achievement of specific performance objectives rather than simple increase in stock price.

Given this evolution, it makes sense for a compensation committee to adopt a flexible incentive plan that permits a variety of award types (often referred to as an "omnibus" plan). Having a more flexible plan in place allows the committee to more precisely tailor individual awards to address the objectives of both the company and its employees.

This part of the chapter describes some of the most common forms of equity-based compensation vehicles, with a focus on their tax and accounting treatment, Section 16 reporting and liability issues, an overview of principal advantages and disadvantages, and a look into the future as to possible trends. Most equity-based awards are long-term incentives in that they provide compensation for performance measured over a period longer than 12 months. However, any of the equity-based incentives discussed in this chapter could be structured as short-term awards, measuring performance over a period of 12 months or less.

Stock Options

Description of Stock Options

A stock option permits the holder to purchase stock at a predetermined price for a specific period of time. Options can be tax-advantaged "incentive stock options" (ISOs) or "nonstatutory stock options" (NSOs).[1] Options that do not comply with the requirements for an ISO or that are otherwise stated not to be ISOs are NSOs.

In order to be considered an ISO, an option must meet all of the following requirements, which are specified in Section 422 of the Internal Revenue Code (Code) and applicable regulations:

1. Only a corporation (including an S corporation, a foreign corporation, or an LLC treated as a corporation) may grant ISOs.
2. Only persons who are employees of the corporation granting the option (or employees of a related parent or subsidiary corporation) are eligible to receive ISOs—consultants and nonemployee directors cannot receive ISOs.
3. An ISO must be granted pursuant to a plan that has been approved by the company's shareholders within 12 months before or after the plan is adopted (certain plan amendments also require shareholder approval).
4. An ISO must be granted within 10 years of the earlier of the date the plan was adopted by the board or the date the plan was approved by the shareholders.
5. The plan under which ISOs are granted must designate a maximum aggregate number of shares that may be issued under the plan in the form of ISOs.
6. The plan under which ISOs are granted must designate the employees or class or classes of employees eligible to receive options or other awards under the plan.
7. The exercise price of an ISO may not be less than 100% of the fair market value of the company's stock as of the date of grant of the option (or, 110% in the case of an optionee who possesses more than 10% of the combined voting power of all classes of stock of the employer corporation or any related parent or subsidiary corporation).
8. An ISO, by its terms, may not be exercisable more than 10 years from the date of grant (or 5 years in the case of an optionee who is a 10% shareholder) or

---

[1]Options granted under an employee stock purchase plan qualified under Code Section 423 (ESPP) are a different type of tax-advantaged option. ESPP options are not discussed in this chapter but are discussed in Chapter 7.

more than 90 days after termination of employment (other than for death or disability).

9. An ISO may not be transferable except in the event of the optionee's death, and is exercisable only by the optionee as long as he or she is living.

10. For any one person, the maximum fair market value of stock subject to ISOs that become exercisable for the first time in any calendar year may not exceed $100,000, which value is measured as of the date of grant.

Tax Treatment of Stock Options

The tax treatment of an option hinges on whether it is an ISO or an NSO.

ISOs   The holder of an ISO is not taxed on the option spread when the option is exercised (but the spread is included for purposes of calculating the optionee's alternative minimum tax for the year of exercise). Instead, the holder of an ISO is taxed when the acquired stock is eventually sold. In short, ISOs provide a tax advantage to optionees that NSOs do not provide—automatic deferral of tax on the gain resulting from the exercise of the option.

Moreover, if stock acquired through the exercise of an ISO is held for a specified period of time—the longer of two years from the date the option is granted or one year after the option is exercised—then any gain on the sale of the stock will be taxed as long-term capital gain. If the stock is not held for the required holding period, the difference between the exercise price and the lesser of (i) the fair market value of the stock on the date of exercise, and (ii) the sales price, will be taxed as ordinary income. Any additional gain will be taxed as long-term or short-term capital gain depending on how long the stock was held.

The employer is not entitled to a tax deduction upon the exercise of an ISO or upon the subsequent sale of the stock if the required holding period is met. If the optionee does not hold the stock for the required holding period, however, the employer will be entitled to a tax deduction equal to the amount of ordinary income recognized by the optionee.

NSOs   The holder of an NSO recognizes taxable income at the time the option is exercised, in an amount equal to the excess of the fair market value of the stock on the exercise date over the exercise price. This amount is taxed at ordinary income tax rates. Any further appreciation in the value of the stock will be taxed when the stock is sold and will be either long-term capital gain or short-term capital gain depending on how long the stock has been held prior to sale. The company is entitled to a tax deduction equal to the amount of ordinary income recognized by the optionee on the exercise of the NSO.

Unlike ISOs, the exercise price of an NSO can be less than the fair market value on the grant date. However, an NSO that is "deeply discounted" may be taxed as if it were an outright award of stock, in which case, the optionee would be taxed on the fair market value of the stock on the date of vesting, rather than as described previously. The IRS has never defined what constitutes a "deep" discount. Based on an array of nonbinding precedents, there is probably a general consensus that (i) a discount of 25% or less is safe, (ii) a discount of between 25% and 50% should pass muster, and (iii) a discount greater than 50% is more apt to be deemed "deeply" discounted.

Limits on Deductibility   Code Section 162(m) prohibits a public company from deducting more than $1 million in compensation paid in any one calendar year to its CEO or any of the next four most highly compensated executive officers (each a "covered employee"). However, compensation that meets the definition of "performance based" within the meaning of Code Section 162(m) and applicable tax regulations is exempt from this annual limit. A special rule under Section 162(m) treats stock options (both ISOs and NSOs) and stock appreciation rights as "performance based" compensation exempt from the deduction limits of Code Section 162(m), provided the award meets all of the following requirements:

1. The option or stock appreciation right is granted under a plan that has been approved by the shareholders of the company, and the plan specifies the maximum number of options or stock appreciation rights that may be granted to any covered employee in a specified time period.
2. The option or stock appreciation right has an exercise price (or base price) of not less than the fair market value of the company's stock on the date the award is granted.
3. The option or stock appreciation right is granted by a committee consisting solely of two or more "outside directors," as defined in the Code Section 162(m) tax regulations. (Most public companies take care to assure that each member of the compensation committee qualifies as an "outside director" for this purpose.)

Accounting Treatment of Stock Options

The favorable accounting treatment for time-vesting, market-priced stock options has been the primary design determinant in equity-based compensation programs for the last two decades. Other types of cash and equity awards, all of which require recognition of expense, simply could not compete with the allure of "free" accounting for stock options. That would change with the mandatory expensing of stock options.

On March 31, 2004, the FASB released its long-anticipated exposure draft indicating that, for fiscal years beginning in 2005, U.S. public companies must recognize an accounting expense for the "fair value" of stock options as of the date of grant. Prior to 2005, corporations have been able to elect to account for equity-based compensation under either the "intrinsic value" method (APB 25) or the "fair value" method (FAS 123). Most companies have elected to follow APB 25 for as long as possible. The discussion in this chapter about APB 25 is primarily of historical relevance. However, an appreciation of the contrast between accounting treatment under APB 25 and FAS 123 is useful to understanding the evolution of plan design. For a detailed description of these two accounting regimes, see Chapter 8. Accounting descriptions that follow in this chapter are based on the FASB exposure draft amending to FAS 123.

Generally, under APB 25, the company would record a compensation expense on its income statement equal to the excess, if any, of (i) the fair market value of the option stock on the "measurement date" (usually the date of grant), over (ii) the exercise price of the option (often resulting in a charge of zero). Thus, market-priced, time-vesting stock options accounted for under APB 25 have enjoyed a financial accounting advantage over all other equity-based and cash-based compensation programs.

In contrast, under FAS 123, the company would record as a compensation expense the "fair value" of a stock option on the date of grant (typically determined by reference to a standard option-pricing model), and such charge would be expensed ratably over the service period (usually the vesting period). This treatment of options is more in line with the current and historical accounting treatment of restricted stock and performance awards.

Companies following APB 25 generally attempt to avoid "variable accounting" of options. "Variable accounting" requires that the company accrue a compensation expense (if such expense must be recorded) based on changes in the market price of the underlying stock. Periodic adjustments are made, until the option is exercised or forfeited, to reflect changes in the market price of the stock (in other words, a mark-to-market approach). While most options accounted for under APB 25 could easily be structured to avoid variable accounting (i.e., to maintain "fixed accounting"), certain design features result in variable accounting, such as having a variable exercise price or making vesting solely contingent on the satisfaction of performance goals. In general, any feature that creates uncertainty in either the number of shares that can be granted upon exercise, or the exercise price of the option, gives rise to variable accounting under APB 25.

Moreover, certain modifications to an otherwise "fixed" option result in variable accounting under APB 25. For example, as discussed later in this chapter, any "repricing" of an option, either by lowering the exercise price or canceling the option and replacing it with a new lower-priced option within six months before or after the cancellation, would cause the repriced or replacement option to be a variable award under APB 25, as would any amendment of an option to add a reload feature. (Note that under FAS 123, a reload option is deemed a new grant resulting in a compensation charge and, therefore, such features are expected to decline in use).

Certain other types of modifications to an outstanding option could result in a new "measurement date" for the option, which under APB 25 would not result in variable accounting but would cause the employer to record a fixed compensation charge equal to the excess of the fair market value of the stock on the date of the modification over the exercise price of the option. Examples of these types of modifications are (i) an acceleration of vesting that was not provided for in the original option agreement, or (ii) an extension of the post-employment exercise period.

As companies begin to expense options under FAS 123, there should be more flexibility in the ability to amend outstanding options without costly accounting effects. For example, under FAS 123, if an option is materially amended, it will be deemed a new grant. If the option was already fully vested at the time of the amendment, the compensation cost would be the excess, if any, of the "fair value" of the option after the amendment over the "fair value" of the option immediately before the amendment, which may be considerably less than the option spread at the date of the amendment (the accounting cost measure under APB 25). To the extent that the option was not fully vested at the time of the amendment, the company must also recognize the previously unexpensed portion of the original grant-date fair value of the option.

Section 16 Reporting and Liability Related to Stock Options

As discussed more fully in Chapter 6, Section 16 of the Securities Exchange Act of 1934 (Exchange Act) imposes short-swing profit liability and reporting requirements on a company's executive officers, directors, and 10% shareholders. A stock option is a derivative security of the company subject to Section 16. The grant of an option to an executive officer or director will generally be treated as an *exempt* acquisition of a derivative security, provided the grant of the option is approved in advance by either the full board of directors or a committee consisting solely of two or more "non-employee" directors, as defined in Rule 16b-3. Most public companies take care to assure that each member of the compensation committee qualifies as a "non-employee" director for this purpose. Two other alternatives for exemption are (i) holding the option or the underlying stock for six months, or (ii) having the individual grant approved or ratified by the shareholders (which is rarely done). Whether or not exempt, the grant of an option to a Section 16 insider must be reported electronically to the SEC on a Form 4 within two business days after the grant of the option.

The exercise of an option by a Section 16 insider is generally an exempt transaction, but must be reported within two business days after the exercise. The sale of any acquired shares will not be exempt and must be reported within two business days after the sale. For example, a broker-assisted cashless exercise of an option involves a nonexempt public sale of some of the option shares, which is matchable with any nonexempt purchase occurring within six months before or after such sale.

See Chapter 6 for a discussion of the relevance of the Sarbanes-Oxley Act with respect to broker-assisted cashless exercises by directors and executive officers.

Advantages and Disadvantages of Stock Options

The primary advantage to the company of granting stock options, as opposed to other equity-based awards, has been the significant accounting advantage under APB 25, which allowed the company in most cases to avoid recognizing any compensation expense. This advantage is neutralized under FAS 123. Under either accounting regime, the primary advantage of stock options to the employee is the risk-free right to appreciation in stock price.

Predictions for the Future of Stock Options

It is reasonable to expect a sharp decline in the use of "plain vanilla" stock options—time-vesting options that have an exercise price equal to grant-date fair market value. In the absence of the highly favorable "free" accounting for such options available under APB 25, there will be little reason to use them, when for example, as discussed later, a stock appreciation right (SAR) settled in stock can provide the same incentive using fewer shares and without the need to pay an exercise price. To the extent that options are used in the future, they are likely to include performance-vesting features, which would have resulted in variable accounting under APB 25 and therefore were rarely used. Examples of option variations that may become more prevalent in the level accounting playing field include:

- *Performance-vesting stock options*, in which the option is forfeited unless predetermined performance criteria (other than based on stock price) are met. These are in contrast to performance-accelerated stock options with an ultimate vest date based solely on continued service, which were sometimes used under APB 25, because the ultimate vesting date preserved the fixed accounting treatment.

- *Premium priced options*, which have an exercise price above the market value at the time of grant. These options could have fixed accounting even under APB 25, but were never widely used. They may become more prevalent under the new accounting regime if the above-market price results in a substantially lower "fair value" of the option on the date of grant, and thus a lower compensation expense than a traditional market-priced option.

- *Discounted stock options*, which have an exercise price below the market value at the time of grant. Since these options result in a compensation expense under APB 25, they have not been widely used. However, they may become more prevalent under the new accounting regime if the perceived value to the optionee is deemed to offset the higher grant-date "fair value" of the option.

• *Indexed options*, which have an exercise price that fluctuates over time depending on the company's stock price relative to a selected index. Because these options would require variable accounting under APB 25, they have been rarely used. Under FAS 123 that is less of an issue, but while indexed options may make sense from an incentive design perspective, they are complex to administer and may not be easily understood by the average employee. These factors may continue to curtail their popularity.

Stock Appreciation Rights

Description of SARs

A stock appreciation right entitles the grantee to a payment (either in cash or stock) equal to the appreciation in value of the underlying stock over a specified time. For example, if the base price of a SAR is equal to the fair market value of the company's stock on the grant date, the grantee will be entitled to a payment upon exercise of the SAR equal to the excess, if any, of the fair market value of the stock at the exercise date over the base price, times the number of SARs being exercised. If the appreciation is settled in cash, it is generally referred to as a cash-based SAR; if the appreciation is settled in shares of stock, it is generally referred to as a stock-based SAR.

Tax Treatment of SARs

The fair market value of the consideration paid to the grantee upon exercise of a SAR (whether settled in cash or stock) constitutes ordinary income to the grantee. The company is entitled to a tax deduction equal to the amount of ordinary income recognized by the grantee at the time of exercise. See the previous discussion under "Tax Treatment of Stock Options" regarding the special designation of SARs as "performance-based compensation" for purposes of the $1 million deduction limit of Code Section 162(m), provided certain conditions are met.

Accounting Treatment of SARs

Under APB 25, SARs are accorded variable accounting treatment, meaning that the company must accrue an expense over the life of the SAR based on changes in the market price of the underlying stock. Periodic adjustments are made, until the exercise date, to reflect changes in the market price of the stock.

Under FAS 123, the accounting treatment depends on whether the SAR is payable in cash or stock. SARs that may be settled in cash (in whole or in part) are accounted for as a liability, which requires mark-to-market adjustments over the life of the SAR, based on changes in the stock price. In contrast, SARs that may be settled only in shares of stock should result in a fixed compensation charge on the date of grant equal to the "fair value" of the award as of the date of grant, and such charge would be expensed ratably over the service period.

Section 16 Reporting and Liability Related to SARs

Similar to options, SARs are derivative securities that must be reported to the SEC on Form 4 within two business days of the date of grant to a Section 16 insider. The grant of a SAR to an executive officer or director will be an exempt acquisition if approved in advance by either the full board of directors or a committee consisting solely of "non-employee" directors or if the SAR is held for at least six months from the date of grant or if the grant is approved or ratified by the shareholders.

The exercise of a SAR that is settled in cash is deemed the simultaneous purchase from the company at the exercise price, and sale back to the company at the market price, of the stock underlying the exercised SAR. The exercise of a SAR that is settled in stock is deemed a purchase from the company of the underlying stock at the exercise price and the simultaneous sale back to the company of a number of shares having a market value equal to the exercise price. In cases where the grant of the SAR to an officer or director was approved in advance by the board of directors or a qualifying committee of non-employee directors (or approved or ratified by the shareholders), both the deemed purchase and sale of stock upon exercise of the SAR should be exempt from short-swing profit liability, but the exercise must be reported on Form 4 within two business days after the exercise date.

Advantages and Disadvantages of SARs

From the grantee's perspective, the principal advantage of a SAR is that the grantee may receive the benefit of appreciation in stock value without having to actually purchase stock. From the company's perspective, the principal advantage is that SARs use fewer shares to deliver essentially the same value as an option. The principal disadvantage of SARs has been the requirement of variable accounting under APB 25 and, going forward, liability accounting for cash-based SARs under FAS 123.

Predictions for the Future of SARs

As companies begin to use FAS 123 to account for equity-based compensation, the use of SARs payable in stock is likely to proliferate, and may even overtake options as the most prevalent form of appreciation-type awards. This is primarily due to the fact that SARs payable in stock use fewer shares to deliver the same value as a stock option, because only the net number of shares is issued upon exercise, while the accounting cost is the same as for options under FAS 123. Moreover, the fact that the grantee (typically) does not have to pay an exercise price to exercise a SAR eliminates the sometimes troublesome aspects of option exercises. See Chapter 6 for a discussion of the relevance of the Sarbanes-Oxley Act with respect to broker-assisted cashless option exercises by directors and executive officers.

Restricted Stock

Description of Restricted Stock

Restricted stock is stock that is awarded to the grantee without cost or for a nominal price. During the restricted period, the shares are not transferable and are subject to a substantial risk of forfeiture. For example, the restricted stock may be forfeited if the grantee terminates employment with the company during a specified period of time. The stock may vest ratably over a period of time or become 100% vested after a stated time period ("cliff" vesting). Alternatively, an award of restricted stock could have performance-related vesting triggers, in addition to or in lieu of an ultimate vesting date. (See the section "Predictions for the Future of Restricted Stock" that follows.) Restricted stock is an example of a "full-value" award, as opposed to an "appreciation" award such as options and SARs.

Tax Treatment of Restricted Stock

The grantee of a restricted stock award is normally taxed when the grantee becomes vested in the stock. The fair market value of the stock at the time of vesting (less any amount paid for the stock) is taxable to the grantee as ordinary income, and the company is entitled to a corresponding tax deduction, subject to applicable limits under Code Section 162(m). The grantee may accelerate the recognition of tax by filing a so-called "Section 83(b) election" with the IRS within 30 days of receiving the restricted stock. If a Section 83(b) election is made, the grantee will recognize ordinary income in the year of grant equal to the fair market value of the stock on the date of grant (less any amount paid for the stock), and the company will be entitled to a corresponding tax deduction, subject to applicable limits under Code Section 162(m). Any subsequent appreciation is taxed as capital gain when the stock is sold. However, if the stock fails to vest and is forfeited, the grantee cannot recover the tax paid. Dividends paid on unvested restricted stock are taxed as compensation.

Accounting Treatment of Restricted Stock

Under APB 25, restricted stock that vests solely on the basis of continued service is accorded fixed accounting treatment. The compensation cost is equal to the fair market value of the shares as of the date of grant, and such cost is recognized over the vesting period. If the restricted stock vests solely on the basis of other performance goals, it is accorded variable accounting treatment (based on fluctuations in the stock price) until the goals are achieved.

Under FAS 123, compensation costs for restricted stock are based on the fair market value of the stock on the date of grant, whether the vesting is based on continued service alone or on other performance requirements. Generally, the cost is recognized over the vesting period. If the award is forfeited before vesting, any compensation charge previously recognized would be reversed. Any dividends paid on unvested restricted stock do not result in additional compensation expense unless the stock is later forfeited and the dividends are not repaid to the company.

Section 16 Reporting and Liability Related to Restricted Stock

The grant of restricted stock to a Section 16 insider must be reported on a Form 4 within two business days after the grant date. A grant to an executive officer or director will be an exempt acquisition if approved in advance by either the full board of directors or a committee consisting solely of "non-employee" directors or if the stock is held for at least six months from the date of grant or if the grant is approved or ratified by the shareholders. The vesting of the award is not reportable and is an exempt transaction.

Advantages and Disadvantages of Restricted Stock

The grantee's principal advantage is that he or she is treated as an owner of the stock from the date of grant (usually including the right to vote the stock and receive dividends), and the grantee typically does not pay anything for the stock award. In addition, the grantee has the ability to accelerate taxation on the shares to avoid a potentially higher tax as the shares vest. From the company's standpoint, the company is able to give an immediate benefit to the grantee and, by imposing performance or service restrictions on the shares, can use the shares to encourage the grantee to meet performance objectives or remain in service. The principal disadvantage is that the company must withhold income taxes at the time the tax liability arises (i.e., when the restrictions lapse or a Section 83(b) election is made). Although the grantee is the owner of the stock, he or she might not have the cash to pay the withholding tax. Therefore, it is common for a company to withhold shares from the award in an amount sufficient to cover the tax liability, but this results in a cash-flow cost to the company, because it must remit cash to the IRS.

Predictions for the Future of Restricted Stock

There has been a significant increase in the use of restricted stock in the last few years. At the forefront of this trend was Microsoft's announcement in July 2003 that its future awards to rank-and-file employees would be in the form of restricted stock or restricted stock units rather than stock options. However, restricted stock, as a full-value award, does not provide as much leverage or as strong an incentive for performance as do stock options or SARs, because the restricted stock continues to have value even if the stock price decreases over the vesting period. A grantee would like to see the value increase, but does not lose all if the stock price declines. However, for this same reason, restricted stock has a stronger retention power than options. For example, an employee might be willing to walk away from an underwater option but not a restricted stock award, which always has value.

As companies are faced with option expensing, it is reasonable to expect to see more performance-based awards, including restricted stock that vests or is granted upon the attainment of predetermined performance goals (other than based on stock price).

Restricted Stock Units or Deferred Stock Units

Description of Restricted Stock Units or Deferred Stock Units

Restricted stock units (RSUs) represent the right to receive stock in the future, subject to the satisfaction of vesting requirements. Deferred stock units represent the right to receive stock at the end of a designated deferral period. It is not unusual to combine the two, such that stock is not delivered at vesting, but is deferred to the grantee's termination of employment or some other deferred date. In both cases, until the stock is delivered, the grantee does not own actual shares of stock, and therefore does not have voting rights or the right to receive dividends. Because of this, such awards are often coupled with dividend equivalent rights, such that phantom dividends are paid in cash or reinvested in additional stock units credited to the grantee's account.

Tax Treatment of Restricted or Deferred Stock Units

The grantee of a stock unit award is normally taxed when he or she receives or has the right to receive the stock. The fair market value of the stock (less any amount the grantee paid for it) is taxable to the grantee at that time as ordinary income, and the company is entitled to a corresponding tax deduction, subject to applicable limits under Code Section 162(m). Because Code Section 83 does not apply to a promise to pay cash or property in the future, unlike for restricted stock, the vesting of RSUs is not a taxable event, and it is not possible to make an early tax election under Code Section 83(b).

Accounting Treatment of Stock Units

Under APB 25, stock units that are payable only in stock and fully vested on grant, or that vest on the basis of continued service, are accorded fixed accounting treatment. The compensation cost is equal to the fair market value of the underlying shares as of the date of grant (less any amount paid by the employee for such stock), and such cost is recognized over the vesting period. If stock units vest solely on the basis of other performance goals, they are accorded variable accounting treatment (based on fluctuations in the underlying stock price) until the goals are achieved. Cash-settled RSUs have variable accounting.

Under FAS 123, compensation cost for stock units payable in stock is based on the fair market value of the underlying stock on the date of grant (less any amount paid by the employee for such award), whether or not the unit is fully vested on the grant date, and whether vesting is based on continued service alone or on other performance requirements. Generally, the cost is recognized over the vesting period, if any. If the award is forfeited before vesting, any compensation charge previously recognized would be reversed. Cash-settled RSUs have variable accounting.

Section 16 Reporting and Liability Related to Stock Units

The grant of stock units to a Section 16 insider must be reported on a Form 4 within two business days after the grant date. A grant of stock units to an officer or director will be an exempt acquisition if approved in advance by either the full board of directors or a committee consisting solely of "non-employee" directors or if the units are held for at least six months from the date of grant or if the grant is approved or ratified by the shareholders. If the stock unit may be settled only in stock (as opposed to cash), the unit is reported on Table I of Form 4 as if it were the acquisition of the actual shares of stock, in which case, the later vesting of the award is not reportable and is exempt. The forfeiture of a stock unit while the grantee is still an officer or director is reportable on Form 4, and would most likely be exempt as part of the terms of the original award. The reinvestment of dividend equivalents into additional stock units would be exempt from reporting and liability if the company maintains a qualifying dividend reinvestment plan for its shareholders that operates in a substantially similar manner. If not, the periodic reinvestment of dividend equivalents into additional stock units must be reported on Form 4, but would most likely be exempt as part of the terms of the original award.

Advantages and Disadvantages of Stock Units

The grantee's principal advantage is that he or she is able to defer taxation until the shares are delivered or are constructively received. Companies sometimes allow unit holders to make a subsequent election to further defer settlement and taxation. The principal disadvantage is that the grantee does not have voting rights in the interim and may not receive dividends (unless the award includes a dividend equivalents feature). From the company's standpoint, (i) an award of stock units uses fewer shares than an option to deliver equivalent value; (ii) deferral of taxation to termination of employment avoids Code Section 162(m) deduction limits; and (iii) by imposing performance or service restrictions on the unit, the company can use the units to drive performance and retention.

Predictions for the Future of Stock Units

Expect to see significant use of stock units in the coming years, as companies and their employees grow familiar with the versatility and tax deferral aspects of stock units.

Performance Awards

Description of Performance Awards

In contrast to options or SARs, which are appreciation awards, performance awards are generally "full-value" awards and can be structured in any number of ways. For example, they may be designated as "performance units" (grants of dollar-denominated units the payment of which is contingent on the satisfaction of predetermined performance goals over a period of time), or as "performance shares" (grants of actual shares or share units that are earned contingent on the satisfaction of predetermined performance goals over a period of time, and which fluctuate in value with the stock over the vesting period). In either case, the settlement of the performance award could be made in cash or stock. The compensation committee typically sets the performance goals and other terms or conditions of the performance awards. As such, these are very flexible awards that allow for a close link between pay and specifically determined performance.

Tax Treatment of Performance Awards

The holder of a performance award generally does not recognize income, and the company is not allowed a tax deduction, at the time performance awards are granted. When the participant receives or has the right to receive payment of cash or stock under the performance award, the cash amount or the fair market value of the stock constitutes ordinary income to the participant, and the company is allowed a corresponding federal income tax deduction at that time, subject to deduction limitations under Code Section 162(m), as discussed previously.

Publicly traded companies may designate any award as a qualified performance-based award in order to make the award fully deductible without regard to the $1 million deduction limit imposed by Code Section 162(m). Market-priced stock options and SARs have special treatment under Code Section 162(m) as discussed earlier. In order for any other type of award to be a qualified performance-based award, a committee consisting entirely of "outside directors" must establish objectively determinable performance goals for the award based on one or more of the performance criteria that have been approved by the company's shareholders (typically such performance criteria are set out in the incentive plan). For example, the list might include some or all of the following financial or non-financial metrics (or others not listed), and the permissible performance targets might be expressed in terms of companywide objectives or in terms of objectives that relate to the performance of a division, affiliate, department, region, or function within the company or an affiliate:

- Revenue
- Sales
- Profit (net profit, gross profit, operating profit, economic profit, profit margins, or other corporate profit measures)
- Earnings (EBIT, EBITDA, earnings per share, or other corporate earnings measures)
- Net income (before or after taxes, operating income, or other income measures)
- Cash (cash flow, cash generation, or other cash measures)
- Stock price or performance
- Total shareholder return
- Return on equity
- Return on assets
- Return on investment
- Market share
- Business expansion or consolidation (acquisitions and divestitures)
- Customer satisfaction ratings

In order to obtain the exemption from Code Section 162(m) limits, the committee must establish the performance goals within the first 90 days (or the first 25%, if shorter) of the period for which such performance goals relate, and the committee may not increase any award or, except in the case of certain qualified terminations of employment, waive the achievement of any specified goal. Any payment of an award granted with performance goals must be conditioned on the written certification of the committee in each case that the performance goals and any other material conditions were satisfied. If the performance targets are not specifically set out in the plan, but are left to the discretion of the committee based on one or more shareholder-approved performance criteria, the plan's performance criteria must be reapproved by the shareholders every five years to maintain the availability of the performance-based exemption.

Accounting Treatment of Performance Awards

Under APB 25, equity-based performance awards (whether they may be settled in cash or stock) are generally accorded variable accounting treatment (based on fluctuations in the underlying stock price) until the goals are achieved.

Under FAS 123, the analysis depends on whether the equity-based performance award may be settled in cash or stock and on other characteristics of the award. For example, an award of performance shares that may be settled only in stock (i.e., the employee will earn shares of stock if performance targets are achieved) will result in a fixed compensation charge equal to the fair market value of the underlying stock on the date of grant (less any amount paid by the employee for such award). The cost is recognized over the requisite service period. If the award is forfeited before vesting, any compensation charge previously recognized would be reversed (except for performance goals based on stock price). Equity-based awards that are settled in cash have variable accounting.

Section 16 Reporting and Liability Related to Performance Awards

The Section 16 analysis of performance awards is complex because it depends on the terms of the award and involves a number of deemed transactions. A performance award whose value is tied solely to the market price of the company's equity securities is a derivative security, whether the award is payable in cash or stock. Such an award must be reported on Form 4 within two business days after grant. Upon settlement for stock, if applicable, a Form 4 must be filed within two business days, reporting both the exempt disposition of the derivative security and the exempt acquisition of the shares. Upon settlement for cash, if applicable, a Form 4 must be filed within two business days, reporting the exempt disposition of the derivative security, the exempt deemed acquisition of the underlying shares, and deemed resale of such shares back to the company. Both the grant of the award and the settlement would be exempt transactions if the award was approved in advance by either the full board of directors or a committee consisting solely of "non-employee" directors, or the award was approved or ratified by the company's shareholders. When a performance award is not tied solely to the market price of the company's equity securities, it is not a derivative security and need not be reported. However, if such an award is settled in stock, the acquisition of the stock must be reported on Form 4 within two days.

Advantages and Disadvantages of Performance Awards

Performance awards can provide an incentive for employees to accomplish a variety of targeted company and individual goals and objectives. In this sense, they can be tailored to encourage a longer-term focus than stock options, SARs, or time-vesting restricted stock, which are increasingly criticized as encouraging a short-term focus based solely on stock price. The principal disadvantage to the company is the challenge of designing meaningful and understandable performance objectives for the awards. Historically, variable accounting under APB 25 has been an additional disadvantage.

Predictions for the Future of Performance Awards

Expect to see an increase in the use of performance shares that combine incentives based on tailored business and individual performance achievement with that of increases in stock value.

REPRICING STOCK OPTIONS

As a result of the sharp decline in the stock markets in the early 2000s, many companies face the dilemma of stock options that are "underwater" in the sense that the exercise price (which was equal to the fair market value of the stock on the date the options were granted) now far exceeds the current stock price. On the one hand, underwater options have little if any remaining incentive or retention value. On the other hand, most shareholders, especially institutional shareholders, strongly oppose repricing underwater options, since that "misaligns" the interests of management with the interests of shareholders (who as a group generally have lost a lot of money). Solving the dilemma is no easy task, and must be considered in light of applicable accounting rules, tax and securities laws, and shareholder sensitivities.

In 1998, the FASB significantly quelled the practice of simply repricing (or replacing) underwater stock options by imposing unfavorable accounting treatment under APB 25 for the repriced or replacement options. Due to these harsh accounting consequences, most companies facing the dilemma of underwater options prior to adopting FAS 123 have generally opted to do nothing or to take one of the following five basic approaches, or a variation of one or more:

1. "Bite the APB 25 accounting bullet" and reprice underwater options to current fair market value or replace them with at-the-money options.
2. Leave underwater options in place and grant additional options at market price.
3. Cancel and replace underwater options with new options after six months.
4. Cancel and replace underwater options with current restricted stock grants.
5. Cash out underwater options.

As companies move to FAS 123 accounting, some of the more perplexing accounting issues for dealing with underwater options become easier, as discussed next.

General "Social" and Fiduciary Duty Considerations

Whether the decision is to reprice, replace, or simply grant additional awards, the compensation committee should consider the following issues:

- Shareholders may well view the replacement of underwater options as an elimination of the risk in what is designed to be a risk-reward mechanism.
- Stock incentives almost universally are promoted as linking executives' interests with those of shareholders. Shareholders may object to the repricing or replacement of executives' options since they, as shareholders, do not get to walk away from losses.
- Many plans by their terms expressly prohibit option repricings without shareholder approval—this is especially true in plans adopted in the 2000s. Many other plans are silent about whether options can or cannot be repriced. Under new

NYSE shareholder approval rules, a plan that is silent about repricing will be deemed to prohibit it, so that if the company does reprice it will be deemed a material plan amendment, which requires shareholder approval.

- Repricing of stock options, directly or indirectly, is a serious "hot button" among institutional investors. In today's environment, shareholders have gained significant clout to exert their influence on matters of corporate governance. In general, a repricing proposal that does not include certain terms favored by shareholders (such as, for example, exclusion of directors and executive officers, imposition of new vesting hurdles on the replacement awards, and a less than one-for-one exchange factor) is not likely to be approved. Obtaining the required shareholder vote may be more difficult now that brokers are not allowed to vote shares held in street name on stock plan proposals absent specific guidance from the beneficial owner.
- Lawsuits alleging "corporate waste" or lack of plan authority are sometimes brought against issuers and their directors for replacing underwater options.
- Repricing or replacing options may create internal inequities among employees. For example, some employees may have already exercised their options but failed to sell the option stock prior to the stock price decline.

Decisions concerning repricings are highly situational. Nevertheless, such decisions should be made on a basis that takes into account a number of factors, including the accounting cost associated with the repricing, the number of underwater options, the exercise price of the underwater options, the responsibilities and performance of the optionholder, and other matters deemed relevant by the compensation committee. Minutes of the committee's meeting should reflect thorough and careful deliberation on these issues.

The process followed by the board or compensation committee in its deliberative and decision-making activity is important in connection with securing the protections of the "business judgment rule" for its actions in this and other areas. See Chapter 5 for a more in-depth discussion of the fiduciary duties of directors in the context of compensation decisions.

The following paragraphs discuss each of the five "repricing" alternatives frequently followed, with comments on the tax, accounting, and securities issues unique to each.

Reprice Underwater Options or Replace Concurrently with New Stock Options

Accounting Issues

Variable Accounting under APB 25   This straightforward approach results in variable (mark-to-market) accounting for the repriced or replaced options under APB 25 and FIN 44. In fact, the mere *offer* to replace underwater stock options with new options in less than six months causes the existing options subject to the offer to become subject to variable accounting, even if the offer is rejected. Moreover, if the offer is accepted and underwater options are cancelled (or if underwater options are simply repriced, which is a deemed cancellation and regrant), then *any* other options granted during the six months before or after such cancellation will be subject to variable accounting, regardless of the price. This harsher treatment is in contrast to the look-forward/look-back replacement treatment where the new options are granted six months and a day later, in which only options granted at a *lower* exercise price during the look-forward/look-back period are subject to variable accounting.

FAS 123   The accounting treatment under FAS 123 is more favorable and straightforward. Under FAS 123, any modification to an outstanding award is treated as a cancellation of the award and the grant of a replacement award. The company incurs a compensation cost equal to (i) the unexpensed value of the original option, if any, based on its fair value as of the original date of grant, plus (ii) the excess of the fair value of the new option immediately after the modification/replacement over the fair value of the original option immediately before the modification/replacement. Therefore, a value-for-value options exchange would result in no additional compensation cost.

Securities Law Issues

Proxy Reporting   Under Item 402 of Regulation S-K, proxy reporting is required if options held by any of a company's "named executive officers" (generally the CEO and four other highest-paid executives) are repriced, whether through amendment, surrender and replacement, or any other means. The compensation committee must explain the repricing in reasonable detail, as well as the basis for the repricing. In addition, the proxy statement must contain a table detailing all repriced stock options and stock appreciation rights held by *any* executive officer over the past 10 years.

Section 16   Whether the existing options are actually surrendered and replaced, or the company simply reduces the exercise price of the underwater options, the transaction would be deemed a surrender of the old option and grant of a new option for purposes of Section 16 of the Exchange Act. In either case, the surrender of outstanding options and grant of new options will be deemed *exempt* transactions under Section 16(b), provided the full board of directors or a committee consisting entirely of "non-employee directors" as defined in Rule 16b-3(b)(3) approves the same in advance, or the shareholders approve or ratify such action. Notwithstanding the Section 16(b) exemptions, both the surrender and replacement of options should be reported pursuant to Section 16(a) on Form 4 within two business days.

Tender Offer Issue   If the optionee is given a choice as to whether to exchange his or her underwater options for lower-priced options (as opposed to the company unilaterally reducing the exercise price), it is likely that this will involve an issuer tender offer. In March, 2001, the SEC's Division of Corporation Finance issued an exemptive order regarding option exchange offers that are conducted for compensatory purposes (e.g., offers to exchange underwater options for new options, restricted stock, cash, or other consideration). The exemptive order was quite narrow in scope and, in practice, served to formalize the SEC's formerly unofficial view that such option exchange offers constitute "issuer tender offers." Issuer tender offers are subject to the relatively rigorous filing requirements of Rule 13e-4 under the Exchange Act. Now that the SEC has taken a formal position on the issue, many companies have made the required filings on Schedule TO. Some companies may have been deterred from such exchange offers, based on the relative expense of such a filing.

Tax Issues

Section 162(m) Limit   For public companies, Code Section 162(m) limits the corporate tax deduction for compensation paid to certain executive officers to $1 million, except that certain performance-based compensation does not count toward the $1 million limit. One example of such exempt performance-based compensation is a stock option granted at fair market value under a plan that has been approved by the shareholders and that, by its terms, limits the number of options that may be granted to any one person in a stated time period. The repricing of options is treated as a grant of new options, such that the repriced options would count double against the maximum grant to a covered employee in the same period. The same analysis would apply if the company simply cancelled the outstanding options and issued new options at fair market value on the date of grant.

Incentive Stock Option (ISO) Issues   An employee may only be eligible for ISO treatment for options that become exercisable for the first time in any calendar year for up to $100,000 worth of stock (based on the fair market value on the date of grant). Replacing existing ISOs with the same number of new ISOs at a lower exercise price should not run afoul of this limit, because the measure would be based on the fair market value of the stock on the date of regrant (i.e., the lower number). However, the $100,000 limitation may restrict the company's ability to provide an accelerated vesting schedule for the replacement options to preserve the prior vesting of the replaced options.

Plan Language

A company's option plans would need to be reviewed to see whether they expressly prohibit, expressly permit, or are silent about the company's ability to reprice or replace options. In light of strong preferences of institutional investors, many recent plans have an express prohibition on repricing (or cancellation and replacement) of stock options. Under 2003 NYSE shareholder approval rules, a plan that is silent about repricing will be deemed to prohibit it, so that if the company does reprice, it will be deemed a material plan amendment that requires shareholder approval. The Nasdaq rules, although less explicit, would probably also require stockholder approval under these circumstances.

Leave Underwater Options in Place and Grant Additional Options at Market Price

Accounting Issues

APB 25   If the new options were for a fixed number of shares and subject only to time-based vesting, they were entitled to favorable "fixed accounting" under APB 25. If the exercise price were equal to or greater than the company's stock price on the date of grant, there would be no accounting charge associated with such options granted to employees or nonemployee directors.

FAS 123   The fair value of the old options would continue to be expensed over their remaining vesting period. The company would have an additional compensation charge equal to the fair value of the new options measured as of the grant date, which would be recognized over the vesting period of the new options.

Securities Law Issues

Proxy Reporting   The grant of additional options should not trigger the special repricing disclosures under the proxy rules. However, the normal rules would apply for reporting option grants during the year to the named executive officers. In addition, the compensation committee should comment in its proxy report on the rationale for the special grant.

Section 16   The grant would be treated like any other grant of options for purposes of Section 16—exempt if approved in advance by either the full board of directors or a committee consisting entirely of "non-employee directors" as defined in Rule 16b-3(b)(3) or approved or ratified by the company's shareholders. Notwithstanding the Section 16(b) exemptions, the grant should be reported pursuant to Section 16(a) on Form 4 by the second business day after grant.

Tax Issues

The tax effects to the company and the optionee with respect to such additional options would be no different than for any grant of options to employees. The tax effects will vary, of course, on whether the new options are incentive stock options or nonstatutory.

Dilution Concerns

If the stock price rebounds to a level above the higher exercise price of the underwater options, the resulting dilution from the increased option overhang could reach unacceptable levels. This would also result in "double compensation."

Plan Share Availability

There may not be sufficient shares under the company's current option plans to double up on existing underwater grants. Under the 2003 NYSE and Nasdaq shareholder approval rules, shareholder approval is required to adopt new plans or amend existing plans to add shares.

Replace Underwater Options with New Options after Six Months

This approach was designed to avoid variable accounting under APB 25 and therefore will not likely be used in the future. Under this approach, the company would give optionees an opportunity to voluntarily surrender their underwater options for a promise to grant them replacement options six months and one day later (at the then fair market value). This approach has the advantage of adding back to the plan share pool the shares covered by the options that are surrendered and reduces the possibility of an unacceptably high overhang.

Accounting Issues

APB 25   To avoid variable accounting under APB 25, there could be no arrangement to make up for any price increase during the six-month waiting period. Moreover, the company must look *backward* for six months from the cancellation date (or the beginning of the exchange offer period, if applicable), as well as *forward* for six months from the option surrender date, to be sure that the optionee did not have a grant of options at a lower exercise price than the surrendered options. If he or she did, those lower-price options would become subject to variable accounting.

One notably adverse consequence of the six-month waiting period is that, during that time, the employees have an incentive to drive the stock price down, so that when the new options are eventually granted, they will have a low exercise price.

FAS 123   Under FAS 123, there would be no need to wait six months to make the replacement grants. There would be a fixed compensation charge as of the date of grant equal to the "fair value" of the new options on the date of grant, less the "fair value" of the cancelled underwater options as of that date. This charge, if any, would be recognized over the vesting period. Any unrecognized expense associated with the original options would also be recognized. As previously noted, a value-for-value options exchange would result in no additional compensation cost.

Securities Issues

As discussed previously with respect to the immediate exchange of underwater options for market-priced options, the SEC takes the position that this type of exchange offer for future options is likely to be an "issuer tender offer" that would require the filing of a Schedule TO under the Exchange Act.

Tax Issues

Tax Treatment of New Options   The tax effects to the company and the optionee with respect to such replacement options would be no different than for any grant of options to employees. The tax effects will depend on whether the new options are incentive stock options or nonstatutory.

Tax Treatment of Old Options   Many tax practitioners once thought that the mere offer to exchange an existing ISO for a new grant (whether an option, restricted stock, or cash) is a "material modification" of the ISO which restarts the ISO holding period—even if the offer is rejected. The ISO holding period—the period prior to sale of the shares that is required in order to obtain the favorable tax treatment of an ISO—is the longer of two years after the date of grant (i.e., in this case, the date of the exchange offer) or one year after the date of exercise. However, the final ISO regulations issued in August 2004 provide that the mere offer of such an exchange would not result in a modification of an ISO that was not exchanged unless the offer remained outstanding for 30 days or more.

Replace Underwater Options with Immediate Grants of Restricted Stock

Many companies have elected to offer optionees the right to surrender their underwater options in exchange for immediate grants of restricted stock, because this did not result in variable accounting and avoided the six-month waiting period under ABP 25. This method has the advantage of adding back to the plan share pool the shares covered by the options that are surrendered and reduces the possibility of an unacceptably high overhang. In most cases, the number of restricted shares offered would be less than the number of options surrendered.

Accounting Issues

APB 25   The new restricted stock awards would result in a compensation charge to the company, but it would be a *fixed* charge based on the fair market value of the restricted shares on the date of grant, which is more predictable than the *variable* charge for repriced options. This fixed charge would be expensed over the vesting period of the restricted stock.

FAS 123   Once again, the treatment under FAS 123 is straightforward. The new restricted stock awards would result in a fixed compensation charge to the company, based on the fair market value of the shares on the date of grant, less the "fair value" of the cancelled underwater options as of the date of grant of the replacement awards. This fixed charge would be expensed over the vesting period of the restricted stock. Any unrecognized expense associated with the original options would also be recognized.

Securities Law Issues

Tender Offer Issue   As discussed previously with respect to an options-for-options exchange, the SEC takes the position that an exchange offer for restricted stock is likely to be an "issuer tender offer" that would require the filing of a Schedule TO under the Exchange Act.

Proxy Reporting   For the named executive officers, the Summary Compensation Table of the proxy statement is required to show the dollar value of restricted stock granted in the last fiscal year, but the disclosure could be footnoted to say, for example, that such value is comparable to the value of stock options surrendered by the executive. The Summary Compensation Table footnotes must also show the number and value of the executive's aggregate restricted stock holdings at the end of the year, and, for any shares of restricted stock that will vest within three years of the date of grant, the company must disclose in a footnote the total number of shares awarded and the vesting schedule. The proxy statement must state whether or not dividends will be paid on the restricted stock.

The report of the compensation committee in the proxy statement should discuss the grant of restricted shares, and could explain that they were made in exchange for the surrender of stock options of equivalent value. This would be a good opportunity to discuss the beneficial reasons for the exchange—increased incentive and retention value, replenishment of shares to the plan, and the like.

The SEC takes the position that this type of exchange offer is a "repricing" of options. Even though it does not fit the model disclosure for repriced options, it is required to be disclosed as such and will trigger the 10-year look-back disclosure for prior repricings, if any.

Section 16   The surrender of the underwater options would be an exempt disposition for purposes of Section 16(b) if it is approved in advance by the compensation committee or the full board, or the shareholders approve or ratify such action. Likewise, the grant of the restricted stock would be an exempt acquisition for purposes of Section 16(b) if it is approved in advance by the compensation committee or the full board, or the shareholders approve or ratify such grant. In both cases, the transactions must be reported on a Form 4 by the end of the second business day thereafter.

Tax Issues

The surrender of the underwater options would have no tax effect to the optionee or the company.

The grant of the restricted stock would have no tax effect to the grantee or the company, unless the grantee filed an election under Code Section 83(b) to be taxed currently on the grant. In that case, the grantee would have ordinary income on the date of grant equal to the then fair market value of the restricted stock, and the company would have a corresponding deduction, subject to the limits of Code Section 162(m).

If an 83(b) election is not filed within 30 days after the grant of the restricted stock, the grantee will have ordinary income as the shares vest, equal to the fair market value of the shares on the various vesting dates. The company would have a corresponding tax deduction at that time, subject to the limits of Code Section 162(m). Note that the restricted stock will not be exempt from the Code Section 162(m) limitations unless it is performance-based.

Cash Out Underwater Options

Accounting Issues

APB 25   The cash payment would result in a *fixed* compensation charge to the company equal to the amount of the cash payment, which is more predictable than the *variable* charge for repriced options under APB 25. The surrendered options would be deemed "cancelled" and would be combined with any other option grant within the six-month "look-back, look-forward" period for purposes of determining whether such other options must be variable awards.

FAS 123   The cash payment to "repurchase" the underwater options would be accounted for as a reduction to equity, to the extent the repurchase amount does not exceed the "fair value" of the options at the repurchase date. Any excess of the purchase price over the fair value of the options as of that date would be recognized as additional compensation cost. If the repurchased option was unvested, any previously measured compensation cost for that unvested portion would be recognized.

Securities Law Issues

Tender Offer Issue   The SEC takes the position that this type of exchange offer for cash is likely to be an "issuer tender offer" that would require the filing of a Schedule TO under the Exchange Act.

Section 16 The surrender of the underwater options would be an exempt disposition for purposes of Section 16(b) *if* it is approved in advance by the compensation committee or the full board, or the shareholders approve or ratify such action. The disposition must be reported on a Form 4 by the end of the second business day after the transaction.

STOCK OWNERSHIP AND RETENTION GUIDELINES

The primary justification for equity-based compensation is to align management's interests with the long-term interests of shareholders. It was this mantra by institutional shareholders, along with their insistence on "pay for performance," that led to the proliferation of stock option grants in the 1990s. However, management's propensity, as it turned out, to exercise options and dispose of the stock at the earliest opportunity undermined the intended link with shareholder interests. In an effort to strengthen that alignment, many public companies adopted stock ownership policies, generally requiring directors and executive officers to acquire and retain a minimum amount of company stock—typically based on a multiple of their base compensation.

However, evolving practices revealed that many such stock ownership policies were anemic, both in terms of magnitude and enforcement. For example, in most cases, equity-based awards to executives far exceeded the required multiple-of-base pay ownership guidelines. Therefore, management was able to sell large quantities of stock while staying well above the minimum holding requirements. Many were couched as mere guidelines with no consequence for failure to comply. These realizations led to a widespread retooling of equity ownership policies. Many companies have instituted stock *retention* policies, in addition to or in lieu of traditional minimum ownership guidelines.

Retention policies generally require an officer or director to retain a designated percentage of all "profit shares" resulting from equity incentive awards (e.g., shares remaining after payment of the option exercise price and tax payment obligations) for a designated period of time. The required holding period varies—it could be a number of years after the vesting or exercise of the award, or could extend to termination of service or beyond. Generally, retention requirements apply to all shares of company stock acquired by the officer or director in the scope of service, even those in excess of the minimum shares required to be owned.

Like ownership guidelines, retention policies are only effective if they are followed. Consideration should be given to designing appropriate consequences for noncompliance, from forfeiture of profits to ineligibility to receive additional equity awards.

Chapter 12

Executive Pension-Benefit, Welfare-Benefit, and Perquisite Programs

This chapter provides a general overview of pension-benefit, welfare-benefit, and perquisite programs in which executives generally participate and with which compensation committee members will need to be familiar. Overall, these programs are essential to any complete executive compensation package; however, there may be a perception that these programs are excessive. Therefore, it is important for the compensation committee to balance the full array of programs and to properly disclose the extent of these programs. The compensation committee should also review the necessity for such programs and whether full disclosure of the program would be negatively perceived by shareholders and the public.

There are numerous examples where the revelation of these programs produced unwanted controversy (e.g., retirement arrangements at a utility company and a financial services company; apartments at an entertainment company and a conglomerate; miscellaneous "small" perquisites at several conglomerates and a lifestyle company). Some companies have chosen to eliminate all or many of these programs; however, such an approach may not be the best approach or the most cost efficient. Accordingly, compensation committees should examine the internal efficacy of the specific program with respect to a specific executive or group of executives, and then externally test the program for market reasonableness.

LIST OF PROGRAMS

Here is a summary of the three arrangements discussed in this chapter:

- Pension-benefit arrangements:
  - Defined-benefit SERPs

- Defined-contribution SERPs
- Excess-benefit SERPs
- Deferred compensation arrangements
- Rabbi trusts and secular trusts
- Other pension arrangements
- Welfare-benefit arrangements:
  - Executive life insurance
  - Key-person life insurance
  - Split-dollar life insurance
  - Executive medical
  - Executive disability
  - Other welfare arrangements
- Perquisites:
  - Relocation and temporary housing
  - Expense accounts
  - Club memberships
  - Air travel
  - Ground travel
  - Security-related arrangements
  - Financial and tax counseling
  - Tax gross-ups
  - Charitable contributions
  - Business machines
  - Annual physicals
  - Other perquisites

PENSION-BENEFIT ARRANGEMENTS

Generally, pension-benefit arrangements are those arrangements that provide for a retirement benefit on or after termination of employment for most or all employees. Pension plans are usually bifurcated into "qualified plans," which apply to most or all employees, and "nonqualified plans," which usually apply only to management. A qualified plan is a plan that is designed to qualify under Internal Revenue Code (Code) Section 401 so that company contributions to the plan are tax deductible when made by the company, but taxation to the plan participants only occurs when the benefits are distributed. To be qualified under the Code, the plan must pass a variety of requirements, such as nondiscrimination, minimum funding levels, contribution and benefit limits, and so on. A nonqualified plan generally is a pension plan that is designed to ignore these "qualified plan" requirements; thus, nonqualified plans discriminate between employees (i.e., between executives and the rank-and-file) and ignore the compensation and benefit limits imposed by the Code.

In many cases, these nonqualified arrangements will be subject to some—but not most—of the rules under ERISA. In order to be outside of most ERISA rules, the nonqualified plan must qualify as a "top-hat" plan. This essentially means that the plan is both only for management and is "unfunded." To be unfunded, the company cannot create a plan trust or do anything that segregates assets intended to be used to pay benefits. For income tax purposes, nonqualified pension benefits are usually taxed as income when the benefit is paid (or distributed) to the executive, and it is only then that the company can take a corresponding deduction. However, funding the arrangement could cause the benefit to be "constructively" received by the executive. Thus, the primary issue is the avoidance of constructive receipt under the tax law. Even if constructive receipt is avoided, under the FICA rules, accrued benefits under these plans may be taxed as "wages" prior to the date of distribution if the benefit is no longer subject to a substantial risk of forfeiture.

Pension-benefit arrangements designed for members of management are commonly known as "SERPs" or "SRPs," which usually stands for Supplemental Executive Retirement Plan/Program or sometimes just Supplement Retirement Plan/Program. Some practitioners distinguish between what are called "true SERPs" and "restoration" or "excess benefit SERPs." A true SERP is an arrangement that "stands on its own" and where the benefit is calculated in accordance with the formula or contribution design contained in the plan. It may incorporate by reference definitions from the company's qualified plans, and the benefit is almost always offset by the benefits paid under the qualified plan. It may be a group arrangement (usually contained in a plan document) or an individual arrangement (very often contained in an employment agreement). The restoration SERP is an arrangement that restores benefit limitations imposed by the tax code (discussed in more detail later). Be aware that the term "SERP" has become somewhat generic, and some may refer to any executive pension arrangement—including basic deferred compensation plans—as a SERP.

Defined-Benefit SERP Arrangements

Defined-benefit pension plans are (or were before 401(k) and cash balance plans became so popular in the late 1990s) the typical pension plan at most companies. A defined-benefit plan pays a lifetime annual pension benefit that is defined by a formula calculated at retirement. The usual formula is $A \times B \times C$, where:

A = a percentage (e.g., 2%, 1.75%)

B = the number of years of employment service

C = the employee's final or average annual compensation

Defined-benefit SERP arrangements generally operate in the same way. Companies implement these plans for a variety of reasons, which include:

- Offering the new executive a "replacement" pension arrangement similar to his or her existing arrangement at the former employer
- Offering the executive payout options not available under the qualified plan (e.g., lump sum distributions, joint and 100% survivorship)
- Changing the normal retirement date from 65 to an earlier age (e.g., 62) so that there is no actuarial reduction of the benefit for retirement prior to age 65
- Providing different features or computational levels to determine the benefit (e.g., actuarial reduction is 1% per year compared with an actuarial reduction of 1.5% per year under the qualified plan, changes in the calculation of final or average compensation, etc.)
- Allowing an executive to have a defined-benefit arrangement while the company's qualified plan is a defined-contribution arrangement

In many circumstances, the defined-benefit pension benefit will be offset and reduced by:

- The pension benefit paid under the company's qualified rank-and-file pension plan (assuming the executive is a participant)
- The pension benefit paid by all other pension arrangements outside the company in which the executive is vested and entitled to receive a benefit

The percentage variable can be fixed (e.g., 2% per year) or variable (e.g., 1.5% for the first 10 years, 1.75% for the next 10 years, and 2% for all years of service over 20). Many defined-benefit SERP arrangements will simply use a "target" final percentage at a specific age (e.g., 60% of final or average compensation at age 62). These final percentages typically range from 50% to 70%, but since the actual benefit is based on the definition of "compensation," these percentages can be misleading.

The number of years of service generally is straightforward in most cases, sometimes capped at 30, 35, or 40 years (usually if the qualified plan is so capped). In many cases where an executive is hired from outside the company, the compensation committees will award the executive "credited" years of service as a "make-whole arrangement." The reason for this is that under most defined-benefit formulas, the final benefit is back-end loaded, since final or average compensation at the end of an executive's career drives the benefit higher. The following examples below illustrate this additional years of service:

Example 1:   Executive X, who is 50 years old, leaves Company A, where he has worked for 20 years, for Company B. X is vested in Company A's qualified pension plan, but is unvested in Company A's SERP (which has a cliff vest at age 60). Company B provides him with a SERP that credits him with 20 years of service from Day 1, but that cliff vests at age 60. Assuming X retires at age 60 from Company B, he will have accrued 30 years of service in computing his benefit.

Example 2:   Same as Example 1, but the company allows Executive X to build up to the additional 20 years by crediting X with 4 years of service for each of the first 5 years of employment. This is in addition to age 60 vesting.

Example 3:   Executive Y (who is Company C's COO and might become Company C's CEO) leaves Company C after 25 years of service with a fully vested SERP to become Company D's CEO. Her final or average compensation is $500,000 and the Company C SERP uses a 2% per year percentage. Thus, her annual benefit is $250,000. Company D has the exact same SERP arrangement as Company C. Y works for 5 years for Company D and retires with final or average compensation of $1,000,000. Without any credited years of service, Y would receive a $250,000 annual benefit from Company C and a $100,000 annual benefit from Company D. However, if Y had stayed at Company C, became CEO and retired with final or average compensation of $1,000,000, her annual benefit would have been $600,000 instead of $350,000. Therefore, Company D, as part of the inducement to bring Y on board, provides her with 25 years of additional credited service (offset by any Company C benefit she receives) to make up this gap.

Final or average compensation is determined in a myriad of ways, and there are several components to consider. First is what makes up the definition of "compensation." It may be salary only (many times this is the case under old qualified pension plans), salary plus annual cash bonus (which is the common arrangement), or even salary and annual cash bonus plus all or some long-term incentives (such as vested restricted stock or exercised options). The second element is whether final or average compensation reflects compensation paid in the last year of employment (which would truly be "final compensation"), or the highest annual compensation paid in the last three or five years of employment prior to retirement ("highest compensation"), or the average of the last 36 or 60 consecutive months of employment prior to retirement ("average compensation"), or the highest average 36 months of compensation over the past 10 years ("highest average compensation"). In many cases, this compensation is calculated by taking the average of the highest three years of compensation paid in the 10 years prior to retirement. Finally, for executives hired outside of the company, there may be a minimum floor for final or average compensation.

As mentioned before, one of the reasons for a SERP is to provide payout options that may not be available under the qualified plan. For example, a lump sum payout is a common feature of SERPs, and may not be permitted under the company's qualified pension plan. Some SERPs may allow a joint and 100% survivor benefit (as compared with a joint and 50% survivor benefit, which is the common payout under a company qualified pension plan), or may use a more favorable formula than under the qualified plan to determine lump sum amounts or actuarial reductions.

Finally, there are always issues associated with any termination of employment. If the executive quits or is terminated for "Cause," then typically the executive is entitled to receive any vested portion of the SERP and all unvested portions are forfeited. Thus, many SERPs are designed to be retention devices and substantially vest at or near age 60 or 65. If, however, there is a termination without Cause (and usually this also applies to a termination for Good Reason), then there may be accelerated vesting, or additional years of service and/or age used to calculate the benefit. In some cases, the SERP's vesting may be the same as under the qualified plan (typically 100% vesting after five years of service) but may provide for benefits to begin only if a specified age and years of service has been achieved. This may be known as the "Rule of 65," which means that benefits can begin only if the executive has 10 years of service and is at least 55, or if the executive is 60 and has at least five years of service, or perhaps if the executive is 50 and has 15 years of service. There are variations of this Rule (e.g., Rule of 70, Rule of 75), and certain limitations may be imposed (e.g., minimum retirement age is 55).

Public companies are required to disclose SERP defined-benefit arrangements in which the company's named executive officers participate in a tabular presentation. In addition, the SERP plan document is required to be publicly filed as a material contract.

Defined-Contribution SERP Arrangements

Defined-contribution plans generally are plans where the benefit is not calculated by a formula but by the value of an account designated to the employee. In these arrangements, the company makes a contribution into the employee's account (usually on an annual basis). The amount of the contribution may be based on salary, other compensation, profits, or a predetermined benefit amount (such as in a "money-purchase" or "target-benefit" pension arrangement). The account is invested in either a fixed or variable vehicle. At retirement, the account is paid out (either in installments, in a lump sum, or to purchase an annuity).

Defined-contribution SERP arrangements operate similarly except the account must be unfunded to avoid being subject to all of the ERISA rules. Thus, the accounts are "notional" bookkeeping accounts where money is hypothetically invested in the fixed or variable instrument. The hypothetical investments are tracked and reported to the executives, but the benefit is simply an unsecured promise to pay by the company. In many cases, a company will actually set up a true account using a rabbi trust (discussed later), but with care so that there is no constructive receipt under the tax code.

Similar to defined-benefit SERPs, these arrangements may be used to replace a similar arrangement at an executive's former employer, or if the company has converted to or implemented a defined-contribution arrangement for most or all employees. Issues relating to timing and form of payout, as well as vesting and what happens on a termination of employment are also similar to those issues under defined-benefit SERPs.

As with defined-benefit SERPs, defined-contribution SERPs in which named executive officers participate must be disclosed by public companies, but the disclosure can be in the Summary Compensation Table and/or a narrative (not tabular) section. These arrangements must also be publicly filed as material contracts.

Excess-Benefit SERP Arrangements

These arrangements are simply "standard" qualified plans, but where the limiting tax rules (i.e., the 2004 annual compensation cap of $205,000 under Code Section 401(a)(17), the 2004 annual contribution cap of $13,000 under Code Section 402(g), the 2004 annual contribution cap of $41,000 under Code Section 415, and the 2004 annual benefit cap of $165,000 under Code Section 415) are ignored. Thus, the benefit is determined as if these rules did not exist, and the SERP benefit is offset by the benefit paid from the qualified plan.

The appeal of these plans is that they are quite simple to design and implement, since the only change is to allow a higher level of contribution and/or a higher level of benefit. Generally, all other terms and conditions remain the same. However, defined-contribution excess benefit plans may become more complicated if there is a variety of investment choices, as is the case under most excess benefit 401(k) plans. If so, the company will need to establish "notional" or "bookkeeping" accounts to track the hypothetical investments, since creating actual accounts would cause the arrangement to be treated as funded and thus subject to all ERISA rules.

Public companies are required to disclose excess-benefit SERPs generally in accordance with the defined-benefit and defined-contribution disclosure rules, as well as the requirement that the plan document be publicly filed.

Deferred Compensation Arrangements

A deferred compensation arrangement, at its core, is where the executive elects to defer the payment or distribution of already earned salary, bonus, or other cash or equity compensation to a future point in time. This point in time could be a certain date (e.g., January 15, 2025), or a contemplated scheduled event (i.e., the first of the month following the executive's 62nd birthday [which is planned retirement]), or an unanticipated date (e.g., immediately following the executive's termination of employment, within 10 days of a change in control, or within 30 days of the date of the executive's death).

Generally, already earned compensation is not subject to forfeiture (and thus would be subject to FICA tax when accrued). In some arrangements, a company may contribute additional amounts of deferred compensation (generally known as matching contributions similar to Section 401(k) arrangements); however, these amounts are often subject to a vesting schedule and—if used as a retention device—such vesting may occur at age 55, 60, or 62.

Rabbi Trusts and Secular Trusts

Because the ERISA rules require that any executive pension that is "funded" will be subject to the discrimination, minimum funding, and other rules, the vast majority of these arrangements are "unfunded"; in other words, the company's obligation is simply a "promise to pay." This means that the executive is vulnerable to either a refusal to pay (commonly referred to as a "change in heart") or a company's inability to pay (i.e., due to insolvency or bankruptcy). To protect executives against a change-in-heart scenario (usually due to a change in control), company's have set up "rabbi trusts." Generally, these are irrevocable grantor trusts established by the company that require the trustee to use the assets of the trust to pay the SERP benefits if the company fails to do so; however, if there is an insolvency or bankruptcy, the trustee is required to cease all benefit payments and to hold the trust assets for the benefit of the company's general unsecured creditors (which would also include the executives who are participants in the SERP). Because the trust's assets are subject to a substantial risk of forfeiture (i.e., in the event of insolvency), the assets are treated as still belonging to the company, and thus the executive is not taxed on the amount until the benefit is distributed and received.

A secular trust is an irrevocable grantor trust usually established by the executive where the assets are not subject to a risk of forfeiture. The assets may indirectly be subject to a clawback if the executive quits or breaches a noncompetition provision or similar covenant. Secular trust contributions are taxed when made (either when actually paid to the executive or when contributed by the company to the trust), and thus the advantages of having a higher rate of return through tax deferral is lost; however, the executive's benefit is secure and the company does take a deduction when the contribution is made.

Other Pension Arrangements

There are, of course, a variety of pension and pension-related arrangements that may be called SERPs. For example, a grant of company restricted stock or restricted stock units that vest on retirement might be called a "stock SERP." There could be a SERP that uses life insurance (discussed next) to provide a benefit at retirement, and there could be an arrangement where a large bonus is paid at or near retirement (which might be called a "bonus SERP"). In other words, there is no limit as to what could be a SERP, as long as the delivery of compensation is designed to begin at and/or after retirement. The important aspect of these "nontraditional" arrangements for compensation committees is to determine whether the compensation will be treated as pension-related and thus subject to ERISA, and the appropriate disclosure (if required).

WELFARE-BENEFIT ARRANGEMENTS

Executive welfare-benefit arrangements usually are "enhanced" welfare-benefit programs. Whether these programs are available to executives depends on the number of participants, the culture of the company, and specific individual executive employment arrangements. If treated as compensation, then public companies may need to disclose such arrangements in their public filings, usually in a footnote to the Summary Compensation Table. While these disclosure rules are not hard and fast, compensation committees should take note of the trend toward "transparency" with respect to all compensation and benefits paid or provided to top executives.

Executive Life Insurance

Most company group life insurance plans have low death benefit levels, perhaps based on a 1x or 2x multiple of salary. Thus, it is common for companies to offer an executive a life insurance program where the executive may be able to purchase a 3x, 4x, or 5x multiple of salary. In these situations, the executive typically pays for the insurance.

Some executives, particularly those hired from outside the company, may negotiate for the company to provide (at its own expense) life insurance to the executive with a $1 million to $10 million death benefit. In many cases, this company-paid benefit is additional compensation, and it is not unusual for executives to ask (and sometimes to receive) a tax gross-up on this amount.

Key-Person Life Insurance

While not an executive welfare-benefit arrangement program for the executive *per se,* key-person life insurance is an executive arrangement where the company buys life insurance on a "key person" (e.g., an executive) for the company's benefit. In this arrangement, the company is the owner and the beneficiary of the death benefit. The rationale behind this type of insurance is that the company will have additional costs if the executive dies, and this death benefit helps pay for these costs. Note that in this situation, the executive does not receive any benefit. If companies are considering providing executives with life insurance, it might be appropriate to consider this key-person insurance (if the company wants itself to have this benefit) at the same time, to deal with underwriting and insurability concerns.

Split-Dollar Life Insurance

Split-dollar life insurance has been around for many years, but has recently undergone radical changes due to new regulations issued by the IRS (see Chapter 7). Essentially, a split-dollar life insurance arrangement is where the policy is shared by the company and the executive (or a trust established by the executive). In almost all situations, the company is entitled to receive all policy premiums it has paid, either through a surrender of the policy's cash value or through death benefits. In some arrangements, the company owns all the cash value (this is usually called "traditional" or "classic" split dollar), and in some cases, the executive (or his or her trust) owns the cash value that exceeds the aggregate of all policy premiums paid by the company (this is usually called "equity" split-dollar). In both arrangements, the company pays all or most of the policy premiums, and the executive pays none or a portion that represents the cost of one-year term life insurance. If the executive pays none, then he or she has imputed income based on the cost of one-year term life insurance. Finally, there was a concept known as reverse split-dollar, where the roles of the company were reversed and artificial premium levels were assumed; however, recent IRS notices have effectively shut down these arrangements.

The equity split-dollar arrangement may be phasing out for two reasons. First, equity split-dollar arrangements may violate Section 402 of the Sarbanes-Oxley Act of 2002, which prohibits personal loans to executive officers and directors. The new IRS regulations require that equity split-dollar be treated as a series of loans from the company to the executive. Thus, at least conceptually, the use of equity split-dollar might be regarded as providing personal loans to executives under federal securities laws. Second, the new IRS regulations requiring below-market loan treatment may not be cost effective.

Traditional split-dollar may still be a viable program for some companies, particularly if it is used to "fund" nonqualified deferred compensation or pension-benefit arrangements, or to provide a life insurance SERP. In addition, traditional split-dollar may be adjusted to provide death benefits exceeding the aggregate premiums paid by the company, which would provide a key-person arrangement.

Executive Medical Benefits

It is not uncommon for executives to have their own medical plan, program, or arrangement. Usually, this is superimposed over the rank-and-file health plan. Compensation committees will need to determine whether such a plan is necessary (based on the benefits and coverage under the rank-and-file plan), is consistent with the company's culture, and will not be regarded as an excessive arrangement. In addition, if the company has these plans, care will be needed to make sure that it complies with IRC Section 105(h).

Executive Disability Benefits

Similar to executive medical benefits, many companies will offer executive disability benefits to its executives. The need for this benefit generally is based on the maximum benefit payable under the company's rank-and-file disability benefit program (which usually ranges from $100,000 to $250,000 per year). Based on a concept that an employee will need 50% to 60% of annual cash compensation if disabled, executives earning $1 million would need at least a $500,0000 annual disability benefit. This benefit may be provided by self-insurance (i.e., the company obligates itself to continue salary—and perhaps bonus—during the disability period), or the company will pay the premiums on individual disability insurance policies. Design of these programs should take into account the general tax rule that premiums paid with after-tax dollars will result in tax-free benefits, while premiums paid by the company, or company-provided benefits, will result in taxable benefits.

Other Executive Welfare Benefits

There may be other executive welfare-benefits arrangements that compensation committees may encounter. However, in most cases (other than severance benefit programs that are discussed in Chapter 9), many of these arrangements most likely fall into the "perquisite" category and are discussed next.

PERQUISITES

Executive perquisites can be an extremely controversial subject, so compensation committees should examine their needs and structure thoroughly before implementing such programs. In most instances, the program will apply to mid-level and senior executives, and thus the CEO may be involved with and be an advocate of the program. Nevertheless, any perquisite program that includes senior executives falls under the auspices of the compensation committee.

Essentially, perquisites need to be viewed as simply another way of delivering compensation to the executive. While there is no argument that certain perquisites are a necessity (e.g., car arrangements), the issue arises as to the level of the perquisite. In other words, there is no question that providing an executive with a car is an important perquisite if it is necessary for the executive to have a car in order to do his or her job. However, whether that executive should be driving a $50,000 car or a $150,000 car needs to be evaluated and ascertained.

Disclosure of perquisites is another factor. The executive compensation disclosure rules require that if the total value of the perquisites exceed the lesser of (1) $50,000 or (2) the sum of salary and bonus, then the total value of the perquisites must be disclosed. In addition, itemized perquisite disclosure is required for any perquisite value that exceeds 25% of the total value of perquisites. Today, however, due to recent controversies and the concept of "transparency," there is an attitude to disclose more than less, and perquisites are falling into that category. An example of this is the trend toward disclosing the value of personal use of corporate-owned or corporate-provided aircraft.

Finally, there is a thin line between providing an executive with an appropriate perquisite consummate with his or her position, title, duties, and responsibilities, and going "over-the-top." Thus, compensation committees need to be prepared to justify their actions with regard to all perquisite programs.

Relocation and Temporary Housing

This perquisite usually applies to a new hire from outside the company, but it may apply to an internal promote. In taking the new job, and with the mutual understanding that the executive will need to move from his or her home in location X to a new home in location Y, the executive will be looking to the company to pay the costs of this relocation. This might consist only of actual "moving" costs; however, more likely, it will also consist of some or most of the following:

- Reimbursement for temporary housing and/or hotel accommodation not only for himself or herself but also for his or her spouse and other members of the executive's family during the "house hunting" phase
- Reimbursement for travel from location X to location Y, not only for himself or herself but also for his or her spouse and other members of the executive's family (although these trips may be limited in frequency or capped in amount)
- Closing costs associated with the purchase of the new home
- An arrangement for the company to purchase the existing home (usually based on an appraisal by a reputable appraiser or the average of three appraisals)
- Other miscellaneous expenses (sometimes subject to a cap)

Finally, while some of these costs/reimbursements may be a working condition fringe benefit and thus not treated as compensation, some of these reimbursements may be treated as compensation and thus taxable. Accordingly, it is not unusual for the executive to ask for a tax gross-up so that the relocation has a neutral financial impact to the executive.

Expense Accounts (Including Sporting and Entertainment Events)

Companies generally have established policies with respect to expense accounts, and reasonable expenses reasonably incurred by the executive in the course of conducting business is a standard and uncontroversial practice. This would even include sporting and entertainment events used for business purposes. However, some executives may ask to have the company obligate itself to specific events or provide a dollar amount to be applied to such events. For example, an executive in the music industry might ask for a commitment from the company for attendance at the Grammys for him or her and 10 clients. Other common examples would be contractual commitments to provide tickets for World Series, Super Bowl, major golfing events, etc. In reviewing these kinds of arrangements, the compensation committee generally should focus on whether there is a legitimate business purpose associated with providing these kinds of perks.

Club Memberships

Generally, club memberships may be divided into country clubs, eating clubs, and health clubs. The company may have a policy that allocates a fixed dollar amount to be applied to a club (any club), or the company may simply provide that it will pay the membership fees and dues for a specific club or a club of the executive's choice. Current taxation of these expenses will need to be examined, since some programs might be structured in such a way that the expenses are not deductible and some programs where the expenses are treated as compensation (and thus deductible).

Air Travel Arrangements

Air travel is usually governed by an established company policy. However, it is not unusual for executives (particularly CEOs) to request and sometimes receive a contractual commitment to first-class air travel or priority rights to corporate aircraft. In addition, personal use of corporate-owned or corporate-provided aircraft may also be contained in such a contractual provision. This is an area where some compensation committees will need to keep their "eye on the ball."

Ground Travel Arrangements

Companies have a variety of automobile arrangements. The questions for most compensation committees will be whether to provide the executive with a car only, a car and driver, and what kind of car. In addition, the company may provide parking as a perquisite, particularly if the executive's office is located in a congested urban area.

Commuting is never tax deductible. However, there are exceptions and arrangements that incorporate the commute into business travel, and these should be explored.

Security-Related Arrangements

The tax regulations allow deductions for a "bona fide security" program. However, this security need must be clearly established. Thus, if a company determines that it needs to provide extra security to its executive (e.g., a car with bulletproof glass), such expense may be deductible, but only to the extent of the cost of the security-related expenses (e.g., the cost of bulletproofing the car's glass, not the entire cost of the car). This is a complex area where compensation committees definitely will need advice from tax counsel.

Financial and Tax Counseling

A common perquisite is to provide executives with financial and tax counseling. Sometimes, a company contracts with a firm to provide this to a group of executives. Sometimes, the company will provide an allowance (usually with a cap). Companies that are trying to minimize their perquisite programs may simply provide a higher base salary to replace this lost perquisite.

Tax Gross-Ups

While not normally considered a perquisite, some executive employment arrangements will provide that if certain benefits or perquisites are treated as compensation (thus resulting in the imposition of income tax), the executive will be provided with a tax gross-up that will leave the executive in an after-tax neutral position. For example, suppose a company agrees to provide an executive with full relocation benefits. The total relocation reimbursements are $50,000, 50% of which will not be treated as compensation under the company's relocation policy, but 50% of which will result in compensation. Using a 45% aggregate tax rate, the company would pay an additional $20,455 to fully gross-up the $25,000 that is treated as compensation.

Charitable Contributions

Executives may suggest or have an arrangement where the company makes a contribution to a charity selected by the executive. This practice appears to be phasing out, as there is a question as to the tax results and the overall optics.

Business Machines

As the business world becomes more dependent on laptops, fax machines, black-berrys, and so forth, more and more companies are providing these machines to their executives. In some cases, the arrangement is that the company simply lets the executive use the machine and that it always remains the property of the company, subject to return upon a termination of employment. Some companies, however, simply give these machines to their executives, or establish an allowance for the purchase of such machines. The tax ramifications will depend on the structure of the program.

Annual Physicals

Annual physicals for executives were a popular perquisite years ago, particularly because they were not provided under standard medical benefit programs. Today, however, most health benefit programs (whether indemnity-based, HMO, PPO, etc.) provide for annual physicals at little or no cost. However, some companies have continued this program, particularly if they have contracted with a doctor-group that caters to these types of physicals. In addition, some company cultures prefer to have a comprehensive physical of its top executive each year (over and above the "standard" physical under the company's health plan).

Other Perquisites

Of course, there are always other uncommon perks that a company may provide its CEO and/or other executives. For example, a defense-related company might allow its CEO (who had been a fighter pilot in the military) to use a company jet fighter. Similarly, a recreational boat company might provide its CEO with use of one of its luxury boats. An insurance company might contractually agree to provide new golf clubs and other golfing equipment every year to its executive if the executive did most of his business on the golf course. A company whose CEO lives in another state and does not relocate might provide a housing allowance with a tax gross-up. Or a company might purchase a residence (perhaps near the company's headquarters, perhaps in a major city) ostensibly for business purposes but which might be used exclusively by the CEO. These types of nontraditional perks, along with any and all other perks, will simply need to be assessed by the compensation committee for cost, reasonableness, tax consequences, and perception by shareholders and the public.

A Glimpse into the Future

Compensation committees have come a long way over the years, but many still have a long way to go. There are initiatives that almost every compensation committee can take to improve its performance, many of which are outlined in this book. Chapter 1, for example, suggests six precepts that can lead to more effective committee performance in the coming years:

1. Get organized
2. Get and stay informed
3. Keep an eye on the big picture
4. Return to reason
5. Consider the shareholders' perspective
6. Communicate effectively

Along with the continuing evolution of the role and purview of the compensation committee, executive compensation practices are undergoing monumental change. For example, the leveling of the playing field resulting from the expected requirement that stock options be expensed opens up whole new opportunities for creative design in equity-based compensation, as discussed in Chapter 11.

Trends highlighted in the first edition published in 2001 continue to gather momentum. Some, such as increased representation of outside directors on boards, are now mandated by the stock exchanges. Others continue because they foster better corporate governance—such as increased board diversity, regular evaluation of board and CEO performance, and closer scrutiny of the link between pay and performance.

The following are some of the trends we see for the years immediately ahead:

Increased profile for the compensation committee. The compensation committee may be the next board committee (after the audit committee) to galvanize public attention. Fully independent compensation committees will expend time and attention in developing compensation strategies and incentive programs that foster the committee's overall compensation philosophy and corporate objectives. There will be more engagement of compensation committees in the processes of CEO evaluation, board evaluation, succession planning, and other key governance processes.

Shareholder transparency will continue. Shareholders will expect to be informed about the company's stance on major governance issues. Expect to see increasing communication in annual reports, proxy statements, and electronic bulletin boards about board practices and activities. There will be more interaction between boards and all corporate constituencies.

Emphasis on ethics. Compensation committees should continue to be proactive in avoiding practices that may have even the appearance of impropriety. Directors are increasingly concerned about shareholders' perception of their actions, especially as they may relate to ethical issues.

Succession planning. CEO turnover will continue as in the past and may even increase. Succession planning will move to the top of the list among the most important board functions. Ideally, succession planning will be a continuous process, integrated into the overall strategic plan. As a consequence, boards should become more willing to replace nonperforming CEOs.

CEO searches will be global and will continue to be industrywide. Companies will continue to seek the best CEO candidates, no matter who and where they are. While many companies are more comfortable with promoting from within, from both a culture and cost perspective, compensation committees must use all resources in filling open management positions. The recent trend is to hire more international executives, and certainly to hire CEOs outside of the industry.

Executive compensation. Companies will continue to pay significant amounts for executive talent, as there will be greater emphasis on innovation, creativity, and accountability of executives. However, the rate of increases in executive compensation most likely will fall from the unsustainable rates that occurred during the last decade, due primarily to the less exuberant stock market. In addition, there is likely to be an adjustment in the mix between cash and equity components, and a more varied mix of award types within the equity component.

Equity-based compensation. With the anticipated expensing of stock options, equity-based compensation is likely to be more concentrated at the upper levels of management, with a reduction in broad-based equity programs. Even employee stock purchase plans, the ultimate broad-based equity program, will be impacted by the new accounting regime for share-based payments and are likely to be eliminated or at least significantly redesigned to limit associated costs. The level playing field created by option expensing will open the door to wider use of other types of equity-based incentive awards. Stock-settled SARs will likely overtake stock options as the most prevalent form of appreciation-type incentive award, and restricted stock units will rival outright grants of restricted stock due to their greater flexibility for tax purposes. Use of reload stock options most likely will be reduced or eliminated due to the unpredictable accounting cost. Option repricing, oddly enough, will become less painful from an accounting perspective and thus may still be used by some companies to "clean up" an underwater stock option or SAR program.

Evaluations will become standard practice. Regular CEO evaluations should become standard practice in the ensuing years, and director evaluations will become more prevalent—especially boardwide evaluations. More and more compensation committees will use the CEO evaluation process to determine CEO pay.

Director compensation. Increasingly higher compensation for directors is expected, as a reflection of increased obligations, time commitment, expertise requirements, and the risk of personal liability. Director compensation is likely to level off after a few years, once a new equilibrium is established.

Director recruitment. The nominating committee is now an essential element of the public company board. Directors are more likely to be selected for how they think, what they know, and how they deliver their knowledge and experience, than for whom they know. Companies will likely turn more often to executive recruiting firms to find qualified independent directors. Even so, members of the nominating committee, and all outside directors, are likely to spend substantial time and energy in the recruitment of new directors.

Certification of directors. Certification of directors is a significant trend outside the United States. While there is some support for this in the United States, there is unlikely to be a national certification signifying "professional" directors. However, institutional investors such as the State of Wisconsin Investment Board are encouraging directors of companies in which they invest to attend director orientation programs. The NACD has a core curriculum for the initial certification of directors, including a continuing education requirement.

Diversity. An increase in women and minority representation on boards is inevitable. For several years, women have made up a slight majority in law school populations. Women also make up a substantial, and increasing, percentage of business school enrollments. The large representation of women in business and law schools should result in a significant increase in their ranks among top corporate offices and on corporate boards. With the move to more fully independent boards, limitations on the number of boards on which a director can serve, higher prevalence of mandatory director retirement ages, and the increase in number of required board committees, the ascension of women and minorities is quite timely to assist public companies seeking to provide the best and brightest new talent to serve on their boards and compensation committees.

Director profiles. For a variety of reasons, including the imposition of mandatory retirement age, directors are likely to be younger and have greater honed skills in finance, management, governance, and technology. There will be more international representation on U.S. boards, and more U.S. executives likely will serve on non-U.S. boards.

Contested director elections. Driven by shareholder activism and the ability to communicate more effectively and quickly over a large group, the election of directors will no longer be a "done deal" when it comes to the shareholder vote. Institutional investors and their advisors are achieving unprecedented efficiency in the review of proxy proposals, including election of directors.

Director training will increase. Pension funds and pension advisory services rate regular director training as an important criterion for their investment. Director orientation programs have emerged across the country to serve the need for new director training. Ongoing training and enrichment will be integrated into the corporate governance process, including both off site professional training programs and programs provided as part of board or committee meetings or retreats.

Board cultures will change for the better. Boards will be more businesslike, more results oriented, more involved and productive, more efficient, more sensitive to time pressure—with less tolerance for unprepared directors.

Global markets and economies will merge. The move toward greater corporate governance continues on a worldwide basis. To compete, every economy will be fostering better boards as a means to better corporate performance. The 100-member Japanese board will be an antiquity. Other countries are evolving better board practices, symbolic of the breadth of the corporate governance revolution. Great Britain's reliance on independent nonexecutive chairs has already affected U.S. practices. The executive talent pools will tend to merge, allowing for more international CEO searches.

Shareholder litigation. Shareholder lawsuits will attempt to show lack of good faith by the board, as an extension of the duty of care (e.g., *Disney, Cendant,* and similar suits). Such a finding would eliminate reliance on the business judgment rule, and most likely would pierce the protections of charter exculpation provisions and make directors unindemnifiable and uninsurable. The best defense to this type of allegation is to pay serious attention to decisionmaking, including seeking outside expert advice and keeping meticulous minutes to document the process actually followed.

Increased responsiveness to shareholders. The focus will remain on greater interaction with and responsiveness to shareholders. Many boards have already formed shareholder relations committees. Shareholders will engage the board directly to encourage reforms of one type or another. Concurrently, directors will learn more about what motivates shareholders to buy or sell their stock holdings, and shareholders, analysts, and investment managers will gain an appreciation of the impact directors have on corporate growth.

Financial analyst activism. Analysts on both the buy and sell sides will recognize the role governance can play in creating shareholder value, and they will prioritize governance as a measure of corporate success. The Association for Investment Management and Research includes corporate governance as part of its Chartered Financial Analyst curriculum. Moody's and Standard & Poor's each has added a substantial corporate governance research group to make corporate governance an element of its review of debt and equity.

THE NEXT EXECUTIVE COMPENSATION CONTROVERSY

If history has taught us anything, it is that executive compensation—and thus compensation committees—will be at the center of controversy every 10 years or so. In the early 1980s, executives receiving excessive severance packages in connection with mergers and acquisitions outraged both the public and the politicians, and the result was the golden parachute tax rules. The recession of the early 1990s focused the country on CEO pay, and the result was the $1 million cap under Code Section 162(m) and a complete redesign by the Securities and Exchange Commission of the executive compensation disclosure rules. And in the beginning of this century, corporate scandals and frauds permeated society, with the result being the Sarbanes-Oxley Act of 2002, new listing requirements at the New York Stock Exchange and at Nasdaq, and the probable mandatory expensing of stock options.

We don't know when the next "executive compensation controversy" will occur, and we don't know who will be the "poster child" of that controversy. But we hope this book will help compensation committees keep themselves and their boards, CEOs, and executives from becoming part of that poster.

Selected SEC Rules, Regulations, Schedules, and Forms

This appendix is a summary listing of SEC regulations, schedules, and forms and stock exchange rules that directly or indirectly impact the duties and responsibilities of compensation committees. The full text of items marked with an asterisk (*) is reproduced following the summary listing.

SECURITIES ACT OF 1933, AS AMENDED

This is the federal law requiring full and fair disclosure and the use of a prospectus in connection with the offer and sale of securities

Selected Relevant Rules under the Securities Act of 1933

Rule 144—Persons Deemed Not to Be Engaged in a Distribution and Therefore Not Underwriters

Rule 701—Exemption for Offers and Sales of Securities Pursuant to Certain Compensatory Benefit Plans and Contracts Relating to Compensation

SECURITIES EXCHANGE ACT OF 1934, AS AMENDED

This is the federal law prohibiting manipulative and abusive practices in the issuance of securities; requires registration of stock exchanges, brokers, dealers, and listed securities; also requires disclosure of certain financial information and insider trading.

Selected Relevant Rules and Regulations under the Securities Exchange Act of 1934

Rule 10b-5—Employment of Manipulative and Deceptive Devices

Rule 10b5-1—Trading "On the Basis of" Material Nonpublic Information in Insider Trading Cases

Rule 10b-18—Purchases of Certain Equity Securities by the Issuer and Others

Rules 16a-1 through 16a-13—Reports of Directors, Officers, and Principal Stockholders

Rules 16b-1 through 16b-8—Exemption of Certain Transactions from Section 16(b)

Regulation 14A—Solicitation of Proxies

Schedule 14A (Rule 14a-101)—Information Required in Proxy Statement

FORMS

Form 8-K—Current Report Pursuant to Section 13 or 15(d) of the Securities Exchange Act of 1934

Form 10-Q—Quarterly Reports

Form 10-K—General Form of Annual Report

Form 144—Notice of Proposed Sale of Securities Pursuant to Rule 144 under the Securities Act of 1933

Form S-8—Registration Under the Securities Act of 1933 of Securities to be Offered to Employees Pursuant to Certain Plans

Form 3—Initial Statement of Beneficial Ownership of Securities

Form 4—Statement of Changes of Beneficial Ownership of Securities

Form 5—Annual Statement of Beneficial Ownership of Securities

Regulation S-K—Standard Instructions for Filing Forms under the Securities Act of 1933 and the Securities Exchange Act of 1934

Item 201(d)—Securities Authorized for Issuance under Equity Compensation Plans (*)

Item 401—Directors, Executive Officers, Promoters and Control Persons (*)

Item 402—Executive Compensation (*)

Item 403—Security Ownership of Certain Beneficial Owners and Management (*)

Item 404—Certain Relationships and Related Transactions (*)

Item 405—Compliance with Section 16(a) of the Exchange Act (*)

Item 601(b)(10)—Exhibits—Material Contracts (*)

SARBANES-OXLEY ACT OF 2002

Section 304—Forfeiture of Certain Bonuses and Profits

Section 306—Insider Trades during Pension Fund Blackout Periods

Section 402—Enhanced Conflict of Interest Provisions

Section 403—Disclosures of Transactions Involving Management and Principal Stockholders

OTHER

Regulation BTR—Blackout Trading Restriction

NYSE Rule 303A.05—Compensation Committee Requirements (*)

Nasdaq Stock Market Rule 4350(c)(3)—Compensation of Officers (*)

Item 201—Market Price of and Dividends on the Registrant's Common Equity and Related Stockholder Matters

d. Securities authorized for issuance under equity compensation plans.

1. In the following tabular format, provide the information specified in paragraph (d)(2) of this Item as of the end of the most recently completed fiscal year with respect to compensation plans (including individual compensation arrangements) under which equity securities of the registrant are authorized for issuance, aggregated as follows:

    i. All compensation plans previously approved by security holders; and

    ii. All compensation plans not previously approved by security holders.

Equity Compensation Plan Information

Plan category	Number of securities to be issued upon exercise of outstanding options, warrants and rights	Weighted-average exercise price of outstanding options, warrants and rights	Number of securities remaining available for future issuance under equity compensation plans (excluding securities reflected in column (a))
	(a)	(b)	(c)
Equity compensation plans approved by security holders			
Equity compensation plans not approved by security holders			
Total			

2. The table shall include the following information as of the end of the most recently completed fiscal year for each category of equity compensation plan described in paragraph (d)(1) of this Item:

    i. The number of securities to be issued upon the exercise of outstanding options, warrants and rights (column (a));

    ii. The weighted-average exercise price of the outstanding options, warrants and rights disclosed pursuant to paragraph (d)(2)(i) of this Item (column (b)); and

    iii. Other than securities to be issued upon the exercise of the outstanding options, warrants and rights disclosed in paragraph (d)(2)(i) of this Item, the number of securities remaining available for future issuance under the plan (column (c)).

3. For each compensation plan under which equity securities of the registrant are authorized for issuance that was adopted without the approval of security holders, describe briefly, in narrative form, the material features of the plan.

Instructions to Paragraph (d) of Item 201.

1. Disclosure shall be provided with respect to any compensation plan and individual compensation arrangement of the registrant (or parent, subsidiary or affiliate of the registrant) under which equity securities of the registrant are authorized for issuance to employees or non-employees (such as directors, consultants, advisors, vendors, customers, suppliers or lenders) in exchange for consideration in the form of goods or services as described in Statement of Financial Accounting Standards No. 123, *Accounting for Stock-Based Compensation,* or any successor standard. No disclosure is required with respect to:

    i. Any plan, contract or arrangement for the issuance of warrants or rights to all security holders of the registrant as such on a pro rata basis (such as a stock rights offering) or

    ii. Any employee benefit plan that is intended to meet the qualification requirements of Section 401(a) of the Internal Revenue Code (26 U.S.C. 401(a)).

2. For purposes of this paragraph, an "individual compensation arrangement" includes, but is not limited to, the following: a written compensation contract within the meaning of "employee benefit plan" under Rule 405 under the Securities Act and a plan (whether or not set forth in any formal document) applicable to one person as provided under Item 402(a)(7)(ii) of Regulation S-K.

3. If more than one class of equity security is issued under its equity compensation plans, a registrant should aggregate plan information for each class of security.

4. A registrant may aggregate information regarding individual compensation arrangements with the plan information required under paragraph (d)(1)(i) and (ii) of this Item, as applicable.

5. A registrant may aggregate information regarding a compensation plan assumed in connection with a merger, consolidation or other acquisition transaction pursuant to which the registrant may make subsequent grants or awards of its equity securities with the plan information required under paragraph (d)(1)(i) and (ii) of this Item, as applicable. A registrant shall disclose on an aggregated basis in a footnote to the table the information required under paragraph (d)(2)(i) and (ii) of this Item with respect to any individual options, warrants or rights assumed in connection with a merger, consolidation or other acquisition transaction.

6. To the extent that the number of securities remaining available for future issuance disclosed in column (c) includes securities available for future issuance under any compensation plan or individual compensation arrangement other than upon the exercise of an option, warrant or right, disclose the number of securities and type of plan separately for each such plan in a footnote to the table.

7. If the description of an equity compensation plan set forth in a registrant's financial statements contains the disclosure required by paragraph (d)(3) of this Item, a cross-reference to such description will satisfy the requirements of paragraph (d)(3) of this Item.

8. If an equity compensation plan contains a formula for calculating the number of securities available for issuance under the plan, including, without limitation, a formula that automatically increases the number of securities available for issuance by a percentage of the number of outstanding securities of the registrant, a description of this formula shall be disclosed in a footnote to the table.

9. Except where it is part of a document that is incorporated by reference into a prospectus, the information required by this paragraph need not be provided in any registration statement filed under the Securities Act.

Item 401—Directors, Executive Officers, Promoters and Control Persons

a. Identification of directors. List the names and ages of all directors of the registrant and all persons nominated or chosen to become directors; indicate all positions and offices with the registrant held by each such person; state his term of office as director and any period(s) during which he has served as such; describe briefly any arrangement or understanding between him and any other person(s) (naming such person(s)) pursuant to which he was or is to be selected as a director or nominee.

Instructions to Paragraph (a) of Item 401.

1. Do not include arrangements or understandings with directors or officers of the registrant acting solely in their capacities as such.

2. No nominee or person chosen to become a director who has not consented to act as such shall be named in response to this Item. In this regard, with respect to proxy statements, see Rule 14a-4(d) under the Exchange Act.

3. If the information called for by this paragraph (a) is being presented in a proxy or information statement, no information need be given respecting any director whose term of office as a director will not continue after the meeting to which the statement relates.

4. With regard to proxy statements in connection with action to be taken concerning the election of directors, if fewer nominees are named than the number fixed by or pursuant to the governing instruments, state the reasons for this procedure and that the proxies cannot be voted for a greater number of persons than the number of nominees named.

5. With regard to proxy statements in connection with action to be taken concerning the election of directors, if the solicitation is made by persons other than management, information shall be given as to nominees of the persons making the solicitation. In all other instances, information shall be given as to directors and persons nominated for election or chosen by management to become directors.

b. *Identification of executive officers.* List the names and ages of all executive officers of the registrant and all persons chosen to become executive officers; indicate all positions and offices with the registrant held by each such person; state his term of office as officer and the period during which he has served as such and describe briefly any arrangement or understanding between him and any other person(s) (naming such person) pursuant to which he was or is to be selected as an officer.

Instructions to Paragraph (b) of Item 401.

1. Do not include arrangements or understandings with directors or officers of the registrant acting solely in their capacities as such.

2. No person chosen to become an executive officer who has not consented to act as such shall be named in response to this Item.

3. The information regarding executive officers called for by this Item need not be furnished in proxy or information statements prepared in accordance with Schedule 14A under the Exchange Act by those registrants relying on General Instruction G of Form 10-K and Form 10-KSB under the Exchange Act, *Provided,* That such information is furnished in a separate item captioned "Executive officers of the registrant" and included in Part I of the registrant's annual report on Form 10-K and Form 10-KSB.

---

c. *Identification of certain significant employees.* Where the registrant employs persons such as production managers, sales managers, or research scientists who are not executive officers but who make or are expected to make significant contributions to the business of the registrant, such persons shall be identified and their background disclosed to the same extent as in the case of executive officers. Such disclosure need not be made if the registrant was subject to section 13(a) or 15(d) of the Exchange Act or was exempt from section 13(a) by section 12(g)(2)(G) of such Act immediately prior to the filing of the registration statement, report, or statement to which this Item is applicable.

d. *Family relationships.* State the nature of any family relationship between any director, executive officer, or person nominated or chosen by the registrant to become a director or executive officer.

Instruction to Paragraph 401(d).

The term "family relationship" means any relationship by blood, marriage, or adoption, not more remote than first cousin.

---

e. Business experience.

1. *Background.* Briefly describe the business experience during the past five years of each director, executive officer, person nominated or chosen to become a director or executive officer, and each person named in answer to paragraph (c) of Item 401, including: Each person's principal occupations and employment during the past five years; the name and principal business of any corporation or other organization in which such occupations and employment were carried on; and whether such corporation or organization is a parent, subsidiary or other affiliate of the registrant. When an executive officer or person named in response to paragraph (c) of Item 401 has been employed by the registrant or a subsidiary of the registrant for less than five years, a brief explanation shall be included as to the nature of the responsibility undertaken by the individual in prior positions to provide adequate disclosure of his prior business experience. What is required is information relating to the level of his professional competence, which may include, depending upon the circumstances, such specific information as the size of the operation supervised.

2. *Directorships.* Indicate any other directorships held by each director or person nominated or chosen to become a director in any company with a class of securities registered pursuant to section 12 of the Exchange Act or subject to the requirements of section 15(d) of such Act or any company registered as an investment company under the Investment Company Act of 1940, naming such company.

Instruction to Paragraph (e) of Item 401.

For the purposes of paragraph (e)(2), where the other directorships of each director or person nominated or chosen to become a director include directorships of two or more registered investment companies that are part of a "fund complex" as that term is defined in Item 22(a) of Schedule 14A under the Exchange Act, the registrant may, rather than listing each such investment company, identify the fund complex and provide the number of investment company directorships held by the director or nominee in such fund complex.

f. *Involvement in certain legal proceedings.* Describe any of the following events that occurred during the past five years and that are material to an evaluation of the ability or integrity of any director, person nominated to become a director or executive officer of the registrant:

1. A petition under the Federal bankruptcy laws or any state insolvency law was filed by or against, or a receiver, fiscal agent or similar officer was appointed by a court for the business or property of such person, or any partnership in which he was a general partner at or within two years before the time of such filing, or any corporation or business association of which he was an executive officer at or within two years before the time of such filing;

2. Such person was convicted in a criminal proceeding or is a named subject of a pending criminal proceeding (excluding traffic violations and other minor offenses);

3. Such person was the subject of any order, judgment, or decree, not subsequently reversed, suspended or vacated, of any court of competent jurisdiction, permanently or temporarily enjoining him from, or otherwise limiting, the following activities:

   i. Acting as a futures commission merchant, introducing broker, commodity trading advisor, commodity pool operator, floor broker, leverage transaction merchant, any other person regulated by the Commodity Futures Trading Commission, or an associated person of any of the foregoing, or as an investment adviser, underwriter, broker or dealer in securities, or as an affiliated person, director or employee of any investment company, bank, savings and loan association or insurance company, or engaging in or continuing any conduct or practice in connection with such activity;

    ii. Engaging in any type of business practice; or

    iii. Engaging in any activity in connection with the purchase or sale of any security or commodity or in connection with any violation of Federal or State securities laws or Federal commodities laws;

4. Such person was the subject of any order, judgment or decree, not subsequently reversed, suspended or vacated, of any Federal or State authority barring, suspending or otherwise limiting for more than 60 days the right of such person to engage in any activity described in paragraph (f)(3)(i) of this section, or to be associated with persons engaged in any such activity; or

5. Such person was found by a court of competent jurisdiction in a civil action or by the Commission to have violated any Federal or State securities law, and the judgment in such civil action or finding by the Commission has not been subsequently reversed, suspended, or vacated.

6. Such person was found by a court of competent jurisdiction in a civil action or by the Commodity Futures Trading Commission to have violated any Federal commodities law, and the judgment in such civil action or finding by the Commodity Futures Trading Commission has not been subsequently reversed, suspended or vacated.

Instructions to Paragraph (f) of Item 401.

1. For purposes of computing the five year period referred to in this paragraph, the date of a reportable event shall be deemed the date on which the final order, judgment or decree was entered, or the date on which any rights of appeal from preliminary orders, judgments, or decrees have lapsed. With respect to bankruptcy petitions, the computation date shall be the date of filing for uncontested petitions or the date upon which approval of a contested petition became final.

2. If any event specified in this paragraph (f) has occurred and information in regard thereto is omitted on the grounds that it is not material, the registrant may furnish to the Commission, at time of filing (or at the time preliminary materials are filed, or ten days before definitive materials are filed in preliminary filing is not required, pursuant to Rule 14a-6 or 14c-5 under the Exchange Act),

as supplemental information and not as part of the registration statement, report, or proxy or information statement, materials to which the omission relates, a description of the event and a statement of the reasons for the omission of information in regard thereto.

3. The registrant is permitted to explain any mitigating circumstances associated with events reported pursuant to this paragraph.

4. If the information called for by this paragraph (f) is being presented in a proxy or information statement, no information need be given respecting any director whose term of office as a director will not continue after the meeting to which the statement relates.

g. *Promoters and control persons.*

1. Registrants, which have not been subject to the reporting requirements of section 13(a) or 15(d) of the Exchange Act for the twelve months immediately prior to the filing of the registration statement, report, or statement to which this Item is applicable, and which were organized within the last five years, shall describe with respect to any promoter, any of the events enumerated in paragraphs (f)(1) through (f)(6) of this section that occurred during the past five years and that are material to a voting or investment decision.

2. Registrants, which have not been subject to the reporting requirements of section 13(a) or 15(d) of the Exchange Act for the twelve months immediately prior to the filing of the registration statement, report, or statement to which this Item is applicable, shall describe with respect to any control person, any of the events enumerated in paragraphs (f)(1) through (f)(6) of this section that occurred during the past five years and that are material to a voting or investment decision.

Instructions to Paragraph (g) of Item 401.

1. Instructions 1. through 3. to paragraph (f) shall apply to this paragraph (g).

2. Paragraph (g) shall not apply to any subsidiary of a registrant which has been reporting pursuant to section 13(a) or 15(d) of the Exchange Act for the twelve months immediately prior to the filing of the registration statement, report or statement.

h. Audit committee financial expert.

1.

    i. Disclose that the registrant's board of directors has determined that the registrant either:

        A. Has at least one audit committee financial expert serving on its audit committee; or

        B. Does not have an audit committee financial expert serving on its audit committee.

    ii. If the registrant provides the disclosure required by paragraph (h)(1)(i)(A) of this Item, it must disclose the name of the audit committee financial expert and whether that person is independent, as that term is used in Item 7(d)(3)(iv) of Schedule 14A under the Exchange Act.

    iii. If the registrant provides the disclosure required by paragraph (h)(1)(i)(B) of this Item, it must explain why it does not have an audit committee financial expert.

Instructions to Paragraph (h)(1) of Item 401.

If the registrant's board of directors has determined that the registrant has more than one audit committee financial expert serving on its audit committee, the registrant may, but is not required to, disclose the names of those additional persons. A registrant choosing to identify such persons must indicate whether they are independent pursuant to Item 401(h)(1)(ii).

---

2. For purposes of this Item, an *audit committee financial expert* means a person who has the following attributes:

    i. An understanding of generally accepted accounting principles and financial statements;

    ii. The ability to assess the general application of such principles in connection with the accounting for estimates, accruals and reserves;

    iii. Experience preparing, auditing, analyzing or evaluating financial statements that present a breadth and level of complexity of accounting issues that are generally comparable to the breadth and complexity of issues that can reasonably be expected to be raised by the registrant's financial statements, or experience actively supervising one or more persons engaged in such activities;

iv. An understanding of internal control over financial reporting; and

v. An understanding of audit committee functions.

3. A person shall have acquired such attributes through:

   i. Education and experience as a principal financial officer, principal accounting officer, controller, public accountant or auditor or experience in one or more positions that involve the performance of similar functions;

   ii. Experience actively supervising a principal financial officer, principal accounting officer, controller, public accountant, auditor or person performing similar functions;

   iii. Experience overseeing or assessing the performance of companies or public accountants with respect to the preparation, auditing or evaluation of financial statements; or

   iv. Other relevant experience.

4. *Safe Harbor.*

   i. A person who is determined to be an audit committee financial expert will not be deemed an *expert* for any purpose, including without limitation for purposes of section 11 of the Securities Act of 1933, as a result of being designated or identified as an audit committee financial expert pursuant to this Item 401.

   ii. The designation or identification of a person as an audit committee financial expert pursuant to this Item 401 does not impose on such person any duties, obligations or liability that are greater than the duties, obligations and liability imposed on such person as a member of the audit committee and board of directors in the absence of such designation or identification.

   iii. The designation or identification of a person as an audit committee financial expert pursuant to this Item 401 does not affect the duties, obligations or liability of any other member of the audit committee or board of directors.

Instructions to Item 401(h).

1. The disclosure under Item 401(h) is required only in a registrant's annual report. The registrant need not provide the disclosure required by this Item 401(h) in a proxy or information statement unless that registrant is electing to incorporate this information by reference from the proxy or information statement into its annual report pursuant to general instruction G(3) to Form 10-K.

2. If a person qualifies as an audit committee financial expert by means of having held a position described in paragraph (h)(3)(iv) of this Item, the registrant shall provide a brief listing of that person's relevant experience. Such disclosure may be made by reference to disclosures required under paragraph (e) of this Item 401.

3. In the case of a foreign private issuer with a two-tier board of directors, for purposes of this Item 401(h), the term *board of directors* means the supervisory or non-management board. In the case of a foreign private issuer meeting the requirements of Rule 10A-3(c)(3) under the Exchange Act, for purposes of this Item 401(h), the term *board of directors* means the issuer's board of auditors (or similar body) or statutory auditors, as applicable. Also, in the case of a foreign private issuer, the term generally accepted accounting principles in paragraph (h)(2)(i) of this Item means the body of *generally accepted accounting principles* used by that issuer in its primary financial statements filed with the Commission.

4. A registrant that is an Asset-Backed Issuer (as defined in Rules 13a-14(g) and 15d-14(g) under the Exchange Act) is not required to disclose the information required by this Item 401(h).

i. Identification of the audit committee.

1. If you meet the following requirements, provide the disclosure in paragraph (i)(2) of this section:

   i. You are a listed issuer, as defined in Rule 10A-3 under the Exchange Act;

   ii. You are filing either an annual report on Form 10-K or 10-KSB, or a proxy statement or information statement pursuant to the Exchange Act if action is to be taken with respect to the election of directors; and

iii. You are neither:

    A. A subsidiary of another listed issuer that is relying on the exemption in Rule 10A-3(c)(2) under the Exchange Act; nor

    B. Relying on any of the exemptions in Rule 10A-3(c)(4) through (c)(7) under the Exchange Act.

2.

    i. State whether or not the registrant has a separately-designated standing audit committee established in accordance with section 3(a)(58)(A) of the Exchange Act, or a committee performing similar functions. If the registrant has such a committee, however designated, identify each committee member. If the entire board of directors is acting as the registrant's audit committee as specified in section 3(a)(58)(B) of the Exchange Act, so state.

    ii. If applicable, provide the disclosure required by Rule 10A-3(d) under the Exchange Act regarding an exemption from the listing standards for audit committees.

j. Describe any material changes to the procedures by which security holders may recommend nominees to the registrant's board of directors, where those changes were implemented after the registrant last provided disclosure in response to the requirements of Item 7(d)(2)(ii)(G) of Schedule 14A or this Item.

Instructions to paragraph (j) of Item 401.

    1. The disclosure required in paragraph (j) need only be provided in a registrant's quarterly or annual reports.

    2. For purposes of paragraph (j), adoption of procedures by which security holders may recommend nominees to the registrant's board of directors, where the registrant's most recent disclosure in response to the requirements of Item 7(d)(2)(ii)(G) of Schedule 14A, or this Item, indicated that the registrant did not have in place such procedures, will constitute a material change.

Item 402—Executive Compensation

---

a. General.

1. **Treatment of specific types of issuers—**

   i. **Small business issuers.** A registrant that qualifies as "small business issuer," as defined by Item 10(a)(1) of Regulation S-B, will be deemed to comply with this item if it provides the information required by paragraph (b) (Summary Compensation Table), paragraphs (c)(1) and (c)(2)(i)-(v) (Option/SAR Grants Table), paragraph (d) (Aggregated Option/SAR Exercise and Fiscal Year-End Option/SAR Value Table), paragraph (e) (Long-Term Incentive Plan Awards Table), paragraph (g) (Compensation of Directors), paragraph (h) (Employment Contracts, Termination of Employment and Change in Control Arrangements) and paragraph (i) (1) and (2) (Report on Repricing of Options/SARs) of this item.

   ii. **Foreign private issuers.** A foreign private issuer will be deemed to comply with this item if it provides the information required by Items 6.B. and 6.E.2 of Form 20-F, with more detailed information provided if otherwise made publicly available.

2. **All compensation covered.** This item requires clear, concise and understandable disclosure of all plan and non-plan compensation awarded to, earned by, or paid to the named executive officers designated under paragraph (a)(3) of this item, and directors covered by paragraph (g) of this item by any person for all services rendered in all capacities to the registrant and its subsidiaries, unless otherwise specified in this item. Except as provided by paragraph (a)(5) of this item, all such compensation shall be reported pursuant to this item, even if also called for by another requirement, including transactions between the registrant and a third party where the primary purpose of the transaction is to furnish compensation to any such named executive officer or director. No item reported as compensation for one fiscal year need be reported as compensation for a subsequent fiscal year.

3. **Persons covered.** Disclosure shall be provided pursuant to this item for each of the following (the "named executive officers"):

   i. All individuals serving as the registrant's chief executive officer or acting in a similar capacity during the last completed fiscal year ("CEO"), regardless of compensation level;

ii. The registrant's four most highly compensated executive officers other than the CEO who were serving as executive officers
at the end of the last completed fiscal year; and

iii. Up to two additional individuals for whom disclosure would
have been provided pursuant to paragraph (a)(3)(ii) of this item
but for the fact that the individual was not serving as an executive officer of the registrant at the end of the last completed
fiscal year.

Instructions to Item 402(a)(3).

1. **Determination of Most Highly Compensated Executive Officers.** The determination as to which executive officers are most
highly compensated shall be made by reference to total annual
salary and bonus for the last completed fiscal year (as required to
be disclosed pursuant to paragraph (b)(2)(iii) (A) and (B) of this
item), but including the dollar value of salary or bonus amounts
forgone pursuant to Instruction 3 to paragraph (b)(2)(iii) (A) and
(B) of this item: *Provided, however,* That no disclosure need be
provided for any executive officer, other than the CEO, whose
total annual salary and bonus, as so determined, does not exceed $100,000.

2. **Inclusion of Executive Officer of Subsidiary.** It may be appropriate in certain circumstances for a registrant to include an executive officer of a subsidiary in the disclosure required by this item.
See Rule 3b-7 under the Exchange Act.

3. **Exclusion of Executive Officer due to Unusual or Overseas
Compensation.** It may be appropriate in limited circumstances for
a registrant not to include in the disclosure required by this item an
individual, other than its CEO, who is one of the registrant's most
highly compensated executive officers. Among the factors that
should be considered in determining not to name an individual
are: (a) the distribution or accrual of an unusually large amount of
cash compensation (such as a bonus or commission) that is not
part of a recurring arrangement and is unlikely to continue; and (b)
the payment of amounts of cash compensation relating to overseas assignments that may be attributed predominantly to such
assignments.

4. **Information for full fiscal year.** If the CEO served in that capacity during any part of a fiscal year with respect to which information is required, information should be provided as to all of his or her compensation for the full fiscal year. If a named executive officer (other than the CEO) served as an executive officer of the registrant (whether or not in the same position) during any part of a fiscal year with respect to which information is required, information shall be provided as to all compensation of that individual for the full fiscal year.

5. **Transactions with third parties reported under Item 404.** This item includes transactions between the registrant and a third party where the primary purpose of the transaction is to furnish compensation to a named executive officer. No information need be given in response to any paragraph of this item, other than paragraph (j), as to any such third-party transaction if the transaction has been reported in response to Item 404 of Regulation S-K.

6. **Omission of table or column.** A table or column may be omitted, if there has been no compensation awarded to, earned by or paid to any of the named executives required to be reported in that table or column in any fiscal year covered by that table.

7. **Definitions.** For purposes of this item:

   i. The term **stock appreciation rights (SARs)** refers to SARs payable in cash or stock, including SARs payable in cash or stock at the election of the registrant or a named executive officer.

   ii. The term **plan** includes, but is not limited to, the following: Any plan, contract, authorization or arrangement, whether or not set forth in any formal documents, pursuant to which the following may be received: cash, stock, restricted stock or restricted stock units, phantom stock, stock options, SARs, stock options in tandem with SARs, warrants, convertible securities, performance units and performance shares, and similar instruments. A plan may be applicable to one person. Registrants may omit information regarding group life, health, hospitalization, medical reimbursement or relocation plans that do not discriminate in scope, terms or operation, in favor of executive officers or directors of the registrant and that are available generally to all salaried employees.

    iii. The term **long-term incentive plan** means any plan providing compensation intended to serve as incentive for performance to occur over a period longer than one fiscal year, whether such performance is measured by reference to financial performance of the registrant or an affiliate, the registrant's stock price, or any other measure, but excluding restricted stock, stock option and SAR plans.

8. **Location of specified information.** The information required by paragraphs (i), (k) and (l) of this item need not be provided in any filings other than a registrant proxy or information statement relating to an annual meeting of security holders at which directors are to be elected (or special meeting or written consents in lieu of such meeting). Such information will not be deemed to be incorporated by reference into any filing under the Securities Act or the Exchange Act, except to the extent that the registrant specifically incorporates it by reference.

9. **Liability for specified information.** The information required by paragraphs (k) and (l) of this item shall not be deemed to be "soliciting material" or to be "filed" with the Commission or subject to Regulations 14A or 14C, other than as provided in this item, or to the liabilities of section 18 of the Exchange Act, except to the extent that the registrant specifically requests that such information be treated as soliciting material or specifically incorporates it by reference into a filing under the Securities Act or the Exchange Act.

b. *Summary Compensation Table.*

1. **General.** The information specified in paragraph (b)(2) of this item, concerning the compensation of the named executive officers for each of the registrant's last three completed fiscal years, shall be provided in a Summary Compensation Table, in the tabular format specified below.

SUMMARY COMPENSATION TABLE

Name and principal position	Year	Annual compensation			Long-term compensation			All other compensation ($)
		Salary ($)	Bonus ($)	Other annual compensation ($)	Awards		Payouts	
					Restricted stock award(s) ($)	Securities underlying options/ SARs (#)	LTIP payouts ($)	
(a)	(b)	(c)	(d)	(e)	(f)	(g)	(h)	(i)
CEO....								
A.........								
B.........								
C.........								
D.........								

301

2. The Table shall include:

    i. The name and principal position of the executive officer (column (a));

    ii. Fiscal year covered (column (b));

    iii. Annual compensation (columns (c), (d) and (e)), including:

        A. The dollar value of base salary (cash and non-cash) earned by the named executive officer during the fiscal year covered (column (c));

        B. The dollar value of bonus (cash and non-cash) earned by the named executive officer during the fiscal year covered (column (d)); and

---

Instructions to Item 402(b)(2)(iii)(A) and (B).

1. Amounts deferred at the election of a named executive officer, whether pursuant to a plan established under Section 401(k) of the Internal Revenue Code, or otherwise, shall be included in the salary column (column (c)) or bonus column (column (d)), as appropriate, for the fiscal year in which earned. If the amount of salary or bonus earned in a given fiscal year is not calculable through the latest practicable date, that fact must be disclosed in a footnote and such amount must be disclosed in the subsequent fiscal year in the appropriate column for the fiscal year in which earned.

2. For stock or any other form of non-cash compensation, disclose the fair market value at the time the compensation is awarded, earned or paid.

3. Registrants need not include in the salary column (column (c)) or bonus column (column (d)) any amount of salary or bonus forgone at the election of a named executive officer pursuant to a registrant program under which stock, stock-based or other forms of non-cash compensation may be received by a named executive in lieu of a portion of annual compensation earned in a covered fiscal year. However, the receipt of any such form of non-cash compensation in lieu of salary or bonus earned for a covered fiscal year must be disclosed in the appropriate column of the Table corresponding to that fiscal year (i.e., restricted stock awards (column

(f)); options or SARs (column (g)); all other compensation (column (i)), or, if made pursuant to a long-term incentive plan and therefore not reportable at grant in the Summary Compensation Table, a footnote must be added to the salary or bonus column so disclosing and referring to the Long-Term Incentive Plan Table (required by paragraph (e) of this item) where the award is reported.

C. The dollar value of other annual compensation not properly categorized as salary or bonus, as follows (column (e)):

1. Perquisites and other personal benefits, securities or property, unless the aggregate amount of such compensation is the lesser of either $50,000 or 10% of the total of annual salary and bonus reported for the named executive officer in columns (c) and (d);

2. Above-market or preferential earnings on restricted stock, options, SARs or deferred compensation paid during the fiscal year or payable during that period but deferred at the election of the named executive officer;

3. Earnings on long-term incentive plan compensation paid during the fiscal year or payable during that period but deferred at the election of the named executive officer;

4. Amounts reimbursed during the fiscal year for the payment of taxes; and

5. The dollar value of the difference between the price paid by a named executive officer for any security of the registrant or its subsidiaries purchased from the registrant or its subsidiaries (through deferral of salary or bonus, or otherwise), and the fair market value of such security at the date of purchase, unless that discount is available generally, either to all security holders or to all salaried employees of the registrant.

Instructions to Item 402(b)(2)(iii)(C).

1. Each perquisite or other personal benefit exceeding 25% of the total perquisites and other personal benefits reported for a named executive officer must be identified by type and amount in a footnote or accompanying narrative discussion to column (e).

2. Perquisites and other personal benefits shall be valued on the basis of the aggregate incremental cost to the registrant and its subsidiaries.

3. Interest on deferred or long-term compensation is above-market only if the rate of interest exceeds 120% of the applicable federal long-term rate, with compounding (as prescribed under section 1274(d) of the Internal Revenue Code) at the rate that corresponds most closely to the rate under the registrant's plan at the time the interest rate or formula is set. In the event of a discretionary reset of the interest rate, the requisite calculation must be made on the basis of the interest rate at the time of such reset, rather than when originally established. Only the above-market portion of the interest must be included. If the applicable interest rates vary depending upon conditions such as a minimum period of continued service, the reported amount should be calculated assuming satisfaction of all conditions to receiving interest at the highest rate.

4. Dividends (and dividend equivalents) on restricted stock, options, SARs or deferred compensation denominated in stock ("deferred stock") are preferential only if earned at a rate higher than dividends on the registrant's common stock. Only the preferential portion of the dividends or equivalents must be included.

---

iv. Long-term compensation (columns (f), (g) and (h)), including:

A. The dollar value (net of any consideration paid by the named executive officer) of any award of restricted stock, including share units (calculated by multiplying the closing market price of the registrant's unrestricted stock on the date of grant by the number of shares awarded) (column (f));

B. The sum of the number of securities underlying stock options granted (including options that subsequently have been transferred), with or without tandem SARs, and the number of freestanding SARs (column (g)); and

C. The dollar value of all payouts pursuant to long-term incentive plans ("LTIPs") as defined in paragraph (a)(7)(iii) of this item (column (h)).

Instructions to Item 402(b)(2)(iv).

1. Awards of restricted stock that are subject to performance-based conditions on vesting, in addition to lapse of time and/or continued service with the registrant or a subsidiary, may be reported as LTIP awards pursuant to paragraph (e) of this item instead of in column (f). If this approach is selected, once the restricted stock vests, it must be reported as an LTIP payout in column (h).

2. The registrant shall, in a footnote to the Summary Compensation Table (appended to column (f), if included), disclose:

   a. The number and value of the aggregate restricted stock holdings at the end of the last completed fiscal year. The value shall be calculated in the manner specified in paragraph (b)(2)(iv)(A) of this item using the value of the registrant's shares at the end of the last completed fiscal year;

   b. For any restricted stock award reported in the Summary Compensation Table that will vest, in whole or in part, in under three years from the date of grant, the total number of shares awarded and the vesting schedule; and

   c. Whether dividends will be paid on the restricted stock reported in column (f).

3. If at any time during the last completed fiscal year, the registrant has adjusted or amended the exercise price of stock options or freestanding SARs previously awarded to a named executive officer, whether through amendment, cancellation or replacement grants, or any other means ("repriced"), the registrant shall include the number of options or freestanding SARs so repriced as Stock Options/SARs granted and required to be reported in column (g).

4. If any specified performance target, goal or condition to payout was waived with respect to any amount included in LTIP payouts reported in column (h), the registrant shall so state in a footnote to column (h).

---

    v. All other compensation for the covered fiscal year that the registrant could not properly report in any other column of the Summary Compensation Table (column (i)). Any compensation reported in this column for the last completed fiscal year shall be identified and quantified in a footnote. Such compensation shall include, but not be limited to:

A. The amount paid, payable or accrued to any named executive officer pursuant to a plan or arrangement in connection with:

1. The resignation, retirement or any other termination of such executive officer's employment with the registrant and its subsidiaries; or

2. A change in control of the registrant or a change in the executive officer's responsibilities following such a change in control;

B. The dollar value of above-market or preferential amounts earned on restricted stock, options, SARs or deferred compensation during the fiscal year, or calculated with respect to that period, except that if such amounts are paid during the period, or payable during the period but deferred at the election of a named executive officer, this information shall be reported as Other Annual Compensation in column (e). See Instructions 3 and 4 to paragraph (b)(2)(iii)(C) of this item;

C. The dollar value of amounts earned on long-term incentive plan compensation during the fiscal year, or calculated with respect to that period, except that if such amounts are paid during that period, or payable during that period at the election of the named executive officer, this information shall be reported as Other Annual Compensation in column (e);

D. Annual registrant contributions or other allocations to vested and unvested defined contribution plans; and

E. The dollar value of any insurance premiums paid by, or on behalf of, the registrant during the covered fiscal year with respect to term life insurance for the benefit of a named executive officer, and, if there is any arrangement or understanding, whether formal or informal, that such executive officer has or will receive or be allocated an interest in any cash surrender value under the insurance policy, either:

1. The full dollar value of the remainder of the premiums paid by, or on behalf of, the registrant; or

2. If the premiums will be refunded to the registrant on termination of the policy, the dollar value of the benefit to the executive officer of the remainder of the premium paid by, or on behalf of, the registrant during the fiscal year. The benefit shall be determined for the period, projected on an actuarial basis, between payment of the premium and the refund.

Instructions to Item 402(b)(2)(v).

1. LTIP awards and amounts received on exercise of options and SARs need not be reported as All Other Compensation in column (i).

2. Information relating to defined benefit and actuarial plans should not be reported pursuant to paragraph (b) of this item, but instead should be reported pursuant to paragraph (f) of this item.

3. Where alternative methods of reporting are available under paragraph (b)(2)(v)(E) of this item, the same method should be used for each of the named executive officers. If the registrant chooses to change methods from one year to the next, that fact, and the reason therefor, should be disclosed in a footnote to column (i).

Instruction to Item 402(b).

Information with respect to fiscal years prior to the last completed fiscal year will not be required if the registrant was not a reporting company pursuant to Section 13(a) or 15(d) of the Exchange Act at any time during that year, except that the registrant will be required to provide information for any such year if that information previously was required to be provided in response to a Commission filing requirement.

---

c. Option/SAR Grants Table.

1. The information specified in paragraph (c)(2) of this item, concerning individual grants of stock options (whether or not in tandem with SARs), and freestanding SARs (including options and SARs that subsequently have been transferred) made during the last

completed fiscal year to each of the named executive officers shall be provided in the tabular format specified as follows:

OPTION/SAR GRANTS IN LAST FISCAL YEAR

| | Individual grants | | | | Potential realizable value at assumed annual rates of stock price appreciation for option term | | Alternative to (f) and (g): grant date value |
Name	Number of securities underlying option/SARs granted (#)	Percent of total options/SARs granted to employees in fiscal year	Exercise or base price ($/sh)	Expiration date	5% ($)	10% ($)	Grant date present value ($)
(a)	(b)	(c)	(d)	(e)	(f)	(g)	(h)
CEO....							
A........							
B........							
C........							
D........							

2. The Table shall include, with respect to each grant:

     i. The name of the executive officer (column (a));

     ii. Number of securities underlying option/SARs granted (column (b));

     iii. The percent the grant represents of total options and SARs granted to employees during the fiscal year (column (c));

     iv. The per-share exercise or base price of the options or SARs granted (column (d)). If such exercise or base price is less than the market price of the underlying security on the date of grant, a separate, adjoining column shall be added showing market price on the date of grant;

     v. The expiration date of the options or SARs (column (e)); and

vi. Either (A) the potential realizable value of each grant of options or freestanding SARs or (B) the present value of each grant, as follows:

A. The potential realizable value of each grant of options or freestanding SARs, assuming that the market price of the underlying security appreciates in value from the date of grant to the end of the option or SAR term, at the following annualized rates:

1. 5% (column (f));

2. 10% (column (g)); and

3. If the exercise or base price was below the market price of the underlying security at the date of grant, provide an additional column labeled 0%, to show the value at grant-date market price; or

B. The present value of the grant at the date of grant, under any option pricing model (alternative column (f)).

Instructions to Item 402(c).

1. If more than one grant of options and/or freestanding SARs was made to a named executive officer during the last completed fiscal year, a separate line should be used to provide disclosure of each such grant. However, multiple grants during a single fiscal year may be aggregated where each grant was made at the same exercise and/or base price and has the same expiration date, and the same performance vesting thresholds, if any. A single grant consisting of options and/or freestanding SARs shall be reported as separate grants with respect to each tranche with a different exercise and/or base price, performance vesting threshold, or expiration date.

2. Options or freestanding SARs granted in connection with an option repricing transaction shall be reported in this table. See Instruction 3 to paragraph (b)(2)(iv) of this item.

3. Any material term of the grant, including but not limited to the date of exercisability, the number of SARs, performance units or other instruments granted in tandem with options, a performance-based condition to exercisability, a reload feature, or a tax-reimbursement feature, shall be footnoted.

4. If the exercise or base price is adjustable over the term of any option or freestanding SAR in accordance with any prescribed standard or formula, including but not limited to an index or premium price provision, describe the following, either by footnote to column (c) or in narrative accompanying the Table: (a) the standard or formula; and (b) any constant assumption made by the registrant regarding any adjustment to the exercise price in calculating the potential option or SAR value.

5. If any provision of a grant (other than an antidilution provision) could cause the exercise price to be lowered, registrants must clearly and fully disclose these provisions and their potential consequences either by a footnote or accompanying textual narrative.

6. In determining the grant-date market or base price of the security underlying options or freestanding SARs, the registrant may use either the closing market price per share of the security, or any other formula prescribed for the security.

7. The potential realizable dollar value of a grant (columns (f) and (g)) shall be the product of:

   a. the difference between:

      i. the product of the per-share market price at the time of the grant and the sum of 1 plus the adjusted stock price appreciation rate (the assumed rate of appreciation compounded annually over the term of the option or SAR); and

      ii. the per-share exercise price of the option or SAR; and

   b. the number of securities underlying the grant at fiscal year-end.

8. Registrants may add one or more separate columns using the formula prescribed in Instruction 7 to paragraph (c) of this item, to reflect the following:

   a. The registrant's historic rate of appreciation over a period equivalent to the term of such options and/or SARs;

   b. 0% appreciation, where the exercise or base price was equal to or greater than the market price of the underlying securities on the date of grant; and

   c. N% appreciation, the percentage appreciation by which the exercise or base price exceeded the market price at grant. Where the grant included multiple tranches with exercise or base prices exceeding the market price of the underlying security by varying degrees, include an additional column for each additional tranche.

9. Where the registrant chooses to use the grant-date valuation alternative specified in paragraph (c)(2)(vi)(B) of this item, the valuation shall be footnoted to describe the valuation method used. Where the registrant has used a variation of the Black-Scholes or binomial option pricing model, the description shall identify the use of such pricing model and describe the assumptions used relating to the expected volatility, risk-free rate of return, dividend yield and time of exercise. Any adjustments for non-transferability or risk of forfeiture also shall be disclosed. In the event another valuation method is used, the registrant is required to describe the methodology as well as any material assumptions.

---

d. *Aggregated option/SAR exercises and fiscal year-end option/SAR value table.*

1. The information specified in paragraph (d)(2) of this item, concerning each exercise of stock options (or tandem SARs) and free-standing SARs during the last completed fiscal year by each of the named executive officers and the fiscal year-end value of unexercised options and SARs, shall be provided on an aggregated basis in the tabular format specified below:

AGGREGATED OPTION/SAR EXERCISES IN LAST FISCAL YEAR AND FY-END OPTION/SAR VALUES

Name	Shares acquired on exercise (#)	Value realized ($)	Number of securities underlying unexercised options/SARs at FY-end (#) Exercisable/ Unexercisable	Value of unexercised in-the-money options/SARs at FY-end ($) Exercisable/ Unexercisable
(a)	(b)	(c)	(d)	(e)
CEO....				
A....				
B....				
C....				
D....				

2. The table shall include:

    i. The name of the executive officer (column (a));

    ii. The number of shares received upon exercise, or, if no shares were received, the number of securities with respect to which the options or SARs were exercised (column (b));

    iii. The aggregate dollar value realized upon exercise (column (c));

    iv. The total number of securities underlying unexercised options and SARs held at the end of the last completed fiscal year, separately identifying the exercisable and unexercisable options and SARs (column (d)); and

    v. The aggregate dollar value of in-the-money, unexercised options and SARs held at the end of the fiscal year, separately identifying the exercisable and unexercisable options and SARs (column (e)).

Instructions to Item 402(d)(2).

1. Options or freestanding SARs are in-the-money if the fair market value of the underlying securities exceeds the exercise or base price of the option or SAR. The dollar values in columns (c) and (e) are calculated by determining the difference between the fair market value of the securities underlying the options or SARs and the exercise or base price of the options or SARs at exercise or fiscal year-end, respectively.

2. In calculating the dollar value realized upon exercise (column (c)), the value of any related payment or other consideration provided (or to be provided) by the registrant to or on behalf of a named executive officer, whether in payment of the exercise price or related taxes, shall not be included. Payments by the registrant in reimbursement of tax obligations incurred by a named executive officer are required to be disclosed in accordance with paragraph (b)(2)(iii)(C)(4) of this item.

---

e. Long-Term Incentive Plan ("LTIP") awards table.

1. The information specified in paragraph (e)(2) of this item, regarding each award made to a named executive officer in the last completed fiscal year under any LTIP, shall be provided in the tabular format specified below:

			Estimated future payouts under nonstock price-based plans		
LONG-TERM INCENTIVE PLANS—AWARDS IN LAST FISCAL YEAR					
Name (a)	Number of shares, units or other rights (#) (b)	Performance or other period until maturation or payout (c)	Threshold ($ or #) (d)	Target ($ or #) (e)	Maximum ($ or #) (f)
CEO....					
A....					
B....					
C....					
D....					

2. The Table shall include:

   i. The name of the executive officer (column (a));

   ii. The number of shares, units or other rights awarded under any LTIP, and, if applicable, the number of shares underlying any such unit or right (column (b));

   iii. The performance or other time period until payout or maturation of the award (column (c)); and

   iv. For plans not based on stock price, the dollar value of the estimated payout, the number of shares to be awarded as the payout or a range of estimated payouts denominated in dollars or number of shares under the award (threshold, target and maximum amount) (columns (d) through (f)).

Instructions to Item 402(e).

1. For purposes of this paragraph, the term "long-term incentive plan" or "LTIP" shall be defined in accordance with paragraph (a)(7)(iii) of this item.

2. Describe in a footnote or in narrative text accompanying this table the material terms of any award, including a general description of the formula or criteria to be applied in determining the amounts payable. Registrants are not required to disclose any factor,

criterion or performance-related or other condition to payout or maturation of a particular award that involves confidential commercial or business information, disclosure of which would adversely affect the registrant's competitive position.

3. Separate disclosure shall be provided in the Table for each award made to a named executive officer, accompanied by the information specified in Instruction 2 to this paragraph. If awards are made to a named executive officer during the fiscal year under more than one plan, identify the particular plan under which each such award was made.

4. For column (d), "threshold" refers to the minimum amount payable for a certain level of performance under the plan. For column (e), "target" refers to the amount payable if the specified performance target(s) are reached. For column (f), "maximum" refers to the maximum payout possible under the plan.

5. In column (e), registrants must provide a representative amount based on the previous fiscal year's performance if the target award is not determinable.

6. A tandem grant of two instruments, only one of which is pursuant to a LTIP, need be reported only in the table applicable to the other instrument. For example, an option granted in tandem with a performance share would be reported only as an option grant, with the tandem feature noted.

---

f. *Defined benefit or actuarial plan disclosure.*

1. **Pension plan table.**

    i. For any defined benefit or actuarial plan under which benefits are determined primarily by final compensation (or average final compensation) and years of service, provide a separate Pension Plan Table showing estimated annual benefits payable upon retirement (including amounts attributable to any defined benefit supplementary or excess pension award plans) in specified compensation and years of service classifications in the format specified below.

PENSION PLAN TABLE

Remuneration	Years of Service				
	15	20	25	30	35
125,000					
150,000					
175,000					
200,000					
225,000					
250,000					
300,000					
400,000					
450,000					
500,000					

ii. Immediately following the Table, the registrant shall disclose:

A. The compensation covered by the plan(s), including the relationship of such covered compensation to the annual compensation reported in the Summary Compensation Table required by paragraph (b)(2)(iii) of this item, and state the current compensation covered by the plan for any named executive officer whose covered compensation differs substantially (by more than 10%) from that set forth in the annual compensation columns of the Summary Compensation Table;

B. The estimated credited years of service for each of the named executive officers; and

C. A statement as to the basis upon which benefits are computed (e.g., straight-life annuity amounts), and whether or not the benefits listed in the Pension Plan Table are subject to any deduction for Social Security or other offset amounts.

2. **Alternative pension plan disclosure.** For any defined benefit or actuarial plan under which benefits are not determined primarily by final compensation (or average final compensation) and years of service, the registrant shall state in narrative form:

    i. The formula by which benefits are determined; and

    ii. The estimated annual benefits payable upon retirement at normal retirement age for each of the named executive officers.

Instructions to Item 402(f).

1. **Pension Levels.** Compensation set forth in the Pension Plan Table pursuant to paragraph (f)(1)(i) of this item shall allow for reasonable increases in existing compensation levels; alternatively, registrants may present as the highest compensation level in the Pension Plan Table an amount equal to 120% of the amount of covered compensation of the most highly compensated individual named in the Summary Compensation Table required by paragraph (b)(2) of this item.

2. **Normal Retirement Age.** The term "normal retirement age" means normal retirement age as defined in a pension or similar plan or, if not defined therein, the earliest time at which a participant may retire without any benefit reduction due to age.

---

g. *Compensation of Directors.*

1. **Standard arrangements.** Describe any standard arrangements, stating amounts, pursuant to which directors of the registrant are compensated for any services provided as a director, including any additional amounts payable for committee participation or special assignments.

2. **Other arrangements.** Describe any other arrangements pursuant to which any director of the registrant was compensated during the registrant's last completed fiscal year for any service provided as a director, stating the amount paid and the name of the director.

Instruction to Item 402(g)(2).

The information required by paragraph (g)(2) of this item shall include any arrangement, including consulting contracts, entered into in consideration of the director's service on the board. The material terms of any such arrangement shall be included.

h. *Employment contracts and termination of employment and change-in-control arrangements.* Describe the terms and conditions of each of the following contracts or arrangements:

1. Any employment contract between the registrant and a named executive officer; and

2. Any compensatory plan or arrangement, including payments to be received from the registrant, with respect to a named executive officer, if such plan or arrangement results or will result from the resignation, retirement or any other termination of such executive officer's employment with the registrant and its subsidiaries or from a change-in-control of the registrant or a change in the named executive officer's responsibilities following a change-in-control and the amount involved, including all periodic payments or installments, exceeds $100,000.

i. *Report on repricing of options/SARs.*

1. If at any time during the last completed fiscal year, the registrant, while a reporting company pursuant to section 13(a) or 15(d) of the Exchange Act, has adjusted or amended the exercise price of stock options or SARs previously awarded to any of the named executive officers, whether through amendment, cancellation or replacement grants, or any other means ("repriced"), the registrant shall provide the information specified in paragraphs (i)(2) and (i)(3) of this item.

2. The compensation committee (or other board committee performing equivalent functions or, in the absence of any such committee, the entire board of directors) shall explain in reasonable detail any such repricing of options and/or SARs held by a named executive officer in the last completed fiscal year, as well as the basis for each such repricing.

3.

   i. The information specified in paragraph (i)(3)(ii) of this item, concerning all such repricings of options and SARs held by any executive officer during the last ten completed fiscal years, shall be provided in the tabular format specified below:

TEN-YEAR OPTION/SAR REPRICINGS

Name	Date	Number of securities underlying options/SARs repriced or amended (#)	Market price of stock at time of repricing or amendment ($)	Exercise price at time of repricing or amendment ($)	New exercise price ($)	Length of original option term remaining at date of repricing or amendment
(a)	(b)	(c)	(d)	(e)	(f)	(g)

   ii. The Table shall include, with respect to each repricing:

     A. The name and position of the executive officer (column (a));

     B. The date of each repricing (column (b));

     C. The number of securities underlying replacement or amended options or SARs (column (c));

     D. The per-share market price of the underlying security at the time of repricing (column (d));

     E. The original exercise price or base price of the cancelled or amended option or SAR (column (e));

     F. The per-share exercise price or base price of the replacement option or SAR (column (f)); and

     G. The amount of time remaining before the replaced or amended option or SAR would have expired (column (g)).

Instructions to Item 402(i).

1. The required report shall be made over the name of each member of the registrant's compensation committee, or other board committee performing equivalent functions or, in the absence of any such committee, the entire board of directors.

2. A replacement grant is any grant of options or SARs reasonably related to any prior or potential option or SAR cancellation, whether by an exchange of existing options or SARs for options or SARs with new terms; the grant of new options or SARs in tandem with previously granted options or SARs that will operate to cancel the previously granted options or SARs upon exercise; repricing of previously granted options or SARs; or otherwise. If a corresponding original grant was canceled in a prior year, information about such grant nevertheless must be disclosed pursuant to this paragraph.

3. If the replacement grant is not made at the current market price, describe the terms of the grant in a footnote or accompanying textual narrative.

4. This paragraph shall not apply to any repricing occurring through the operation of:

   a. A plan formula or mechanism that results in the periodic adjustment of the option or SAR exercise or base price;

   b. A plan antidilution provision; or

   c. A recapitalization or similar transaction equally affecting all holders of the class of securities underlying the options or SARs.

5. Information required by paragraph (i)(3) of this item shall not be provided for any repricings effected before the registrant became a reporting company pursuant to section 13(a) or 15(d) of the Exchange Act.

j. *Additional information with respect to Compensation Committee Interlocks and Insider Participation in compensation decisions.* Under the caption "Compensation Committee Interlocks and Insider Participation,"

1. The registrant shall identify each person who served as a member of the compensation committee of the registrant's board of directors (or board committee performing equivalent functions) during the last completed fiscal year, indicating each committee member who:

   i. was, during the fiscal year, an officer or employee of the registrant or any of its subsidiaries;

   ii. was formerly an officer of the registrant or any of its subsidiaries; or

   iii. Had any relationship requiring disclosure by the registrant under any paragraph of Item 404 of Regulation S-K. In this event, the disclosure required by Item 404 shall accompany such identification.

2. If the registrant has no compensation committee (or other board committee performing equivalent functions), the registrant shall identify each officer and employee of the registrant or any of its subsidiaries, and any former officer of the registrant or any of its subsidiaries, who, during the last completed fiscal year, participated in deliberations of the registrant's board of directors concerning executive officer compensation.

3. The registrant shall describe any of the following relationships that existed during the last completed fiscal year:

   1. An executive officer of the registrant served as a member of the compensation committee (or other board committee performing equivalent functions or, in the absence of any such committee, the entire board of directors) of another entity, one of whose executive officers served on the compensation committee (or other board committee performing equivalent functions or, in the absence of any such committee, the entire board of directors) of the registrant;

      ii. An executive officer of the registrant served as a director of another entity, one of whose executive officers served on the compensation committee (or other board committee performing equivalent functions or, in the absence of any such committee, the entire board of directors) of the registrant; and

    iii. An executive officer of the registrant served as a member of the compensation committee (or other board committee performing equivalent functions or, in the absence of any such committee, the entire board of directors) of another entity, one of whose executive officers served as a director of the registrant.

4. Disclosure required under paragraph (j)(3) of this item regarding any compensation committee member or other director of the registrant who also served as an executive officer of another entity shall be accompanied by the disclosure called for by Item 404 with respect to that person.

Instruction to Item 402(j).

For purposes of this paragraph, the term "entity" shall not include an entity exempt from tax under section 501(c)(3) of the Internal Revenue Code.

---

k. Board compensation committee report on executive compensation.

1. Disclosure of the compensation committee's compensation policies applicable to the registrant's executive officers (including the named executive officers), including the specific relationship of corporate performance to executive compensation, is required with respect to compensation reported for the last completed fiscal year.

2. Discussion is required of the compensation committee's bases for the CEO's compensation reported for the last completed fiscal year, including the factors and criteria upon which the CEO's compensation was based. The committee shall include a specific discussion of the relationship of the registrant's performance to the CEO's compensation for the last completed fiscal year, describing each measure of the registrant's performance, whether qualitative or quantitative, on which the CEO's compensation was based.

3. The required disclosure shall be made over the name of each member of the registrant's compensation committee (or other board committee performing equivalent functions or, in the absence of any such committee, entire board of directors). If the board of directors modified or rejected in any material way any action or recommendation by such committee with respect to such decisions in the last completed fiscal year, the disclosure must so indicate and explain the reasons for the board's actions, and be made over the names of all members of the board.

Instructions to Item 402(k).

1. Boilerplate language should be avoided in describing factors and criteria underlying awards or payments of executive compensation in the statement required.

2. Registrants are not required to disclose target levels with respect to specific quantitative or qualitative performance-related factors considered by the committee (or board), or any factors or criteria involving confidential commercial or business information, the disclosure of which would have an adverse effect on the registrant.

l. *Performance Graph.*

1. Provide a line graph comparing the yearly percentage change in the registrant's cumulative total shareholder return on a class of common stock registered under section 12 of the Exchange Act (as measured by dividing (i) the sum of (A) the cumulative amount of dividends for the measurement period, assuming dividend reinvestment, and (B) the difference between the registrant's share price at the end and the beginning of the measurement period; by (ii) the share price at the beginning of the measurement period) with

  i. the cumulative total return of a broad equity market index assuming reinvestment of dividends, that includes companies whose equity securities are traded on the same exchange or NASDAQ market or are of comparable market capitalization; *provided, however,* that if the registrant is a company within the Standard & Poor's 500 Stock Index, the registrant must use that index; and

    ii. the cumulative total return, assuming reinvestment of dividends, of:

        A. A published industry or line-of-business index;

        B. Peer issuer(s) selected in good faith. If the registrant does not select its peer issuer(s) on an industry or line-of-business basis, the registrant shall disclose the basis for its selection; or

        C. Issuer(s) with similar market capitalization(s), but only if the registrant does not use a published industry or line-of-business index and does not believe it can reasonably identify a peer group. If the registrant uses this alternative, the graph shall be accompanied by a statement of the reasons for this selection.

2. For purposes of paragraph (l)(1) of this item, the term "measurement period" shall be the period beginning at the "measurement point" established by the market close on the last trading day before the beginning of the registrant's fifth preceding fiscal year, through and including the end of the registrant's last completed fiscal year. If the class of securities has been registered under section 12 of the Exchange Act for a shorter period of time, the period covered by the comparison may correspond to that time period.

3. For purposes of paragraph (l)(1)(ii)(A) of this item, the term "published industry or line-of-business index" means any index that is prepared by a party other than the registrant or an affiliate and is accessible to the registrant's security holders; provided, however, that registrants may use an index prepared by the registrant or affiliate if such index is widely recognized and used.

4. If the registrant selects a different index from an index used for the immediately preceding fiscal year, explain the reason(s) for this change and also compare the registrant's total return with that of both the newly selected index and the index used in the immediately preceding fiscal year.

Instructions to Item 402(l).

1. In preparing the required graphic comparisons, the registrant should:

    a. Use, to the extent feasible, comparable methods of presentation and assumptions for the total return calculations required by paragraph (l)(1) of this item; *provided, however,* that if the registrant constructs its own peer group index under paragraph (l)(1)(ii)(B), the same methodology must be used in calculating both the registrant's total return and that on the peer group index; and

    b. Assume the reinvestment of dividends into additional shares of the same class of equity securities at the frequency with which dividends are paid on such securities during the applicable fiscal year.

2. In constructing the graph:

    a. The closing price at the measurement point must be converted into a fixed investment, stated in dollars, in the registrant's stock (or in the stocks represented by a given index), with cumulative returns for each subsequent fiscal year measured as a change from that investment; and

    b. Each fiscal year should be plotted with points showing the cumulative total return as of that point. The value of the investment as of each point plotted on a given return line is the number of shares held at that point multiplied by the then-prevailing share price.

3. The registrant is required to present information for the registrant's last five fiscal years, and may choose to graph a longer period; but the measurement point, however, shall remain the same.

4. Registrants may include comparisons using performance measures in addition to total return, such as return on average common shareholders' equity, so long as the registrant's compensation committee (or other board committee performing equivalent functions or in the absence of any such committee, the entire board of directors) describes the link between that measure and the level of executive compensation in the statement required by paragraph (k) of this Item.

5. If the registrant uses a peer issuer(s) comparison or comparison with issuer(s) with similar market capitalizations, the identity of those issuers must be disclosed and the returns of each component issuer of the group must be weighted according to the respective issuer's stock market capitalization at the beginning of each period for which a return is indicated.

Item 403—Security Ownership of Certain Beneficial Owners and Management

a. *Security ownership of certain beneficial owners.* Furnish the following information, as of the most recent practicable date, substantially in the tabular form indicated, with respect to any person (including any "group" as that term is used in section 13(d)(3) of the Exchange Act) who is known to the registrant to be the beneficial owner of more than five percent of any class of the registrant's voting securities. The address given in column (2) may be a business, mailing or residence address. Show in column (3) the total number of shares beneficially owned and in column (4) the percentage of class so owned. Of the number of shares shown in column (3), indicate by footnote or otherwise the amount known to be shares with respect to which such listed beneficial owner has the right to acquire beneficial ownership, as specified in Rule 13d-3(d)(1) under the Exchange Act.

(1) Title of class	(2) Name and address of beneficial owner	(3) Amount and nature of beneficial ownership	(4) Percent of class

b. *Security ownership of management.* Furnish the following information, as of the most recent practicable date, in substantially the tabular form indicated, as to each class of equity securities of the registrant or any of its parents or subsidiaries other than directors' qualifying shares, beneficially owned by all directors and nominees, naming them, each of the named executive officers as defined in Item 402(a)(3), and directors and executive officers of the registrant as a group, without naming them. Show in column (3) the total number of shares beneficially owned and in column (4) the percent of class so owned. Of the number of shares shown in column (3), indicate, by footnote or otherwise, the amount of shares with respect to which such persons have the right to acquire beneficial ownership as specified in Rule 13d-3(d)(1).

(1) Title of class	(2) Name of beneficial owner	(3) Amount and nature of beneficial ownership	(4) Percent of class

c. *Changes in control.* Describe any arrangements, known to the registrant, including any pledge by any person of securities of the registrant or any of its parents, the operation of which may at a subsequent date result in a change in control of the registrant.

Instructions to Item 403.

1. The percentages are to be calculated on the basis of the amount of outstanding securities, excluding securities held by or for the account of the registrant or its subsidiaries, plus securities deemed outstanding pursuant to Rule 13d-3(d)(1) under the Exchange Act. For purposes of paragraph (b), if the percentage of shares beneficially owned by any director or nominee, or by all directors and officers of the registrant as a group, does not exceed one percent of the class so owned, the registrant may, in lieu of furnishing a precise percentage, indicate this fact by means of an asterisk and explanatory footnote or other similar means.

2. For the purposes of this Item, beneficial ownership shall be determined in accordance with Rule 13d-3 under the Exchange Act. Include such additional subcolumns or other appropriate explanation of column (3) necessary to reflect amounts as to which the beneficial owner has (A) sole voting power, (B) shared voting power, (C) sole investment power, or (D) shared investment power.

3. The registrant shall be deemed to know the contents of any statements filed with the Commission pursuant to section 13(d) or 13(g) of the Exchange Act. When applicable, a registrant may rely upon information set forth in such statements unless the registrant knows or has reason to believe that such information is not complete or accurate or that a statement or amendment should have been filed and was not.

4. For purposes of furnishing information pursuant to paragraph (a) of this Item, the registrant may indicate the source and date of such information.

5. Where more than one beneficial owner is known to be listed for the same securities, appropriate disclosure should be made to avoid confusion. For purposes of paragraph (b), in computing the aggregate number of shares owned by directors and officers of the registrant as a group, the same shares shall not be counted more than once.

6. Paragraph (c) of this Item does not require a description of ordinary default provisions contained in the charter, trust indentures or other governing instruments relating to securities of the registrant.

7. Where the holder(s) of voting securities reported pursuant to paragraph (a) hold more than five percent of any class of voting securities of the registrant pursuant to any voting trust or similar agreement, state the title of such securities, the amount held or to be held pursuant to the trust or agreement (if not clear from the table) and the duration of the agreement. Give the names and addresses of the voting trustees and outline briefly their voting rights and other powers under the trust or agreement.

Item 404—Certain Relationships and Related Transactions

---

a. *Transactions with management and others.* Describe briefly any transaction, or series of similar transactions, since the beginning of the registrant's last fiscal year, or any currently proposed transaction, or series of similar transactions, to which the registrant or any of its subsidiaries was or is to be a party, in which the amount involved exceeds $60,000 and in which any of the following persons had, or will have, a direct or indirect material interest, naming such person and indicating the person's relationship to the registrant, the nature of such person's interest in the transaction(s), the amount of such transaction(s) and, where practicable, the amount of such person's interest in the transaction(s):

1. Any director or executive officer of the registrant;

2. Any nominee for election as a director;

3. Any security holder who is known to the registrant to own of record or beneficially more than five percent of any class of the registrant's voting securities; and

4. Any member of the immediate family of any of the foregoing persons.

Instructions to Paragraph (a) of Item 404.

1. The materiality of any interest is to be determined on the basis of the significance of the information to investors in light of all the circumstances of the particular case. The importance of the interest to the person having the interest, the relationship of the parties to the transaction with each other and the amount involved in the transactions are among the factors to be considered in determining the significance of the information to investors.

2. For purposes of paragraph (a), a person's immediate family shall include such person's spouse; parents; children; siblings; mothers and fathers-in-law; sons and daughters-in-law; and brothers and sisters-in-law.

3. In computing the amount involved in the transaction or series of similar transactions, include all periodic installments in the case of any lease or other agreement providing for periodic payments or installments.

4. The amount of the interest of any person specified in paragraphs (a)(1) through (4) shall be computed without regard to the amount of the profit or loss involved in the transaction(s).

5. In describing any transaction involving the purchase or sale of assets by or to the registrant or any of its subsidiaries, otherwise than in the ordinary course of business, state the cost of the assets to the purchaser and, if acquired by the seller within two years prior to the transaction, the cost thereof to the seller. Indicate the principle followed in determining the registrant's purchase or sale price and the name of the person making such determination.

6. Information shall be furnished in answer to paragraph (a) with respect to transactions that involve remuneration from the registrant or its subsidiaries, directly or indirectly, to any of the persons specified in paragraphs (a)(1) through (4) for services in any capacity unless the interest of such person arises solely from the ownership individually and in the aggregate of less than ten percent of any class of equity securities of another corporation furnishing the services to the registrant or its subsidiaries.

7. No information need be given in answer to paragraph (a) as to any transactions where:

    A. The rates or charges involved in the transaction are determined by competitive bids, or the transaction involves the rendering of services as a common or contract carrier, or public utility, at rates or charges fixed in conformity with law or governmental authority;

    B. The transaction involves services as a bank depositary of funds, transfer agent, registrar, trustee under a trust indenture, or similar services; or

    C. The interest of the person specified in paragraphs (a)(1) through (4) arises solely from the ownership of securities of the registrant and such person receives no extra or special benefit not shared on a pro rata basis.

8. Paragraph (a) requires disclosure of indirect, as well as direct, material interests in transactions. A person who has a position or relationship with a firm, corporation, or other entity that engages in a transaction with the registrant or its subsidiaries may have an indirect interest in such transaction by reason of such position or relationship. Such an interest, however, shall not be deemed "material" within the meaning of paragraph (a) where:

   A. The interest arises only: (i) From such person's position as a director of another corporation or organization which is a party to the transaction; or (ii) from the direct or indirect ownership by such person and all other persons specified in paragraphs (a)(1) through (4), in the aggregate, of less than a ten percent equity interest in another person which is a party to the transaction; or (iii) from both such position and ownership;

   B. The interest arises only from such person's position as a limited partner in a partnership in which the person and all other persons specified in paragraphs (a)(1) through (4) have an interest of less than ten percent; or

   C. The interest of such person arises solely from the holding of an equity interest or a creditor interest in another person that is a party to the transaction with the registrant or any of its subsidiaries, and the transaction is not material to such other person.

9. There may be situations where, although these instructions do not expressly authorize nondisclosure, the interest of a person specified in paragraphs (a)(1) through (4) in a particular transaction or series of transactions is not a direct or indirect material interest. In that case, information regarding such interest and transaction is not required to be disclosed in response to this paragraph.

---

b. *Certain business relationships.* Describe any of the following relationships regarding directors or nominees for director that exist, or have existed during the registrant's last fiscal year, indicating the identity of the entity with which the registrant has such a relationship, the name of the nominee or director affiliated with such entity and the nature of such nominee's or director's affiliation, the relationship between such entity and the registrant and the amount of the business done between the registrant and the entity during the registrant's last full fiscal year or proposed to be done during the registrant's current fiscal year:

1. If the nominee or director is, or during the last fiscal year has been, an executive officer of, or owns, or during the last fiscal year has owned, of record or beneficially in excess of ten percent equity interest in, any business or professional entity that has made during the registrant's last full fiscal year, or proposes to make during the registrant's current fiscal year, payments to the registrant or its subsidiaries for property or services in excess of five percent of (i) the registrant's consolidated gross revenues for its last full fiscal year, or (ii) the other entity's consolidated gross revenues for its last full fiscal year;

2. If the nominee or director is, or during the last fiscal year has been, an executive officer of, or owns, or during the last fiscal year has owned, of record or beneficially in excess of ten percent equity interest in, any business or professional entity to which the registrant or its subsidiaries has made during the registrant's last full fiscal year, or proposes to make during the registrant's current fiscal year, payments for property or services in excess of five percent of (i) the registrant's consolidated gross revenues for its last full fiscal year, or (ii) the other entity's consolidated gross revenues for its last full fiscal year;

3. If the nominee or director is, or during the last fiscal year has been, an executive officer of, or owns, or during the last fiscal year has owned, of record or beneficially in excess of ten percent equity interest in, any business or professional entity to which the registrant or its subsidiaries was indebted at the end of the registrant's last full fiscal year in an aggregate amount in excess of five percent of the registrant's total consolidated assets at the end of such fiscal year;

4. If the nominee or director is, or during the last fiscal year has been, a member of, or of counsel to, a law firm that the issuer has retained during the last fiscal year or proposes to retain during the current fiscal year; *provided, however,* that the dollar amount of fees paid to a law firm by the registrant need not be disclosed if such amount does not exceed five percent of the law firm's gross revenues for that firm's last full fiscal year;

5. If the nominee or director is, or during the last fiscal year has been, a partner or executive officer of any investment banking firm

that has performed services for the registrant, other than as a participating underwriter in a syndicate, during the last fiscal year or that the registrant proposes to have perform services during the current year; *provided, however,* That the dollar amount of compensation received by an investment banking firm need not be disclosed if such amount does not exceed five percent of the investment banking firm's consolidated gross revenues for that firm's last full fiscal year; or

6. Any other relationships that the registrant is aware of between the nominee or director and the registrant that are substantially similar in nature and scope to those relationships listed in paragraphs (b)(1) through (5).

Instructions to Paragraph (b) of Item 404.

1. In order to determine whether payments or indebtedness exceed five percent of the consolidated gross revenues of any entity, other than the registrant, it is appropriate to rely on information provided by the nominee or director.

2. In calculating payments for property and services the following may be excluded:

   A. Payments where the rates or charges involved in the transaction are determined by competitive bids, or the transaction involves the rendering of services as a common contract carrier, or public utility, at rates or charges fixed in conformity with law or governmental authority;

   B. Payments that arise solely from the ownership of securities of the registrant and no extra or special benefit not shared on a pro rata basis by all holders of the class of securities is received; or

   C. Payments made or received by subsidiaries other than significant subsidiaries as defined in Rule 1-02(w) of Regulation S-X, provided that all such subsidiaries making or receiving payments, when considered in the aggregate as a single subsidiary, would not constitute a significant subsidiary as defined in Rule 1-02(w).

3. In calculating indebtedness the following may be excluded:

   A. Debt securities that have been publicly offered, admitted to trading on a national securities exchange, or quoted on the automated quotation system of a registered securities association;

   B. Amounts due for purchases subject to the usual trade terms; or

   C. Indebtedness incurred by subsidiaries other than significant subsidiaries as defined in Rule 1-02(w) of Regulation S-X, provided that all such subsidiaries incurring indebtedness, when considered in the aggregate as a single subsidiary, would not constitute a significant subsidiary as defined in Rule 1-02(w).

4. No information called for by paragraph (b) need be given respecting any director who is no longer a director at the time of filing the registration statement or report containing such disclosure. If such information is being presented in a proxy or information statement, no information need be given respecting any director whose term of office as a director will not continue after the meeting to which the statement relates.

---

c. *Indebtedness of management.* If any of the following persons has been indebted to the registrant or its subsidiaries at any time since the beginning of the registrant's last fiscal year in an amount in excess of $60,000, indicate the name of such person, the nature of the person's relationship by reason of which such person's indebtedness is required to be described, the largest aggregate amount of indebtedness outstanding at any time during such period, the nature of the indebtedness and of the transaction in which it was incurred, the amount thereof outstanding as of the latest practicable date and the rate of interest paid or charged thereon:

   1. Any director or executive officer of the registrant;

   2. Any nominee for election as a director;

   3. Any member of the immediate family of any of the persons specified in paragraph (c)(1) or (2);

   4. Any corporation or organization (other than the registrant or a majority-owned subsidiary of the registrant) of which any of the persons specified in paragraph (c)(1) or (2) is an executive officer

or partner or is, directly or indirectly, the beneficial owner of ten percent or more of any class of equity securities; and

5. Any trust or other estate in which any of the persons specified in paragraph (c)(1) or (2) has a substantial beneficial interest or as to which such person serves as a trustee or in a similar capacity.

Instructions to Paragraph (c), of Item 404.

1. For purposes of paragraph (c), the members of a person's immediate family are those persons specified in Instruction 2 to Item 404(a).

2. Exclude from the determination of the amount of indebtedness all amounts due from the particular person for purchases subject to usual trade terms, for ordinary travel and expense payments and for other transactions in the ordinary course of business.

3. If the lender is a bank, savings and loan association, or broker-dealer extending credit under Federal Reserve Regulation T [12 CFR part 220] and the loans are not disclosed as nonaccrual, past due, restructured or potential problems (see Item III.C. 1. and 2. of Industry Guide 3, Statistical Disclosure by Bank Holding Companies), disclosure may consist of a statement, if such is the case, that the loans to such persons were made in the ordinary course of business, were made on substantially the same terms, including interest rates and collateral, as those prevailing at the time for comparable transactions with other persons, and did not involve more than the normal risk of collectibility or present other unfavorable features.

4. If any indebtedness required to be described arose under section 16(b) of the Exchange Act and has not been discharged by payment, state the amount of any profit realized, that such profit will inure to the benefit of the registrant or its subsidiaries and whether suit will be brought or other steps taken to recover such profit. If, in the opinion of counsel, a question reasonably exists as to the recoverability of such profit, it will suffice to state all facts necessary to describe the transactions, including the prices and number of shares involved.

---

d. Transactions with promoters. Registrants that have been organized within the past five years and that are filing a registration statement on Form S-1 under the Securities Act or on Form 10 and Form 10-SB under the Exchange Act shall:

1. State the names of the promoters, the nature and amount of anything of value (including money, property, contracts, options or rights of any kind) received or to be received by each promoter, directly or indirectly, from the registrant and the nature and amount of any assets, services or other consideration therefore received or to be received by the registrant; and

2. As to any assets acquired or to be acquired by the registrant from a promoter, state the amount at which the assets were acquired or are to be acquired and the principle followed or to be followed in determining such amount and identify the persons making the determination and their relationship, if any, with the registrant or any promoter. If the assets were acquired by the promoter within two years prior to their transfer to the registrant, also state the cost thereof to the promoter.

Instructions to Item 404.

1. No information need be given in response to any paragraph of Item 404 as to any compensation or other transaction reported in response to any other paragraph of Item 404 or to Item 402 of Regulation S-K or as to any compensation with respect to which information may be omitted pursuant to Item 402.

2. If the information called for by Item 404 is being presented in a registration statement filed pursuant to the Securities Act or the Exchange Act, information shall be given for the periods specified in the Item and, in addition, for the two fiscal years preceding the registrant's last fiscal year.

3. A foreign private issuer will be deemed to comply with Item 404 if it provides the information required by Item 7.B of Form 20-F.

Item 405—Compliance with Section 16(a) of the Exchange Act

Every registrant having a class of equity securities registered pursuant to section 12 of the Exchange Act, every closed-end investment company registered under the Investment Company Act of 1940, and every holding company registered pursuant to the Public Utility Holding Company Act of 1935 shall:

a. Based solely upon a review of Forms 3 and 4 and amendments thereto furnished to the registrant pursuant to Rule 16a-3(e) during its most recent fiscal year and Forms 5 and amendments thereto furnished to the registrant with respect to its most recent fiscal year, and any written representation referred to in paragraph (b)(2)(i) of this Item.

   1. Under the caption "Section 16(a) Beneficial Ownership Reporting Compliance," identify each person who, at any time during the fiscal year, was a director, officer, beneficial owner of more than ten percent of any class of equity securities of the registrant registered pursuant to section 12 of the Exchange Act, or any other person subject to section 16 of the Exchange Act with respect to the registrant because of the requirements of section 30 of the Investment Company Act or section 17 of the Public Utility Holding Company Act ("reporting person") that failed to file on a timely basis, as disclosed in the above Forms, reports required by section 16(a) of the Exchange Act during the most recent fiscal year or prior fiscal years.

   2. For each such person, set forth the number of late reports, the number of transactions that were not reported on a timely basis, and any known failure to file a required Form. A known failure to file would include, but not be limited to, a failure to file a Form 3, which is required of all reporting persons, and a failure to file a Form 5 in the absence of the written representation referred to in paragraph (b)(2)(i) of this section, unless the registrant otherwise knows that no Form 5 is required.

Note:

The disclosure requirement is based on a review of the forms submitted to the registrant during and with respect to its most recent fiscal year, as specified above. Accordingly, a failure to file timely need only be disclosed once. For example, if in the most recently concluded fiscal year a reporting person filed a Form 4 disclosing a transaction that took place in the prior fiscal year, and should have been reported in that year, the registrant should disclose that late filing and transaction pursuant to this Item 405 with respect to the most recently concluded fiscal year, but not in material filed with respect to subsequent years.

---

b. With respect to the disclosure required by paragraph (a) of this Item:

    1. A form received by the registrant within three calendar days of the required filing date may be presumed to have been filed with the Commission by the required filing date.

    2. If the registrant (i) receives a written representation from the reporting person that no Form 5 is required; and (ii) maintains the representation for two years, making a copy available to the Commission or its staff upon request, the registrant need not identify such reporting person pursuant to paragraph (a) of this Item as having failed to file a Form 5 with respect to that fiscal year.

Item 601—Exhibits

---

b. *Description of exhibits.* Set forth below is a description of each document listed in the exhibit tables.

  10. *Material contracts.*

  i. Every contract not made in the ordinary course of business which is material to the registrant and is to be performed in whole or in part at or after the filing of the registration statement or report or was entered into not more than two years before such filing. Only contracts need be filed as to which the registrant or subsidiary of the registrant is a party or has succeeded to a party by assumption or assignment or in which the registrant or such subsidiary has a beneficial interest.

  ii. If the contract is such as ordinarily accompanies the kind of business conducted by the registrant and its subsidiaries, it will be deemed to have been made in the ordinary course of business and need not be filed unless it falls within one or more of the following categories, in which case it shall be filed except where immaterial in amount or significance:

  A. Any contract to which directors, officers, promoters, voting trustees, security holders named in the registration statement or report, or underwriters are parties other than contracts involving only the purchase or sale of current assets having a determinable market price, at such market price;

  B. Any contract upon which the registrant's business is substantially dependent, as in the case of continuing contracts to sell the major part of registrant's products or services or to purchase the major part of registrant's requirements of goods, services or raw materials or any franchise or license or other agreement to use a patent, formula, trade secret, process or trade name upon which registrant's business depends to a material extent;

  C. Any contract calling for the acquisition or sale of any property, plant or equipment for a consideration exceeding 15 percent of such fixed assets of the registrant on a consolidated basis; or

    D. Any material lease under which a part of the property described in the registration statement or report is held by the registrant.

iii. A. Any management contract or any compensatory plan, contract or arrangement, including but not limited to plans relating to options, warrants or rights, pension, retirement or deferred compensation or bonus, incentive or profit sharing (or if not set forth in any formal document, a written description thereof) in which any director or any of the named executive officers of the registrant, as defined by Item 402(a)(3) of Regulation S-K, participates shall be deemed material and shall be filed; and any other management contract or any other compensatory plan, contract, or arrangement in which any other executive officer of the registrant participates shall be filed unless immaterial in amount or significance.

    A. Any compensatory plan, contract or arrangement adopted without the approval of security holders pursuant to which equity may be awarded, including, but not limited to, options, warrants or rights (or if not set forth in any formal document, a written description thereof), in which any employee (whether or not an executive officer of the registrant) participates shall be filed unless immaterial in amount or significance. A compensation plan assumed by a registrant in connection with a merger, consolidation or other acquisition transaction pursuant to which the registrant may make further grants or awards of its equity securities shall be considered a compensation plan of the registrant for purposes of the preceding sentence.

    B. Notwithstanding paragraph (b)(10)(iii)(A) above, the following management contracts or compensatory plans, contracts or arrangements need not be filed:

        1. Ordinary purchase and sales agency agreements.

        2. Agreements with managers of stores in a chain organization or similar organization.

        3. Contracts providing for labor or salesmen's bonuses or payments to a class of security holders, as such.

4. Any compensatory plan, contract or arrangement which pursuant to its terms is available to employees, officers or directors generally and which in operation provides for the same method of allocation of benefits between management and nonmanagement participants.

5. Any compensatory plan, contract or arrangement if the registrant is a foreign private issuer that furnishes compensatory information on an aggregate basis as permitted by General Instruction 1 to Item 402 or by Item 11 of Form 20-F.

6. Any compensatory plan, contract, or arrangement if the registrant is a wholly owned subsidiary of a company that has a class of securities registered pursuant to section 12 or files reports pursuant to section 15(d) of the Exchange Act and is filing a report on Form 10-K and Form 10-KSB or registering debt instruments or preferred stock which are not voting securities on Form S-2.

Instruction 1 to Paragraph (b)(10).

With the exception of management contracts, in order to comply with paragraph (iii) above, registrants need only file copies of the various compensatory plans and need not file each individual director's or executive officer's personal agreement under the plans unless there are particular provisions in such personal agreements whose disclosure in an exhibit is necessary to an investor's understanding of that individual's compensation under the plan.

Instruction 2 to Paragraph (b)(10).

If a material contract is executed or becomes effective during the reporting period reflected by a Form 10-Q or Form 10-K, it shall be filed as an exhibit to the Form 10-Q or Form 10-K filed for the corresponding period. See paragraph (a)(4) of this Item. With respect to quarterly reports on Form 10-Q, only those contracts executed or becoming effective during the most recent period reflected in the report shall be filed.

Nasdaq Stock Market Rule 4350(c)(3)—Compensation of Officers

(c) Independent Directors

   (3) Compensation of Officers

      (A) Compensation of the chief executive officer of the company must be determined, or recommended to the Board for determination, either by:

         (i) a majority of the independent directors, or

         (ii) a compensation committee comprised solely of independent directors.

The chief executive officer may not be present during voting or deliberations.

      (B) Compensation of all other executive officers must be determined, or recommended to the Board for determination, either by:

         (i) a majority of the independent directors, or

         (ii) a compensation committee comprised solely of independent directors.

      (C) Notwithstanding paragraphs 3(A)(ii) and (3)(B)(ii) above, if the compensation committee is comprised of at least three members, one director who is not independent as defined in Rule 4200 and is not a current officer or employee or a Family Member of an officer or employee, may be appointed to the compensation committee if the board, under exceptional and limited circumstances, determines that such individual's membership on the committee is required by the best interests of the company and its shareholders, and the board discloses, in the proxy statement for the next annual meeting subsequent to such determination (or, if the issuer does not file a proxy, in its Form 10-K or 20-F), the nature of the relationship and the reasons for the determination. A member appointed under this exception may not serve longer than two years.

NYSE Rule 303A.05—Compensation Committee Requirements

5. (a) Listed companies must have a compensation committee composed entirely of independent directors.

   (b) The compensation committee must have a written charter that addresses:

   (i) the committee's purpose and responsibilities—which, at minimum, must be to have direct responsibility to:

   (A) review and approve corporate goals and objectives relevant to CEO compensation, evaluate the CEO's performance in light of those goals and objectives and, either as a committee or together with the other independent directors (as directed by the board), determine and approve the CEO's compensation level based on this evaluation; and

   (B) make recommendations to the board with respect to non-CEO compensation, incentive-compensation plans and equity-based plans; and

   (C) produce a compensation committee report on executive compensation as required by the SEC to be included in the company's annual proxy statement or annual report on Form 10-K filed with the SEC;

   (ii) an annual performance evaluation of the compensation committee.

Commentary: In determining the long-term incentive component of CEO compensation, the committee should consider the company's performance and relative shareholder return, the value of similar incentive awards to CEOs at comparable companies, and the awards given to the listed company's CEO in past years. To avoid confusion, note that the compensation committee is not precluded from approving awards (with or without ratification of the board) as may be required to comply with applicable tax laws (i.e., Rule 162(m)).

The compensation committee charter should also address the following items: committee member qualifications; committee member appointment and removal; committee structure and operations (including authority to delegate to subcommittees); and committee reporting to the board.

Additionally, if a compensation consultant is to assist in the evaluation of director, CEO or senior executive compensation, the compensation committee charter should give that committee sole authority to retain and terminate the consulting firm, including sole authority to approve the firm's fees and other retention terms.

Boards may allocate the responsibilities of the compensation committee to committees of their own denomination, provided that the committees are composed entirely of independent directors. Any such committee must have a published committee charter.

Nothing in this provision should be construed as precluding discussion of CEO compensation with the board generally, as it is not the intent of this standard to impair communication among members of the board.

List of Organizations and Periodicals

Many organizations provide information of interest to compensation committees. This appendix lists organizations that provide information on compensation, roles of the board and directors, corporate governance, and shareholder issues of various types. Some of these organizations offer memberships for a nominal fee; others provide free access to their Web sites. Also included is a list of relevant periodicals, some of which are free. Please also refer to the Bibliography for further reading on the similar subjects.

Exhibit B.1 List of Organizations

Organization	Address and Other Information	Contacts
WorldatWork	1440 N. Northsight Boulevard Scottsdale, AZ 85260-3601 www.worldatwork.org	Anne C. Ruddy, CPCU Executive Director Charles Allen, Director of Compensation Group
	Tel#: (480) 922-2020 (800) 951-9191 Fax#: (480) 483-8352	
American Management Association	1601 Broadway New York, NY 10019-7420 www.amanet.org	Edward T. Reilly, President and CEO
	Tel#: (800) 262-9699 Fax#: (518) 891-0368	

(continues)

Exhibit B.1   Continued

Organization	Address and Other Information	Contacts
The American Society of Corporate Secretaries	521 Fifth Avenue New York, NY 10175 Dfox@ascs.org www.ascs.org Tel#: (212) 681-2000 Fax#: (212) 681-2005	David W. Smith, President Deborah Fox Administrator, Membership
Business Roundtable	1615 L Street, NW, Suite 1100 Washington, DC 20036 rob@businessroundtable.org www.businessroundtable.org Tel#: (202) 872-1260 Fax#: (202) 466-3509	Johanna I. Schneider Executive Director, External Relations
California Public Employees' Retirement System (CalPERS)	Lincoln Plaza 400 P Street Sacramento, CA 95814 www.calpers.org Tel#: (888) 225-7377 Fax#: (916) 326-3507	Fred Buenrostro, Chief Executive Officer
The Conference Board	845 Third Avenue New York, NY 10022-6679 info@conference_board.org www.conference-board.org Tel#: (212) 339-0345 Fax#: (212) 836-9740	Richard E. Cavanagh, President and CEO
Corporate Governance	9295 Yorkship Court Elk Grove, CA 95758 jm@corpgov.net www.corpgov.net Tel#: (916) 869-2402	Mr. James McRitchie
Corporate Governance Center at Kennesaw State College	1000 Chastain Road Kennesaw, GA 30144 www.coles-kennesaw.edu Tel#: (770) 423-6587 Fax#: (770) 423-6606	Professor Paul Lapides

Exhibit B.1 Continued

Organization	Address and Other Information	Contacts
The Corporate Library	40 Exchange Street Suite 201 Portland, ME 04101 nminow@thecorporatelibrary.co www.thecorporatelibrary.com Tel#: (207) 874-6921 Fax#: (207) 874-6925	Nell Minow, Editor
Council of Institutional Investors	1730 Rhode Island Avenue, N.W. Suite 512 Washington, DC 20036 info@cii.org www.ciicentral.com Tel#: (202) 822-0800 Fax#: (202) 822-0801	Sarah A.B. Teslik, Executive Director
Attorneys for Family-Held Enterprise	4405 Pleasant View Drive Williamsburg, VA 23188 afhe@afhe.com www.afhe.com Tel#: (757) 565-5297 Fax# (757) 565-5298	Sarah E. Spiers, Executive Director
Foundation for Enterprise Development	1919 Pennsylvania Avenue NW Suite 650 Washington, DC 20006 Fed@fed.org www.fed.org Tel#: (202) 530-8920 Fax#: (202) 530-5702	Ray Smilor, President David Binns, Vice President
Institutional Shareholder Services	2099 Gaither Road Suite 501 Rockville, MD 20850-4045 www.issproxy.com Tel#: (301) 556-0500 Fax#: (301) 556-0491	Jamie Heard, Vice Chairman Partrick S. McGurn, Senior Vice President, and Special Counsel

(continues)

Exhibit B.1   Continued

Organization	Address and Other Information	Contacts
Investor Responsibility Research Center	1350 Connecticut Ave., Suite 700 Washington, DC 20036-1702 marketing@irrc.com www.irrc.org Tel#: (202) 833-0700 Fax#: (202) 833-3555	Linda Crompton, President and CEO
National Association of Corporate Directors	Two Lafayette Centre 1133 21st Street NW Washington, DC 20036 info@nacdonline.org www.nacdonline.org Tel#: (202) 775-0509 Fax#: (202) 775-4857	Roger W. Raber, President and CEO Peter R. Gleason Chief Operating Officer and Director of Research
National Association of Stock Plan Professionals	P.O. Box 21639 Concord, CA 94521-0639 www.nasspp.com Tel#: (925) 685-9271 Fax#: (925) 685-5402	Jesse Brill, Chair
The National Center for Employee Ownership	1736 Franklin Street 8th Floor Oakland, CA 94612-3445 nceo@nceo.org www.nceo.org Tel#: (510) 208-1300 Fax#: (510) 272-9510	Corey Rosen, Executive Director Ed Carberry, Director of Communications Pam Chernoff Director of Equity Compensation Projects
National Investor Relations Institute	8020 Towers Crescent Drive Suite 250 Vienna, VA 22182 info@niri.org www.niri.org Tel#: (703) 506-3572 Fax#: (703) 506-3571	Louis M. Thompson, Jr., President and CEO

Exhibit B.1 Continued

Organization	Address and Other Information	Contacts
The New York Society of Security Analysts	1601 Broadway, 11th Floor New York, NY 10019-7406 membership@nyssa.org www.nyssa.org Tel#: (212) 541-4530 Fax#: (212) 541-4677	Joan Shapiro Green, Executive Director Eileen Budd, Director of Programming and Education
TIAA-CREF	730 Third Avenue New York, NY 10017-3206 www.tiaa-cref.org Tel#: (800) 842-2252	Herbert M. Allison, Jr., Chairman, President, and CEO

PERIODICALS

Name of Periodical	Publisher	Editor(s)	Frequency	Address/E-mail/Web Site Telephone Number
WorldatWork Journal	WorldatWork	Andrea Ozozias	Quarterly	1440 N. Northsight Boulevard Scottsdale, AZ 85260-3601 www.worldatwork.org Tel#: (480) 922-2038 (800) 951-9191 Fax#: (480) 483-8352
Workspan	WorldatWork	Andrea Ozozias	Monthly	440 N. Northsight Boulevard Scottsdale, AZ 85260-3601 www.worldatwork.org Tel#: (480) 922-2038 (800) 951-9191 Fax#: (480) 483-8352
Across The Board	The Conference Board	A. J. Vogl	Monthly	845 Third Avenue New York, NY 10022-6679 www.conference-board.org Tel#: (212) 339-0345 Fax#: (212) 836-9740

Publication	Publisher	Author	Frequency	Contact
Board Leadership: A bimonthly workshop	Jossey-Bass Publisher	John and Miriam Carver	Bi-monthly	P.O. Box 13007 Atlanta, GA 30324-0007 www.carvergoverance.com Tel#: (404) 728-9444 Fax#: (404) 728-0060
Corporate Board Member	Corporate Board Member Magazine	Deborah Scally	Monthly	475 Park Ave. South 19th Floor New York, NY 10016 www.boardmember.com Tel#: (212) 686-1805 Fax#: (212) 686-3041
Boardroom INSIDER	Ralph Ward	Ralph Ward	Monthly	P.O. Box 196 Riverdale, MI 48877 www.boardroominsider.com Tel#: (989) 833-7615 Fax#: (989) 833-7615
BusinessWeek's Annual Executive Compensation Survey	BusinessWeek	Louis Lavelle	Annually published in early April	1221 Avenue of the Americas New York, NY 10020-1095 www.businessweek.com Tel#: (212) 512-2511 Fax#: (212) 512-4589

(continues)

Name of Periodical	Publisher	Editor(s)	Frequency	Address/E-mail/Web Site Telephone Number
The Corporate Board	Vanguard Publications	Ralph D. Ward	Monthly	4440 South Hagadorn Road Okemos, MI 48864-2414 Info@corporateboard.com www.corporateboard.com Tel#: (517) 336-1700 Fax#: (517) 336-1705
The Corporate Counsel	Executive Press, Inc.	Jesse Brill or Broc Romonek	Bi-monthly	P.O. Box 21639 Concord, CA 94521-0639 www.thecorporatecounsel.net Tel#: (925) 685-5111 Fax#: (925) 685-5402
The Corporate Executive	Executive Press, Inc.	Jesse Brill or Broc Romonek	Bi-monthly	P.O. Box 21639 Concord, CA 94521-0639 www.thecorporatecounsel.net Tel#: (925) 685-5111 Fax#: (925) 685-5402
Corporate Governance	Corporate Governance.Net	James McRitchie	As needed	2461 Second Avenue Sacramento, CA 95818 Jm@corpgov.net www.corpgov.net Tel#: (530) 542-5338

Corporate Governance Bulletin	Investor Responsibility Research Center	Maryanne Moore	Quarterly	1350 Connecticut Avenue, Suite 700 Washington, DC 20036-1702 www.irrc.org Tel#: (202) 833-0700 Fax#: (202) 833-3555
Corporate Monitoring Newsletter	Mark Latham	Mark Latham	Quarterly	1755 Robson St. #469 Vancouver, B.C. Canada V6 G 387 www.corpmon.com Tel#: (604) 608-9779
The Corporate Secretary	The American Society of Corporate Secretaries	David Smith	Quarterly	521 Fifth Avenue New York, NY 10175 hjohnson@ascs.org www.ascs.org Tel#: (212) 681-2000 Fax#: (212) 681-2005
Crystal Column	Bloomberg Information	Graef Crystal	Monthly	3519 Daybreak Court Santa Rosa, CA 95404-2042 www.crystalreport.com Tel#: (707) 591-0464 Fax#: (707) 591-0645

(continues)

Name of Periodical	Publisher	Editor(s)	Frequency	Address/E-mail/Web Site Telephone Number
Directors & Boards Magazine	MLR Holdings LLC	James Kristie	Quarterly	1845 Walnut Street Suite 900 Philadelphia, PA 19103-4709 www.directorsandboards.com Tel#: (800) 637-4464 Fax#: (215) 405-6078
Board Alert	Money Media, Inc.	Michael D. Griffin	Monthly	211 East 43rd St. 13th Floor New York, NY 10017 www.boardalert.net Tel#: (212) 949-4288 Fax#: (212) 949-6121
Directors Monthly	The National Association of Corporate Directors	Deborah J. Davidson	Monthly	Two Lafayette Centre 1133 21st Street NW Suite 700 Washington, DC 20036 www.nacdonline.org Tel#: (202) 775-0509 Fax#: (202) 775-4857
Directorship	The Directorship Search Group, Inc.	J. P. Donlon	Monthly	8 Sound Shore Drive Greenwich, CT 06830 info@directorship.com www.directorship.com Tel#: (203) 618-7040 Fax#: (203) 618-7007

Executive Compensation Resources Newsletter	Towers Perrin, HR Services	Judith Fischer	Twice monthly	2107 Wilson Blvd Suite 500 Arlington, VA 22201 ecrinfo@ecronline.com www.ecronline.com Tel#: (800) 391-0045 Fax#: (703) 837-9501
Forbes' Magazine Annual Executive Compensation Survey	Forbes	Scott DeCarlo	Annually published in May	60 Fifth Avenue New York, NY www.forbes.com Tel#: (212) 620-2338 Fax#: (212) 620-1863
Insights: The Corporate Securities Law Advisor	Aspen Publishers	Amy L. Goodman	Monthly	1185 Avenue of the Americas New York, NY 10036 www.aspenpublishers.com Tel#: (212) 597-0200 Fax#: (212) 597-0338
Investor Relations Newsletter	Kennedy Information, Inc.	David Beck	Monthly	One Phoenix Mill Lane 5th Floor Petersborough, NH 03458 www.kennedyinfo.com Tel#: (800) 531-8007 Fax#: (603) 924-4034

(continues)

Name of Periodical	Publisher	Editor(s)	Frequency	Address/E-mail/Web Site Telephone Number
Investor Relations Quarterly	National Investor Relations Institute	Beth Carty	Quarterly	8020 Towers Crescent Drive Suite 250 Vienna, VA 22182 www.niri.org Tel#: (703) 506-3570 Fax#: (703) 506-3571
IR Update	National Investor Relations Institute	Beth Carty	Monthly	8020 Towers Crescent Drive Suite 250 Vienna, VA 22182 www.niri.org Tel#: (703) 506-3572 Fax#: (703) 506-3571
The ISS Friday Report	Institutional Shareholder Services	Stephen Deane	Weekly	2099 Gaither Road Suite 501 Rockville, MD 20850-8041 www.issproxy.com Tel#: (301) 556-0500 Fax#: (301) 556-0491
The Journal of Compensation and Benefits	West Publishers, Inc.	Jeffrey D. Manorsky	Bi-monthly	P.O.B. 64833 St. Paul, MN 55164-0833 www.westthomson.com Tel#: (800) 328-4880 Fax#: (800) 340-9378

Publication	Organization	Contact	Frequency	Address
Journal of Employee Ownership Law and Finance	The National Center for Employee Ownership	Scott Rodrick	Quarterly	1736 Franklin Street 8th Floor Oakland, CA 94612-1217 www.nceo.org Tel#: (510) 208-1300 Fax#: (510) 272-9510
The Stock Plan Advisor	The National Association of Stock Plan Professionals	Jesse Brill	Monthly	P.O. Box 21639 Concord, CA 94521-0639 www.nasspp.com Tel#: (925) 685-9271 Fax#: (925) 685-5402
The Employee Ownership Report (NCEO Newsletter)	The National Center for Employee Ownership	Scott Rodrick	Bi-monthly	1736 Franklin Street 8th Floor Oakland, CA 94612-1217 www.nceo.org Tel#: (510) 208-1300 Fax#: (510) 272-9510
The Wall Street Journal's Annual Chief Executive Officer Compensation Survey	The Wall Street Journal	Joann S. Lublin	Annually published in early April	200 Liberty Street New York, NY 10281 www.wsj.com Tel#: (212) 416-2000 Fax#: (212) 416-2653

List of Directors Colleges and Other Training Opportunities

Sponsoring Organization	The Conference Board
Name of Program	Directors' Institute
Length of Program	Varies, see contact information.
Cost of Program	Varies, see contact information.
Description of Course	The Directors' Institute conducts highly interactive sessions for corporate directors only. Directors' Institute programs meet director education needs by providing high-level forums for public company directors to review real-world governance and business challenges.

The Directors' Institute offers intensive, one-day Director Dialogue Sessions throughout the year focusing on corporate governance, audit committees, and compensation committees: |

Corporate Governance Sessions & New Director Orientation	*Audit Committee Sessions*	*Compensation Committee Sessions*
Fiduciary Responsibilities & Challenges	Legislative & Regulatory Landscape	Compensation Issues & Trends
Enterprise Risk Assessment	Financial Risk Assessment	Structuring "Pay for Performance"

Description of Course (cont.)	*Corporate Governance Sessions & New Director Orientation*	*Audit Committee Sessions*	*Compensation Committee Sessions*
	Board Evaluation	Evaluation of the Audit Process	Evaluating Management Performance
	Director Liability Issues	Recognizing "Red Flags"	Use of Compensation Consultants
	Institutional Investor Expectations	Committee Effectiveness	Committee Effectiveness

The Directors' Institute's intensive one-day sessions focus on interactive discussion among directors. Experienced public company directors serve as discussion leaders, supplemented by expert presentations in key areas such as legal, insurance, governance, ethics, regulations, finance, auditing, and accounting. Sessions are strictly limited to 25 directors.

Contact Information	Dr. Carolyn Kay Brancato Director The Conference Board 845 Third Avenue New York, NY 10022 E-mail: carolyn.brancato@conference-board.org Phone: 1-212-339-0413 Fax: 1-212-836-9711 www.conference-board.org/knowledge/govern/govInstitute.cfm
Sponsoring Organization	Harvard Business School Executive Education
Name of Program	Compensation Committees: Preparing for the Challenges Ahead
Length of Program	3 days
Cost of Program	$3,500
Description of Course	The program is designed as a timely, action-oriented opportunity for directors to think deeply about the root causes of many compensation issues—and to identify possible solutions to the difficulties their particular boards and companies are facing. Given these challenges, the program emphasizes the growing demand for compensation committees to exhibit greater knowledge, independence, and accountability.

Description of Course (cont.)	This intensive learning experience provides an educational, interactive environment for directors to:

- Identify and address critical issues pertaining to employment agreements, overall pay, incentive compensation, stock ownership, and stock compensation—then determine to what extent their own board's compensation plans need to be demolished and rebuilt.
- Define the characteristics of a well-functioning compensation committee—then review and rethink their respective committee charters in regard to purpose, processes, roles, responsibilities, and review procedures.
- Prepare to operate successfully in the new age of accountability by becoming knowledgeable of current issues, acting independently of management, and diligently discharging all duties.

Contact Information	Executive Education Programs Harvard Business School Soldiers Field Boston, MA 02163-9986 E-mail: executive_education@hbs.edu Phone: 1-800-HBS-5577 (1-617-495-6555) Fax: 1-617-495-6999 www.exed.hbs.edu/programs
Sponsoring Organization	Harvard Business School Executive Education
Name of Program	Making Corporate Boards More Effective
Length of Program	3 days
Cost of Program	$6,000
Description of Course	The program addresses critical issues facing boards today, including:

- Changing legal responsibilities of directors
- Board composition and director selection
- Setting time-efficient agendas
- Conducting dynamic, constructive board meetings
- Effective use of committees
- Role of the board in strategic planning and as an agent of positive change
- Designing performance scorecards to monitor business strategy and management performance

Description of *Course (cont.)*	• Role of the board and audit committee in formulating an external financial reporting and disclosure strategy • CEO evaluation and compensation • CEO succession • Evaluation of the board and its members • Director compensation and stock ownership

These issues will be examined in the overall context of structuring a corporate governance system that facilitates cooperation between the board and management, thereby achieving real benefits for the enterprise. Particular attention will be devoted to helping participants develop action plans for improving their own boards. Participants will have the opportunity to discuss their plans with both their peers and the faculty.

Contact *Information*	Executive Education Programs Harvard Business School Soldiers Field Boston, MA 02163-9986 E-mail: executive_education@hbs.edu Phone: 1-800-HBS-5577 (1-617-495-6555) Fax: 1-617-495-6999 www.exed.hbs.edu/programs
Sponsoring *Organization*	University of Chicago Graduate School of Business, Stanford Law School, and the Wharton Business School (The University of Pennsylvania)
Name of Program	The Director's Consortium
Length of Program	3 days
Cost of Program	$5,550
Description of *Course*	The Directors' Consortium is a joint offering by The University of Chicago Graduate School of Business, Stanford Law School, and The Wharton School of the University of Pennsylvania. The Directors' Consortium offers even experienced directors the benefit of a research-based, comprehensive approach to the complex decisions that board members must make. Taught by faculty from accounting, finance, law, public policy, and strategic management, this program will help you build a best practices framework for thinking about and making informed board decisions.

Description of Course (cont.)	The program outline:
	• Policy and Strategy
	• Seeing Red Flags: How to Spot Early Warning Signs of Management Problems
	• Nominating Committee Issues and CEO Succession
	• Compensation Committee Issues
	• Audit Committee—Qualifications, Responsibilities, and Content
	• Finance
	• Directors' Fiduciary Duties: The Core Duties of Directors, and What They Mean in Practice
	This program's location rotates among Chicago, Stanford, and Wharton.
Contact Information	www.directorsconsortium.net
Sponsoring Organization	National Association of Corporate Directors
Name of Program	The NACD offers a variety of one-day programs for compensation committees and board directors in general. Current program offerings are listed below. Please check the NACD Web site for availability.
Length of Program	1 day
Cost of Program	$795.00 for NACD members $1,395.00 for others
Listing of Courses	• Effective Compensation Committees
	• Annual Corporate Governance Conference
	• Audit Committee: Improving Quality, Independence, and Performance
	• Director Finance: What Every Director Should Know
	• Director Professionalism
	• Role of the Board in Corporate Strategy and Risk Oversight
	• Role of the Governance Committee: Raising the Bar on Board Policies, Practices and Board Evaluations
	• Small Company Governance: Building Board Value
	• What the Board Really Expects from the General Counsel and Corporate Secretary

Contact Information	Cynthia J. Magill Director of Education National Association of Corporate Directors 1133 21st Street, NW, Suite 700, Washington, DC 20036 E-mail: cjmagill@nacdonline.org Phone: 202-775-0509, ext 2081 Fax: 202-775-4857 www.nacdonline.org
Sponsoring Organization	Terry College of Business Executive Education (University of Georgia) and the National Association of Corporate Directors (Atlanta Chapter)
Name of Program	Terry/NACD Directors' College
Length of Program	2 days
Cost of Program	$1800 ($1500 for NACD members or +1 participant from the same organization)

Description on of Course	The Terry College of Business/NACD Directors' College focuses the increasingly critical and challenging role corporate boards play in business organizations. The program develops the skills and insight needed to function as an informed, contributing board director. By combining the practical knowledge of experienced business executives with conceptual frameworks developed by highly acclaimed Terry College of Business faculty, the program highlights the strategic significance of the corporate board and the tools required to effectively monitor company performance.
	
	An overview of the course materials:
	
	• Compliance issues
	  • Shareholder law suits
	  • Business judgment rule
	  • Recent court cases and how they may apply to you
	  • Board minutes
	  • D&O liability coverage
	• What do financial statements show and what directors should know about them
	  • Brief overview of financial statements
	  • Case studies relating to fraud and legal actions
	  • Signs of trouble and indications of fraud
	  • What the board can do about it

Description of
Course (cont.)
	• Ways in which the board can improve corporate performance
	   • Relationship between corporate governance and corporate performance
	   • Executive compensation
	   • CEO evaluation
	   • Succession planning
	   • Board evaluation
	   • Importance of independence and diversity
	• Roles, responsibilities, and expectations of directors
	   • Legal obligations
	   • Duty of care and loyalty
	   • Different oversight committees
	• Emerging issues
	   • Regulation FD
	   • SEC actions and rules
	   • Institutional investor activism
	   • Stock analyst' focus on the board
	   • Size and composition of the board

Contact *Information*	Richard L. Daniels Associate Dean for Executive Programs, Professor of Management Terry College of Business 278 Brooks Hall Athens, GA 30602-6262 E-mail: rdaniels@terry.uga.edu Phone: 706-542-8393 Fax: 706-542-3835 www.terry.uga.edu/exec_ed/director_education/index.php

Annotated Form of Compensation Committee Charter

This Appendix contains an annotated form of compensation committee charter, as well as the compensation committee charters for Amgen, Apple Computer, Goldman Sachs, General Electric, and Revlon.

[CORPORATE NAME]
COMPENSATION COMMITTEE CHARTER

Purpose and Responsibilities[1]

The Compensation Committee (the "Committee") shall be responsible for:

- Discharging the Board of Directors responsibilities relating to the compensation of [corporate name] (the "Company") executives.
- Producing an annual report on executive compensation for inclusion in the Company's [proxy statement for the annual meeting of [stockholders] [shareholders[2]]] [annual report filed on Form 10-K with the Securities and Exchange Commission], in accordance with applicable rules and regulations.

Composition of the Committee

The members of the Committee shall be independent[3] directors meeting the requirements of the [New York Stock Exchange[4]][Nasdaq National Market[5]] and

---

[1]*See* NYSE Rule 303A.5(b)(i).
[2]*See* corporate code of state of incorporation for proper term.
[3]*See* NYSE Rule 303A.5(a) and Nasdaq Rule 4350(c)(3)(A)(ii) and 4350(c)(3)(C).
[4]*See* NYSE Rule 303A.2(a) and (b) for independence requirements.
[5]*See* Nasdaq Rule 4200(a)(15) for independence requirements.

appointed by the Board of Directors on the recommendation of the Nominating and Corporate Governance Committee.[6] The Chairman of the Committee shall be designated by the Board of Directors. In the absence of the Chairperson, the members of the Committee may designate a chairman by majority vote. The Board of Directors may at any time remove one or more directors as members of the Committee and may fill any vacancy on the Committee.[7] The Committee may form and delegate authority to subcommittees when appropriate. At least two of the directors appointed to serve on the Committee shall be "nonemployee directors" (within the meaning of Rule 16b-3 promulgated under the Securities Exchange Act of 1934, as amended) and "outside directors" (within the meaning of Section 162(m) of the Internal Revenue Code of 1986, as amended, and the regulations thereunder).

Operations of the Committee

The Committee shall:

- Annually review and approve all Company goals and objectives relevant to the chief executive officer's compensation (as directed by the board)
- Annually evaluate the chief executive officer's performance in light of the Company's goals and objectives
- Annually [together with the other independent directors] determine and approve the chief executive officer's base salary and incentive compensation levels based on the Committee's evaluation of the chief executive officer's performance relative to the Company's goals and objectives[8]
- Annually review, evaluate and [determine] [make recommendations to the Board of Directors with respect to] the base salary level and incentive compensation levels of other executive officers of the Company[9]

---

[6]*See* NYSE Rule 303A.4. Also note that current Nasdaq rules do not require listed companies to have a nominating/corporate governance committee and do not require the adoption of corporate governance guidelines.

[7]*See* second paragraph of commentary to NYSE Rule 303A.5.

[8]*See* NYSE Rule 303A.5(b)(i)(A) and Nasdaq Rule 4350(c)(3)(A). Under NYSE standards, the compensation committee alone may approve the corporate goals and objectives relative to CEO compensation and evaluate the CEO's performance in light of such goals and objectives, but the Board may direct that the other independent directors may participate in determining and approving the CEO's compensation level based on this evaluation. Under Nasdaq standards, compensation of the CEO may be determined, or recommended to the Board for determination, either by the compensation committee or a majority of the independent directors, and the chief executive officer may not be present during voting or deliberations.

- Make recommendations to the Board of Directors with respect to the Company's incentive-compensation plans and equity-based compensation plans[10]
- Make regular reports to the Board of Directors concerning the activities of the Committee[11]
- Perform an annual performance evaluation of the Committee[12]
- Perform any other activities consistent with this Charter, the Company's [Certificate][Articles][13] of Incorporation and Bylaws and governing law as the Committee or the Board of Directors deem appropriate

To these ends, the Committee shall have and may exercise all the powers and authority of the Board of Directors to the extent permitted under Section [Authorizing Statute of State of Incorporation] of the [State of Incorporation][General Corporation Law].

The Committee may determine, from time to time, the advisability of retaining a compensation consultant to assist in the evaluation of chief executive officer or other executive officer compensation. The Committee has the authority to retain, at Company expense, and terminate a compensation consultant, including sole authority to approve the consultant's fees and other retention terms.[14]

Committee Meetings

The Committee shall meet at least [two] times per year. One such meeting shall be held at a time when the Committee can review and recommend annual base salary and incentive awards as described previously. The other meeting[s] shall be held at the discretion of the Chairperson of the Committee. Minutes of each of these meetings shall be kept.

---

[9]*See* NYSE Rule 303A.5(b)(i)(A) and Nasdaq Rule 4350(c)(3)(B). Under NYSE standards, the compensation committee may itself determine, or may make recommendations to the Board with respect to, compensation of executive officers other than the CEO. Under Nasdaq standards, compensation of the non-CEO executive officers may be determined, or recommended to the Board for determination, either by the compensation committee or a majority of the independent directors, and the chief executive officer may be present during voting or deliberations.

[10]*See* NYSE Rule 303A.5(b)(i)(B).

[11]*See* second paragraph of commentary to NYSE Rule 303A.5.

[12]*See* NYSE Rule 303A.5(b)(ii).

[13]*See* corporate code of state of incorporation for proper term.

[14]*See* third paragraph of commentary to NYSE Rule 303A.5.

AMGEN, INC.
COMPENSATION AND MANAGEMENT DEVELOPMENT COMMITTEE
OF THE BOARD OF DIRECTORS CHARTER

Purpose

The Compensation and Management Development Committee (the "Committee") of the Board of Directors (the "Board") assists the Board in fulfilling its fiduciary responsibilities with respect to the oversight of the Company's affairs in the areas of compensation plans, policies, and programs of the Company, especially those regarding executive compensation, employee benefits, and producing an annual report on executive compensation for inclusion in the Company's proxy materials in accordance with applicable rules and regulations and assists the Board in oversight of Executive Talent Management. The Committee shall ensure that compensation programs are designed to encourage high performance, promote accountability and adherence to Company values and the code of conduct, assure that employee interests are aligned with the interests of the Company's stockholders, serve the long-term best interests of the Company, and that the Executive Management Development processes are designed to attract, develop, and retain talented leadership to serve the long-term best interests of the company.

The Committee shall have the authority to undertake the specific duties and responsibilities described below and the authority to undertake such other duties as are assigned by law, the Company's certificate of incorporation or bylaws, or by the Board.

Membership

The Committee shall be composed of at least three (3) members of the Board, one of whom shall be designated by the Board as the Chair.

Each member of the Committee shall (1) qualify as independent under the Nasdaq listing requirements, (2) be a "nonemployee director" within the meaning of Rule 16b-3 of the Securities Exchange Act of 1934, as amended, (3) be an "outside director" under the regulations promulgated under Section 162(m) of the Internal Revenue Code of 1986, as amended (the "Code"), and (4) be otherwise free from any relationship that, in the judgment of the Board, would interfere with his or her exercise of business judgment as a Committee member.

Meetings and Procedures

The Committee shall hold at least four (4) regularly scheduled meetings each year.

In discharging its responsibilities, the Committee shall have sole authority to, as it deems appropriate, select, retain, and/or replace, as needed, compensation and benefits consultants and other outside consultants to provide independent advice to the Committee. In addition, the Committee shall have free access to Company staff personnel to provide data and advice in connection with the Committee's review of management compensation practices and policies and leadership development processes and practices.

The Committee shall maintain written minutes or other records of its meetings and activities. Minutes of each meeting of the Committee shall be distributed to each member of the Committee and other members of the Board. The Secretary of the Company shall retain the original signed minutes for filing with the corporate records of the Company.

The Chair of the Committee shall report to the Board following meetings of the Committee and as otherwise requested by the Chairman of the Board.

Responsibilities

The Committee shall be responsible for:

1. Overseeing succession planning for senior management of the Company, including consulting on an ongoing basis with the chief executive officer and the Board to remain abreast of management development activities, including a review of the performance and advancement potential of current and future senior management and succession plans for each and reviewing the retention of high-level, high-potential succession candidates.

2. Assessing the overall compensation structure of the Company and adopting a written statement of compensation philosophy and strategy, selecting an appropriate peer group, and periodically reviewing executive compensation in relation to this peer group.

3. Reviewing and approving corporate goals and objectives relating to the compensation of the Chief Executive Officer, evaluating the performance of the Chief Executive Officer in light of the goals and objectives, and making appropriate recommendations for improving performance. The Committee shall establish the compensation of the Chief Executive Officer based on such evaluation. In performing the foregoing functions, the Chair of the Committee shall solicit comments from the other members of the Board and shall lead the Board in an overall review of the Chief Executive Officer's performance in an executive session of nonemployee Board members. Final determinations regarding the performance and compensation of the Chief Executive Officer will be conducted in an executive session of the Committee and be reported by the Chair of the Committee to the entire Board during an independent session of the Board.

4. Reviewing and approving all compensation for all other officers of the Company; evaluating the responsibilities and performance of other executive officers and making appropriate recommendations for improving performance.

5. Recommending policies to the Board regarding minimum retention and ownership levels of Company common stock by officers.
6. Administering and reviewing all executive compensation programs and equity-based plans of the Company. The Committee shall have and shall exercise all the authority of the Board of Directors with respect to administering such plans, including approving amendments thereto.
7. Making recommendations to the Board with respect to incentive compensation plans and equity-based plans.
8. Approving, amending, and terminating ERISA-governed employee benefit plans.
9. Preparing and approving the Report of the Compensation Committee to be included as part of the Company's annual proxy statement.
10. Conducting an annual evaluation of the effectiveness of the Committee.

The Committee shall have the authority to delegate its functions to a subcommittee thereof.

For purposes of this Charter, "compensation" shall include, but not be limited to, cash or deferred payments, incentive and equity compensation, benefits and perquisites, employment, retention and/or termination/severance agreements, and any other programs that pursuant to the regulations of the Securities and Exchange Commission or Internal Revenue Service (or successor organizations, if applicable), would be considered compensation. In addition, "officer" shall be as defined in Section 16 of the Securities Exchange Act of 1934, and Rule 16a-1 thereunder.

The Committee shall review and reassess the Committee's charter on a periodic basis and submit any recommended changes to the Board for its consideration.

The Committee shall perform such other functions and have such other powers as may be necessary or convenient in the efficient discharge of the foregoing.

APPLE COMPUTER, INC.
COMPENSATION COMMITTEE CHARTER

There shall be a Committee of the Board of Directors to be known as the Compensation Committee with purpose, composition, duties, and responsibilities, as follows:

Purpose of the Committee. The Committee shall (i) establish and modify compensation and incentive plans and programs, and (ii) review and approve compensation and awards under compensation and incentive plans and programs for elected officers of the Corporation, and (iii) be the administering committee for certain stock option and other stock-based plans as designated by the Board.

Composition. The members of the Committee shall be appointed by the Board of Directors. The Committee will be composed of not less than three Board members. Each member shall be "independent" in accordance with applicable law, including the rules and regulations of the Securities and Exchange Commission and the rules of the Nasdaq Stock Market. The Chairman of the Committee shall be designated by the Board of Directors. The Chairman of the Board, any member of the Committee, or the Secretary of the Corporation may call meetings of the Committee.

Authority and Resources. The Committee may request any officer or employee of the Corporation or the Corporation's outside counsel to attend a Committee meeting. The Committee has the right at any time to obtain advice, reports, or opinions from internal and external counsel and expert advisors and has the authority to hire independent legal, financial, and other advisors as it may deem necessary, at the Corporation's expense, without consulting with, or obtaining approval from, any officer of the Corporation in advance.

Duties and Responsibilities. The duties of the Committee shall include:

- Review periodically and approve all compensation and incentive plans and programs (other than those administered by the Benefits Committee).
- Conduct and review with the Board of Directors an annual evaluation of the performance of all executive officers, including the Chief Executive Officer (CEO).
- Review periodically and fix the salaries, bonuses, and perquisites of elected officers of the Corporation and its subsidiaries, including the CEO.
- Act as administering committee of the Corporation's various stock plans and equity arrangements that may be adopted by the Corporation from time to time, with such authority and powers as are set forth in the respective plans' instruments, including but not limited to the granting of options to employees.
- Review for approval or disapproval special hiring or termination packages for officers and director-level employees of the Corporation and its subsidiaries that go beyond the Board's adopted criteria for management authority, if it is determined by the members of the Committee that approval by the full Board is not necessary.
- To the extent it deems necessary, recommend to the Board of Directors the establishment or modification of employee stock-based plans for the Corporation and its subsidiaries.
- To the extent it deems necessary, review and advise the Board of Directors regarding other compensation plans.
- To prepare an annual Compensation Committee Report for inclusion in the Corporation's proxy statement.

- Review the Committee charter, structure, process, and membership requirements at least once a year.
- Report to the Board of Directors concerning the Committee's activities.

The Committee can delegate any of its responsibilities to the extent allowed under applicable law.

Exceptions. Notwithstanding any implication to the contrary above:

- The Committee shall not be empowered to review or approve broad-based employee benefit plans (such as medical or insurance plans) not specifically delegated to the Committee, and the consideration and approval of any such plans shall remain the responsibility of the Board, the Benefits Committee, or the officers of the Corporation and its subsidiaries, depending on the amounts involved.
- In making its determination regarding compensation and plans that it is responsible for administering, the Committee shall take into account compensation received from all sources, including plans or arrangements that it is not responsible to administer.
- The Committee should take into consideration the tax-deductibility requirements of Section 162(m) of the Internal Revenue Code when reviewing and approving compensation for executive officers and, if deemed advisable, have such compensation approved by no less than two outside Committee members. If the Committee does not have two outside directors as defined in Section 162(m) of the Internal Revenue Code, such compensation should be approved by a majority of the outside Board members.
- The Committee shall not be empowered to approve matters that applicable law, the Corporation's charter, or the Corporation's bylaws require be approved by a vote of the whole Board.

THE GOLDMAN SACHS GROUP, INC.
COMPENSATION COMMITTEE CHARTER

Amended and restated as of January 2004

Purpose of Committee

The purpose of the Compensation Committee (the "Committee") of the Board of Directors (the "Board") of The Goldman Sachs Group, Inc. (the "Company") is to:

a. Determine and approve the compensation of the Company's Chief Executive Officer (the "CEO")

b. Make recommendations to the Board with respect to non-CEO compensation, incentive-compensation plans and equity-based plans

c. Assist the Board in its oversight of the development, implementation, and effectiveness of the Company's policies and strategies relating to its human capital management function, including but not limited to those policies and strategies regarding recruiting, retention, career development, and progression, management succession (other than that within the purview of the Corporate Governance and Nominating Committee), diversity, and employment practices

d. Prepare any report on executive compensation required by the rules and regulations of the Securities and Exchange Commission (the "SEC").

Committee Membership

The Committee shall consist of no fewer than three members of the Board. The members of the Committee shall each have been determined by the Board to be "independent" under the rules of the New York Stock Exchange, Inc. At least two members of the Committee should qualify as "Nonemployee Directors" for the purposes of Rule 16b-3 under the Securities Exchange Act of 1934, as in effect from time to time ("Rule 16b-3"), and as "outside directors" for the purposes of Section 162(m) of the Internal Revenue Code, as in effect from time to time ("Section 162(m)"). No member of the Committee may (except in his or her capacity as a member of the Committee, the Board or any other Board committee) receive, directly or indirectly, any consulting, advisory or other compensatory fee from the Company, other than fixed amounts of compensation under a retirement plan (including deferred compensation) for prior service with the Company (provided that such compensation is not contingent in any way on continued service).

Members shall be appointed by the Board based on the recommendations of the Corporate Governance and Nominating Committee and shall serve at the pleasure of the Board and for such term or terms as the Board may determine.

Committee Structure and Operations

The Board, taking into account the views of the Chairman of the Board, shall designate one member of the Committee as its chairperson. The Committee shall meet at least three times a year, with further meetings to occur, or actions to be taken by unanimous written consent, when deemed necessary or desirable by the Committee or its chairperson.

The Committee may invite such members of management and other persons to its meetings as it may deem desirable or appropriate. The Committee shall report regularly to the Board summarizing the Committee's actions and any significant issues considered by the Committee.

Committee Duties and Responsibilities

The following are the duties and responsibilities of the Committee:

1. In consultation with senior management, to make recommendations to the Board as to the Company's general compensation philosophy and to oversee the development and implementation of compensation programs.

2. To review and approve those corporate goals and objectives established by the Board that are relevant to the compensation of the CEO, evaluate the performance of the CEO in light of those goals and objectives, and determine and approve the CEO's compensation level based on this evaluation. As part of this evaluation, the Committee shall consider the evaluation of the CEO conducted by the Corporate Governance and Nominating Committee. In determining the long-term incentive component of CEO compensation, the Committee shall consider, among other factors, the Company's performance and relative shareholder return, the value of similar incentive awards to chief executive officers at the Company's principal competitors and other comparable companies, and the awards given to the CEO in past years.

3. To review and approve the annual compensation of the Company's executives and any new compensation programs applicable to such executives, to make recommendations to the Board with respect to the Company's non-CEO compensation, incentive compensation plans, and equity-based plans, including the Amended and Restated Stock Incentive Plan, the Defined Contribution Plan, the Partner Compensation Plan, and the Restricted Partner Compensation Plan, to oversee the activities of the individuals and committees responsible for administering these plans, and to discharge any responsibilities imposed on the Committee by these plans.

4. To review periodically, as it deems appropriate:

   - Benefits and perquisites provided to the Company's executives

   - Employment agreements, severance arrangements, and change-in-control agreements and provisions relating to the Company's executives

5. To review annually the application of the compensation process to the Company's investment research professionals and assess whether that process remains consistent with the Company's Investment Research Principles and the requirements of Section I.5 of Addendum A to the global research settlement to which the Company is a party.

6. To review the Company's policies on the tax deductibility of compensation paid to "covered employees" (as defined by Section 162(m)), and, as and when required, to administer plans, establish performance goals, and certify that performance goals have been attained for purposes of Section 162(m).

7. To discuss with management periodically, as it deems appropriate:
   - Reports from management regarding the development, implementation, and effectiveness of the Company's policies and strategies relating to its human capital management function, including but not limited to those policies and strategies regarding recruiting, retention, career development and progression, management succession (other than that within the purview of the Corporate Governance and Nominating Committee), diversity, and employment practices
   - Reports from management relating to compensation guarantees
   - Reports from management regarding the Company's regulatory compliance with respect to compensation matters
8. To prepare and issue the report and evaluation required under "Committee Reports" below.
9. To discharge any other duties or responsibilities delegated to the Committee by the Board from time to time.

Committee Reports

The Committee shall produce the following report and evaluation and provide them to the Board:

1. An annual Report of the Compensation Committee on Executive Compensation for inclusion in the Company's annual proxy statement in accordance with applicable SEC rules and regulations.
2. An annual performance evaluation of the Committee, which evaluation shall compare the performance of the Committee with the requirements of this charter. The performance evaluation shall also include a review of the adequacy of this charter and shall recommend to the Board any revisions the Committee deems necessary or desirable, although the Board shall have the sole authority to amend this charter. The performance evaluation shall be conducted in such manner as the Committee deems appropriate.

Delegation to Subcommittee

The Committee may, at its discretion, delegate all or a portion of its duties and responsibilities to a subcommittee of the Committee, whether or not such delegation is specifically contemplated under any plan or program. In particular, the Committee may delegate the approval of award grants and other transactions and other responsibilities regarding the administration of compensatory programs to a subcommittee consisting solely of members of the Committee who are (i) "Non-employee Directors" for the purposes of Rule 16b-3, and/or (ii) "outside directors" for the purposes of Section 162(m).

Resources and Authority of the Committee

The Committee shall have the resources and authority appropriate to discharge its duties and responsibilities, including the authority to select, retain, terminate, and approve the fees and other retention terms of special counsel or other experts or consultants, as it deems appropriate, without seeking approval of the Board or management. With respect to compensation consultants retained to assist in the evaluation of CEO or executive compensation, this authority shall be vested solely in the Committee.

GENERAL ELECTRIC COMPANY
MANAGEMENT DEVELOPMENT AND COMPENSATION
COMMITTEE CHARTER

The Management Development and Compensation Committee of the board of directors of General Electric Company shall consist of a minimum of three directors. Members of the committee shall be appointed by the board of directors upon the recommendation of the Nominating and Corporate Governance Committee and may be removed by the board of directors in its discretion. All members of the committee shall be independent directors, and shall satisfy GE's independence guidelines for members of the Management Development and Compensation Committee.

The purpose of the committee shall be to carry out the board of directors' overall responsibility relating to executive compensation.

In furtherance of this purpose, the committee shall have the following authority and responsibilities:

1. To assist the board in developing and evaluating potential candidates for executive positions, including the chief executive officer, and to oversee the development of executive succession plans.
2. To review and approve on an annual basis the corporate goals and objectives with respect to compensation for the chief executive officer. The committee shall evaluate at least once a year the chief executive officer's performance in light of these established goals and objectives, and based upon these evaluations shall set the chief executive officer's annual compensation, including salary, bonus, incentive, and equity compensation.
3. To review and approve on an annual basis the evaluation process and compensation structure for the company's officers. The committee shall evaluate the

performance of the company's senior executive officers and shall approve the annual compensation, including salary, bonus, incentive, and equity compensation, for such senior executive officers. The committee shall also provide oversight of management's decisions concerning the performance and compensation of other company officers.

4. To review the company's incentive compensation and other stock-based plans and recommend changes in such plans to the board as needed. The committee shall have and shall exercise all the authority of the board of directors with respect to the administration of such plans.

5. To maintain regular contact with the leadership of the company. This should include interaction with the company's leadership development institute, review of data from the employee survey, and regular review of the results of the annual leadership evaluation process.

6. To prepare and publish an annual executive compensation report in the company's proxy statement.

The committee shall have the authority to delegate any of its responsibilities to subcommittees as the committee may deem appropriate in its sole discretion.

The committee shall have authority to retain such compensation consultants, outside counsel, and other advisors as the committee may deem appropriate at its sole discretion. The committee shall have sole authority to approve related fees and retention terms.

The committee shall report its actions and any recommendations to the board after each committee meeting and shall conduct and present to the board an annual performance evaluation of the committee. The committee shall review at least annually the adequacy of this charter and recommend any proposed changes to the board for approval.

REVLON, INC.
COMPENSATION COMMITTEE CHARTER

In accordance with Article IV of the By-Laws of Revlon, Inc. (the "Company") and applicable laws, rules and regulations, there will be a standing committee of the Board of Directors of the Company (the "Board") known as the Compensation and Stock Plan Committee (the "Compensation Committee").

I. Organization

The Compensation Committee will consist of three or more directors of the Company.

The Board will endeavor to ensure that the Compensation Committee will at all times have at least two members who are "outside directors" pursuant to Section 162(m) of the Internal Revenue Code, as amended, and as defined in Treasury Reg. Section 1.162-27(e)(3), as may be amended from time to time. Further, the Board will endeavor to ensure that at least two members of the Compensation Committee are "nonemployee directors" pursuant to Rule 16b-3(b))(3)(i) under the Securities and Exchange Act of 1934, as amended from time to time.

The Board will appoint the members of the Compensation Committee annually. Each member will serve until his or her successor is appointed.

II. Meetings

The Compensation Committee will meet as often as it determines is necessary or desirable, but not less frequently than quarterly. The Compensation Committee may from time to time decide to act by unanimous written consent in lieu of a meeting.

The Chairman of the Compensation Committee will preside at each meeting of the Compensation Committee and, in consultation with the other members of the Compensation Committee and the Company's Secretary, will set the agenda of items to be addressed at each upcoming meeting. Each member of the Compensation Committee may suggest the inclusion of items on such agenda, and may raise at any Compensation Committee meeting appropriate and relevant business subjects that are not on the agenda for that meeting. The Chairman of the Compensation Committee and the Company's Secretary will endeavor to ensure, to the extent feasible, that the agenda for each upcoming meeting of the Compensation Committee is circulated to each member of the Compensation Committee in advance of the meeting.

III. Authority and Responsibilities

The Compensation Committee will have the following authority and principal direct responsibilities:

a. Reviewing and approving corporate goals and objectives relevant to the compensation of the Company's Chief Executive Officer, evaluating the CEO's performance in light of those goals and objectives and determining, either as a committee or together with the Board's other independent directors (as directed by the Board), the CEO's compensation level based on such evaluation

b. Reviewing and approving the compensation plans, incentive compensation plans, and equity-based plans established for the Company's and its subsidiaries' Section 16 officers other than the CEO and such other employees of the Company as the Compensation Committee may determine to be necessary or desirable from time to time

c. Producing the Board's annual Compensation Committee Report on Executive Compensation for inclusion in the Company's proxy statement, in accordance with applicable rules and regulations

d. Administering the Revlon, Inc. Fourth Amended and Restated 1996 Stock Plan, the Revlon, Inc. 2002 Supplemental Stock Plan, and the Revlon Executive Bonus Plan, in each case as may be amended and in effect from time to time, as well as any other stock plans, executive bonus plans, or other incentive compensation plans or arrangements of the Company and its subsidiaries, as may be in effect from time to time

e. Conducting an annual self-evaluation

f. Appointing subcommittees to perform any or all of its functions and to delegate to appropriate Company officers execution of certain actions as may be appropriate from time to time

g. Performing any other activities consistent with this Charter and the Company's By-Laws or as required under the rules and regulations of the Securities and Exchange Commission and the New York Stock Exchange, as in effect from time to time

Publication Date: January 31, 2004

Sample Compensation Committee Reports

This Appendix contains the compensation committee reports for Pfizer, Intel, and General Electric contained in those companies' proxy statements filed with the Securities and Exchange Commission in 2004.

PFIZER INC. COMPENSATION COMMITTEE REPORT

Overview of Compensation Philosophy and Program

The Compensation Committee establishes the salaries and other compensation of the executive officers of the Company, including its Chairman and CEO and other executive officers named in the Compensation Table (the "Named Executive Officers"). The Committee consists entirely of independent Directors who are not officers or employees of the Company. There were eleven meetings of the Committee in 2003, of which three involved executive sessions with no Pfizer employees present for all or a portion of the meeting. In accordance with the Committee's Charter, the Committee engages an independent compensation consultant to advise the Committee on all matters related to CEO and other executive compensation.

The Company's executive compensation program consists of salaries, Executive Annual Incentive Awards and long-term incentive compensation and is designed to:

- retain executive officers by paying them competitively, motivate them to contribute to the Company's success and reward them for their performance;

- link a substantial part of each executive officer's compensation to the performance of both the Company and the individual executive officer; and

- encourage significant ownership of Company common stock by executive officers.

The Committee also intends that all incentive compensation paid to the Named Executive Officers will be deductible for federal income tax purposes.

Evaluation of Executive Performance in 2003

The Committee does not rely solely on predetermined formulas or a limited set of criteria when it evaluates the performance of the Chairman and CEO and the Company's other executive officers.

In 2003, the Committee considered management's continuing achievement of its short and long-term goals, including:

- the financial, operational and strategic merits of business development, notably the acquisition of Pharmacia;

- improving operating margins;

- revenue growth versus industry;

- earnings-per-share growth;

- exceeding the merger-related synergy/cost savings targets relating to the Pharmacia merger;

- continued optimization of organizational effectiveness and productivity;

- managing increased scale;

- responding to customer value expectations;

- the breadth of the current product portfolio, and the acceptance of those products in the marketplace, which drove considerable sales growth, resulting in furthering the Company's position as the number one pharmaceutical company;

- the number of promising product candidates under development by the Company; and

- the development of talent and leadership throughout the Company.

The Committee also considers management's responses to the changes occurring within the global marketplace for health-care products and services. The discovery by the pharmaceutical industry of innovative medicines that effectively treat chronic as well as acute health problems has focused attention on the issues of access and adequate third-party coverage for prescription drugs, particularly for low-income individuals and the elderly, both in the U.S. and other key markets (e.g., Japan). It is the Committee's opinion that management continues to effectively develop and implement strategies within the marketplace and at the local and federal levels of government to address these issues, enabling the Company to remain a leader in the health-care industry. The success of these efforts and their benefits to the Company cannot, of course, be quantifiably measured, but the Committee believes they are vital to the Company's continuing success.

Total Compensation

To establish target total compensation levels of Company executives, the Committee considers total compensation in the competitive market. The total compensation package for each executive is broken down into the three basic components of salary, annual incentive, and long-term incentive, as discussed in more detail below. No executive officer of the Company is receiving compensation from any subsidiary or affiliated organization of the Company. The Company intends to continue its strategy of compensating its executives through programs that emphasize performance-based incentive compensation. To that end, Dr. McKinnell's compensation is tied directly to the performance of the Company and is structured so that, due to the nature of the business, there is an appropriate balance between the long-term and short-term performance of the Company. We believe that it is imperative to balance these pay components. Target salary and bonus levels are generally set at the median of the Peer Group (as described with the Performance Graph) and a select group of large global companies, based on available survey data, after adjusting the data to reflect Pfizer's scale and scope relative to that of the comparison companies. For 2003, the actual total compensation of Dr. McKinnell and the other Named Executive Officers generally fell in the upper quartile of total compensation paid to executives holding equivalent positions in these companies. The Committee believes that this position was consistent with the outstanding performance and relative market capitalization of the Company compared to these companies.

Salaries

The 2003 salaries of the Named Executive Officers are shown in the "Salary" column of the Summary Compensation Table. Dr. McKinnell received a salary of $2,042,700 for 2003. For 2004, it has been set at $2,270,500, effective April 1. This effective date of April 1 represents a change from the previous effective date for merit increases of January 1, used in 2003 and earlier. In order to consolidate the planning of merit increases for all U.S. employees, which has historically occurred at various times throughout the year for different sites and employee groups, we have transitioned those various merit increase dates to a common effective date of

April 1. As a result of this change in effective date, the merit increases for the Named Executive Officers, along with a large portion of the U.S. employee population, reflect a 15-month period since their last merit increase. All affected employees will receive a single payment to mitigate the impact of this change in effective date. This payment for Dr. McKinnell will be in the amount of $11,350, and will be paid to him shortly after April 1, 2004.

Executive Annual Incentive Awards

In 1997, the Board of Directors adopted and the shareholders approved the Pfizer Inc. Executive Annual Incentive Plan. Under the terms of this Plan, a maximum award of 0.3% of Adjusted Net Income as defined in the Plan was established for each employee participating in the Plan. This maximum exceeds the current level of Annual Incentive Awards made by the Committee, and the Committee will continue to base the awards on Company and individual performance criteria within the established maximum.

For 2003, an Annual Incentive Award of $4,607,400 for Dr. McKinnell was approved by the Committee and confirmed by the Board. The Annual Incentive Awards for 2003 paid to each of the Named Executive Officers are shown in the "Bonus" column of the Summary Compensation Table.

Long-Term Incentive Compensation

In 2003, Dr. McKinnell and the other executive officers participated in the Company's long-term incentive compensation program which consists of stock options and Performance-Contingent Share Awards. Stock options granted to Dr. McKinnell and the other Named Executive Officers, when combined with the value of the Performance-Contingent Shares that these officers may potentially earn, have, until 2003, been targeted to fall at the median of the value of long-term incentives granted by the Peer Group to executive officers holding comparable positions. In 2003, the Company began moving the targeted positioning toward the 75th percentile of the comparison companies in order to emphasize and support sustained exceptional performance, given the long-term, high-risk nature of our core business.

In 2003, the Committee granted restricted stock to certain executives of the Company for retention purposes. Dr. McKinnell did not receive this award; however, the other Named Executive Officers received awards as shown in the Summary Compensation Table and its related footnotes.

As a result of the acquisition of Pharmacia, the Committee has recommended to the Board of Directors that a new Stock Plan be submitted for shareholder approval. This plan, included in Annex 6 and described in Item 3 of this Proxy Statement, will provide a basis for future stock options and awards, which are designed to attract, retain and motivate our employees. If the new Plan is approved by shareholders, no future awards will be granted from the current plans; however, stock options and awards granted prior to the adoption of the new Plan will continue to be governed by the current Plans.

For 2004, the Compensation Committee has reduced the target stock option award for the CEO by 40% and has increased the target Performance-Contingent Share Award by an equivalent value to emphasize the importance of Company performance on both measures (total shareholder return and change in earnings per share) relative to the performance of the Peer Group. The target awards for Dr. McKinnell in 2004 are 300,000 options and 265,000 performance-contingent shares.

(a) Stock Options

The Committee granted stock options to each executive officer in February 2003 under the Company's 2001 Stock and Incentive Plan.

The Named Executive Officers were awarded the number of stock options shown in the table headed "Option Grants in 2003." As shown in the table, the stock option grants vest ratably on the third, fourth and fifth anniversary of the stock option grant. Dr. McKinnell was awarded 1,000,000 stock options in 2003.

(b) Performance-Contingent Share Awards

The Committee established awards for Dr. McKinnell and other executive officers, including the other Named Executive Officers, for the 2003-2007 performance period under the 2001 Performance-Contingent Share Award Plan. Payments pursuant to the awards are determined by using a non-discretionary formula comprised of the following two performance criteria measured over the applicable performance period relative to the performance of the Peer Group:

- total shareholder return; and
- Diluted earnings per share growth.

The performance formula weighs the two criteria equally. If our performance in both measures is below the threshold level relative to the Peer Group, then no Performance-Contingent Shares will be earned. To the extent that the Company's performance on either or both measures exceeds the threshold performance level relative to the Peer Group, a varying amount of shares of common stock up to the maximum will be earned.

The total number of shares earned by each of the Named Executive Officers for the performance periods ending December 31, 2003 is shown in footnote 4 to the "LTIP Payouts" column of the Summary Compensation Table. The number of Performance-Contingent Shares that the Named Executive Officers may earn at the end of the five-year performance period 1/1/2003-12/31/2007 is shown in the table headed "Long-Term Incentive Plan Awards in 2003." Dr. McKinnell earned 75,060 shares for the 1999-2003 performance period, and the number of Performance-Contingent Shares that Dr. McKinnell may earn at the end of the five-year performance period (1/1/2003-12/31/2007) will range from 0 to 330,000. In reviewing the Company's performance relative to the Peer Group and the resulting awards under the program, the Committee determined that the reduction in the program awards due to the Pharmacia purchase accounting-related costs were inappropriate, given the substantial favorable impact of the acquisition on Pfizer Inc. and its shareholders. Therefore, the Committee will grant shares of restricted stock under the 2001 Pfizer Stock and Incentive Plan to the program participants, based on the difference in the actual program awards and the awards that would have been earned if the financial impact of non-cash charges associated with the acquisition are excluded. The grants will be determined and awarded shortly after the release of all of the Peer Group companies' annual reports on Form 10-K, which will not be filed with the SEC until after the publication of this Proxy Statement. These restricted shares, if any, will not be deductible by the Company for tax purposes for the Named Executive Officers and will be disclosed in the Summary Compensation Table that will be included in the Proxy Statement relating to our 2005 Annual Meeting of Shareholders.

Stock Ownership Program

The Company maintains stock ownership requirements for its executive and other officers. "Stock ownership" is defined as stock owned by the officer directly or through the Company's Savings Plan, or awarded pursuant to the 2001 Performance-Contingent Share Award Plan or its predecessor Performance-Contingent Share Award Program, and subsequently deferred. Under the current guidelines of the program established by the Committee, employee Directors (currently Dr. McKinnell) are required to own Company common stock equal in value to at least five times their annual salaries. The program also extends to the other Named Executive Officers and other members of the Pfizer Leadership Team, who are required to own Company common stock equal in value to at least four times their annual salaries. All other elected corporate officers are required to own Company stock with a value equivalent to three times their annual salaries, and all other participants in the 2001 Performance-Contingent Share Award Plan are required to own an amount equal in value to their annual salaries. The Committee has determined that, as of December 31, 2003, all employees covered by these guidelines met their ownership targets.

The Compensation Committee:

Mr. Burns (Chair)
Mr. Lorch
Dr. Mead
Mr. Raines

INTEL CORPORATION

Report of the Compensation Committee on Executive Compensation

The Compensation Committee (the "Committee") administers Intel's executive compensation program. In this regard, the role of the Committee is to oversee our compensation plans and policies, annually review and approve all executive officers' compensation decisions, and administer our stock option plans (including reviewing and approving stock option grants to executive officers). The Committee's charter reflects these various responsibilities, and the Committee and the Board periodically review and revise the charter. The Committee's membership is determined by the Board and is composed entirely of independent directors. The Committee meets at scheduled times during the year, and it also considers and takes action by written consent. The Committee Chairman reports on Committee actions and recommendations at Board meetings. The Compensation and Benefits Group in Intel's Human Resources Department supports the Committee in its work and in some cases acts pursuant to delegated authority to fulfill various functions in administering Intel's compensation programs. In addition, the Committee has the authority to engage the services of outside advisers, experts and others to assist the Committee. For the past two years, the Committee has directly engaged an outside compensation consulting firm to assist the Committee in its review of the compensation for the executive officers.

General Compensation Philosophy

Our general compensation philosophy is that total cash compensation should vary with Intel's performance in achieving financial and non-financial objectives, and that any long-term incentive compensation should be closely aligned with the stockholders' interests. This philosophy applies to all Intel employees, with a more significant level of variability and compensation at risk as an employee's level of responsibility increases. In 2003, the Committee engaged in a review of the executive compensation philosophy, with the goal of ensuring the appropriate mix of fixed and variable compensation linked to individual and corporate performance. In the course of this review, the Committee sought the advice and input of both an outside compensation consultant and Intel management. Through this review, the Committee also identified the key strategic compensation design priorities for Intel: employee retention, cost management, the egalitarian treatment of employees, alignment with stockholder interests and continued focus on corporate governance. The Committee also considered whether any changes should be made to Intel's cash compensation and stock option programs in support of these strategic priorities. Intel's egalitarian focus caused the Committee to decide against consideration of equity vehicles that may differ between the executive officers and the broad-based employee population, and endorse the continued use of stock options for long-term incentive and retention for all employees. This compensation review confirmed that our compensation program elements individually and in the aggregate strongly support and reflect the compensation philosophy and strategic design priorities, both on a cash and long-term incentive basis.

In 2003, the Committee directly engaged an outside compensation consultant to provide an independent analysis of Intel's executive compensation program and practices. The results of the analysis completed by this independent consultant, and corroborated by management and the Committee, included the following observations about Intel's 2003 executive compensation:

- Base salaries are less than the competitive norm.
- Performance-based cash incentives are higher than the market, but when coupled with base salaries provide total cash compensation that is lower than the market.
- Annual stock option grants, as an incentive for future performance, are targeted at less than competitive levels.
- Additional stock grants at approximately seven-year intervals, with vesting beginning no earlier than five years from the grant date, are another means for long-term incentive and retention.

Both the Committee's review and the outside compensation consultant's review of Intel's executive compensation practices suggest that our executive compensation has a higher proportion of total compensation delivered through pay-for-performance incentive and long-term equity compensation, equating to more compensation risk for Intel's executives than for the executives of competitor companies. This higher risk is due to the combination of lower-than-market base salaries and higher-than-market annual pay-for-performance incentive targets and the infrequent, long-vesting stock option grants. The higher-than-market compensation variability employed by Intel is closely linked to the company's annual financial results through lower-than-market total cash compensation in times of poor financial performance. Conversely, in times of excellent performance, the compensation variability yields higher total cash compensation, rewarding employees for excellent performance. Our philosophy is to pay higher-than-market average compensation over periods of sustained excellent performance. Despite improved company performance in 2003, our total executive cash compensation remained below the market average because our compensation philosophy requires that we consistently outperform the market to deliver above-market compensation. We have several performance-based compensation programs in which the majority of our employees are eligible to participate. Most Intel employees who are not compensated on a commission basis participate in a broad-based variable cash incentive program. Executive officers participate in the Executive Officer Incentive Plan (the "EOIP," formerly known as the Executive Officer Bonus Plan).

Total annual cash compensation for the majority of Intel's employees, including its executive officers, consists of the following components:

- Base salary;
- An annual pay-for-performance cash incentive dependent on Intel's earnings per share ("EPS") and performance against business group objectives for the performance period, and an individual incentive target; and
- A semiannual cash award payment based upon company profitability.

Long-term incentive compensation is realized through the grant of stock options. All general full-time and part-time employees are eligible to receive stock options, including executive officers. Stock options require Intel stock price appreciation in order for the employees to realize any benefit, thus directly aligning employee and stockholder interests.

Our employees can also acquire Intel stock through a tax-qualified employee stock purchase plan, which is generally available to all employees. This plan allows participants to buy Intel stock at a discount to the market price with up to 10% of their salary and incentives (subject to certain limits), with the objective of allowing employees to profit when the value of Intel stock increases over time.

Setting Executive Compensation

In setting the annual base salary and individual EOIP pay-for-performance incentive target amount (together, base salary and incentive target are referred to as "BSIT") for each executive officer, the Committee reviews executive compensation information derived from nationally recognized compensation surveys. The Committee utilizes a cross-industry subset of companies as well as a technology industry subset of companies generally considered to be comparable to Intel, most of which are included in the Dow Jones Technology Index. Although the Committee does not use a specific formula to set pay in relation to this market data, it generally sets executive officer BSIT below the average salaries for comparable jobs in the marketplace. However, when Intel's business groups meet or exceed certain predetermined financial and non-financial goals, amounts paid under the performance-based compensation programs may lead to total cash compensation levels that are higher than the average cash compensation for comparable jobs. Conversely, total cash compensation levels may be reduced and become further behind competitive cash compensation averages in times of poor performance. While our philosophy is to pay higher-than-market-average compensation in times of excellent performance (due to higher-than-market pay at risk), in 2003, despite the successful achievement of business goals and a significant EPS increase, total executive cash compensation remained lower than the market average.

The Committee reviews the executive officers' compensation levels for internal consistency relative to the 100 most highly paid Intel employees. In January 2004, the Committee reviewed the total remuneration that each of the top five most highly compensated executive officers could potentially receive in each of the next ten years, under scenarios of continuing employment with the company or upon retirement from the company. Total remuneration included all aspects of the executive officer's future cash-convertible benefits, total cash compensation (base salary plus incentive) from continuing employment, the future value of stock options under varying stock price growth assumptions and including as applicable the impact of accelerated vesting upon retirement, and the value of any deferred compensation and profit sharing retirement benefits.

Section 162(m) of the Internal Revenue Code of 1986, as amended (the "Tax Code"), places a limit of $1,000,000 on the amount of compensation that Intel may deduct in any one year with respect to each of its five most highly paid executive officers. Certain performance-based compensation approved by stockholders is not subject to the deduction limit. Intel's stockholder-approved 1984 Stock Option Plan and the EOIP are qualified so that awards under such plans constitute performance-based compensation not subject to Section 162(m) of the Tax Code. To maintain flexibility in compensating executive officers in a manner designed to promote varying corporate goals, the Committee has not adopted a policy that all compensation must be deductible.

Base Salary

The Committee reviews the history of and proposals for the compensation of each of Intel's executive officers, including cash and equity-based components. In accordance with our compensation philosophy that total cash compensation should vary with company performance, the Committee establishes executive officers' base salaries at levels that it believes are below the average base salaries of executives of companies it considers comparable to Intel. The Committee also sets executive officers' base salaries as a percentage of BSIT, taking into account each officer's level and amount of responsibility. As a result, a large part of each executive officer's potential total cash compensation is variable and dependent upon Intel's performance.

In general, executive officers with the highest level and amount of responsibility have the lowest percentage of their BSIT fixed as base salary and the highest percentage of their BSIT variable as their individual incentive target amount. For example, in 2003, the base salary for Dr. Barrett, Chief Executive Officer, was 50% of his total BSIT. The other executives' base salaries were determined in the same manner, but for 2003, the base salary as a percentage of their BSIT ranged from 50% to 65%, depending on their job responsibilities. Once base salary is fixed, it does not depend on Intel's performance.

Performance-Based Compensation

Executive Officer Incentive Plan (EOIP)

The EOIP is a cash-based pay-for-performance incentive program, and its purpose is to motivate and reward eligible employees for their contributions to Intel's performance by making a large portion of their cash compensation variable and dependent upon Intel's performance. EOIP participants have a higher proportion of their total cash compensation delivered through this pay-for-performance incentive, which equates to more compensation risk for Intel's executives than for those of competitor companies due to the relative mix of lower-than-market base salary and higher-than-market annual EOIP pay-for-performance incentive targets. The higher-than-market compensation variability employed by Intel is closely linked to the company's annual financial results through lower-than-market total cash compensation in times of poor financial performance. Conversely, in times of excellent performance, the higher variability yields higher-than-market total cash compensation, motivating and rewarding employees for excellent performance. While our philosophy is to pay higher-than-market-average compensation in times of excellent performance, in 2003, despite the successful achievement of business goals and a significant EPS increase, total cash compensation for all corporate officers, on average, remained lower than the market average.

The incentive formula has three variables: (1) the executive officer's annual incentive target, (2) Intel's EPS and (3) a factor pre-established each year by the Committee (the "Performance Factor"), all of which are further explained below. At the end of each year, the individual's incentive target is multiplied by Intel's EPS for the year and the Performance Factor to calculate the actual EOIP amount for that year. The EOIP has a cap limiting each individual's incentive payment to a maximum annual limit of $5,000,000. After the individual incentive amounts are calculated, the Committee reviews and authorizes each participant's actual incentive payments and has the discretion to reduce (but not increase) a participant's incentive payment. The EOIP does not specify criteria that the Committee must use in exercising its discretion to reduce EOIP payments, and it also does not require the Committee to make any reductions. The Committee has often reduced the incentive amounts below what the EOIP formula would allow, and, as described below, it did so for the 2003 incentive payments.

For purposes of this formula, EPS is the greater of (x) Intel's operating income or (y) Intel's net income divided by Intel's weighted average common and common equivalent shares outstanding. The Committee may adjust Intel's operating income or Intel's net income based on objective criteria selected by the Committee in its sole discretion and in compliance with IRS regulations. These adjustments may include, but are not limited to: asset write-downs; litigation; claim judgments, settlements or tax settlements; the effects of tax law changes, changes in accounting principles or other such laws or provisions affecting reported results; accruals for reorganization and restructuring programs; unrealized gains or losses on investments; and any extraordinary non-recurring items as described in Accounting Principles Board Opinion No. 30 and/or in management's discussion and analysis of financial condition and results of operations appearing in Intel's annual report to stockholders for the applicable year. Operating income does not include gains or losses on equity securities or interest and other income earned by Intel, and does not include a deduction for interest expense and income taxes; as a result, EPS based on operating income generally exceeds EPS based on net income. The Performance Factor applied to EPS as mentioned above is a predetermined factor that considers BSIT market competitiveness, forecasted EPS growth and performance probability, with the purpose of setting challenging employee performance expectations.

In January 2003, the Committee established individual incentive targets ranging from $135,000 to $610,000 for each of the executive officers (representing a range of 35% to 50% of BSIT) and set the Performance Factor as 3.50 for the 2003 performance period, unchanged from 2002 with expectations of a delayed financial market recovery. The 2003 financial results yielded an EPS based on operating income of $1.14*, which exceeded adjusted net income per share of $0.83* and led to an EPS value, as defined, of $1.14* to be used in the formula for determining the maximum incentive amount (EPS for 2003 under generally accepted accounting principles was $0.85 per share). The Committee adjusted down net income

---

Both operating income per share and adjusted net income per share are not defined under generally accepted accounting principles and are not deemed alternatives to measure performance under GAAP. As explained above, the EOIP is based on either operating income or net income, both of which can be adjusted by the Committee at its discretion. We have presented EPS based on operating income and EPS based on adjusted net income per share solely to indicate the inputs to the EOIP formula for 2003 and the discretionary adjustments made by the Committee. EPS under GAAP was $0.85 for 2003. To arrive at adjusted net income per share of $0.83, GAAP net income was adjusted on a per share basis to exclude a fourth-quarter goodwill impairment charge of $611 million and exclude $758 million in tax benefits related to the 2003 divestitures. EPS based on operating income adds to GAAP net income per share, the per share impact of income tax expense of $1,801 million, loss on equity securities, net of $283 million and subtracts interest and other, net of $192 million.

EPS to remove the positive effects of divestiture-related tax benefits in 2003. The Committee adjusted up net income EPS for a goodwill impairment charge for certain executive officers, but excluded the top four most highly paid executives and one other executive, holding them accountable for the strategic decisions from which the goodwill impairment stemmed.

For the 2003 performance period, the Committee exercised its discretion to reduce incentive payments below what would have been allowed under the EOIP. These incentives were limited to the amounts that would have resulted from calculating the incentives under the broad-based employee plan, with the exception of the incentives for certain executives, which were further reduced below this level, including the incentives for the top four most highly paid executives and one other executive. The broad-based plan also takes into account whether certain business groups have met their objectives over the performance period. The goals are set annually and vary from year to year. In determining incentives payable to the executive officers with responsibility for Intel's overall performance, such as the Chief Executive Officer and the President, the Committee takes into account the corporate average score on achievement of business objectives. For executive officers with specific responsibility for a particular business group, achievement scores are based on either the individual business group's score or a combination of the group's score and the corporate average score. The broad-based plan also uses a Performance Factor in its calculation, as generally described above; the Performance Factors for the broad-based plan and the EOIP plan may differ. Incentives paid to executive officers for 2003 under the EOIP were on average 33% higher than incentive payments for

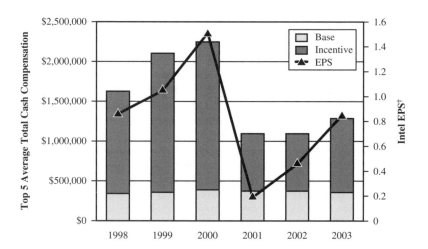

†EPS is net income divided by Intel's weighted average common shares outstanding, assuming dilution.

2002, which is in general accordance with the intent of the EOIP to reflect the relative level of Intel's financial performance from year to year, consistent with the significant earnings growth achieved in 2003. Incentives paid to executive officers for 2002 were approximately flat with the incentives for 2001.

Semiannual Cash Award

The semiannual cash award offers cash incentive payments to employees, including executive officers, based on corporate profitability. Twice a year, eligible employees receive 0.55 day of pay (calculated based on eligible earnings for the six-month period, including one-half of incentive targets as applicable) for every two percentage points of corporate pretax margin (pretax profit as a percentage of revenue), or a total payment based on 4% of net income, whichever is greater. Cash award payments are made in the first and third quarters of each year based on corporate performance for the preceding two quarters. The plan also has a provision for rewarding employees for helping Intel achieve customer satisfaction goals under Intel's Customer Excellence Program, and this provision resulted in an extra day of pay for each employee in 2003. Cash award payments earned in 2003 totaled 18.4 days of pay per employee.

Profit Sharing Retirement Plans

Intel has both tax-qualified and non-qualified capital accumulation/retirement plans ("Profit Sharing Retirement Plans"). The tax-qualified plans are available to eligible employees in the U.S., and there are similar plans for certain of Intel's non-U.S. subsidiaries. The non-qualified plan is a supplemental, deferred compensation plan that provides eligible U.S. employees with the opportunity for contributions that could not be credited to their individual accounts under the qualified plan because of Tax Code limitations. The Profit Sharing Retirement Plans are defined contribution plans designed to accumulate retirement funds for employees, including executive officers, and to allow Intel to make contributions or allocations to those funds. Intel's contributions are made at its discretion and may vary with the company's financial performance, particularly revenue and income. Company contributions made under the plans vest beginning after three years of service in 20% annual increments until the employee is 100% vested after seven years. Additional company contributions made after the seven-year period are immediately vested. All company contributions are invested in a diversified equity portfolio. For 2003, Intel's discretionary contributions (including allocation of forfeitures) to the Profit Sharing Retirement Plans for all eligible employees, including executive officers, equaled 8% of eligible salary (which includes actual incentive payments as applicable). The Tax Code limits contributions to individual accounts for the qualified plan. Where Tax Code limits applied, Intel allocated the excess, up to 8% of eligible salary, to the non-qualified plan for eligible employees, including executive officers.

Stock Options

To reward and retain employees in a manner that best aligns employees' interests with stockholders' interests, Intel uses stock options as its primary incentive vehicle. The use of stock options was affirmed by Intel management and the Committee through the compensation philosophy analysis completed in March 2003, as being the best equity vehicle for Intel with its continued focus on growth and innovation. Stock options align employees' interests precisely with those of other stockholders, because when the price of the stock declines from the price at the grant date, the employee obtains no value. On the other hand, restricted stock vehicles have value to an employee regardless of the company's performance (unless the stock price falls to $0). If the stock price drops from the price at which restricted stock was granted, the restricted stock simply has less value. As an example, if our executives received restricted shares while the broad-based employee population received stock options, in a declining stock price environment, the broad-based employee population may be holding options having no value, because the market price would be below the exercise price, while the executives would be holding shares of restricted stock with a value equivalent to the then-current Intel stock price. Our belief in the egalitarian treatment of all employees caused us to decide against the use of equity vehicles that may differ between the executive officers and the broad-based employee population. Performance shares were also decided against due to the high level of pay-for-performance variability already included in the elements of our compensation program, the strong belief in the egalitarian treatment of all employees, and the fact that we believe that stock options directly link a portion of an employee's compensation to stockholders' interests by providing an incentive to maximize stockholder value over the long-term period. Unless stockholder value increases, stock options yield no increased compensation to the employees.

Intel's stock option programs are broad-based and in 2003, more than 90% of our full-time employees received stock option grants. Approximately 98% of the options covered by those grants went to employees other than the top five most highly compensated executive officers in 2003; for the period 1999 to 2003, only 1.2% of all options granted were granted to the top five most highly compensated executive officers. The percentage of stock option grants to the top five most highly paid executives is higher for 2003 than for the preceding five-year period as a result of infrequent long-term stock option grants to two executives. This percentage is expected to be lower in 2004. The Compensation Committee has established a policy that in any one year Intel may not grant more than 5% of total options granted to the Chief Executive Officer and the next four most highly compensated executive officers. (See the "Option Grants in Last Fiscal Year" table under the heading "Executive Compensation.")

Intel has two stock option plans under which it grants stock options. The stockholder-approved 1984 Stock Option Plan, as amended, expires in May 2004 and is generally used for making annual grants to officers and directors as a part of Intel's executive performance review process, and is also used for infrequently granted long-term executive performance incentive and retention grants. The 1997 Stock Option Plan, under which the majority of Intel's stock options are granted, is used for stock options that are granted to employees other than officers and directors, and is not a stockholder-approved plan. Annual stock option grants for executives are a key element of market-competitive total compensation. In 2003, the Committee approved annual stock option grants for the executive officers and long-term executive performance incentive and retention grants for two of the executive officers. Individual grant amounts were based on internal factors, such as the size of prior grants, relative job scope and contributions made during the past year, as well as a review of publicly available data on senior management compensation at other companies. The long-term executive performance incentive and retention grants are generally granted to an executive every six to seven years, vesting 25% annually beginning five or six years after the date of grant. These long-term incentive and retention grants are a critical component of the executive officer total compensation program. The delayed vesting of these grants requires focus on Intel's long-term performance and stock price appreciation.

In general, initial grants that employees receive when they begin employment at Intel are exercisable in 20% annual increments over a five-year period. Grants subsequent to hire generally become exercisable in 25% annual increments over a four-year period. Prior to 2003, grants subsequent to hire became exercisable five years after the date of grant (for example, options granted in 2002 become exercisable in 2007). The 2003 Committee-approved change of the standard vesting schedule to the linear format, in which 25% of a grant is vested each year over a four-year period, was made in the belief that it would make Intel's option grants more competitive with those of other companies and help reduce the effects of market price volatility on any grants vesting within any particular year. The impact of market price volatility is reduced by having, in a given year, a percentage of options granted over a period of several years, each vesting with a different grant price. Stock options under the 1984 and 1997 plans are granted at a price equal to the market price on the date of grant.

With the upcoming expiration of the 1984 Stock Option Plan, we are submitting for stockholder approval a new equity plan that upon approval will replace both the 1984 and 1997 Stock Option Plans. If stockholders approve the new equity plan, we will cancel any remaining shares available for grant under the 1997 Stock Option Plan and make no further grants from this plan. This new equity plan will be significantly shorter in duration than the existing plans—two years rather than the ten-year terms of the current plans—providing stockholders with more frequent opportunities to approve Intel's equity plan. The new equity plan will also allow for very limited use of additional equity vehicles in the future should the Committee determine that there is a need to do so; however, our intent is to continue to offer a broad-based stock option program.

Stockholding Guidelines

Because the Committee believes in linking the interests of management and stock-holders, the Board approved stockholding guidelines for Intel's executive officers in 2003. The holding guidelines specify a number of shares that the executive officers must accumulate and hold within five years of the later of the effective date of the program or the date of appointment as an officer. The specific share requirements are based on a multiple of annual target total cash compensation ranging from 3X to 5X, with the higher multiples applicable to Intel's executive officers having the highest levels of responsibility.

Personal Benefits

Intel seeks to maintain an egalitarian culture in its facilities and operations. Officers are not entitled to operate under different standards than other Intel employees. We do not provide officers with reserved parking spaces or separate dining or other facilities, nor do we have programs for providing personal-benefit perquisites to officers, such as permanent lodging or defraying the cost of personal entertainment or family travel. Our health care and other insurance programs are the same for all eligible employees, including officers. Our loan programs, although modest in nature, are not available to executive officers. There are no outstanding loans of any kind to any executive officer, and since 2002, federal law has prohibited any new company loans to executive officers. We expect our officers to be role models under our Corporate Business Principles, which are applicable to all employees, and officers are not entitled to operate under lesser standards.

Company Performance and CEO Compensation

Intel's compensation program is designed to promote the achievement of corporate and business objectives. This pay-for-performance program is most clearly exemplified in the compensation of our Chief Executive Officer, Dr. Barrett. Dr. Barrett's BSIT is determined in the same manner as described for all executive officers. In setting compensation levels for the Chief Executive Officer, the Committee considers comparative compensation information from other companies for the prior year. However, consistent with the Committee's general practice and discretionary authority, Dr. Barrett's 2003 salary and individual pay-for-performance incentive target were not tied directly to the comparative compensation data but set at levels believed to be below average. In January 2003, Dr. Barrett's base salary and pay-for-performance incentive target were set at levels that were 49% of the competitor company average for base salary, 35% of the competitor company average for target incentive-based compensation and 41% of the competitor company average for BSIT.

Under the EOIP, Dr. Barrett's actual pay-for-performance incentive for 2003 (paid in 2004) was $1,421,300. This incentive, like the incentives paid to each of the other executive officers under the EOIP, was less than the maximum amount payable under the EOIP formula. Although Dr. Barrett's BSIT was 41% of the average total target compensation disclosed by peer companies, due to the higher variability in Intel's total compensation program, his actual cash compensation (base salary and incentive) for 2003 was 71% of the average total actual cash compensation disclosed by the peer companies.

In 2003, the Committee awarded Dr. Barrett the following stock options: (1) a January 2003 long-term stock option grant to purchase 1,000,000 shares of stock, which becomes exercisable 25% annually in each of 2009 through 2012 and requires long-term stock price appreciation for Dr. Barrett to benefit from this grant, and (2) an April 2003 annual stock option grant to purchase 350,000 shares of stock, which becomes exercisable in 2004 through 2007 in 25% annual increments. Both the January 2003 and the April 2003 stock grants expire 10 years from the grant date. In 2003, Intel also contributed $16,000 to Dr. Barrett's account under the tax-qualified retirement plan and allocated $118,800 to Dr. Barrett's account under the non-qualified retirement plan. In general, Dr. Barrett's retirement plan accounts are available to Dr. Barrett only upon retirement or termination from Intel as an employee, or upon disability or death.

The Committee is pleased to submit this report to Intel's stockholders and believes that Intel's pay-for-performance executive compensation sets the standard for best-in-class executive compensation practices.

Compensation Committee:

Reed E. Hundt, Chairman   Winston H. Chen
E. John P. Browne   David S. Pottruck

GENERAL ELECTRIC COMPANY
COMPENSATION COMMITTEE REPORT

Each member of our management development and compensation committee is an independent director as determined by our board of directors, based on the New York Stock Exchange listing rules and GE's stricter independence guidelines. These independence rules and guidelines are discussed in Sections 4 and 7 of GE's corporate governance principles which are set forth in the Appendix of this proxy statement at pages 66 and 68. This committee's charter and key practices are published on the governance section of the GE website at www.ge.com.

We approve all of the policies under which compensation is paid or awarded to our executives, and individually review the performance of, and all compensation actions affecting, our senior executive officers—the chief executive officer, the vice chairmen and the senior vice presidents. We oversee and regularly evaluate the effectiveness of our overall executive compensation program. All stock-based long-term performance awards are made under the GE 1990 Long-Term Incentive Plan, which shareowners approved in 1990 and again in 1997. The plan limits total annual awards to less than 1% of issued shares. Historically, the committee has awarded only about half of the authorized amount.

• Executive Compensation Philosophy

Our key compensation goals are to hire, motivate, reward and retain executives who create long-term investor value. We use a variety of compensation elements to achieve these goals, including:

• salary and bonus: we pay salaries that are designed to attract and retain superior leaders, and we pay annual bonuses to reward exceptional performance;
• stock options and stock appreciation rights: we award these to provide incentives for superior long-term performance and to retain top executives because the awards are forfeited if the executive leaves before they become fully exercisable five years after grant;
• restricted stock units: we grant RSUs to more closely align executives' interests with investors' long-term interests, and to retain top executives because the awards are paid out only to executives who remain with the company for extended periods; and
• long-term performance awards: we use these to provide a strong incentive for achieving specific performance measurements over multi-year periods.

We discuss below how we have used these awards and a number of other steps to strengthen the alignment of our executives' interests with the long-term interests of investors and other stakeholders.

• Compensation Elements for Executive Officers

As noted above, the basic elements of our executive compensation approach are:

1. Salary and bonus. Salary is paid for ongoing performance throughout the year. Bonuses are paid in February for the prior year's performance and are based upon our evaluation of each executive officer's individual performance in the prior year in the context of our assessment of the overall performance of the company and the executive's business unit. This includes an assessment of the executive's contribution to the achievement of financial performance and other key goals we established for the company during the performance year. The salaries and bonuses we paid to our five most highly paid executive officers for the past three years are shown in the table on page 30.

2. Stock options and stock appreciation rights payable in stock (SARs). Stock options and SARs provide incentives for long-term superior performance and have the same economic value to the executive and the same cost to the company. Each stock option permits the executive to purchase one share of GE stock from the company at the market price of GE stock on the date of grant. SARs payable in stock permit the executive to receive shares of GE stock from the company equal in value to the difference between the price of GE stock on the day the SARs were granted and the price on the day they were exercised, multiplied by the number of SARs exercised. SARs are exercisable in five equal annual installments beginning one year after the grant date. The number of SARs granted to our five most highly paid executives in 2003, and the estimated grant date value of the awards, are shown in the table on page 29. The number of stock options and SARs granted to our five most highly paid executive officers in the last three years are shown in the table on page 31. Stock options granted during and after 2002 generally become exercisable in five equal annual installments beginning one year after the grant date. Stock options granted before 2002 generally become exercisable in two equal installments, three and five years after they were granted.

3. Restricted stock units (RSUs). We periodically make special RSU grants to key performers to provide strong incentives for continued superior service. RSUs are forfeited if the executive leaves GE prior to the lapse of restrictions, and the value of the RSU changes with the market value of GE stock. Each RSU entitles the executive to receive regular quarterly payments from the company equal to the quarterly dividend on one share of GE stock. Also, provided the executive is still employed by GE when the restrictions lapse, the executive will receive one share of GE stock from the company in exchange for each RSU. For most special RSUs granted during and after 2002, restrictions on 25% lapse after three, five and ten years, with the final 25% lapsing at retirement. For most special RSUs granted before 2002, restrictions on 25% lapse after three and seven years and the remaining 50% lapse at retirement.

In September 2003, for the first time, we granted annual RSUs in lieu of portion of our executives' regular annual stock option or SAR award. We discuss on page 24 our reasons for making these annual RSU grants. The RSUs granted annually in combination with stock options or SARs under this new policy have essentially the same terms and conditions as the special RSUs described above, except that the restrictions on half of these RSUs will lapse after three years, and the other half after five years. The grant date market value of all RSUs awarded in the last three years to the five most highly paid executive officers is shown in the table on page 31.

4. Contingent long-term performance awards. We also periodically grant contingent long-term performance awards to select operating managers and executives. These awards are based on the attainment of specific financial measurements over a three-year period, which are designed to enhance long-term shareowner value.

We granted these awards in 1994, 1997, 2000 and 2003. The table on page 31 shows the amounts paid last year to our five most highly paid executive officers under the 2000 award.

- Recent Executive Compensation Policy Actions

A. Actions Affecting Our Senior Executive Officers. We consider our CEO, vice chairmen and senior vice presidents to be our senior executive officers and have recently taken a number of actions to further align their interests with investor long-term interests.

    1. CEO five-year performance share units. As we explain in our discussion on page 25 of the basis for the compensation awards we made to Mr. Immelt last year, and summarized in the table on the next page, we granted him 250,000 five-year performance share units in September 2003 in lieu of stock options, SARs and RSUs, so that the performance share units were the only stock-based incentive we awarded to him in 2003. Half of the performance share units provide an incentive for sustained superior operating cash flow growth and the other half provide an incentive to produce long-term shareowner returns that exceed a broad market index. Each of the 125,000 performance share units linked to operating cash flow growth will entitle Mr. Immelt to receive one share of GE stock from the company in 2008 if GE's operating cash flow, adjusted to exclude the effect of unusual events, increases an average of 10% or more per year during the five-year period from 2003 through 2007. These performance share units will be cancelled if GE's operating cash flow growth fails to achieve the specified growth rate. Each of the 125,000 performance share units linked to broad market performance will entitle Mr. Immelt to receive one share of GE stock from the company in 2008 if GE's total shareowner return for the five-year period from 2003 through 2007 meets or exceeds the total share owner return of the S&P 500 for the same period. These performance share units will be cancelled if GE's total shareowner return is less than the S&P 500 total shareowner return for the period. For this purpose, "total shareowner return" means the cumulative total return on GE stock and the S&P 500 index, respectively, from December 31, 2002 to December 31, 2007, calculated in the same manner as the five-year performance graph on page 32 of this proxy statement. Mr. Immelt will receive quarterly cash payments on each performance share unit equal to GE's quarterly per share dividend.

Long-Term Incentive Plans—Awards in Last Fiscal Year

Name	Number of Units	Performance Period Until Payout	Maximum Future Payout
Jeffrey R. Immelt	250,000	2003–2007	250,000 Shares

In summary, Mr. Immelt will receive no shares in 2008 if the company fails to meet or exceed both targets for cash flow growth and total shareholder return. He will receive 125,000 shares if the company meets or exceeds only one of the two performance targets. He will receive 250,000 shares only if the company meets or exceeds both performance targets.

2. Stock option holding period. In 2002, we decided that senior executives should be required to hold for at least one year the net shares of our stock that they receive by exercising stock options. For this purpose, "net shares" means the number of shares obtained by exercising stock options, less the number of shares the executive sells: (a) to cover the exercise price of the options; and (b) to pay the company withholding taxes.

3. SARs payable in stock. In September 2003, in lieu of stock options, we granted our vice chairmen and senior vice presidents SARs payable only in GE stock. As described on page 21, these SARs have the same economic value to the senior executive, and the same cost to the company, as stock options, but are payable only in shares of GE stock. The senior executives will also pay the same taxes for SAR exercises as they would for stock option exercises, and grants and exercises of these awards will be publicly reported in the same manner as stock options. SARs payable in stock enable the company to deliver to the senior executive the number of "net shares" that the senior executive would have retained after exercising the same number of stock options and selling enough shares to cover the exercise price and withholding taxes. This will facilitate the senior executive's compliance with the holding period requirement described above, which we also apply to SAR exercises, by delivering only the "net shares" that he or she will be required to hold for at least one year, and will also result in less dilution when exercised because fewer shares will be issued to the executive.

4. Stock ownership requirement. In 2002, we established the following stock ownership requirements, as a multiple of the executive's base salary, that must be held by senior executive officers:

Position	Multiple	Time to Attain
CEO	6X	3 years
Vice Chairmen	5X	4 years
Senior VPs	4X	5 years

The number of shares of GE stock that must be held is determined by multiplying the executive's annual base salary rate in September 2002, when the requirement was adopted by the board, or, for senior executives elected after September 2002, their base salary rate at the end of the month in which they were elected to a senior executive position, by the applicable multiple shown above and dividing the result by the average closing price of our stock during the immediately preceding 12 months. The number of shares to be held will change only if the executive is promoted into a higher level position. In 2003, Mr. Immelt acquired over 425,000 shares of GE stock, including over 293,000 shares he bought in the open market with his own funds or elected to receive in GE stock from a long-term award payout. He currently owns over 600,000 shares of GE stock, more than satisfying his stock ownership requirement.

B. Actions Affecting All Executive Compensation Grants. In addition to the actions described above with respect to our senior executive officers, we have also recently taken the following actions that affect executive compensation awards made to those executives and to all other executives as well.

1. Stock option/RSU grants. In September 2003, we decided to replace 40% of the estimated value of new grants of stock options or SARs with RSUs on a basis intended to provide comparable value to the executive at a comparable cost to the company. RSUs will result in less dilution because we grant fewer RSUs than the number of options they replace in view of the fact that, when granted, RSUs have more value than stock options. Also, RSUs are effective incentives for our superior performers to remain with the company and continue that performance during periods of stock market fluctuations, when stock options may have no realizable value. The cost of combined grants of stock options and RSUs is comparable to the cost of granting only stock options or SARs.

2. Expensing stock options. In 2002, we recommended, and our full board approved, the policy of expensing stock options to respond to investor views that this would improve the transparency of our financial statements.

3. Prohibition on repricing stock options. In 2002, we also reaffirmed our long-standing policy of prohibiting the repricing of stock options.

• Factors We Considered in Making Specific Compensation Decisions

As in prior years, all of our judgments regarding executive compensation last year were based primarily upon our assessment of each executive officer's leadership performance and potential to enhance long-term shareowner value. We rely upon judgment and not upon rigid guidelines or formulas or short-term changes in our stock price in determining the amount and mix of compensation elements for each executive officer.

Key factors affecting our judgments included the nature and scope of the executive officers' responsibilities, their effectiveness in leading our initiatives to increase customer value, productivity and growth, and their success in creating a culture of unyielding integrity and compliance with applicable law and our ethics policies. We also considered the compensation levels and performances of a comparison group of major companies that are most likely to compete with us for the services of executive officers.

Based upon all the factors we considered relevant, and in light of our strong financial and operating performance in an extraordinarily challenging global economic environment, we believe it was in your best long-term interest for us to ensure that the overall level of our salary, bonus and other incentive compensation awards was competitive with companies in the comparison group. Quite simply, we continue to believe that the quality, skills and dedication of our executive leaders are critical factors affecting the long-term value of our company. Therefore, we continue to try to maintain an executive compensation program that will attract, motivate and retain the highest level of executive leadership possible.

Our decisions concerning the specific 2003 compensation elements for individual executive officers, including the chief executive officer, were made within this framework and after consultation with an executive compensation expert. We also considered each executive officer's level of responsibility, performance, current salary, prior-year bonus and other compensation awards. As noted above, in all cases our specific decisions involving 2003 executive officer compensation were ultimately based upon our judgment about the individual executive officer's performance and potential future contributions—and about whether each particular payment or award would provide an appropriate incentive and reward for performance that sustains and enhances long-term shareowner value.

- Basis for Chief Executive Officer Compensation

For 2003, we paid Mr. Immelt $3,000,000 in salary, which is the annual salary rate that has been in effect for him since April 2001. We also paid him a cash bonus of $4,325,000 for 2003, a 10.9% increase over his bonus for 2002.

We considered this level of pay and bonus appropriate for the following reasons: his execution of our strategy to change our portfolio of businesses to enhance long-term investor value through better profit margins and higher returns on equity; his actions to ensure that the company has a strong capital structure and cash flow; his role in leading us to solid financial results in an extremely challenging global economic environment; his actions in making the company a leader in integrity, transparency and corporate governance; and his leadership in driving growth initiatives and reorganizing our businesses around markets to simplify our operations and strengthen our relationships with our customers.

In September 2003 we granted Mr. Immelt 250,000 performance share units in lieu of stock options, SARs and restricted stock units. These performance share units are intended to recognize the unique position of the GE CEO. The committee believes that the CEO of GE needs no retention compensation, and that his equity compensation should be focused entirely on performance and alignment with investors. As described more fully above in our discussion at page 22 of recent changes in our executive compensation policies, 125,000 of the performance share units will convert into shares of GE stock only if GE's cash flow from operating activities has grown an average of 10% or more per year over the five-year period from 2003 through 2007. The remaining 125,000 performance share units will convert into GE stock only if GE's total shareowner return meets or exceeds that of the S&P 500 over that period. If one or both performance criteria are not met, the associated performance share units will be cancelled.

Linking 50% of Mr. Immelt's 2003 equity award directly to the company's cash generation performance underscores GE's commitment to strong operating discipline, our triple-A rating and the GE dividend. The remaining 50% of the equity award is based solely on successfully delivering to GE's shareholders total returns equal to or better than the broader market. When these awards were granted last September, 250,000 shares of GE stock had a market value of about $7.5 million, which means that the performance share units had a grant date value of either zero, about $3.75 million or about $7.5 million, depending on whether neither, one or both performance criteria are ultimately met. In other words, the full value of that grant is at risk, based on GE's cash flow performance and GE stock price performance from 2003 through 2007.

In 2003, we also granted Mr. Immelt, and certain other executives, a three-year contingent performance incentive award. The awards will be payable only if the company achieves, on an overall basis for the three-year 2003-2005 period, specified goals for one or more of the following four measurements, all as adjusted by the committee to remove the effects of unusual events and the effect of pensions on income: average earnings per share growth rate; average revenue growth rate; average return on total capital; and cumulative cash generated. In summary, more than 75% of Mr. Immelt's potential compensation for 2003 was at risk, including his bonus, these three-year contingent performance incentive awards and the performance share units we granted to Mr. Immelt last September.

****

The foregoing report on executive compensation for 2003 is provided by the undersigned members of the management development and compensation committee of the board of directors.

Ralph S. Larsen (Chairman)	Andrew C. Sigler
Claudio X. Gonzalez	Douglas A. Warner III
Andrea Jung	

Glossary

ABA.   Abbreviation for *American Bar Association.*

Accounting Principles Board (APB).   A board convened in 1959 by the American Institute of Certified Public Accountants (AICPA) to determine and publish accounting principles. This group was terminated in 1973 and replaced by the Financial Accounting Standards Board (FASB). All opinions of the APB remain in effect unless superseded by FASB announcements.

accredited investors.   Sophisticated investors who, under the securities laws, can participate in private placements of unregistered securities. Individuals fall into this category if they have certain wealth and income characteristics, such as a net worth (alone or with a spouse) of $1 million.

accrued compensation expense.   Incurred and charged expense that has not yet been paid. This expense would be reflected on the balance sheet and will show on the income statement.

actuarial assumptions.   An actuary's prediction of future measures that will have an impact on pension cost. Examples include life expectancy, investment returns, inflation, and mortality rates.

actuary.   Mathematician employed by a life insurance company or consulting firm to calculate life insurance premiums, reserves, policy dividend payments, insurance, pension amounts, pension balances, annuity rates, and the like, using mortality rates and other risk factors obtained from experience. These experience tables of mortality are based on mortality and life insurance claims.

ADEA.   Abbreviation for *Age Discrimination in Employment Act of 1967.*

ADR.   Abbreviation for *American depositary receipt.*

affiliate.   An individual in a position to influence corporate policies. Includes directors, officers, 10% or more owners, members of families that own more than 10%, and close associates of these groups. The term often applies to people who live in the same household. Restrictions and reporting requirements on company stock sales under Rule 144 under the Securities Act of 1933 apply to affiliates. Also known as a "control persons."

AFL-CIO.   Voluntary federation of America's labor unions, formed in 1955 by the merger of the American Federation of Labor and the Congress of Industrial Organizations.

AFR.   Abbreviation for *applicable federal rate.*

Age Discrimination in Employment Act (ADEA) of 1967 (amended 1978, 1986, and 1990). Makes nonfederal employees age 40 and over a protected class relative to treatment in pay, benefits, and other personnel actions. The 1990 amendment is called the *Older Workers Benefit Protection Act.*

agency theory. A theory of motivation that depicts exchange relationships in terms of two parties: agents and principals. According to the theory, both sides of the exchange will seek the most favorable exchange possible, and will act opportunistically if given a chance. As applied to executive compensation, agency theory expects the executive (agent) to act in the best interests of the shareholders (principals), rather than in the executive's own self-interests.

agent. Individual authorized by another person, called the principal, to act on the latter's behalf in transactions involving a third party. In a corporation, the agent is management, and the principal is the board (which is elected by the owners). Agents (management) have three basic characteristics: (1) they act on behalf of and are subject to the control of the principal (board or shareholders); (2) they do not have title to the principal's (shareholders') property; and (3) they owe the duty of obedience to the principal's (board's) orders.

aggregate exercise price. The exercise or strike price of an option times the number of underlying securities subject to the option.

alternative minimum tax (AMT). An alternative method of calculating income tax liability that requires the taxpayer to include in his or her taxable income certain tax preference items that are deductible under the regular income tax rules.

American Bar Association (ABA). An association of the legal profession in the United States.

American depositary receipt (ADR). Receipt for the shares of a foreign-based corporation held in the care of a U.S. bank and entitling the shareholder to all dividends and capital gains of the stock. Instead of buying shares directly on the foreign stock exchange, ADR shareholders buy shares in the United States in the form of an ADR. ADRs are available on hundreds of stocks on numerous exchanges. The SEC requires limited disclosure for ADRs. ADRs are also called *"American depositary shares."*

American Institute of Certified Public Accountants (AICPA). The national, professional organization for all certified public accountants. Its mission is to supply members with the resources, information, and leadership that enable them to provide valuable services in the highest professional manner, to benefit the public as well as employers and clients.

American option. An option contract that may be exercised at any time between the date of purchase or vesting date and the expiration date of the option.

American Stock Exchange (AMEX). An open-auction market similar to the New York Stock Exchange, where buyers and sellers compete in a centralized marketplace. The AMEX typically lists small- to medium-cap stocks of younger or smaller companies. Until 1921 it was known as the New York Cumulative Exchange. The AMEX merged with Nasdaq in the late 1990s.

AMEX. Abbreviation for *American Stock Exchange.*

AMT. Abbreviation for *alternative minimum tax.*

analyst. Person in a brokerage house, bank trust department, or mutual fund group who studies a number of companies and makes buy or sell recommendations on the securities of particular companies and industry groups.

annual incentive. A lump-sum payment (cash, stock, etc.) made in addition to base salary for a fiscal year, based on achievement of performance goals.

annual meeting. Once-a-year meeting where the managers of a company report to shareholders on the year's results directors stand for election for the next year. The chief executive officer usually comments on the outlook for the coming year and, with other senior executives, answers questions from shareholders. Shareholders can also request that all those owning stock in the company vote on resolutions regarding corporate policy. Shareholders unable to attend the annual meeting may vote for directors and other proposals through the use of proxy material, which is legally required to be mailed to all shareholders of record.

annual report. A publication that is issued yearly by all publicly held corporations and is freely available to all shareholders. It reveals the company's assets, liabilities, revenues, expenses, and earnings for the past year, along with other financial data. This is often accompanied by a glossy presentation of the company's achievements and philosophy, but it is the accounting information that is required by law to allow investors to gauge the financial health of the company.

annuity. A contract sold by life insurance companies that guarantees a fixed or variable payment to the annuitant at some future time, usually retirement. In a fixed annuity, the amount will ultimately be paid out in regular installments, varying with the payout method elected. In a variable annuity, the payout is based on a guaranteed number of units; unit values and payments depend on the value of the underlying investments. All capital in the annuity grows tax-deferred. Key considerations when buying an annuity are the financial soundness of the insurance company, the returns it has paid in the past, and the levels of fees and commissions.

APB. Abbreviation for *Accounting Principles Board.*

applicable federal rate (AFR). Interest rates, which are published monthly, set by the U.S. Treasury for determining imputed interest and for other specified purposes.

appreciation. Increase in value of an asset (typically the price of publicly traded stock).

appreciation rights. The right to receive the appreciation in value of an instrument (typically common stock) over time, which appreciation can be paid in the form of cash or stock.

arbitrage. A technique used by stock traders, now aided by sophisticated computer programs, to profit from minute price differences for the same security on different markets.

arm's-length transaction. An exchange between parties who are independent of each other, and who are acting in their own best interests.

articles of incorporation (also called certificate of incorporation or charter). Document filed with a U.S. state by the founders of a corporation setting forth such information as the corporation's legal name, business purpose, number of authorized shares, and number and identity of directors. The corporation's powers derive from the laws of the state of incorporation and the provisions of the charter.

attestation. An affidavit or declaration of share ownership by which an option holder exercising an option by a stock swap can avoid surrendering a physical stock certificate for the shares used to exercise the option.

audit report. Often called the "accountant's opinion"; the statement of the auditor as to whether the company's financial statements present fairly the results of its operations in conformity with GAAP.

average.   Arithmetic mean of reported data; sum of the values divided by the number of cases.

balance sheet.   A financial statement that shows total assets, total liabilities, and owners' equity. Also referred to as a "statement of financial position."

Barone-Adesi and Whaley value.   The value derived by a method for pricing tradable call options on dividend-paying stock. Uses the stock price, the exercise price, the risk-free interest rate, the time to expiration, the expected standard deviation of the stock return, and the dividend yield. Developed by Giovanni Barone-Adesi and Robert E. Whaley. See Giovanni Barone-Adesi and Robert E. Whaley, "Efficient Analytic Approximation of American Option Values," *Journal of Finance* 42 (1987): 301–320.

base salary.   A major element of compensation; the basic compensation that an employer pays for work performed. Tends to reflect the value of work itself and typically ignores differences in individual contributions.

basis.   See *tax basis*.

bear.   An investor who believes that a stock price or the overall market will decline. A bear market is a prolonged period of falling stock prices, usually by 20% or more.

bear market.   Any market in which prices are in a declining trend, usually accompanied by a drop in stock prices of 20% or more.

bearish.   A viewpoint that anticipates a price decline, referring either to an individual security or to the entire market.

benchmarking.   A company's use of information about other firms in the same industry; used for comparisons and to set standards and goals.

beneficial owner.   For most purposes under the federal securities laws, any person or entity with sole or shared power to vote or dispose of the stock. This SEC definition is intended to include a holder who enjoys the economic benefits of ownership although the shares may be held in another's name. For example, one spouse is generally deemed the beneficial owner of shares held by the other spouse.

best pay practices.   Compensation practices that allow employers to gain preferential access to superior human resources talent, which in turn influences the strategies the organization adopts.

beta.   A mathematical measure of the sensitivity of rates of return on a stock compared with the broader stock market. Higher betas indicate higher stock price volatility. In specific, a coefficient measuring a stock's relative volatility. The beta is a covariance of the stock in relation to the rest of the stock market. The Standard & Poor's 500 Stock Index has a beta coefficient of 1. Any stock with a higher beta is more volatile than the market, and any with a lower beta can be expected to rise and fall more slowly than the market. A conservative investor whose main concern is preservation of capital should focus on stocks with low betas, whereas one willing to take high risks in an effort to earn high rewards should look for high-beta stocks.

binomial option pricing model.   A model for pricing stock options. Fundamental to the binomial option pricing model is the idea that stock price movements are well approximated by assuming the stock price can only move to two possible values in a short interval of time. A price tree is constructed that describes the probability of future stock price movements.

Black-Scholes model. A "closed" option pricing model that incorporates both the intrinsic value (the spread in the option) and the time value of the option (the term of the option) to determine the option's total market value.

blackout period. A period of time prior to the release of annual or quarterly financial information by a publicly held company during which insiders are restricted from trading the company's stock.

BLS. Abbreviation for *Bureau of Labor Statistics.*

blue chip. Common stock of a nationally known company that has a long record of profit growth and dividend payments and a reputation for quality management, products, and services. Examples of blue-chip stocks include IBM, General Electric, and DuPont. Blue-chip stocks typically are relatively high priced and low yielding.

blue sky laws. A popular name for various state laws enacted to protect the public against securities fraud.

board of directors. The governing body of a corporation, as elected by the shareholders. Among other things, the board of directors has the power to appoint the corporation's officers, to appoint committees, to issue shares of stock, to grant equity awards, and to adopt stock plans.

board of trustees. A group of people responsible for the oversight of a nonprofit organization.

bonus plan. An annual program established to regulate the funding and distribution of annual or short-term cash bonus payments. Also referred to as "short-term incentive plan."

book-value stock (BVS). Stock for which the value is based on a formula such as book value.

book-value stock option (BVSO). Options for which the exercise price is based on a formula such as book value.

broad-banding. A compensation strategy that collapses salary grades or classes into a few salary bands. The bands are usually 70% to 150% wide and encompass numerous occupational groups at a comparable organizational level. Broad-bands are often used to support skill/competency-based or -influenced pay programs. The effect of broad-banding is to shift the focus from vertical to horizontal career movement and place more responsibility for salary administration at the manager level.

budget. A plan or a schedule that a businessperson seeks to meet. Also, a standard against which managers' actual expenditures, revenue, or profit are evaluated.

Bureau of Labor Statistics (BLS). The principal fact-finding agency for the federal government in the broad field of labor economics and statistics. The BLS is a major source of compensation data. It also publishes the Consumer Price Index.

burn rate. The percentage of options a company grants per year of either the total number of options authorized or shares outstanding.

buy-sell agreement. An arrangement between two or more parties that obligates one party to buy the business and another party to sell the business upon the death, disability, or retirement of one of the owners.

bylaws. Rules governing the management of an organization, which are usually prepared at the time of incorporation. The bylaws, which usually can be amended by the board, cover such points as the election of directors, the appointment of executive and finance committees, the duties of officers, and how share transfers may be made.

cafeteria benefit plan.   A benefit plan that gives employees a choice as to the benefits they receive, within some dollar limit. Usually a common core benefit package is required (e.g., specific minimum levels of health, disability, retirement, and death benefit) plus elective programs from which the employee may elect a set dollar amount. Additional coverage may be available through employee contributions. Also referred to as a "flexible benefit plan."

call option (call).   A derivative security giving the holder the right to buy the underlying securities at a fixed price. An employee stock option is a type of call option, in that the employee has the right to buy the stock at a fixed price for a set number of years (see *put option*).

capital.   Permanent money invested in a business. Also can mean the long-term assets of a company.

Capital Asset Pricing Model (CAPM).   A model used to evaluate a publicly held stock. The underlying principle of the model is that investors demand a return that equals the risk-free rate of return plus a nominal risk premium for equity investment times the risk factor (beta) of the particular stock. In other words, higher investor risk requires higher investor return.

capital gain (loss).   Profit (or loss) from the sale of a capital asset. Capital gains may be short term (held 12 months or less) or long term (held more than 12 months). Capital losses are used to offset capital gains to establish a net position for tax purposes.

capital loss limitation.   Net long-term capital losses and net short-term capital losses may be used to offset up to $3,000 of ordinary income. To reach the net amounts to determine deductibility, total all capital gains and losses. Amounts of more than $3,000 can be carried forward to future years until all of the net capital losses are used.

CAPM.   Abbreviation for *Capital Asset Pricing Model.*

carried interest.   Total shares in which the owner or option holder has an interest or financial stake in the appreciation of the value of the company.

cash balance pension plan.   A defined benefit plan that maintains individual employee accounts like a defined contribution plan.

cash flow.   Total funds that are generated internally for investment and working capital. Cash flow is often calculated as operating profits (e.g., profits before interest, taxes, depreciation, and amortization).

cash surrender value.   The amount that an insurance policyholder is entitled to receive when he or she discontinues coverage. Policyholders are usually able to borrow against the surrender value of a policy from the insurance company. Loans that are not repaid will reduce the policy's death benefit.

cashless exercise/same-day sale.   A brokerage transaction in which an option holder exercises a stock option and simultaneously sells some or all of the shares, with a portion of the sale proceeds delivered to the company by the broker to pay the exercise price.

CBOE.   Abbreviation for *Chicago Board Options Exchange.*

CBOT.   Abbreviation for *Chicago Board of Trade.*

CEO.   Abbreviation for *chief executive officer.*

certified public accountant (CPA). An accountant who has met specified professional requirements established by the AICPA and local state societies. A key service provided by CPAs is the performance of independent audits of financial statements for publicly traded companies.

CFO. Abbreviation for *chief financial officer.*

chairman (chair). Sometimes referred to as "Chairman of the Board." A member of a corporation's board of directors who presides over its meetings and who is the highest-ranking officer in the corporation. The chairman may or may not have the most actual executive authority in a company.

change in control (CIC) of ownership agreement. A contractual agreement that provides certain guarantees to the covered executive when ownership of the company changes as specified by a CIC trigger. This is sometimes referred to "change of control (COC) of ownership," although CIC is the prevalent term.

charitable remainder trust. Involves the irrevocable transfer of assets, such as company stock, to a trust. The income stream from the assets goes to an individual or individuals (who may include the transferee of the assets); a qualified charity receives the assets at the expiration of the trust period.

The contributor of the assets receives a charitable tax deduction at the time of the transfer, equal to the present value of the charity's remainder interest. The transferred property will escape federal estate tax, as it is removed from the donor's estate.

cheap stock. Stock options granted to employees at a low exercise price relative to a planned IPO offering price. The SEC will require an IPO company to take an earnings charge as a compensation expense for part of the spread between the exercise price and the offering price.

Chicago Board of Trade (CBOT). Formed in 1948 as a central marketplace for the midwestern grain trade, the CBOT is now the oldest and largest futures exchange in the world.

Chicago Board Options Exchange (CBOE). Founded in 1973, the CBOE was established for the trading of call options on listed stock.

chief executive officer (CEO). The officer of a company principally responsible for its activities and performance. The CEO often holds the additional title of chairman of the board and/or president.

chief financial officer (CFO). The executive officer who is responsible for handling funds, signing checks, keeping financial records, and financial planning for the company. The CFO is in charge of accounting, finance, budgeting, tax, and cash management functions of a company.

chief operating officer (COO). The officer of a company principally responsible for day-to-day management. The COO reports to the CEO.

CIC. Abbreviation for *"change in control."*

Civil Rights Act. Title VII of the Civil Rights Act of 1964 prohibits discrimination in terms and conditions of employment (including benefits), based on race, color, religion, sex, or national origin.

Civil Rights Act of 1991. Reestablishes the standards for proving discrimination, which had been in general use before the 1989 Supreme Court rulings. Allows jury trials and damage awards.

classified board. A corporate board structure in which only a portion of the board of directors is elected each year, often used to discourage takeover attempts.

closing price. The last price paid for a security on any trading day.

COBRA. Abbreviation for *Consolidated Omnibus Budget Reconciliation Act.*

COC. Abbreviation for change of control. See *change in control.*

Code. Abbreviation for *Internal Revenue Code.*

coefficient of correlation (r). Measures the strength of a relationship between the independent and dependent variables in a *regression* (e.g., an element of compensation and revenues). This figure of merit ranges from –1 to 1. A correlation of 0 denotes that there is no relationship between the independent and dependent variables. A correlation of –1 denotes that there is a perfect inverse relationship, and a correlation of +1 denotes that there is a perfect positive relationship.

coefficient of determination (r²). Measures the ability of the *regression* to explain the variance in a regression. It is equal to the square of the *coefficient of correlation.*

COLA. Abbreviation for *cost of living adjustment.*

COLI. Abbreviation for *corporate-owned life insurance.*

common stock. Units of ownership of a corporation. Common shareholders are typically entitled to vote on the selection of directors and other matters. Distinguished from *preferred stock,* which generally has more favorable dividend and liquidation rights, although often has more limited voting rights.

compa-ratio. An index that helps assess how managers actually pay employees in relation to the midpoint of the pay ranges established for jobs. It estimates how well actual practices correspond to intended policy.

compensable factors. Job attributes that provide the basis for evaluating the relative worth of jobs inside an organization. A compensable factor must be work related, business related, and acceptable to the parties involved.

compensation. All forms of financial returns and tangible services and benefits employees receive as part of an employment relationship. Compensation elements include salary, bonus, long-term incentive, health and welfare benefits, pension entitlements, and perquisites.

compensation committee. At many companies, a committee of the board of directors, generally made up of outside directors, that is responsible for executive compensation matters, including stock plans. In public companies, the committee's report on executive compensation appears in the proxy statement each year.

competency. Basic units of knowledge and abilities employees are expected to acquire or demonstrate in order to successfully perform the work, satisfy customers, and achieve business objectives.

compression. Narrow pay differentials among jobs at different levels as a result of wages for jobs filled from the outside increasing faster than the internal pay structure.

Consolidated Omnibus Budget Reconciliation Act (COBRA).   A federal law requiring employers with more than 20 employees to offer terminated or retired employees the opportunity to continue their health insurance coverage for 18 months at the employee's expense. Coverage may be extended to the employee's dependents for 36 months in the case of divorce or death of the employee.

constructive receipt.   Refers to the time that compensation is taxable to the employee because he or she has control over and access to the payment.

constructive sale.   Tax term referring to when the IRS recharacterizes as a sale a transaction that eliminates the risk of loss and the opportunity for gain. This concept, which first appeared in the 1997 Taxpayer Relief Act, eliminated certain long-term stock hedging strategies, such as short-against-the-box and many equity swaps.

Consumer Price Index (CPI).   An index published by the Bureau of Labor Statistics U.S. Department of Labor. The CPI measures the changes in prices of a fixed basket of goods and services purchased by a typical average family.

control stock.   Stock held by affiliates, which is subject to sale restrictions under Rule 144.

COO.   Abbreviation for *chief operating officer.*

corporate governance.   The relationship between the shareholders, directors, and management of a company, as defined by the corporate charter, bylaws, formal policy, and rule of law.

corporate owned life insurance (COLI).   An insurance policy of which an organization is the owner and beneficiary. Should the insured executive die while covered, the company pays a comparable noninsured sum to selected survivors. Policy loans associated with the insurance are accessible to the organization.

cost of living adjustment (COLA).   Across-the-board wage and salary increases or supplemental payments based on changes in some index of prices, usually the Consumer Price Index. If included in a union contract or an employment agreement, COLA adjustments will automatically increase compensation levels for the life of the contract/agreement.

Council of Institutional Investors.   Founded in 1985, the Council of Institutional Investors (CII) is an organization of large public, Taft-Hartley and corporate pension funds formed to address investment issues that affect the size or security of plan assets.

covered employee.   Under Internal Revenue Code Section 162(m)(3), any employee of a company who, as of the close of a taxable year, is the CEO of the company (or an individual acting in such capacity), or whose total compensation for the taxable year is required to be reported to shareholders under the Securities Exchange Act of 1934 by reason of such employee being among the four highest compensated officers for the taxable year.

CPA.   Abbreviation for *certified public accountant.*

CPI.   Abbreviation for *Consumer Price Index.*

credited service.   A length of employment prior to or subsequent to the effective plan date that is recognized as service for plan purposes. This would include such issues as determination of benefit amounts, benefits entitlement, and/or vesting.

cumulative voting.   A method of stock voting that permits shareholders to cast all votes for one candidate. A voting system that gives minority shareholders more power, by allowing them to cast all of their board-of-director votes for a single candidate, as opposed to regular or statutory voting, in which shareholders must vote for a different candidate for each available seat.

current ratio.   Current assets divided by current liabilities. This ratio measures liquidity as it measures a company's ability to pay current liabilities from current assets.

CUSIP.   The trademark for a system that uniquely identifies securities trading in the United States. It was developed in the late 1960s by the American Bankers Association as a way to standardize the identification and tracking of securities. The CUSIP number consists of nine digits—the first six identify the issuer and the last three identify the issue. CUSIP numbers are a trademark of the American Bankers Association.

Davis-Bacon Act of 1931.   Requires most federal contractors to pay wage rates prevailing in the area where the work is performed.

DCF.   Abbreviation for *discounted cash flow*.

dead-hand poison pill.   An antitakeover device designed to prevent the acquisition of a company even if a majority of shareholders favor the acquisition. Dead-hand poison pills can be removed only by incumbent directors or their chosen successors.

deferred compensation.   Earned compensation that is payable in the future. May include contributions to retirement plans.

deferred compensation program.   Provides income to an employee at some future time as compensation for work performed now.

defined benefit pension plan.   A pension plan that promises to pay a specified amount to each person who retires after a set number of years of service. Such plans pay no taxes on their investments. In almost all cases, the employer makes all contributions to this plan.

defined contribution pension plan.   Pension plan that specifies the employer's contribution based on a formula that includes such factors as age, length of service, employer's profits, and compensation levels. FASB Statement No. 87 does not deal with these types of plans except for disclosure requirements. The pension expense is the amount funded each year.

Department of Labor (DOL).   A department in the U.S. executive branch, responsible for the administration and enforcement of more than 180 federal statutes. These legislative mandates and the regulations produced to implement them cover a wide variety of workplace activities for nearly 10 million employers and well over 100 million workers. In specific, the DOL protects workers' wages, health and safety, employment and pension rights; equal employment opportunity; job training, unemployment insurance, and workers' compensation programs. It also collects, analyzes, and publishes labor and economic statistics.

Depository Trust Company (DTC).   The world's largest securities depository, with more than $10 trillion of securities in custody. DTC is a national clearinghouse for the settlement of trade in corporate and municipal securities and performs securities custody-related services for its participating banks and broker-dealers.

derivative security.   An option, warrant, convertible security, stock appreciation right, or similar right with an exercise or conversion privilege at a price related to an *equity security,* or similar securities with a value derived from the value of an equity security.

dilution. Refers to the effect that the grant of equity awards has upon the other share-holders of a company. For example, each time an option is granted, an existing share-holder's ownership interest in the company is potentially reduced, because at exercise, the value of the stock is greater than the cash paid to exercise the option. In effect, this results in a transfer of economic value from existing shareholders to the option holder.

direct compensation. Pay received directly in the form of cash (e.g., salary and annual bonus).

director. Person elected by shareholders, usually during an annual meeting, to serve on the board of directors of a corporation. The directors appoint the president, vice presidents, and all other operating officers. Directors decide, among other matters, if and when dividends shall be paid.

directors and officers (D&O) liability insurance. Professional liability coverage for legal expenses and liability to shareholders, bondholders, creditors, or others due to actions or omissions by a director or officer of a corporation or nonprofit organization.

discount stock option. The opposite of premium options; discount stock options have an exercise price *below* market value at the time of grant. They are often used when cash compensation is to be deferred by converting it into stock options.

discounted cash flow (DCF). Present value of future expected cash flow. The discount rate is an important factor in this analysis. The accuracy and validity of a DCF analysis diminish with the time horizon of the analysis, because the discount rate and/or the future cash flow will be more likely to deviate from estimated amounts.

discretionary bonus. An informal incentive award not based on a performance-related formula or specific measurable criteria.

disqualifying disposition (of incentive stock options). A sale, gift, or exchange of ISO shares within two years from the grant date or one year from the exercise date. Upon a disqualifying disposition, the employee recognizes taxable ordinary income, and the company is entitled to claim a deduction equal to the excess of the fair market value on the exercise date or the sale price, whichever is lower, over the exercise price.

dividend. The payment designated by the board of directors to be distributed pro rata among the shares outstanding. For preferred shares, the dividend is usually a fixed amount. For common shares, the dividend varies with the fortunes of the company and the amount of cash on hand, and may be omitted if business is poor or if the directors determine to with-hold earnings to invest in plant and equipment. Sometimes, a company will pay a dividend out of past earnings even if it is not currently operating at a profit.

dividend equivalent rights. The right to be credited with cash or additional shares under a stock option or other stock award for the value of dividends that the company has paid on its shares while the option or award is outstanding.

DJIA. Abbreviation for *Dow Jones Industrial Average.*

D&O. Abbreviation for directors & officers. Usually used in context of *D&O liability insurance.*

DOL. Abbreviation for *Department of Labor.*

dollar cost averaging. A system of buying securities at regular intervals with a fixed dollar amount. Under this system, investors buy by the dollars' worth rather than by the number of shares. If each investment is of the same number of dollars, payments buy more shares when the price is low and fewer when it rises. Temporary downswings in price benefit investors if they continue periodic purchases in both good times and bad and the price at which the shares are sold is more than their average cost.

double trigger. A term used in connection with a change in control of ownership; refers to how a CIC, together with a subsequent event, such as termination of the employee by the company or termination by the employee for good reason, might trigger accelerated vesting of a stock option or other benefits. A *double* trigger means that vesting or payment will not occur until the second event takes place.

Dow Jones Industrial Average (DJIA). An index used to measure the performance of the U.S. financial markets. Introduced on May 26, 1896, by Charles H. Dow, it is the oldest stock price measure in continuous use. Over the past century, "the Dow" has become the most widely recognized stock market indicator in the United States and probably in the world.

DTC. Abbreviation for *Depository Trust Company.*

due diligence. An investigation into the financial, legal, and business affairs of a company undertaken by the underwriters and their counsel prior to a public offering by the company, or by the buyer in the purchase of a company.

early exercisable options. Options that are immediately exercisable (i.e., before vesting), but that typically do not start vesting until six months to a year after grant. The underlying shares received at exercise are restricted and subject to a repurchase right by the company at the exercise price until they are vested. Early exercise starts the capital gain clock ticking for a later resale. No gains are realized on the spread from the option exercise until vesting or until a Section 83(b) election is filed. Sometimes referred to as *reverse vesting.*

earnings before interest and taxes (EBIT). All profits (operating and nonoperating) before deduction of interest and income taxes.

earnings before interest, taxes, depreciation, and amortization (EBITDA). Concerns the cash flow of a company; by not including interest, taxes, depreciation, and amortization, one can see clearly the amount of money a company is bringing in.

earnings per share (EPS). Net income for the fiscal year divided by the total number of shares outstanding, with adjustments for common stock equivalents.

EBIT. Abbreviation for *earnings before interest and taxes.*

EBITDA. Abbreviation for *earnings before interest, taxes, depreciation, and amortization.*

EBP. Abbreviation for *excess benefit plan.*

economic indicator. A key statistic in the overall economy that may be used as a yardstick to predict the performance of the stock market.

economic profit. A calculation of profits that exceed the expected return to shareholders. Normally calculated by subtracting the cost of capital from an adjusted profit number. Many variations of the calculation exist.

Economic Recovery Tax Act (ERTA) of 1981 (1981 Tax Act). ERTA emphasized the deferral of compensation, and also reduced ordinary income tax rates.

economic value added (EVA). A concept copyrighted by Stern Stewart & Co. EVA is net operating profit minus an appropriate charge for the opportunity cost of all capital invested in an enterprise. As such, EVA is an estimate of true "economic" profit, or the amount by which earnings exceed or fall short of the required minimum rate of return that shareholders and lenders could get by investing in other securities of comparable risk.

EDGAR—Electronic Data Gathering, Analysis and Retrieval System. The system through which companies electronically file reports and registration statements with the SEC. This requires converting the paper or word-processing document to be filed into a universal ASCII format, a process known as "EDGAR-izing" the document. The public can then access the filings through the SEC's Web site on the Internet.

EEOC. Abbreviation for *Equal Employment Opportunity Commission.*

EITF. Abbreviation for *Emerging Issues Task Force.*

Emerging Issues Task Force (EITF). Organization affiliated with FASB that addresses new and emerging accounting issues. The EITF was formed in 1984 in response to the recommendations of the FASB's task force on timely financial reporting guidance and an FASB Invitation to Comment on those recommendations.

employee stock purchase plan (ESPP). A type of broad-based plan that permits employees to purchase stock of the company, usually at a discount price and by payroll deduction. ESPPs may or may not qualify as tax-advantaged plans under Section 423 of the Code.

employment agreement. A legal agreement between a company and an executive that sets forth the terms and conditions of employment, often including severance arrangements.

EPA. Abbreviation for *Equal Pay Act.*

EPS. Abbreviation for *earnings per share.*

Equal Employment Opportunity Commission (EEOC). A commission of the federal government charged with enforcing the provision of the Civil Rights Act of 1964 and the EPA of 1963 as it pertains to sex discrimination in pay.

Equal Pay Act (EPA) of 1963. An amendment to the Fair Labor Standards Act of 1936, prohibiting pay differentials on jobs that are substantially equal in terms of skills, efforts, responsibility, and working conditions, except when the variances are the result of bona fide seniority, merit, or production-based systems, or any other job-related factor other than gender.

equity collar. Hedging strategy involving offsetting puts and calls on an equity position, often used to diversify concentrated stock positions. The collar can be structured so that the premium received for the sale of the call and the money paid for purchase of the put net each other out (a "zero cost" collar).

    This strategy allows an executive to hold stock after an option exercise for long-term capital gains, minimizes the risk of stock price fluctuations, finances the cost of the put (zero-cost collar), or brings in more or less cash than the cost of the put. However, it has uncertain legal and tax ramifications; it is prohibited by many companies, and the executive gives up the benefit of future price increases beyond the collar price.

equity security. An ownership interest in a company. Common and preferred stock are types of equity securities. Equity securities can be distinguished from debt securities, such as bonds, and from derivative securities, such as stock options.

ERISA.   Abbreviation for *Employee Retirement Income Security Act of 1974.*

ERISA excess plan.   A type of pension plan for key executives to restore benefits that were reduced by the enactment of ERISA. The company makes up the difference between what an executive accrues under the company pension plan and the amount he or she is allowed to receive under ERISA restrictions.

ESOP.   Abbreviation for *employee stock ownership plan.*

ESPP.   Abbreviation for *employee stock purchase plan.*

European option.   A stock option that may be exercised only on its expiration date.

EVA.   Abbreviation for *economic value added.*

evergreen agreement.   An agreement that does not expire. The agreement is usually automatically renewed if not canceled by a certain date each year.

evergreen stock option reserve.   An employee stock plan funding mechanism that authorizes annual increases (generally expressed as a percentage of outstanding common stock) to the number of shares available for stock grants and awards.

excess benefit plan.   See *ERISA excess plan.*

ex-dividend.   A synonym for "without dividend." The buyer of an ex-dividend stock is not entitled to the next dividend payment. Dividends are paid on a set date to all those shareholders recorded on the books of the company as of a previous date of record. For example, a dividend may be declared as payable to stockholders of record on a given Friday. Since three business days are allowed for delivery of stock in a regular transaction on the New York Stock Exchange, the NYSE would declare the stock "ex-dividend" as of the opening of the market on the preceding Wednesday. That means anyone who bought it on or after that Wednesday would not be entitled to that dividend. When stocks go ex-dividend, the stock tables include the symbol "x" following the name.

executive perquisite.   Special benefit made available to top executives (and sometimes other managerial employees). May be taxable income to the executive. Company-related perquisites may include company-paid club memberships, first-class air travel, use of corporate aircraft, company car, home computer, cellular phone, and other amenities related to work. Personal perquisites include such items as low-cost loans for various reasons, and personal tax planning and legal counsel. Since 1978, the IRS has required companies to value these special benefits and require executives to pay tax on the imputed income associated with the benefit.

exercisable.   Describes options that, because of the passage of time or the meeting of specified performance targets, have vested and may now be exercised by the option holder. Options often become exercisable in increments over time. In some option plans one can exercise unvested options subject to a company repurchase right under a vesting-like schedule. See "early exercise options."

exercise.   The act of acquiring the underlying securities subject to a stock option by paying the exercise price.

exercise period.   The date or dates specific stock options are available for exercise.

expatriate.   Employee assigned outside of the base country for any period of time in excess of one year.

face value. Refers to the number of shares times the share price. For example, 100 shares at $50 per share have a face value of $5,000.

Fair Labor Standards Act of 1936 (FLSA). A federal law that establishes minimum wage, overtime pay, recordkeeping, and child labor standards that affect more than 100 million full- and part-time workers in the private sector and in federal, state, and local governments. FLSA applies to enterprises that have employees who are engaged in interstate commerce; producing goods for interstate commerce; or handling, selling, or working on goods or materials that have been moved in or produced for interstate commerce.

fair market value (FMV). The value that would as closely as possible approximate the value of a particular instrument or share of stock as determined by a willing buyer and a willing seller in an arms' length transaction. For public companies, FMV is often determined by, or based on, the quoted market price. With a private company, the fair market value measure is more subjective, and often may be based on a recent round of financing or set by an outside valuation.

fair value. The amount for which an asset could be bought or sold in a current transaction between willing parties; that is, other than in a forced liquidation sale. Quoted market prices in active markets are the best evidence of fair value and are to be used as the basis for measurement, if available. If quoted market prices are not available, the estimate of fair value is based on the best information available. The estimate of fair value considers prices for similar amounts and the results of valuation techniques to the extent available. Examples of valuation techniques include the present value of estimated future cash flows using a discount rate commensurate with the risks involved, option-pricing models, matrix pricing, option-adjusted spread models, and fundamental analysis.

Family Medical Leave Act (FMLA) of 1993. Entitles an eligible employee to receive unpaid leave of up to 12 weeks per year for specified family or medical reasons, such as caring for ill family members or adopting a child.

FAS. Abbreviation for *Financial Accounting Statement.*

FASB. Abbreviation for *Financial Accounting Standards Board.*

Federal Insurance Contributions Act (FICA). The statute that established social security contribution withholding requirements. The FICA payments are made equally by the employer and employee.

Federal Unemployment Tax Act (FUTA). A law enacted more than 60 years ago to guarantee financing for a national employment security system. The idea was that employers would pay the cost of administering the new unemployment compensation system, along with a national job placement system, to help them recruit new workers and to get laid-off workers and unemployment compensation claimants into new jobs as quickly as possible. FUTA is administered by the DOL.

FICA. Abbreviation for *Federal Insurance Contributions Act.*

Financial Accounting Standards Board (FASB). An organization that develops accounting standards on a wide range of financial topics, including stock compensation. Since 1973, the FASB has been the designated organization in the private sector for establishing standards of financial accounting and reporting. Those standards govern the preparation of financial reports. These accounting standards are officially recognized as authoritative by the

Securities and Exchange Commission (Financial Reporting Release No. 1, Section 101) and the American Institute of Certified Public Accountants (Rule 203, Rules of Conduct, as amended May 1973 and May 1979).

Financial Accounting Statement No. 123 (FAS 123). Accounting standard that originally recommended expensing of all stock-based compensation using stock fair market value to value stock awards and a recognized option-pricing model (typically Black-Scholes) to value options. FAS 123, however, was not mandatory, and companies could elect to continue to expense stock-based compensations under APB 25. In March 2004, the FASB released an exposure draft (Share-Based Payment) amending FAS 123, which will require, for tax years beginning in 2005, all U.S. companies to recognize an accounting expense for the "fair value" of stock options as of the date of grant.

financial statements. The balance sheet, income statement, statement of changes in financial position, statement of changes in owners' equity accounts, and notes thereto.

fiscal year. Any consecutive 12-month period of financial accountability for a corporation or government.

fixed accounting. A method of accounting for share-based employee compensation under which a non-varying charge to earnings is recorded and amortized over the service period. FAS 123 uses the term *fixed award* in an somewhat different sense than APB Opinion 25, which distinguishes between fixed awards and variable awards. FAS 123 only distinguishes between fixed awards and liabilities.

fixed award. See *fixed accounting.*

fixed grant guidelines. Guidelines under which a company determines grant size according to a set number of shares or a set percentage of shares outstanding rather than a value for the shares granted.

FLSA. Abbreviation for *Fair Labor Standards Act of 1936.*

FMLA. Abbreviation for *Family Medical Leave Act of 1993.*

FMV. Abbreviation for *fair market value.*

forgivable stock option exercise loan. A full-recourse loan extended by the company to employee (or company-secured third-party financing) for purchase of company stock. The loan must be repaid upon voluntary termination and may be forgiven based on future company service and/or performance.

Form 3. The initial form filed with the SEC pursuant to Section 16(a) of the Securities Exchange Act of 1934 by directors, officers, and 10% owners to report initial holdings in company equity securities.

Form 4. Form filed with the SEC to report changes in an insider's ownership of company stock, such as a purchase or sale.

Form 5. Year-end form filed with the SEC pursuant to Section 16(a) of the Securities Exchange Act of 1934 to report certain transactions exempt from Form 4 reporting and any changes not previously reported by the insider on Form 3 or Form 4.

Form 8-K. A report required to be filed with the SEC to publicly disclose certain material corporate events, such as a change in control, a significant acquisition, a bankruptcy, or a change in the company's fiscal year or accounting firms.

Form 10-K.   Annual report required to be filed with the SEC after the end of the fiscal year. The 10-K includes a description of the company's business and properties, the audited financial statements, and management's discussion and analysis (MD&A) of the financials. The 10-K must be signed by a majority of the board of directors.

Form 10-Q.   Quarterly report required to be filed with the SEC after the end of each of the first three fiscal quarters. Form 10-Q is less comprehensive than the Form 10-K annual report and does not require that financial statements be audited. It covers the specific quarter and the year to date.

Form 144.   The notice of sale required when an executive officer, director, or other affiliate of a company sells that company's stock. It must be filed with the SEC at the time an order is placed with a broker to sell the stock. Form 144 is not required if both the number of shares does not exceed 500 *and* the aggregate sale price does not exceed $10,000.

Form 1099-B.   Form provided by a broker detailing the amount received from securities sales, such as the proceeds from a cashless exercise. This amount, along with the person's tax basis, is used to calculate gain or loss for tax purposes on Schedule D.

Form 1099-MISC.   Tax form provided to nonemployees (e.g., consultants, independent contractors) that reports income/compensation.

Form S-1.   A registration statement under the Securities Act of 1933, which a company files with the SEC to register its stock for sale. Form S-1 is generally the form used by a private company that is going public. It contains the prospectus, along with a number of exhibits and other information about the company. The SEC staff reviews the Form S-1 and provides comments that must be resolved with the staff before the public offering can go forward.

Form S-3.   A shorter form of registration statement than the Form S-1, that can be used by certain already-public companies to sell additional shares. It is also the form most often used to cover resales of restricted securities by selling shareholders.

Form S-4.   A form of registration statement used when a company is issuing its shares in connection with a merger or acquisition.

Form S-8.   A very brief form of registration statement filed with the SEC to register shares to be issued under an employee benefit plan. Does not require filing of a prospectus.

Form W-2.   See *W-2.*

Form W-8.   See *W-8.*

Form W-9.   See *W-9.*

formula plan.   A plan in which both the recipients and the number of shares to be granted are set by the terms of the plan itself rather than being left to the discretion of the compensation committee.

formula-value stock.   Simulated stock, also called *phantom stock,* used to measure the performance of companies or business units that do not have publicly traded shares. The value of the stock is determined by a formula.

founders' stock.   A pre-IPO stock grant.

fundamental research.   Analysis of industries and companies based on such factors as sales, assets, earnings, products or services, markets, and management. As applied to the economy, fundamental research includes consideration of gross national product, interest rates, unemployment, inventories, savings, and so forth.

funding formula. The performance level required, as defined by the board, for bonuses to be paid and the percentage of profits above the threshold that will go toward bonuses.

FUTA. Abbreviation for *Federal Unemployment Tax Act.*

going public. When a privately held company first offers its shares to the investing public; also known as an IPO or initial public offering.

golden bungee. Refers to executive "severance" benefits after a change in control of ownership when the executive agrees to stay with the new organization and receive additional pay in various forms.

golden handcuffs. Refers to compensation and benefits that could be lost upon voluntary termination of the executive.

golden hello. See *sign-on bonus.*

golden parachute. A phrase commonly used to refer to a severance arrangement between a company and an employee that provides benefits triggered by termination of employment in connection with a change in control of the company.

grant. The issuance of an award under a stock plan, such as a stock option or shares of restricted stock.

grant date. The date on which a stock award is granted.

grant multiple. The multiple of aggregate stock option award (options shares times option exercise price) as a function of the grantee's salary.

grant price. The price per share at which a stock option is granted and that must be paid to exercise the stock option. The grant price is typically the fair market value of the stock on the date of grant. Also known as the *exercise price* or *strike price.*

hedging. Investments made in an attempt to reduce the risk of adverse price fluctuations in a security, by taking an offsetting position in a related security.

hold. Refers to an exercise transaction in which the option holder holds the shares received upon exercise (rather than selling them for cash).

immaculate option exercise. A form of cashless exercise in which the option exercise price is paid by instructing the company to withhold from the total number of shares issuable upon an option exercise a number of shares equal to the exercise price. The option holder is left with just the number of shares equal to the option spread. As a result of the advent of broker-assisted cashless exercise/same-day sale programs, and concerns over the potential for variable accounting treatment, the immaculate exercise programs are not used.

imputed interest. Interest that the IRS assumes has been paid on a loan if the stated interest is below a minimum interest rate (the applicable federal rate).

incentive stock option (ISO). A stock option that has met certain tax requirements that entitle the option holder to favorable tax treatment. Such an option is free from regular tax at the date of grant and the date of exercise (when a nonqualified option would become taxable). If two holding-period tests are met (two years after the date and one year after the exercise date), the profit on the option qualifies as a long-term capital gain rather than ordinary income. If the holding periods are not met, there has been a disqualifying disposition, and the holder incurs ordinary income.

indexed stock option. Option that has an exercise price which may fluctuate *above* or *below* market value at grant, depending on the company's stock price performance relative to a specified index (e.g., the Standard & Poors 500 Stock Index) or the movement of the index itself. Indexed options differ from performance options in that the exercise price of indexed options typically remains variable until the option is exercised.

Individual Retirement Account (IRA). An individual pension fund that anyone may open with a bank. An IRA permits investment of contributed funds, through intermediaries such as mutual funds, insurance companies, and banks; or directly in stocks and bonds, through stockbrokers. Because it is intended for retirement, money in an IRA enjoys many tax advantages over traditional investments, but may not be withdrawn early without heavy penalty fees.

initial public offering. The process of going public.

insider. An officer, director, or principal shareholder of a publicly owned company and members of his or her immediate family. The term may also include other people who obtain nonpublic information about a company and owe a duty not to use it for personal gain.

insider trading. Trading in a company's securities by company insiders or others with access to material, nonpublic information.

Insider Trading and Securities Fraud Enforcement Act of 1988. Federal legislation that greatly increased the penalties for trading on material inside information.

installment exercise. A form of stock option exercise right that can be executed at certain times and with certain limits during its term.

institutional investor. Organization whose primary purpose is to invest its own assets or those entrusted to it by others. The most common such investors are employee pension funds, insurance companies, mutual funds, university endowments, and banks.

internal equity. Refers to the pay relationships among jobs or skill levels within a single organization and focuses attention on employee and management acceptance of those relationships. It involves establishing equal pay for jobs of equal worth and acceptable pay differentials for jobs of unequal worth.

Internal Revenue Service (IRS). U.S. agency charged with collecting federal taxes, including personal and corporate income taxes, social security taxes, and excise, estate, and gift taxes. The IRS administers the rules and regulations that are the responsibility of the U.S. Treasury Department and investigates and prosecutes (through the U.S. Tax Court) tax illegalities.

intrinsic value. The difference between the exercise price and/or strike price of an option and the market value of the underlying security.

Investment Advisers Act of 1940. This act, which falls under the purview of the SEC, regulates investment advisers. With certain exceptions, this act requires that firms or sole practitioners compensated for advising others about securities investments must register with the SEC and conform to regulations designed to protect investors. Since the act was amended in 1996, generally only advisers who have at least $25 million of assets under management or advise a registered investment company must register with the SEC.

investment bank.   Also known as underwriter; investment banks serve as intermediaries between corporations issuing new securities and the buying public. Normally one or more investment banks buy the new issue of securities from the issuing company for a negotiated price. The company walks away with this new supply of capital, while the investment banks form a syndicate and resell the issue to their customer base and the investing public. Investment banks perform a variety of other financial services, such as merger and acquisition advice and market analysis.

Investment Company Act of 1940.   This act, which falls under the purview of the SEC, regulates the organization of companies, including mutual funds that engage primarily in investing, reinvesting, and trading in securities and whose own securities are offered to the investing public. The regulation is designed to minimize conflicts of interest that arise in these complex operations. The act requires these companies to disclose their financial condition and investment policies to investors when stock is initially sold and, subsequently, on a regular basis.

IRA.   Abbreviation for *individual retirement account.*

IRC.   Abbreviation for *Internal Revenue Code.*

irrevocable trust.   Trust that cannot be changed or terminated by the one who created it without the agreement of the beneficiary of the trust.

IRS.   Abbreviation for *Internal Revenue Service.*

ISO.   Abbreviation for *incentive stock option.*

job evaluation.   The process for determining the relative worth of a position within an organization based on the factors valued by the organization. The end result of the job evaluation process is the assignment of jobs to some form of pay hierarchy.

job family.   A collection of jobs that have common skills, occupational qualifications, technology, working conditions, and so on. Often, a job family represents increasingly complex levels of a job.

joint and survivor (J&S) annuity.   A common form of pension plan payout, which pays over the life of the retiree and his or her spouse after the retiree dies. The retiree and his or her spouse usually must specifically choose not to accept this payment form.

J&S.   Abbreviation for *joint & survivor.*

junior stock.   Stock with limited or no voting stock or dividend rights; convertible into regular common stock if performance goals (or other stated events such an initial public offering) are met.

Labor-Management Reporting and Disclosure Act.   Law dealing with the relationship between a union and its members. It safeguards union funds and requires reports on certain financial transactions and administrative practices of union officials, labor consultants, and the like. The Office of Labor-Management Standards administers the act, which is part of the Employment Standards Administration. This act is also known as the *Landrum-Griffin Act.*

LCN.   Abbreviation for *Local Country National.*

legend.   A notice on a stock certificate that the shares represented by that certificate are restricted in some manner.

leverage. Any means of increasing value and return by borrowing funds or committing less of one's own. For corporations, it refers to the ratio of debt (in the form of bonds and preferred stock outstanding) to equity (in the form of common stock outstanding) in the company's capital structure. The more long-term debt there is, the greater the financial leverage. Shareholders benefit from this financial leverage to the extent that the return on the borrowed money exceeds the interest costs of borrowing it. Because of this effect, financial leverage is popularly called "trading on the equity." For individuals, leverage can involve debt, as when an investor borrows money from a broker on margin and so is able to buy more stock than he or she otherwise could. If the stock goes up, the investor repays the broker the loan amount and keeps the profit. By borrowing money, the investor has achieved a higher return on his or her investment than if he or she had paid for all the stock personally. Rights, warrants, and option contracts also provide leverage, not through debt but by offering the prospect of a high return for little or no investment.

leveraged stock option. Often used after the restructure of a corporation; the company will match some multiple of stock options to the employee's purchase of a fixed number of shares (e.g., company provides four options for one share purchased).

liquidity. (1) The ability to convert an asset into cash quickly and without any price discount. (2) The ability of the market in a particular security to absorb a reasonable amount of buying or selling at reasonable price changes.

limited offering. Sales of securities exempt from registration pursuant to certain exemptions that limit the size of the offering and the number of purchasers.

limited stock appreciation right (LSAR). Similar to a SAR, but only exercisable in the case of a change in control or up to a certain value. Usually granted in tandem with a stock option.

listed stock. The stock of a company that is traded on a securities exchange.

living trust. A trust created by a person during his or her lifetime.

Local Country Nationals (LCNs). Citizens of countries in which a U.S. foreign subsidiary is located. LCNs' compensation is tied either to local wage rates or to the rate of U.S. expatriates performing the same job. Each practice of paying LCNs has different internal equity and external equity implications.

lock-up. An agreement between investment bankers and the companies that they take public. This agreement restricts the resale of shares owned by founders, employees, and venture capitalists immediately after the IPO. Typically lasts for 180 days, but could last for a shorter or longer period.

look-back feature. Option provision typically used in a Code § 423 employee stock purchase plan (ESPP). The purchase price (with or without a discount) is based on the *lower* of the market price at the beginning or end of the purchase period (a typical plan purchase period might run for six months). For example, for a plan with a look-back feature and a 15% discount, if the stock price is $10 at the beginning of the purchase period and goes up to $20 at the end, your purchase price is just $8.50 ($10–15%).

margin. The amount paid by the customer when using a broker's credit to buy or sell a security. Under Federal Reserve regulations, the initial margin required since 1934 has ranged from 40% of the purchase price up to 100%. The current rate of 50% has been in effect since 1974.

market share.   Sales of a particular product or product line as a percentage of total sales of the product or product line.

material information.   Information that would affect a reasonable investor's decision to buy or sell a security if the information was known to him or her. Examples might include a corporate takeover, a divestiture, significant management changes, and new product introductions.

mean.   The sum of a set of data reported divided by the number of observations. Also referred to as the average.

measurement date.   When the fair value of a stock-based employee award is known and fixed, according to current FASB rules, the first date on which the stock award can be measured. It is the first date on which both the number of shares and the option or purchase price are known.

median.   The middle value of a variable in a distribution of numbers. Thus, the median of (1, 2, 3, 10, and 100) is 3. The mean (or average) of these values is 23.2. The median is generally preferred to the mean as a measure of typical values, because extreme values (very high or very low) will tend to skew the mean.

medical savings account (MSA).   The general concept of a medical savings account is for an employer, or the government in the case of Medicare, to enable an insured individual to obtain and pay for a high-deductible catastrophic health insurance policy. The employer or the government would pay a fixed premium to the catastrophic insurance company, and the insured individual would share the cost of the premium. The difference between what the employer or government would customarily pay for traditional coverage and the premium of the catastrophic health insurance coverage would be put into an individual's MSA for his or her qualified medical expenses.

mega-grant.   An exceptionally large share-based award.

minimum value.   An amount attributed to an option that is calculated without considering the expected volatility of the underlying stock. Minimum value may be computed without using a standard option-pricing model and a volatility of zero. It also may be computed as (1) the current price of the stock reduced to exclude the present value of any expected dividends during the option's life minus (2) the present value of the exercise price. Different methods of reducing the current price of the stock for the present value of the expected dividend payments, if any, may result in different computed minimum values.

minimum value stock valuation model.   A model that estimates the value of a stock option; it considers the same factors as the Black-Scholes model, with the exception of (1) the stochastic estimation of future stock price, and (2) the volatility of the stock. This model is defined as the current stock price less the present value of (a) expected dividends, and (b) exercise price.

monetize.   To convert illiquid value such as stock option spread to cash. See *hedging, costless collar,* and *zero premium collar.*

MSA.   Abbreviation for *medical savings account.*

mutual fund.   A portfolio of stocks, bonds, or other securities administered by a team of one or more managers from an investment company who make buy and sell decisions on component securities. Capital is contributed by smaller investors who buy shares in the mutual fund rather than the individual stocks and bonds in its portfolio. The return on the fund's holdings is distributed back to its contributors, or shareholders, minus various fees and commissions. This system allows small investors to participate in the reduced risk of a large and diverse portfolio that they could not otherwise build themselves. They also have the benefit of professional managers overseeing their money who have the time and expertise to analyze and pick securities.

named executive officers (NEOs). The five highest paid executive officers, whose prior fiscal year compensation is reflected in the Summary Compensation Table in a publicly held company's annual proxy statement, pursuant to SEC disclosure requirements.

National Association of Securities Dealers (NASD). An association of securities broker/dealers, including all of the major brokerage firms as members. The NASD establishes uniform practices in the securities industry for trading in the over-the-counter market in order to protect investors. The NASDR is the regulatory arm of the NASD.

Nasdaq. The National Association of Securities Dealers Automated Quotation, a global intranet providing brokers and dealers with price quotations on trades over-the-counter. Unlike the NYSE auction market, where orders meet on a trading floor, Nasdaq orders are paired and executed on a computer network.

national market system. A system mandated by the Securities Act Amendments of 1975. Eight markets—the American, Boston, Cincinnati, Chicago, New York, Pacific, Philadelphia, and NASD over-the-counter markets—are linked electronically by computers. This allows traders at any exchange to seek the best available price on all other exchanges that a particular security is eligible to trade on. The national market system also includes a consolidated electronic tape, which combines last-sale prices from all markets into a single stream of information.

negative discretion. Provision in an incentive plan that permits the compensation committee to reduce, but not to increase, an employee's formula-generated bonus payment.

New York Stock Exchange (NYSE). Oldest (established in 1792) and largest securities exchange in the United States. The NYSE marketplace blends public pricing with assigned dealer responsibilities. Aided by advanced technology, public orders meet and interact on the trading floor with a minimum of dealer interference. The result is competitive price discovery at the point of sale. Liquidity in the NYSE auction market system is provided by individual and institutional investors, member firms trading for their own accounts, and assigned specialists. The NYSE is linked with other markets trading listed securities through the Intermarket Trading System (ITS).

NYSE-assigned dealers, known as specialists, are responsible for maintaining a fair and orderly market in the securities assigned to them. Most trading, however, is conducted by brokers acting on behalf of customers, rather than by dealers trading for their own account. For this reason, the NYSE is often described as an agency auction market. The interaction of natural buyers and sellers determines the price of an NYSE-listed stock.

nonqualified deferred compensation plan. A nonqualified plan is an employer-sponsored retirement or other deferred compensation plan that does not meet the tax-qualification requirements under the Code.

nonqualified stock option (NQSO). An employee stock option not meeting the IRS criteria for ISOs (incentive stock options) and therefore triggering a tax upon exercise. This type of option requires withholding of state and federal income tax, Medicare, and FICA/FUTA on the excess of the fair market value over the exercise price on the exercise date.

NQSO.   Abbreviation for *nonqualified stock option.*

NYSE.   Abbreviation for *New York Stock Exchange.*

NYSE Composite Index.   A market-value weighted index of all stocks on the NYSE. The Composite Index consists of all common stocks listed on the NYSE and four subgroup indexes—Industrial, Transportation, Utility, and Finance.

Occupational Safety and Health Act (OSH Act).   The law administered by the Occupational Safety and Health Administration (OSHA). Safety and health conditions in most private industries are regulated by OSHA or OSHA-approved state systems. Employers must identify and eliminate unhealthful or hazardous conditions; employees must comply with all rules and regulations that apply to their own workplace conduct.

off-hours trading.   Trading that takes place after the close of the regular session. On June 13, 1991, the NYSE introduced off-hours trading in the form of two post-4:00 P.M. crosses. Crossing Session I introduced a 5:00 P.M. cross in individual stocks at the NYSE regular day closing price; Crossing Session II facilitates the crossing of portfolios until 5:15 P.M.

omnibus stock plan.   A long-term incentive plan that provides the flexibility to use a number of long-term incentive vehicles, such as stock options, stock appreciation rights, restricted stock, performance shares, and performance units. A list of performance measures usually is included in such a plan to satisfy Code § 162(m) purposes.

option gain deferral.   A technique for postponing taxation on stock option gains. The optionee pays the exercise price by surrendering previously-owned shares. The option shares in excess of that amount ("profit shares") are deferred in the form of stock units payable in stock at a later date.

option holder.   A person who has been granted a stock option. Also referred to as an *optionee.*

option spread.   The amount by which the value of stock underlying an option grant, exceeds the exercise price. The aggregate spread is determined by multiplying the number of shares by the amount by which the market price per share exceeds the option's exercise price per share. Also referred to as *intrinsic value.*

optionee.   A person who has been granted a stock option. Also referred to as an *option holder.*

out of the money.   A term used to describe an employee stock option when the current market price is below the option exercise price. When an option is out of the money, it would cost more than the underlying stock is worth to exercise the option. Such options are also described as being *underwater.*

outside director.   A board member who is neither a current employee nor a former employee.

over the counter.   A market, including Nasdaq, in which securities transactions are conducted through a computer network connecting dealers in stocks and bonds, rather than on the floor of an exchange.

ownership guidelines. Requirements at some companies that executives, directors, and key employees own a specified amount of company stock so that their financial interests are clearly aligned with those of shareholders. The most commonly used guidelines require stock ownership with a value based on some multiple of salary (e.g., 3x salary). A minority of companies express ownership as a specific number of shares. The guidelines are tiered by position so that the CEO has the highest-level ownership requirement.

PARSAP. Abbreviation for *performance-accelerated restricted stock award plan.*

pay differential. Pay differences among levels within the organization, such as the difference in pay between adjacent levels in career path, between supervisors and subordinates, and between executive and nonexecutive employees.

penny stocks. Low-priced issues, often highly speculative, selling at less than $1 a share. Frequently used as a term of disparagement, although some penny stocks have developed into investment-caliber issues.

performance condition (performance award). An award of stock-based employee compensation for which vesting depends on both (a) an employee's rendering services to the employer for a specified period of time, and (b) the achievement of a specified performance target. A performance condition may pertain either to the performance of the enterprise as a whole or to some part of the enterprise, such as a division.

performance share. Grants of actual shares of stock or phantom stock whose payment is contingent on performance as measured against predetermined objectives over a period of time; same as performance units except that the value paid fluctuates with stock price changes as well as performance against objectives. Payout may be settled in cash or stock.

performance stock option. Options for which some aspect of vesting or exercise price is subject to specified performance criteria. Options with performance vesting provisions often become exercisable at or near the end of the option term, regardless of performance, to secure favorable accounting treatment under APB 25.

performance unit. Cash earned by an executive at the end of a performance period if certain preestablished financial objectives are achieved. Similar to performance shares, except that payments are not related to stock price and units are earned on the basis of internal financial performance measures.

performance-accelerated restricted stock award plan (PARSAP). Also known as *performance-accelerated restricted stock* (PARS) and *time-accelerated restricted stock award plans* (TARSAPs). Grants of restricted stock or restricted stock units that may vest early upon attainment of specified performance objectives. Otherwise, a time-vesting schedule would remain in effect.

performance-based compensation. Under Internal Revenue Code Section 162(m)(4)(C), remuneration that is payable solely on account of the attainment of one or more performance goals, but only if the performance goals are determined by a compensation committee of the board of directors, which is comprised solely of two or more "outside directors," the material terms under which the remunderation is to be paid (including the performance goals) are disclosed to and approved by stockholders, and the compensation committee certifies that the performance goals and any other material terms were satisfied before any payment of such remuneration.

permanent discount purchase plan. A stock purchase plan that enables employees to purchase restricted stock at a set dollar discount from the then-current market price of the stock. The discount is usually significant relative to the market price at the date of purchase. If the employee subsequently wishes to sell the stock, the employer typically has a right to repurchase the shares at the then market price, less the original discount.

perquisites. See *executive perquisite.*

phantom stock award. A type of incentive grant in which the recipient is not issued actual shares of stock on the grant date, but instead receives an account credited with a certain number of hypothetical shares. The value of the account increases or decreases over time based on the appreciation or depreciation of the stock price and the crediting of phantom dividends. Payout may be settled in cash or stock.

poison pill. A device designed to prevent a hostile takeover by increasing the takeover cost, usually through the issuance of new preferred shares that carry severe redemption provisions.

pooling of interests. A merger accounting method (now obsolete) whereby the balance sheets of the two merging companies are combined line by line without a tax impact.

preferred stock. A class of stock that typically pays a fixed dividend, regardless of corporate earnings, and has priority over common stock in the payment of dividends. However, it often carries no voting rights. The fixed income stream of preferred stock makes it similar in many ways to bonds.

Pregnancy Discrimination Act of 1978. An amendment to Title VII of the Civil Rights Act. It requires a company to extend to pregnant employees or spouses the same disability and medical benefits provided other employees or spouses of employees.

premium-priced stock option. Options that have an exercise price above market value at the time of grant.

present value (PV). Value today of a future payment, or stream of payments, discounted at some appropriate compound interest or discount rate. The present-value method, also called the discounted cash-flow method, is widely used to compare alternative investments of cash-flow streams.

price earnings (P/E) ratio. A popular measure for comparing stocks selling at different prices in order to single out over- or undervalued issues. The P/E ratio is the price per share divided by the company's earnings per share.

price index. Overall measure of how much prices have increased over a period of time. Prices are expressed as some percentage of the prices prevailing during a base period.

primary offering. An offering of as-yet unissued securities.

principal stockholder. An investor that either (1) owns 10% or more of an entity's common stock or (2) has the ability, directly or indirectly, to control or significantly influence the entity.

private placement. Sales of securities not involving a public offering pursuant to certain exemptions.

program trading. A wide range of portfolio trading strategies involving the purchase or sale of 15 or more stocks having a total market value of $1 million or more.

prospectus. A legal document offering securities or mutual fund shares for sale, required by the Securities Act of 1933. It must explain the offer, including the terms, issuer, objectives (if mutual fund) or planned use of the money (if securities), historical financial information, and other information that could help an individual decide whether the investment is appropriate for him or her. Also called "offering circular."

proxy. Refers either to (1) a person, such as a member of management, who is designated by a shareholder to vote on behalf of the shareholder at a meeting; or (2) a signed card or other document that designates such a person. Corporate matters are typically voted on via proxy because it would be impractical to assemble all of the shareholders at one time to vote in person.

proxy battle. Strategy used by an acquiring company in a hostile takeover attempt, whereby the acquirer challenges the target company's management and solicits support from the target company's shareholders for proposals that would effectively give the acquiring company control of the target without having to pay a premium. Also known as a "proxy fight."

proxy fight. See *proxy battle.*

proxy statement. Information document that the SEC requires to be provided to shareholders before they vote by proxy on corporate matters. The proxy statement contains biographical information on the members of the board of directors; the top five executive officers' salaries, bonus, and stock compensation; and any proposals from management or shareholders to be acted upon at the meeting.

prudent person rule. An investment standard that dictates the type of security, or specific securities, in which a fiduciary or trustee may invest money. Generally, it implies that a fiduciary or trustee may invest in a security only if it is one that a prudent person of discretion and intelligence would buy.

Public Utility Holding Company Act of 1935. Interstate holding companies engaged, through subsidiaries, in the electric utility business or in the retail distribution of natural or manufactured gas are subject to regulation under this act. These companies, unless specifically exempted, are required to submit reports providing detailed information concerning the organization, financial structure, and operations of the holding company and its subsidiaries.

put option (put). A derivative security giving the holder the right to sell securities at a fixed price (see *call option*). A protective put strategy allows holders of concentrated stock positions to have protection against share price drops. By purchasing a put, if the stock price is below the strike price at expiration, the holder will receive a payment for the difference. For example, the current market price per share is $50, and a put is purchased with a $35 downside strike price. At expiration, when the price is $30, a $5 cash payment will be made.

PV. Abbreviation for *present value.*

pyramid exercise. A type of stock swap option exercise in which a small number of previously owned shares is surrendered to the company to pay a portion of the exercise price, for which a slightly larger number of option shares may be purchased. The newly purchased shares are then immediately surrendered back to the company to pay additional amounts of the exercise price, and so on until the full option price has been paid and the option holder is left with just the number of shares equal to the option spread. With the advent of broker-assisted cashless exercise/same-day sale programs, pyramiding has fallen out of favor.

qualified plan. Generally, a plan that meets qualifications under the applicable sections of the Internal Revenue Code. A plan whereby the employer can take a tax deduction with respect to accrual of an as-yet-unpaid benefit. For example, a qualified defined benefit pension allows a company to take a tax deduction for the accrual of a pension benefit.

qualified stock option. A stock option that meets the requirements established by Internal Revenue Code Section 422. Usually referred to as an ISO.

qualifying disposition. Transfer (e.g., by gift or sale) of ISO or ESPP shares after the required holding period of two years from the grant date and one year from the purchase/exercise date.

rabbi trust. A nonqualified fund for holding deferred compensation tax-free until either the company gives up the right to recall the money, the beneficiary collects, or the funds are made available to the general creditors of the company in the event of a bankruptcy.

real estate investment trust. See *REIT.*

record date. The date set by the board of directors for the transfer agent to close the company's books to further changes in registration of stock, in order to identify the shareholders entitled to receive the next dividend or to vote at an upcoming meeting. A shareholder must officially own shares as of the record date to receive the dividend or vote at the meeting.

record owner. The shareholder of record of shares of stock, which may be different from the beneficial owner of those shares.

registration. Before a company may make a public offering of new securities, the securities must be registered under the Securities Act of 1933. A registration statement is filed with the SEC by the issuer. It must disclose pertinent information relating to the company's operations, securities, management, and purpose of the public offering. Before a security may be admitted to dealings on a national security exchange, it must be registered under the Securities Exchange Act of 1934. The company issuing the securities must file the application for registration with the exchange and the SEC.

registration statement. A disclosure document filed with the SEC to register shares of stock for sale to the public. Forms S-1, S-2, S-3, and S-8 are common types of registration statements. Form S-8 is used for employee benefit plans.

regression. A common statistical approach used to determine the relationship between pay and factors that may affect pay, such as revenue size, number of employees, and so on. The most common type of regression is a single regression.

Regulation T. Federal Reserve Board regulations governing the extension of credit by broker/dealers, including their participation in cashless exercise/same-day sale transactions.

REIT (real estate investment trust). An organization similar to an investment company in some respects, but concentrating its holdings in real estate investments. The yield is generally liberal because REITs are required to distribute as much as 90% of their income annually.

reload stock option (RSO). A replacement stock option granted by some companies to option holders upon a stock swap. The number of reload options granted is equal to the number of shares delivered to exercise the option plus, in some cases, any shares withheld for tax withholding obligations. The exercise price of the new option is the current market price; the reload option generally expires on the same date that the original option would have.

repricing. The exchange of previously granted, now out-of-the-money stock options for lower-priced options at the current market price. The actual exchange can be structured in different ways and with different ratios of old-to-new stock options.

restricted securities. The term used under SEC Rule 144 for securities issued privately by the company or an affiliate, without the benefit of a registration statement. Restricted securities are subject to a holding period before they can be sold, under Rule 144. The term is also commonly used to refer to any securities held by affiliates that must be sold under Rule 144, regardless of whether the stock is registered, although the technical terms is "control securities."

restricted stock award. Grants of shares of stock subject to restrictions on transfer and risk of forfeiture until vested by continued employment or by reaching a performance target. Restricted stock typically vests in increments over a period of several years. Dividends may be paid, and award holders may have voting rights during the restricted period.

return on assets (ROA). A profitability ratio measured by net income divided by assets, This is equivalent to return on sales multiplied by capital turnover.

return on equity (ROE). A profitability ratio measured by net income divided by equity. This is equivalent to return on assets (ROA) multiplied by leverage (the ratio of assets to shareholders' equity).

return on invested capital (ROIC). Amount, expressed as a percentage, earned on a company's total capital.

return on sales (ROS). Net income as a percentage of sales. ROS is a useful measure of overall operational efficiency when compared with prior periods or with other companies in the same line of business. ROS varies widely from industry to industry.

reverse vesting. A technique (also known as *early exercise*) most often found in stock option plans offered by pre-IPO companies. Under this type of arrangement, the optionee would be allowed to exercise options before they are vested. For each option exercised, the optionee would receive a share of restricted stock, which is subject to vesting based on the original vesting schedule of the option.

ROA. Abbreviation for *return on assets.*

ROC. Abbreviation for *return on capital.*

ROE. Abbreviation for *return on equity.*

ROIC. Abbreviation for *return on invested capital.*

ROS. Abbreviation for *return on sales.*

ROSE. Abbreviation for *return on shareholders' equity.*

RSO. Abbreviation for *reload stock option.*

Rule 10b-5. An SEC rule that prohibits trading by insiders on material nonpublic information. This is also the rule under which a company may be sued for false or misleading disclosure.

Rule 13d.   An SEC rule that requires holders of 5% or more of a company's stock to disclose their security holdings and any changes in a Schedule 13D filing.

Rule 144.   An SEC rule that applies to public resales of restricted securities, as well as all sales by affiliates. The requirements include:

1. Current public information about the issuer.
2. A one-year holding period for restricted securities.
3. Unsolicited brokers' transactions.
4. An amount limitation—the greater of 1% of the outstanding stock or the average weekly trading volume may be sold during any three-month period.
5. A Form 144 filing in most cases.

Rule 701.   SEC registration exemption used for private company equity plans.

SAB.   Abbreviation for *Staff Accounting Bulletin.*

same-day sale.   A same-day option exercise and sale transaction, effected through a broker. The broker uses the proceeds of the sale to pay to (1) the company the exercise price and any tax withholding and (b) the option holder the net shares or cash (less any brokerage commissions or fees).

SAR.   Abbreviation for *stock appreciation right.*

Schedule 13D, 13G.   Disclosure forms required to be filed with the SEC and the company by a shareholder or group of shareholders that owns more than 5% of a public company. Schedule 13G is a short-form version of the 13D and may generally (but not always) be used only by institutional investors.

SEC.   Abbreviation for *Securities and Exchange Commission.*

Section 16(a).   Provision of the Securities Exchange Act of 1934 that requires company insiders to file periodic reports disclosing their holdings and changes in beneficial ownership of the company's equity securities. See *Forms 3, 4,* and *5.*

Section 16(b).   Provision of the Securities Exchange Act of 1934 that requires any profit realized by a company insider from the purchase and sale, or sale and purchase, of the company's equity securities within a period of less than six months to be returned to the company. Section 16(b) is also known as the "short-swing profit rule."

Section 162(m).   The section of the Code imposing a $1 million cap on deductible compensation paid by a publicly held corporation to its *named executive officers* (see also *named executive officers*).

Section 423.   The Internal Revenue Code section that regulates employee stock purchase plans.

Section 83(b) election.   An election filed by an employee to be taxed on a restricted stock grant as of the date of grant. This voluntary election must be made within 30 days of the date of grant to be effective.

secular trust.   A trust fund for holding deferred compensation. Differs from a rabbi trust in that contributions are taxable to the recipient as they accumulate. The trust usually begins to pay out when the trust beneficiary retires. The trust assets are not subject to claims of creditors in the event of a bankruptcy.

Securities Act of 1933. Federal legislation enacted to protect potential purchasers of stock by requiring companies to register their public stock offerings and make full disclosure to purchasers. Often referred to as the "truth in securities" law, the Securities Act of 1933 has two basic objectives:

- Require that investors receive financial and other significant information concerning securities being offered for public sale; and

- Prohibit deceit, misrepresentations, and other fraud in the sale of securities.

Securities and Exchange Commission (SEC). The government agency responsible for the supervision and regulation of the securities industry and markets, as well as public securities offerings and the ongoing disclosure obligations of public companies.

Securities Exchange Act of 1934. This act gives the SEC broad authority over all aspects of the securities industry, including the power to register, regulate, and oversee brokerage firms, transfer agents, and clearing agencies as well as the nation's securities self-regulatory organizations (SROs). The various stock exchanges, such as the New York Stock Exchange and American Stock Exchange, are SROs. The National Association of Securities Dealers, which operates the Nasdaq system, is also an SRO. The act also identifies and prohibits certain types of conduct in the markets and provides the SEC with disciplinary powers over regulated entities and persons associated with them. The act also empowers the SEC to require periodic reporting of information by companies with publicly traded securities.

security. Includes any note, stock, treasury stock, bond, debenture, evidence of indebtedness, certificate of interest, or participation in any profit-sharing agreement. Also includes collateral-trust certificate; preorganization certificate or subscription; transferable share; investment contract; voting-trust certificate; certificate of deposit for a security; fractional undivided interest in oil, gas, or other mineral rights; any put, call, straddle, option, or privilege on any security, certificate of deposit, or group or index of securities (including any interest therein or based on the value thereof); or any put, call, straddle, option, or privilege entered into on a national securities exchange relating to foreign currency. In general, any interest or instrument commonly known as a "security," or any certificate of interest or participation in, temporary or interim certificate for, receipt for, guarantee of, or warrant or right to subscribe to or purchase any of the foregoing.

self-funding/self-insurance. A health care benefit financing technique in which an employer pays claims out of an internally funded pool, as permitted under ERISA. Self-funded companies might or might not also be self-administered, meaning they perform the administrative tasks associated with the benefit as opposed to purchasing such services from an outside firm.

sequential exercise. The exercise of employee stock options in the order in which they were granted.

SERP. Abbreviation for *supplemental executive retirement plan.*

seventy-fifth percentile. Also referred to as the "third quartile," "upper quartile," or "Q3"; represents the dividing point between the upper 25th percentile and the lower 75th percentile of reported data.

share repurchase plan. A program by which a corporation buys back its own shares in the open market. It is usually done when the common shares are undervalued. Because it reduces the number of shares and thus increases earnings per share, it tends to elevate the market value of the remaining shares held by shareholders.

shareholder proposal.   A recommendation or requirement, proposed by a shareholder holding at least $2,000 market value or 1% of the company's voting shares, that the company and/or its board of directors take action presented for a vote by other shareholders at the company's annual meeting.

shareholder value.   Usually calculated as market capitalization—the stock price multiplied by the number of shares. Changes in shareholder value reflect both dividends and appreciation of the stock.

shareholders' agreement.   An agreement among the shareholders of a company governing any of a number of possible topics, such as buy-out terms and voting rights.

shares outstanding.   The number of company shares currently held by shareholders, as tracked by the transfer agent.

short-against-the-box.   A short sale by an investor who also owns the stock being sold is referred to as a sale "against the box," meaning it is a sale versus the broker's "box" position, not the stock in the account of the person who is short-selling. Strategies of this type are generally referred to as hedging strategies.

To defer capital gain recognition until the next tax year, the short sale must be:

• Covered before the end of January of the next year.

• The shares held must continue to be held for at least 60 days after the short is closed.

• The shares held must not be otherwise protected from loss by an alternate hedge strategy.

Thus, the short is closed by buying back the stock (to cover) and, in order to get the favorable tax treatment, holding the owned stock for at least 60 days.

short sale.   The sale of a security that is not owned by the seller at the time of the trade, necessitating a purchase or delivery some time in the future to cover the sale. Investors who believe the stock being sold will decline in value between the time it is sold short and the time it is covered use the strategy. By being able to cover at a price lower than the short sale price, the investor profits on the difference in price.

To sell short, the investor must borrow stock from a broker in order to meet the delivery requirements of the sale, which has potential risks.

short-swing transaction.   Any purchase and sale (or sale and purchase) of the issuer's equity securities by an insider within a period of less than six months. See *Section 16(b)*.

SIC.   Abbreviation for *Standard Industrial Classification code*.

Sign-on bonus.   An amount of cash or stock granted at the time an employment agreement is executed. Also referred to as a *golden hello*.

S&P 500.   A capitalization weighted index of 500 stocks. Standard and Poor's 500 stock index represents the price trend movements of the major common stock of U.S. public companies. It is used to measure the performance of the entire U.S. domestic stock market.

spinoff.   The separation of a subsidiary or division of a corporation from its parent by issuing shares in a new corporate entity. Shareholders in the parent receive shares in the new company in proportion to their original holding, and the total value remains approximately the same.

split. The division of the outstanding shares of a corporation into either a larger or smaller number of shares, without any immediate effect on individual shareholders equity. For example, a 3-for-1 forward split by a company with 1 million shares outstanding results in 3 million shares outstanding. Each holder of 100 shares before the split would have 300 shares (each worth less) after the split, although the proportionate equity in the company would stay the same. A reverse split would reduce the number of shares outstanding and each share would be worth more.

split dollar life insurance. An arrangement between a company and an executive whereby the parties agree to allocate the benefits and costs of a life insurance contract.

spread. Depending on the context, refers either to (1) the difference between the bid and ask prices for an over-the-counter stock, or (2) the difference between an option's exercise price and the market price of the underlying shares (i.e., the profit component of the option).

Staff Accounting Bulletin (SAB). Promulgation that reflects the SEC staff's views regarding accounting-related disclosure practices. SABs represent interpretations and policies followed by the Division of Corporation Finance and the Office of the Chief Accountant in administering the disclosure requirements of the federal securities laws. SABs do not represent official positions of the SEC.

staggered board. A corporate board structure whereby only a portion of the board of directors is elected each year, often used to discourage takeover attempts.

stakeholders. All parties interested in the performance of a company. Stakeholders range from the owners of a company to the local taxing authorities, to company employees, and also to residents concerned about the company's impact on the environment.

Standard Industrial Classification code (SIC). Four-digit code used by the Securities and Exchange Commission to categorize and identify a company's type of business.

STI. Abbreviation for *short-term incentive.*

stock appreciation right (SAR). A contractual right, often granted in tandem with an option, that allows an individual to receive cash or stock of a value equal to the appreciation of the stock from the grant date to the date the SAR is exercised.

stock award. Generally refers to a grant of unrestricted common shares.

stock bonus plan. A plan that provides for periodic awards of stock based upon the company's performance.

stock depreciation right. A right that protects an option holder, who exercises a stock option, from price declines for a specified period (normally the first six months) that he or she holds the stock. These types of plans are designed to protect the employee from price declines during mandatory holding period requirements for either tax or regulatory purposes.

The employer agrees to make a cash payment to the employee equal to the amount of any decline in the fair market value of the acquired stock from the date of exercise to the end of the six-month period. Also known as "stock indemnification right."

stock dividend. A dividend paid in securities rather than cash. The dividend may be additional shares of the issuing company, or shares of another company (usually a subsidiary) held by the company.

stock exchange. Organized marketplace in which members of the exchange, acting as agents (brokers) and as principals (dealers or traders) trade stocks, common stock equivalents, and bonds. Such exchanges have a physical location where brokers and dealers meet to execute orders to buy and sell securities. Each exchange sets its own requirements for membership.

stock grant.   See *stock award.*

stock option.   A contractual right granted by the company, generally under a stock option plan, to purchase a specified number of shares of the company's stock at a specified price (the exercise price) for a specified period of time (generally 5 or 10 years). The option will become more valuable if the market price goes up over the term of the option. The option effectively gives the option holder the right to buy stock in the future at a discount. This definition describes an employee stock option, as distinguished from a listed or exchange-traded option.

Stock options come in several forms, including the following, each of which is defined separately in this glossary: *performance stock options, premium-priced stock options, discount stock options,* and *indexed stock options.*

stock option exercise rescission.   An agreement between a company and certain employees to rescind the previous exercise of a stock option. In the transaction, employees agree to return to the company shares acquired from an option exercise that occurred earlier in the same taxable year (plus any dividends received on those shares since exercise), and the company agrees to reimburse the employees for the previously remitted exercise price. The company then reinstates the previously exercised option according to the option's original terms (i.e., the same number of shares, exercise price, vesting schedule, exercise term, etc.). The intent of the transaction is to treat the previous exercise as if it had never occurred for income tax purposes (including the alternative minimum tax). This will eliminate employee tax liabilities incurred earlier in the year when stock prices were high, but which cannot be funded by sale of the underlying stock because of subsequent declines in stock price. A potentially negative consequence of the rescission is that the company loses the income tax benefit (or deduction) it would otherwise have received had the original exercise not been rescinded.

stock split.   When a company increases the number of shares outstanding by splitting existing shares. A 2-for-1 split means that every shareholder gets two new shares for each one they own; a 3-for-2 split means they get three shares for every two they own. The price of an individual share falls, but shareholders do not lose money because they are being given the equivalent number of new shares.

In a reverse stock split, a company reduces the number of the shares outstanding by consolidating existing shares. A 1-for-5 reverse split, for example, means that for each five shares owned, the shareholder receives a single new share instead. The price of the new shares is five times higher, but only to reflect the shortened supply. If a company's stock is trading at a very low price, this process makes the company look more attractive to investors.

stock swap.   Also known as a "stock-for-stock" exercise. A form of cashless exercise transaction in which shares of company stock already owned are delivered, either physically or by attestation, in lieu of cash to pay for the exercise of stock options.

stock withholding.   A cashless method of satisfying the exercise price or withholding taxes for an equity award, by authorizing the company to withhold from the shares otherwise due a number of shares the value of which is equal to the exercise price and/or taxes.

street name. Securities held in the name of a broker instead of a customer's name are said to be carried in "street name." This occurs when the securities have been bought on margin or when the customer wishes the security to be held by the broker.

strike price. Also known as the *exercise price* or grant price, the price per share at which a stock option is granted and that must be paid to exercise a stock option. The strike price is typically the fair market value of the stock on the date of grant.

substantial risk of forfeiture. Tax term that applies when rights to compensation are conditioned upon future performance of services (e.g., working X years for a company) or the occurrence of some activity (e.g., reaching a performance or stock price goal). As it relates to restricted stock, income is not recognized while the stock is subject to a risk of forfeiture (e.g., vesting), unless a Section 83(b) election is filed with the IRS within 30 days of when a grant is received.

Summary Compensation Table. A required table for all publicly held companies as part of their proxy statement. This table should include salary, bonus earned in the prior fiscal year, number of stock options, all other annual compensation, and all compensation. The top five most highly paid executives who earn more than $100,000 in total salary and bonus should appear in this table.

supplemental executive retirement plan (SERP). A nonqualified plan for retirement benefits or deferred compensation.

TARSAP. Abbreviation for *time-accelerated restricted stock award plan.*

tax basis. Cost of stock for calculating gains or losses for tax purposes. For equity compensation, the basis includes the costs plus any compensation income reported (e.g., amount for ordinary income tax on NQSO spread).

tax preference items. Various tax breaks available under the regular income tax system that are added back to income to determine alternative minimum tax (AMT).

Without regard to the AMT calculation, the option spread is not included in the regular income tax liability calculation. Other preference items include state and local taxes, interest on second mortgages, and medical expenses.

Tax Reform Act of 1976 (1976 Tax Act). Federal legislation that tightened several provisions and benefits relating to taxation, beginning in the 1976 tax year. Highlights of this act included creation of the individual retirement account, change of the treatment of the exercise of a stock option from capital gains to ordinary income, and increase of the maximum net capital loss to $3,000 starting in tax year 1978.

TC. Abbreviation for *total compensation.*

TCC. Abbreviation for *total cash compensation.*

Teachers Insurance and Annuity Association–College Retirement Equities Fund (TIAA-CREF). The premier pension system among education and research institutions in the United States; the largest portable pension system in the world, with over $500 billion in total assets under management.

technical research. Analysis of the market and stocks based on supply and demand. The technician studies price movements, volume, trends, and patterns, which are revealed by charting these factors, and attempts to assess the possible effects of current market action or future supply and demand for securities and individual issues.

tender offer. An offer to purchase outstanding shareholders' securities, often made in an attempt to gain control of another company.

testamentary trust. A trust established by a will that takes effect upon death. A revocable trust is a trust in which the creator reserves the right to modify or terminate the trust; an irrevocable trust may not be modified or terminated by the trustor after its creation.

third-party administrator (TPA). An independent company or person who contracts with an employer to provide administrative functions associated with a benefit or benefits, but does not assume or underwrite risk.

TIAA-CREF. Abbreviation for *Teachers Insurance and Annuity Association–College Retirement Equities Fund.*

tick. The direction in which the price of a stock moved on its last sale. An up-tick means the last trade was at a higher price than the one before it and a down-tick means the last sale price was lower than the one before it. A zero-plus tick means the transaction was at the same price as the one before, but still higher than the nearest preceding different price.

ticker symbol. A system of letters used to uniquely identify a stock or mutual fund. Symbols with up to three letters are used for stocks that are listed and trade on an exchange. Symbols with four letters are used for Nasdaq stocks. Symbols with five letters are used for Nasdaq stocks other than single issues of common stock. Symbols with five letters ending in X are used for mutual funds.

time-accelerated restricted stock award (TARSAP). A restricted stock plan that combines both time-lapse and performance vesting restrictions while still allowing fixed accounting treatment under APB 25. Using such an approach, the restricted stock will vest at the earlier of a stated period of time or upon the achievement of certain performance targets.

top-hat plan. A plan maintained by an employer that primarily provides deferred compensation for highly compensated employees or certain members of upper management.

total capital. Common and preferred equity plus long-term debt. Long-term debt is debt due one or more years later.

total cash compensation (TCC). The total of salary and bonus.

total compensation (TC). The complete pay package for employees, including all forms of cash, stock, benefits, services, and in-kind payments. *Net total compensation* refers to *salary, bonus,* and *long-term incentive.*

total reward system. Includes financial compensation, benefits, opportunities for social interaction, security, status and recognition, work variety, appropriate work load, importance of work, authority/control/autonomy, advancement opportunities, feedback, hazard-free working conditions, and opportunities for personal and professional development. An effective compensation system will use many of these rewards.

TPA. Abbreviation for *third-party administrator.*

transfer agent. An agent who keeps a record of the name of each registered shareowner, his or her address, and the number of shares owned, and sees that the certificates presented for transfer are properly cancelled and new certificates issued in the name of the new owner.

transferable stock options. Options providing, by their terms, that they may be transferred by the option holder, generally only to a family member or to a trust, limited partnership, or other entity for the benefit of family members, or to a charity.

tranche.   A set of stock options as part of a larger grant. For example, if options vest in 25% blocs over four years, each 25% bloc of options is a tranche.

treasury stock.   Stock reacquired by the issuing company and available for retirement or resale. Generally, treasury stock is issued but not outstanding, cannot be voted, neither pays nor accrues dividends, and is not included in any of the financial ratios measuring values per common share. Among the reasons treasury stock is created are: (1) to provide an alternative to paying dividends, because the decreased amount of outstanding shares increases the per-share value and often the market price; and (2) to provide a source of shares for the exercise of stock options and the conversion of convertible securities.

trigger.   As relates to stock compensation, an event that causes change or acceleration in the stock grant. For example, some stock plans accelerate vesting upon a merger, or new management (i.e., change in control). Other plans may require a double trigger of a change in control followed by termination of employment.

trust.   A legal entity in which one person or institution holds the right to manage property or assets for the benefit of someone else. Types of trusts include:

- Testamentary trust—A trust established by a will that takes effect upon death.
- Living trust—A trust created by a person during his or her lifetime.
- Revocable trust—A trust in which the creator reserves the right to modify or terminate the trust.
- Irrevocable trust—A trust that may not be modified or terminated by the trustor after its creation.

Trust Indenture Act of 1939.   This act, which falls under the purview of the SEC, applies to debt securities such as bonds, debentures, and notes offered for public sale. Even though such securities may be registered with the SEC, they may not be offered for sale to the public unless a formal agreement between the issuer of bonds and the bondholder, known as the "trust indenture," conforms to the standards of this act.

trustee.   An individual or institution appointed to administer a trust for its beneficiaries.

underwater.   A term used to describe an employee stock option when the current market price is below the option exercise price. When an option is underwater, it would cost more than the underlying stock is worth to exercise the option. For example, the exercise price is $25 when the stock market price is $15. In this situation, it would be cheaper to buy the stock on the open market than to exercise the option. Such options are also described as being *out of the money.*

underwriter.   An investment banking firm that actually buys the shares from the company in a public offering and then resells them (at a higher price) to its customers.

Uniformed Services Employment and Reemployment Rights Act.   The act giving certain persons who serve in the U.S. armed forces a right to reemployment with the employer they were with when they entered service. This includes those called up from the reserves or National Guard. The Veterans' Employment and Training Service administer these rights.

unreasonable (excessive) compensation.   The IRS may challenge executive compensation as excessive or unreasonable, and as a distribution of corporate profits rather than salary.

unvested.   Unvested stock options have not vested and, therefore, are not exercisable.

variable accounting.   Under APB 25, "variable accounting" requires that the issuer accrue a compensation expense over time based on changes in the market price of the underlying stock. As opposed to "fixed accounting," in which the compensation charge is calculated upon the measurement date (typically, the grant date), variable accounting requires periodic adjustments, until the option is exercised or forfeited, to reflect changes in the market price of the stock (in other words, a mark-to-market approach). In general, any feature that creates uncertainty in either the number of shares subject to the option, or the exercise price of the option, can give rise to variable accounting under APB 25.

variable annuity.   A life insurance policy under which the annuity premium (a set amount of dollars) is immediately turned into units of a portfolio of stocks. Upon retirement, the policyholder is paid according to accumulated units, the dollar value of which varies according to the performance of the stock portfolio. Its objective is to enhance, through stock investment, the purchasing value of the annuity, which otherwise is subject to erosion through inflation.

variable compensation.   The portion of pay that is determined by performance. Typical variable compensation includes annual bonuses, options, and performance shares and units. Also referred to as "variable incentive pay." This type of compensation is payable in cash or stock, or at a certain period of time.

variable grant guidelines.   Under these guidelines, a company determines grant size according to a target dollar value rather than a target number of shares.

variable plan.   See *variable accounting.*

variable stock award plan.   A plan in which either the number of shares and/or the price at which they will be issued is not known on the grant date.

variable universal life insurance.   A type of life insurance that combines a death benefit with a savings element that accumulates tax-deferred at current interest rates. Under a variable universal life insurance policy, the cash value in the policy can be placed in a variety of subaccounts with different investment objectives. The policyholder can transfer funds among the subaccounts as he or she wishes. Fees are charged after a certain number of transfers.

vesting period.   A waiting period, after the award of an equity award, that must elapse before the award is no longer subject to forfeiture.

vesting schedule.   Schedule setting forth when, and to what extent, options become exercisable, or restricted stock or stock units are no longer subject to forfeiture (for example, 20% per year over five years). The schedule may be based on continued employment or may be based in whole or in part on meeting performance targets.

volatility.   An amount, expressed as a percentage of the stock price, that reflects recent fluctuation of the stock price. The moving average of this parameter is used in certain option pricing models to calculate the fair value of options. Volatility is generally expressed as the annual standard deviation of the daily price changes in the security.

The volatility of a stock is the standard deviation of the continuously compounded rates of return on the stock over a specified period. That is the same as the standard deviation of the differences in the natural logarithms of the stock prices plus dividends, if any, over the period. The higher the volatility, the more the returns on the stock can be expected to vary—up or down. Volatility is typically expressed in annualized terms that are comparable regardless of the time period used in the calculation (for example, daily, weekly, or monthly price observations).

volume. The number of shares or contracts traded in a security or an entire market during a given period. Volume is normally considered on a daily basis, with a daily average being computed for longer periods.

voting right. The common shareholders' right to vote their stock in the affairs of a company. Preferred stock usually has the right to vote when preferred dividends are in default for a specified period. The right to vote may be delegated by the shareholder to another person.

W-2. IRS form that reports income paid and taxes withheld by an employer for a particular employee during a calendar year.

W-8. Certificate of Foreign Status form required by the IRS to tell the payer, transfer agent, broker, or other intermediary that an employee is a nonresident alien or foreign entity that is not subject to U.S. tax reporting or backup withholding rules.

W-9. Request for Taxpayer Identification Number and Certification form required by the IRS to furnish the payer, transfer agent, broker, or other intermediary with an employee's social security or taxpayer identification number. The filing of this form allows the employee not to be subject to backup withholding because of underreporting of interest and dividends on his or her tax return.

waiting period. A specified length of time after an option has been granted during which the option cannot be exercised.

WARN. Abbreviation for *Worker Adjustment and Retraining Notification* act.

warrants. Financial instruments that are usually given to financial backers, other corporations, and underwriters as part of a funding or business arrangement. In most respects, warrants are like stock options. The rules governing their exercise and sale often attempt to reflect the deal that was struck between the investors and management. Warrants are often very complex and each round of warrants may have its own peculiar rules.

when issued. A short form of "when, as, and if issued." The term indicates a conditional transaction in a security authorized for issuance but not as yet actually issued. All "when issued" transactions are on an "if" basis, to be settled if and when the actual security is issued and the exchange or National Association of Securities Dealers rules the transactions are to be settled.

whole life insurance. A type of life insurance that offers a death benefit and also accumulates cash value, tax-deferred, at fixed interest rates. Whole life insurance policies generally have a fixed annual premium that does not rise over the duration of the policy. Whole life insurance is also referred to as "ordinary" or "straight" life insurance.

Wilshire 5000. A capitalization weighted index of all U.S.-headquartered companies (currently about 6,800). The capitalization of the portfolio is the sum of the market capitalizations of all the companies.

Worker Adjustment and Retraining Notification Act (WARN). Mandates that employees be given early warning of impending layoffs or plant closings. The DOL's Employment and Training Administration administers this law.

WorldatWork.   WorldatWork, formerly the American Compensation Association, is a global, not-for-profit professional association of compensation, benefits, and human resources professionals. Founded in 1955, WorldatWork is dedicated to knowledge leadership in compensation, benefits, and total rewards disciplines associated with attracting, retaining, and motivating employees.

yield.   In general, the amount of current income provided by an investment. For stocks, the yield is calculated by dividing the total of the annual dividends by the current price. For bonds, the yield is calculated by dividing the annual interest by the current price. The yield is distinguished from the return, which includes price appreciation or depreciation.

zero premium collar.   Hedging strategy used for high-value, concentrated stock positions, previously referred to as a "costless collar."

Bibliography

Abelson, Reed. "Who Profits if the Boss is Overfed?" *New York Times*, 20 June 1999, 9.

Ackerman, Elise. "Optionaires, Beware!" *U.S. News & World Report*, 6 March 2000, 25.

Alpern, Richard. *Guide to Change of Control: Protecting Companies and Their Executives.* Alexandria, Virginia: Executive Compensation Advisory Services, 2001.

American Bar Association. *Corporate Directors Guidebook*, 4th Ed. Chicago: American Bar Association, Committee on Corporate Laws, Section of Business Law, 2004.

American Law Institute. *Principles of Corporate Governance: Analysis and Recommendations*. Vols. 1 and 2. St. Paul, Minn: American Law Institute, 1994.

American Society of Corporate Secretaries. Directors: *Selection, Orientation, Compensation, Evaluation, and Termination.* New York: American Society of Corporate Secretaries, 2000.

―――. *Compensation Committees*. New York: American Society of Corporate Secretaries, 2000.

―――. *Board Committees: Considerations, Structures, and Uses in Effective Governance.* New York: American Society of Corporate Secretaries, 2000.

―――. *Corporate Governance Principles: A Representative Sampling.* New York: American Society of Corporate Secretaries, 2000.

―――. *Corporate Secretary's Resource Guide for the New Public Company.* New York: American Society of Corporate Secretaries, 2000.

―――. *Current Board Practices, 3rd Study.* New York: American Society of Corporate Secretaries, 2000.

―――. *Corporate Minutes: A Monograph for the Corporate Secretary.* New York: American Society of Corporate Secretaries, 1996.

Ang, James S., Shmuel Hauser, and Beni Lauterbach. "Top Executive Compensation Under Alternative Ownership and Governance Structures: Evidence from Israel," in Hirschey and Marr, *Advances in Financial Economics* 3, 1997.

Balsam, Steven. *An Introduction to Executive Compensation.* San Diego: Academic Press, 2002.

Bernard, Tara Siegel. "It's Your Choice." *Wall Street Journal's Special Report on Executive Pay*, 12 April 2004, R3.

Bernstein, Peter. *Against the Gods: The Remarkable Story of Risk.* New York: John Wiley & Sons, 1996.

Bhagat, Sanjai, Dennis Carey, and Charles Elson. "Director Ownership, Corporate Performance, and Management Turnover."*Business Lawyer* 54, no. 3 (May 1999): 885–919.

Bischoff, Bill. "Now That's an Interesting Option." *SmartMoney.com,* 23 August 2000.

Black, Fischer and Myron Scholes. "The Pricing of Options and Corporate Liabilities." *Journal of Political Economy* 81 (May/June 1973): 637–54.

Blair, Margaret. *Ownership and Control: Rethinking Corporate Governance for the Twenty-First Century.* Washington, D.C.: The Brookings Institution, 1995.

Block, Stanley. "A Study of Financial Analysts: Practice and Theory." *Financial Analysts Journal* 55, no. 4 (July/August 1999): 86–95.

Bogan, Christopher, and Michael English. *Benchmarking for Best Practices: Winning Through Innovative Adaptation.* New York: McGraw-Hill, 1994.

Bogle, John. "Bogle on Mutual Fund Investment Policies and Corporate Governance." Speech before the New York Society of Security Analysts, Washington, D.C., 20 October 1999.

———. "Creating Shareholder Value: BY Mutual Funds . . . or FOR Mutual Fund Shareholders." Speech before the Annual Conference for the Investor Responsibility Research Center, Washington, D.C., 26 October 1998.

Bok, Derek. *The Cost of Talent: How Executives Are Paid and How It Affects America.* New York: Free Press, 1993.

Booth, Richard. "Seven Myths About Stock Options." *Directors & Boards* (Summer 1999): 35–38.

Brancato, C. K., ed., *Institutional Investor Report.* New York: The Conference Board, January 1998.

Brickley, James, Clifford Smith, and Jerold Zimmerman. *Managerial Economics and Organizational Architecture.* Boston: Irwin-McGraw Hill, 1997.

Brinkley, Christina and Joann Lublin. "ITT Brass to Get 'Golden Bungee' in Takeover." *Wall Street Journal,* 12 February 1998, B1.

Buck Consultants, Inc. *Review of CEO Employment Arrangements.* New York: Buck Consultants, 2001.

Bulkeley, William. "Decompensation: Executives Ordered to Return Millions; Computer Associates Forgot About Those Stock Splits; Still, 'No Mere Bagatelle.'" *Wall Street Journal,* 10 November 1999, A1.

Business Roundtable. "Statement of the Business Roundtable on the American Law Institute's Proposed 'Principles of Corporate Governance and Structure.'" New York: Business Roundtable, 1998.

Byrd, John, Robert Parrino, and Gunnar Pritsch. "Stockholder-Manager Conflicts and Firm Value." *Financial Analysts Journal* 54, no. 3 (May/June 1998): 14–30.

Byrne, John. "How to Reward Failure: Reprice Stock Options." *BusinessWeek,* 12 October 1998, 50.

———. "The Teddy Roosevelts of Corporate Governance." *BusinessWeek,* 31 May 1999, 75–79.

Byrnes, Tracy. "Stock Options Lost Value? Little-Known Provision May Be a Life Preserver." *TheStreet.com,* 11 May 2000.

California Public Employees' Retirement Equities Fund Home Page. *Barriers to Good Corporate Governance.* 1999. www.calpers.com.

Carey, Dennis, Dayton Ogden, and Judith A. Roland. *CEO Succession: A Window on How Boards Can Get It Right When Choosing a New Executive.* New York: Oxford University Press, 2000.

Cartano, David. *Taxation of Compensation and Employee Benefits.* New York: Panel Publishers, Inc., 1999.

Carver, John, and Miriam Carver. *Reinventing Your Board: A Step-by-Step Guide to Implementing Policy Governance.* San Francisco: Jossey-Bass, 1997.

Carver, John. *Corporate Boards that Create Value.* San Francisco: Jossey-Bass, 2002.

Ceron, Gaston. "The Company We Keep." *Wall Street Journal's Special Report on Executive Pay*, 12 April 2004, R4.

Charan, Ram. *Boards at Work: How Corporate Boards Create Competitive Advantage.* San Francisco: Jossey-Bass, 1998.

Charan, Ram and Geoffrey Colvin. "Why CEOs Fail." *Fortune*, 21 June 1999, 69–78.

Chew, Donald and Stuart L. Gillan, (eds.), *Corporate Governance at the Crossroads: A Book of Readings.* New York: McGraw-Hill Irwin, 2005.

Chingos, Peter and KPMG Peat Marwick LLP. *Paying for Performance: A Guide to Compensation Management.* New York: John Wiley & Sons, 1997.

Ciampa, Dan, and Michael Watkins. "The Successor's Dilemma." *Harvard Business Review* (November/December 1999): 161–65.

Colvin, Geoffrey. "The Great CEO Pay Heist." *Fortune*, 25 June 2001, 64–68.

Conger, Jay, Edward Lawler, and David Finegold. *Corporate Boards: New Strategies for Adding Value at the Top.* San Francisco: Jossey-Bass, 2001.

Cook, Frederic. "Do Stock Options Dilute Shareholder Interests?" *ACA Journal* 7, no. 1 (Spring 1998): 67–72.

Council of Institutional Investors. *Does Shareholder Activism Make a Difference?* Washington, D.C.: Council of Institutional Investors Monograph, 1998.

Cox, John, and David Larcker. "Performance Consequences of Requiring Target Stock Ownership Levels." Philadelphia: Wharton School Working Paper, revised December 7, 1999.

Cox, John, S. A. Ross, and M. Rubenstein. "Option Pricing: A Simplified Approach." *Journal of Financial Economics* 7 (September 1979): 239–63.

Crystal, Graef, and Ira Kay. "Contrasting Perspectives: Do Stock Options Affect Performance?" *ACA Journal* 7, no. 1 (Spring 1998): 102–08.

Day, Kathleen. "Defying Gravity." *Washington Post*, 1 April 2001, B1.

"Does Good Governance Create Better Corporate Performance? Interview with Charles Elson." *Directorship* 25, no. 1 (January 1999): 5–6.

Delves, Donald P. *Stock Options and the New Rules of Corporate Accountability: Measuring, Managing, and Rewarding Executive Performance.* New York: McGraw-Hill, 2004.

Donaldson, Gordon, and Jay Lorsch. *Decision Making at the Top.* New York: Basic Books, 1983.

Duca, Diane. *Nonprofit Boards: Roles, Responsibilities and Performance.* New York: John Wiley & Sons, 1996.

Ellig, Bruce R. *The Complete Guide to Executive Compensation.* New York: McGraw-Hill Trade, 2001.

Ellin, Abby. "When the Glitter of Stock Options Turns to Dust." *New York Times*, 22 August 1999, C10.

Elson, Charles. "Director Compensation and the Management-Captured Board—The History of a Symptom and a Cure." *SMU Law Review* 50, no. 1 (September/October 1996): 127–74.

———. "Courts and Boards: The Top 10 Cases." *Directors and Boards* (Fall 1997): 26–32.

Ermann, David, and Richard Lundman. *Corporate and Governmental Deviance*. New York: Oxford University Press, 1978.

Fierman, Jaclyn. "The People Who Set The CEO's Pay. (Chief Executive Officer, The Compensation Committee)." *Fortune*, 12 March 1990, 58–62.

Frederic W. Cook & Co. *Reload Stock Options: The First 10 Years*. New York: Frederic W. Cook & Co., 1998.

Foundation for Enterprise Development. *The Entrepreneur's Guide to Equity Compensation*, 2nd Ed. Washington, D.C.: Foundation for Enterprise Development, 1998.

Gay, Christopher. "Hard to Lose: Reload options promote stock ownership among executives. But critics say they're a lot more costly than shareholders realize." *Wall Street Journal's Special Report on Executive Pay*, 8 April 1999, R6.

Gogoi, Pallavi. "False Impressions: More companies require top executives to own stock. The result isn't what everybody expected." *Wall Street Journal's Special Report on Executive Pay*, 8 April 1999, R3.

Gross, Bill. "The New Math of Ownership." *Harvard Business Review* 76, no. 6 (November/December 1998): 68–74.

Hall, Brian J. and Kevin J. Murphy. "The Trouble with Stock Options," *Journal of Economic Perspectives 2003*. Vol. 17, 49–70.

Hallock, Kevin. "Reciprocally Interlocking Boards of Directors and Executive Compensation." *Journal of Financial and Quantitative Analysis* 32, no. 3 (September 1997): 331–34.

———. "Dual Agency: Corporate Boards with Reciprocally Interlocking Relationships," in *Executive Compensation and Shareholder Value: Theory and Evidence*, by Jennifer Carpenter and Yermack, Kluwer, 1999, 55–75.

Hallock, Kevin, and Paul Oyer. "The Timeliness of Performance Information in Determining Executive Compensation," *Journal of Corporate Finance* 5 (December 1999): 303–321.

Hankins, Melissa. "Battle Over the Boardroom: Should Directors Get Paid Based on Corporate Performance?" *Wall Street Journal*, 12 April 2001, R6.

Heath, Chris, Steven Huddart, and Mark Lang. "Psychological Factors and Stock Option Exercise." *Quarterly Journal of Economics* 114, no. 2 (May 1999): 601–27.

Heidrick, Robert. "Board Evaluations: Who Does Them, Who Doesn't and Why." *Corporate Board* 20, no. 115 (March/April 1999): 23–26.

Hemmer, T., S. Matsunaga, and T. Shevlin. "An Empirical Examination of Reload Employee Stock Options." Working paper, University of Washington, October 1996.

———. "Optimal Exercise and the Cost of Employee Stock Options with a Reload Provision." *Journal of Accounting Research* 36 (Fall 1998): 231–35.

Hewitt Associates LLC. *Research Report: Unleashing the Power of Employee Ownership*. Lincolnshire, IL: Hewitt Associates, 1998.

———. *Survey Findings: Executive Employment Contracts*. Lincolnshire, IL: Hewitt Associates, 1998.

Huddart, Steven. "Employee Stock Options." *Journal of Accounting and Economics* 18 (1994): 207–31.

———. "Options 101: Planning for Stock Option Wealth." Presentation before the 55th Pennsylvania State University Tax Conference, May 2001.

———. "Patterns of Stock Option Exercise in the United States." Durham, NC: The Fuqua School of Business Working Paper, revised November 24, 1997.

Huddart, Steven, Bin Ke and Kathy Petroni. "What Insiders Know about Future Earnings and How They Use It: Evidence from Insider Trades." *Journal of Accounting & Economics* 35:3 (August 2003) 315–346.

Huddart, Steven and John S. Hughes. "Public Disclosure and Dissimulation of Insider Trades." *Econometrica* 69:3 (May 2001) 665–681.

Huddart, Steven, and Mark Lang. "Employee Stock Option Exercises: An Empirical Analysis." *Journal of Accounting and Economics* 21 (1996), 5–43.

———. "Information Distribution Within Firms: Evidence from Stock Option Exercises." *Journal of Accounting & Economics* 34:1–3 (January 2003) 3–31.

Jacobs, Karen. "Enough Is Enough: Computer Associates Offers a Cautionary Example of High Pay." *Wall Street Journal's Special Report on Executive Pay*, 8 April 1999, R8.

Jensen, Michael and Kevin Murphy. "CEO Incentives—It's Not How Much You Pay, But How." *Harvard Business Review* (1 May 1990).

Johnson, Carrie. "Some Shocked at Tax Bills on Options." *Washington Post*, 16 March 2001, E1.

Johnson, Mike. *Building and Retaining Global Talent: Towards 2002*. London: The Economist Intelligence Unit, 1998.

Keasey, Kevin, Steve Thompson, and Mike Wright. *Corporate Governance: Economic, Management and Financial Issues*. New York: Oxford University Press, 1997.

Khurana, Rakesh. "The Curse of the Superstar CEO." *Harvard Business Review*, September 2002, 23.

Kotter, John, and James Heskett. *Corporate Culture and Performance*. New York: Free Press, 1992.

Lavelle, Louis. "The Artificial Sweetener in CEO Pay." *BusinessWeek*, 26 March 2001, 102–03.

"Leapfrogging Pay Packages." *Executive Compensation Reports* 19, no. 15 (1 December 1999): 1–2.

Lederer, Jack, Susan Lowry, and Dennis Carey. "Compensation Committee: 10 Best Practices." *Directors & Boards* (Summer 1999): 44–45.

Leonhardt, David. "Law Firms' Pay Soars to Stem Dot-Com Defections." *New York Times*, 2 February 2000, A1, E2.

Lipton, Martin, and Jay Lorsch. "A Modest Proposal for Improved Corporate Governance," *Business Lawyer* 70, no. 48 (November 1992): 59–72.

Lorsch, Jay, and Rakesh Khurana. "Changing Leaders: The Board's Role in CEO Succession." *Harvard Business Review* 77, no. 3, (May/June 1999): 96–105.

Lorsch, Jay, and Elizabeth MacIver. *Pawns or Potentates: The Reality of America's Corporate Boards*. Boston: Harvard Business School, 1989.

Lowenstein, Roger. "Heads I Win, Tails I Win." *The New York Times Magazine*, 9 June, 2002, 9.

Lublin, Joann. "Here Comes Politically Correct Pay." *Wall Street Journal's Special Report on Executive Pay*, 12 April 2004, R1.

———. "In Whose Interest?: Compensation committees are supposed to be independent. That may be tough when the CEO is a member." *Wall Street Journal's Special Report on Executive Pay*, 8 April 1999, R4.

Lublin, Joann, and Leslie Scism. "Stock Options at Firms Irk Some Investors." *Wall Street Journal*, 12 January 1999, C1, C4.

Lyons, Dennis. "CEO Casualties: A Battlefront Report." *Directors & Boards* (Summer 1999): 43–44.

MacDonald, Elizabeth. "Fears About Hidden Earnings Overstatements Caused by Stock Options Appear Overblown." *Wall Street Journal*, 11 October 1999.

Martin, Roger. "Taking Stock." *Harvard Business Review* (1 January 2003).

McConnell, Pat, Janet Pegg, and David Zion. *Employee Stock Option Expense Pro Forma Impact on EPS and Operating Margins*. New York: Bear Stearns Equity Research, 1 May 1998.

Milkovich, George, and Jerry Newman. *Compensation, 7th ed.* Chicago: Irwin, 2001.

Millstein, Ira, and Paul MacAvoy. "The Active Board of Directors and Performance of the Large Publicly Traded Corporation." *Columbia Law Review* 98, no. 5 (June 1998): 1283–1321.

Monks, Robert. "Stock Options Don't Work: If CEOs Want Shares, Let' Em Buy Some." *Fortune*, 18 September 1995: 230.

Monks, Robert, and Nell Minow. *Corporate Governance*. Malden, MA: Blackwell Business, 1995.

Morgenson, Gretchen. "Why Not Restate Bonuses." *New York Times*, 25 April 2004, C1.

———. "Executive Pay: A Special Report; Two Pay Packages, Two Different Galaxies." *New York Times*, 4 April 2004, C1.

———. "Dispelling the Myth That Options Help Shareholders." *New York Times*, 29 July 2001, C1.

———. "Hidden Costs of Stock Options May Soon Come Back to Haunt." *New York Times*, 13 June 2000, A1.

———. "Holding Executives Answerable to Owners." *New York Times*, 29 April 2001, E1.

———. "Investors May Now Eye Costs of Stock Options." *New York Times*, 29 August 2000, E1.

———. "Options Seem to Be Coming Home to Roost." *New York Times*, 8 October 2000, E1.

———. "Rumblings of an Avalanche." *New York Times*, 15 August 1999, E1.

———. "Stock Options Are Not a Free Lunch." *Forbes*, 18 May 1999, 212–17.

Napolitano, Gabriel, and Abby Cohen. *The Controversy Surrounding Employee Stock Options*. New York: Goldman Sachs Investment Research, 4 May 1998.

———. "The NACD Blue Ribbon Commission on Executive Compensation and the Role of the Compensation Committee." Washington, D.C., NACD, 2003.

National Association of Corporate Directors (NACD). *2003–2004 Public Company Governance Survey*. Washington, D.C.: NACD, 2003.

National Association of Corporate Directors (NACD). *Report of the NACD Blue Ribbon Commission on Director Professionalism.* Washington, D.C.: NACD, 2001.

———. *Report of the NACD Best Practices Council: Coping with Fraud and Other Illegal Activity.* Washington, D.C.: NACD, 1998.

National Association of Corporate Directors (NACD). *Report of the NACD Blue Ribbon Commission on Executive Compensation: Guidelines for Corporate Directors.* Washington, D.C.: NACD, 1993.

National Center for Employee Ownership. *The Stock Options Book.* Oakland, CA: NCEO, 1999.

Neff, Thomas, James Citrin, and Paul Brown. *Lessons from the Top: The Search for America's Best Business Leaders.* New York: Currency Doubleday, 1999.

"Optional Logic." *Wall Street Journal,* 21 September 1998, A28.

Ottenstein, Robert, and Nina Scheller. *Paine Webber Specialty Chemicals Research Report. Corporate Governance: Update on Executive Compensation, Incentive Programs and Stock Ownership.* New York: Paine Webber, 1998.

Overton, Bruce and Susan E. Stoffer. *Executive Compensation Answer Book,* 5th Ed. New York: Panel, 2003.

Pastore, Robert. *Stock Options: An Authoritative Guide to Incentive and Nonqualified Stock Options.* San Francisco: PCM Capital Publishing, 1999.

Pearl Meyer & Partners, Inc. *2003 Equity Stake, Study of Management Equity Participation in the Top 200 Corporations.* New York: Pearl Meyer & Partners, 2004.

Peterson, Pamela, and David Peterson. *Company Performance and Measures of Value Added.* Charlottesville, VA: The Research Foundation of the Institute of Chartered Financial Analysts, December 1996.

Phillips, Robert. *Stakeholder Theory and Organizational Ethics.* San Francisco: Berrett-Koehler Publishers, Inc., 2003.

Porter, Michael. *Competitive Advantage: Creating and Sustaining Superior Performance.* New York: The Free Press, 1985.

Post, James E. et.al. *Redefining the Corporation: Stakeholder Management and Organizational Wealth.* Stanford: Stanford University Press, 2002.

Rappaport, Alfred. *Creating Shareholder Value: A Guide for Managers and Investors.* New York: Free Press, 1998.

———. "New Thinking on How to Link Executive Pay with Performance." *Harvard Business Review* (March/April 1999): 91–101.

Reda, James F. "Till Wealth Do Us Part: The Truth Behind Executive Employment Arrangements." *World at Work Journal,* 11 no. 2 (Second Quarter 2002): 34–43.

———. "Committees: A Glimpse at the Future Boardroom." *Corporate Board* 23, no. 133 (March/April 2002): 21–25.

———. "CEO Stock Ownership Guidelines." *Directors & Boards* 25, no. 1 (Fall 2000): 46–7.

———. "Change-in-Control Severance Arrangements: Practical Considerations." *Journal of Compensation and Benefits* 15, no. 2 (September/October 1999): 21–26.

———. "The Compensation Committee: A Potential Strategic Asset." *ACA Journal* 9, no. 1 (First Quarter 2000): 39–46.

———. "Executive Pay Today and Tomorrow." *Corporate Board* 22, no. 126 (January/February 2001): 18–21.

———. "The New World of the Compensation Committee." *Corporate Board* 20, no. 119 (November/December 1999): 18–21.

———. "The Six Habits of a Highly Effective Compensation Committee." *Directorship* 26, no. 1 (January 2000): 6–9, 12–13, 16.

———. "What's New in Accounting for Executive Stock Awards." *Journal of Taxation of Employee Benefits* 6, no. 5 (January/February 1999): 214–20.

———. "What You Need to Know about Pooling of Interests Accounting." *Journal of Compensation and Benefits* 15, no. 2 (March/April 1999): 33–39.

Reda, James, and John Chandler. "Imperatives for Compensation Committees." *National Association of Corporate Directors' Monthly* 23, no. 10 (October 1999): 1–5.

Reda, James, and Thomas Hemmer. "Reload Stock Options: Facts and Fictions." *Journal of Compensation and Benefits* 14, no. 6 (May/June 1999): 38–43.

Reda, James, and Stewart Reifler. "Repricing Stock Options: Current Trends and Dangers." *Journal of Compensation and Benefits* 14, no. 3 (November/December 1998): 5–10.

Reda, James, James McMahon, and Eric Lane. *2000 Pay to Win: How America's Most Successful Companies Pay Their Executives*. San Diego: Harcourt, 2000.

———. "Repricing Stock Options: How to Win a Loser's Game." *Journal of Taxation of Employee Benefits* 7, no. 1 (May/June 1999); 45–48.

Reifler, Stewart. "New Golden Parachute Rules." *Mergers and Acquisitions* 3, no. 1 (May 2002): 3.

———. "New IRS Rules for Split-Dollar Life Insurance Arrangements." *Corporation Business Taxation Monthly* 4, no. 8 (May 2003): 20.

———. "New IRS Rules Will Impact Private Split-Dollar Life Insurance Arrangements." *Estate Tax Planning Advisor* 2, no. 4 (April 2003): 1.

Reifler, Stewart and Atief Heermance. "SEC Adopts Revised Rules Requiring Shareholder Approval of Equity Compensation Plans." Securities Regulatory Update 6, no. 14 (21 July, 2003): 1.

Reifler, Stewart and James Reda. "Repricing Stock Options: Surviving the Great American Blowout." *Director's Monthly* 22 (December 1998): 7.

Reifler, Stewart, Mary Hevener, Helyn Goldstein and Rachel Rimland. "Section 162(m) Outside Director Sample Questionnaire." *The Tax Executive* 48 (July/August 1996): 283.

Reifler, Stewart and Mary Hevener. "Taxation: Section 162(m) Final Regulations." *The National Law Journal,* 25 March 1996, B5.

———. "Final Tax Regulations Issued Governing the $1 Million Deduction Limitation on Executive Compensation." *The Metropolitan Corporate Counsel,* 13 February 1996, 13.

Reingold, Jennifer. "Nice Option if You Can Get It." *BusinessWeek*, 4 May 1998, 111,114.

———. "What Keeps the Pay Merry-Go-Round Whirling." *BusinessWeek*, 19 April 1999, 81.

———. "Options Plan Your CEO Hates." *BusinessWeek*, 28 February 2000, 82–5.

———. "As Long as You're Up, Get Me a Restricted Stock Grant: When Prices Fall, Execs Find Such Awards Preferable to Options." *BusinessWeek*, 3 April 2000, 42.

Richard, J. *Compensation Committee Manual*. Half Moon Bay, CA: J. Richard & Co., 1999.

Richtel, Matt. "Stock Option Blues: Slide Leaves Little But a Big Tax Bill." *New York Times*, 18 February 2001, C1.

Rothwell, William. *Effective Succession Planning: Ensuring Leadership Continuity and Building Talent from Within*. AMOCOM: New York, 2001.

Sagalow, Ty. *Directors and Officers Liability Insurance: A Director's Guide*. NACD: Washington, D.C., 2000.

Sahlman, William A. "Expensing Options Solves Nothing." *Harvard Business Review* (December 2002).

Salter, Malcolm S. "Tailor Incentive Compensation to Strategy." *Harvard Business Review* (March 1973).

Saly, Jane, Ravi Jagananathan, and Steven Huddart. "Valuing the Reload Features of Executive Stock Options." *Accounting Horizons* 13, no. 3 (September 1999): 219–40.

Schellhardt, Timothy. "More Directors Are Raking in Six-Figure Pay" *Wall Street Journal*, 29 October 1999, B1.

———. "National Presto Comes Under Microscope: Analysts Study Governance Issues." *Wall Street Journal*, 28 July 1999, C1, C4.

———. "Relocating Mom: A Primer of New Perks." *Wall Street Journal*, 23 June 1998, B1, B6.

Serven, Lawrence. *Value Planning: The New Approach to Building Value Every Day*. New York: John Wiley & Sons, 1998.

Sherman, Hugh, and Rajeswarao Chaganti. *Corporate Governance and the Timeliness of Change: Reorientation in 100 American Firms*. Westport, CT: Quorum Books, 1998.

Shultz, Susan. *The Board Book: Making Your Corporate Board a Strategic Force in Your Company's Success*. New York: AMACOM, 2001.

Smith, David. "The Case for a Chief Governance Officer." Speech before the National Association of Corporate Directors' Directors Summit, Madison, Wisconsin, 6 September 2001.

Sonnenfeld, Jeffrey. *The Hero's Farewell: What Happens When CEOs Retire*. New York: Oxford University Press, 1988.

Spellman, Howard. *Corporate Directors: A Treatise on the Principles of the Law Governing*. New York: Prentice-Hall, 1931.

Stanton, Elizabeth, "Executive Pay: A Power Behind the Pay Surge." *New York Times*, 1 April 2001, C2.

Strauss, Gary. "Good Year or Not, Execs Clean Up: Performance, Compensation Often Unlinked." *USA Today*, 4 October 2000, 3B.

———. "CEO Pay: Fair or Foul." *USA Today*, 6 April 2001, 1B.

———. "Forget the Brass Rings—Execs Grab for Gold: Golden Contracts Give Bigwigs Beaucoup Bucks to Stay . . . or Sometimes to Go." *USA Today*, 20 March 2001, 1B.

———. "Many Execs Pocket Perks Aplenty." *USA Today*, 20 June 2001, 1B.

———. "Spotlight on Corporate Performance Burns CEOs." *USA Today*, 14 November 2000, 1B.

Teachers Insurance and Annuity Association—College Retirement Equities Fund. *TIAA-CREF Policy Statement on Corporate Governance*. New York: TIAA-CREF, 1999.

Teitelbaum, Richard. "Greenspan Weighs in on Options and Earnings." *New York Times*, 29 August 1999, C1.

Thatcher, Laura. "Analysis and Perspective: Prohibition on Trading During Blackout Periods under the Sarbanes-Oxley Act." *BNA, Inc. Daily Tax Report*, 24 February 2003.

———. "Analysis and Perspective: Executive Compensation Aspects of the Sarbanes-Oxley Act of 2002." *BNA, Inc. Daily Tax Report,* 19 February 2003.

———. "Analysis and Perspective: Prohibition on Trading During Blackout Periods under Section 306(a) of the Sarbanes-Oxley Act of 2002." *BNA, Inc. Corporate Accountability Report,* 14 February 2003.

———. "Analysis and Perspective: Executive Compensation Aspects of the Sarbanes-Oxley Act of 2002." *BNA, Inc. Corporate Accountability Report,* 24 January 2003.

———. "Special Report: Executive Compensation." *BNA, Inc. Corporate Accountability Report,* 17 October 2003.

———. "Insider Issues in Spin-off Transactions." *Executive Compensation Reports* (November/December 2000).

———. "Securities Considerations in Offering Company Stock as an Investment Alternative in Participant-Directed Plans." *Journal of Deferred Compensation* (Winter 1998).

Thatcher, Laura, Michael Brink and Mark Williamson. "Legislative/Regulatory Developments: IRS Issues Notice on Split-Dollar Life Insurance." *Journal of Deferred Compensation* (Spring 2001).

———. "SERP Swap—Continuing the Evolution of Executive Benefits." *Journal of Deferred Compensation* (Winter 2001).

Thomas, Kaye. *Consider Your Options: Get Most from Your Equity Compensation.* Lisle, IL: Fairmark Press, 1999.

Varallo, Gregory, and Daniel Dreisbach. *Fundamentals of Corporate Governance: A Guide for Directors and Corporate Counsel.* Chicago: American Bar Association, 1996.

Wagner, Richard H. *Executive Compensation 2004 Guide.* New York: Kennedy Information, 2004.

Ward, John. *Creating Effective Boards for Private Enterprises.* Marietta, GA: Business Owner Resources, 1997.

Ward, Ralph. *Improving Corporate Boards: The Boardroom Insider Guidebook.* New York: John Wiley & Sons, 2000.

Ward, Ralph. *21st Century Corporate Board.* New York: John Wiley & Sons, 1997.

Watson Wyatt Worldwide. *Stock Option Overhang: Shareholder Boon? Or Shareholder Burden?* Bethesda, MD: Watson Wyatt Worldwide, 1998.

Weisbach, M. S. "Outside Directors and CEO Turnover." *Journal of Financial Economics* 20, no. 1–2 (January/March 1988): 431–60.

Weston, Fred, Kwang Chung, and Juan Siu. *Takeovers, Restructuring, and Corporate Governance.* Upper Saddle River, NJ: Prentice-Hall, 1997.

Whittlesey, Fred. "Indexed Stock Options: A Solution to the Excessive Pay Issue." *ACA News,* September 1999, 6.

"Who Wants to be a Billionaire? Stock Options Have Made Many American Bosses Rich—But Not Necessarily Any Better at Their Jobs." *Economist,* 8 May 1999, 12–15.

Williamson, Oliver. *The Mechanisms of Governance.* New York: Oxford University Press, 1996.

Worthy, James and Robert Nueschel. *Emerging Issues in Corporate Governance.* Evanston, IL: Northwestern University Press, 1983.

Yavitz, Boris, and William Neuman. *Strategy in Action: The Execution, Politics, and Pay of Business Planning.* New York: Free Press, 1982.

Zehnder, Egon. "A Simpler Way to Pay." *Harvard Business Review,* (April 2001): 53.

Index